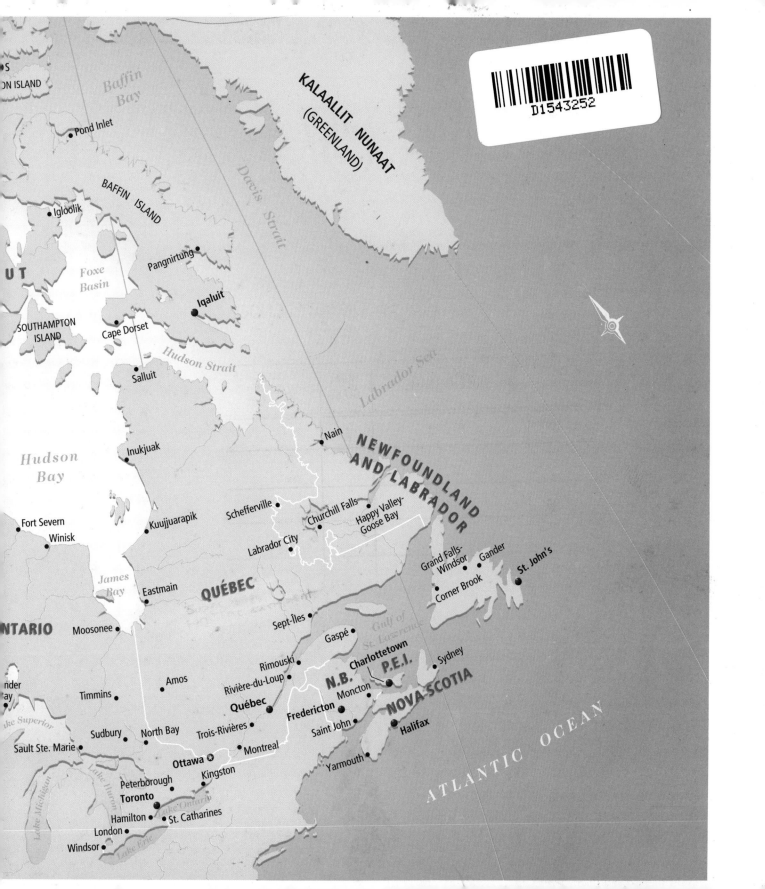

Baffin Bay

ON ISLAND

KALAALLIT NUNAAT
(GREENLAND)

• Pond Inlet

BAFFIN ISLAND

• Igloolik

UT

Foxe Basin

Pangnirtung •

**Iqaluit**

SOUTHAMPTON ISLAND

• Cape Dorset

*Davis Strait*

*Hudson Strait*

• Salluit

*Hudson Bay*

• Inukjuak

*Labrador Sea*

• Nain

**NEWFOUNDLAND AND LABRADOR**

• Fort Severn

• Winisk

• Kuujjuarapik

• Schefferville

• Churchill Falls

Happy Valley-
Goose Bay •

• Labrador City

Grand Falls-
Windsor •    • Gander

• Corner Brook     **St. John's** •

*James Bay*

• Eastmain

**QUÉBEC**

**NTARIO**

• Moosonee

Sept-Îles •

*Gulf of St. Lawrence*

Gaspé •

nder
ay

• Timmins

Amos •

Rimouski •

Rivière-du-Loup •

**N.B.**   Charlottetown   **P.E.I.**   • Sydney

Moncton •

*Lake Superior*

• Sudbury   • North Bay

**Québec** •

Trois-Rivières •

**Fredericton** •

**NOVA SCOTIA**

• Sault Ste. Marie

Saint John •

• Halifax

**ATLANTIC OCEAN**

Montreal •

**Ottawa** ⊛

Yarmouth •

Peterborough •    Kingston •

**Toronto**

*Lake Michigan*

Hamilton •   • St. Catharines

*Lake Huron*

London •

Windsor •    *Lake Erie*

*Lake Ontario*

01 - 06

YORK REGION BOARD OF EDUCATION
STOUFFVILLE DISTRICT SECONDARY SCHOOL

Book No.............................

| SCHOOL YEAR | STUDENT'S NAME | HOME CLASS | CONDITION WHEN GIVEN OUT |
|---|---|---|---|
| | | | |
| | | | |
| | | | |
| | | | |
| | | | |

# Continuity and Change
# Canada

## A History of Our Country from 1900 to The Present

Don Bogle
Eugene D'Orazio
Fred McFadden
Don Quinlan

**Fitzhenry & Whiteside**
Markham, Ontario

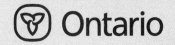

# Canada, Continuity and Change

© 2000 Fitzhenry & Whiteside Limited
195 Allstate Parkway, Markham, Ontario L3R 4T8

*Editor:* Elizabeth Ballantyne
*Designer:* Wycliffe Smith Design Inc.
*Cartographer:* Deborah Crowle
*Illustrator:* Steven Hutchings

*Cover design:* Wycliffe Smith
*Cover photo illustration:* Catherine Chatterton
*Electronic page production:* Cara Scime, Wycliffe Smith Design Inc.

*Cover images: Background image © First Light; partial reproduction of Ozias Leduc's "L'Enfant au Pain" © Estate of Ozias Leduc/SODRAC, 2000; Sam Hughes NAC C-2468; Frederick Banting NAC C-37756; Gabrielle Roy NAC C-18347; Wayne Gretzky CP; Montreal Rally CP; Aboriginal Woman Glenbow Archives NC-7-852*

Fitzhenry & Whiteside acknowledges with thanks the support of the Government of Canada through its Book Publishing Industry Development Program.

**Canadian Cataloguing in Publication Data**
Canada, Continuity and Change
Rev. Edition
Previous edition published under title: Canada, the twentieth century
Includes index
ISBN 1-55041-475-5

1. Canada—History—20th century. I. McFadden, Fred, 1928-1993. II. Title:
Canada, the twentieth century

FC600.M32 2000          971.06          C00-931250-1
F1034.2.M339 2000

The book is dedicated to
*Bridget Fitzhenry and Fred McFadden*

# Contents

# Introduction

Students frequently ask, "Why do we have to study history?" The study of the history of a country has often been compared to the examination of an individual's memory. You could not make wise decisions today if you did not remember what had happened to you previously. In the same way, citizens cannot make wise decisions unless they know something of their nation's past.

Your study of Canadian history should increase your knowledge of some of the important developments in Canada's history. It should make you aware of some of the issues, tensions, questions, and problems that have emerged. You will see the gradual changes in our population, our society, our laws, and our way of life, that have contributed to our present-day Canadian society. You will also see the roles of the many leaders who have both shaped the events of the past, and been shaped by them.

An intelligent citizen needs not only knowledge of the past, but the skills to act upon that knowledge. Your course will provide you with the opportunities to develop your abilities to communicate—by writing, by discussing, and by making oral presentations. You will have opportunities to go beyond this text to develop your research skills. You will be required to think, to analyze, to compare, and to evaluate the ideas of the past. You will be asked to participate with your fellow students in cooperative learning activities, to solve problems and, to present solutions.

All of these skills are not only the necessary skills of a student, but also of the successful citizen as well.

We hope that your study of Canada in the twentieth century is interesting, useful, enjoyable, and challenging.

# METHODS OF HISTORICAL INQUIRY

## A New Century Dawns

**Skill:** Primary and Secondary Sources
**Practice:** Distinguishing Between Primary and Secondary Sources
- Locating Information
- Creative Writing
- Writing a Biography

## War and Recognition

**Skill:** Analysis, Evaluation and Communication
**Practice:** Recording Information in Paragraph Form

## The Radio Age

**Skill:** The Inquiry Process and Causation
**Practice:** Constructing a Chronology
- Cause and Effect
- Writing a Newspaper Account

## The World on Trial

**Skill:** The Inquiry Process and the Research Essay
**Practice:** The Research Essay

## The Baby Boom

**Skill:** Researching and Recording Information
**Practice:** Researching Information
- Recording Information
- Group Work
- The Oral Report

## Canada Comes of Age

**Skill:** Notation Methods
**Practice:** Endnotes, Footnotes and Bibliography

## One Nation or Two

**Skill:** Computer Technology
**Practice:** Using the Internet for Research

## Sleeping With an Elephant

**Skill:** Comparisons
**Practice:** Assessing Bias and Distinguishing Fact from Opinion

## Hands Around the World

**Skill:** Assessing Bias
**Practice:** Making Comparisons
- Formulating Conclusions
- Culminating Activity

# Introduction

**C**ANADA BECAME A NATION IN 1867 AND, LIKE ALL NEW COUNTRIES, faced several important challenges during its formative years. Prime Ministers John A. Macdonald and Wilfrid Laurier were responsible for building the fledgling country. Macdonald brought Manitoba and British Columbia into Confederation. Laurier established the provinces of Alberta and Saskatchewan. Both worked to build transcontinental railways—the most important influence on Canada's growth in the early part of the century.

Life was not easy, nor was it without conflict. Aboriginal Canadians were **marginalized** as their way of life was disrupted by the hordes of Europeans settling the West. Women were oppressed and undervalued. They could not vote or own property. They had no legal rights. Indeed, they were not even considered "persons" under the law. Minority groups faced discrimination and racism. Chinese immigrants had to pay a head tax to enter the country.

Canadians struggled to find a common identity. The new immigrants tried to find a place for themselves as "free" Canadians. English Canadians fostered ties with Britain. French Canadians did not feel this loyalty to the British Empire. They saw themselves as "Canadien," with a long history and a rich culture. The rift was a serious one and caused unity problems, especially during the debates over Canada's participation in the Boer War and Laurier's desire for a Canadian Navy.

## METHODS OF HISTORICAL INQUIRY

### Primary and Secondary Sources

Reconstructing past events is a difficult task. Historians must gather information from a variety of places which are categorized as either **primary** or **secondary** sources. Primary sources are original documents, such as government or parliamentary records, personal journals and letters—things written by the people involved in the event. Secondary sources are texts that have been interpreted by someone. Newspaper and magazine articles, books, encyclopedias and most information on the Internet are all good examples. Public and university libraries contain a good amount of both primary and secondary sources. Provincial and national archives have mostly primary sources. The Internet provides mainly secondary sources, although primary sources are sometimes available.

# Chapter One:
## A New Century

# Expectations

## General Expectations:
**By the end of this chapter, you will be able to:**

- compare life in Canada at the start of the twentieth century with life in Canada at the start of the twenty-first century—your century

- demonstrate an awareness of the changing nature of the people of Canada

- understand the impact of technological development on Canada and Canadians

- read and analyze primary and secondary source documents

## Specific Expectations:
**By the end of this chapter, you will be able to:**

- describe Canadian life at the turn of the century

- assess the roots of Canada's remarkable economic growth in the twentieth century

- identify major groups who have immigrated to Canada

- compare contemporary immigration patterns with historical ones

- describe the impact of Canadian immigration on Aboriginal communities, particularly the Métis

- understand the role played by Canadian women in building a more equitable society

- describe the influence of Great Britain and the United States on Canada's policies at the turn of the last century

- trace the growing divisions between French and English Canadians

## WORD LIST

| | | | |
|---|---|---|---|
| Assimilation | Interpretation | Reciprocity | Tariff |
| British Empire | Marginalized | Residential schools | Unions |
| Head tax | Métis | Self-determination | |
| Conscription | Oral history | Suffragette | |

# *Advance* Organizer

**1**

At the turn of the twentieth century, Canada was largely a rural society. Most people were farmers, fishers, fur trappers, loggers, or construction workers. The local community was the centre of most activities. Baseball and hockey games, songfests and church get-togethers were major social events. The horse and buggy was the most common method of local transportation, whereas trains were the best form of long-distance travel. The automobile was slowly becoming known as a new, strange alternative. No one could imagine the impact this invention was to have on the new century.

**2**

In 1896, Minister of the Interior, Clifford Sifton, put out a call for settlers to break new land in the Canadian West. Many people from eastern and southern Europe answered the call and, for the first time in Canada's history, a large number of immigrants settled in the Canadian West. Most of these pioneer families became wheat farmers. Farming methods were changing: horse-drawn and steam-powered machinery was replacing the rake and sickle; windmills pumped water; iron ploughs were widely used; and barbed wire became the most common fencing for maintaining livestock herds. The opening of the West had a profound impact on Canada's Aboriginal population, starting with the so-called "numbered treaties" from 1870 to 1921. By the terms of these treaties, Canada's Aboriginal peoples were often uprooted and forced to settle on federally-controlled reserves. Many concerns expressed by First Nation peoples throughout the twentieth century stem from the westward migration of European settlers after 1880.

**3**

Industry found new uses for Canada's natural resources and revolutionary methods of processing them. Timber supplied both building material, and pulp and paper. Minerals such as copper, iron and nickel were used in construction, and in the manufacture of machinery. They also found wide use in the railway-building boom. Railway expansion continued until the start of World War I in 1914.

**4**

Cities grew. Factories and stores thrived. People found jobs in construction and manufacturing. These jobs were usually poorly paid. Most cities became places of startling contrast. Factory and storeowners lived in large comfortable houses, while their employees were usually forced to live in slum districts. Workers banded together to form and strengthen their unions in order to improve their wages and working conditions. Gradually, a middle class emerged — merchants and professional people.

**6**

Many Canadians wanted freer trade with the United States— competition would lower prices. Big business was against free trade. The

Liberals wanted freer trade: opposition leader Robert Borden sided with business. Borden's Conservatives defeated Laurier's Liberals in the 1911 election.

**5**

Most French Canadians opposed Canada's involvement in the Boer War (1899-1902), a war between England and the Dutch Boers in South Africa. Many were against helping to strengthen Britain's navy. English Canadians sided with Britain. The country was divided. Prime Minister Laurier sought compromises to both issues.

**7**

Women wanted the right to vote. Canada's most active suffragettes lived on the Prairies, where they were supported by farmers' organizations. Nellie McClung was a key figure in the suffragettes' struggle, both in Manitoba and in Alberta. Manitoba granted the vote to women in 1916. Other provinces soon followed, but Quebec refused women the vote until 1940. Aboriginal women did not get the right to vote until 1960.

# Canadians at the Turn of the Century

## The People

What was Canadian life like in 1900? Try to place yourself back in time. Your life would have been quite different from what it is today. As you read this section, consider whether life at the turn of the twentieth century was better or worse than life at the turn of the twenty-first century. Try to note the major differences and similarities. Would you consider changing places with a young Canadian in 1900?

In 1900, Canada consisted of only six provinces. Most Canadians lived on farms. Many young people left school early. In the country, they were needed on the farm. In the city, their wages helped pay for the family's food and rent. The work was hard, and the hours long. People tended to marry young and start raising families early. Adult responsibilities came quickly. As well, Canada began to receive waves of immigrants, many of whom chose to settle and develop the vast stretches of the fertile, but underpopulated West. Canada's Aboriginal peoples faced new challenges as they struggled to maintain their identity, lands and rights in a world dominated by European arrivals. Canadian women began to claim new roles and respect for themselves as fuller partners in Canada's changing society. When one looks back, it is clear that the turn of the twentieth century was a new beginning for Canada and Canadians.

This map of Canada shows what the country looked like at the turn of the twentieth century. How is it different today?

Life revolved around such institutions as the town band, the local baseball or hockey team, and the church.

## A Rural Society

By 1900 the population of Canada was 5,200,000. Toronto, Montreal and Halifax were the largest cities. Vancouver was the boomtown of the West Coast, but not many people lived west of Winnipeg. Regina, Calgary and Edmonton were still small pioneer cities.

*A "caboose" taking children to school one wintry morning in the early part of the twentieth century.*

Most people still earned their living by the sweat of their brow. The hours were long, salaries were poor and conditions difficult. Farming was the main occupation in 1900. Other Canadians worked in logging camps to provide lumber for the growing cities, the railways and the treeless prairies. Fishing was an important occupation in the coastal areas of the Maritime provinces. Still other people worked in construction—on the rapidly expanding railways or on the roads, sewers and buildings of the new cities. Women worked in factories, as servants for the rich, as teachers and store clerks, and on their own farms and in their own homes.

## Living Close to Home

Most people depended on the horse and buggy for local travel and the train for long journeys. By 1885, Canada was linked from sea to sea by railroads.

Automobiles were so rare that people did not have driving licences. There were no speed limits, no stop signs and no traffic lights. People usually spent their lives close to home where interest was centred on the local community. Life revolved around such institutions as the town band, the local baseball or hockey team, and the church. There were few telephones, no supermarkets, no radios and no television. Many people did not have newspapers to bring them news from the rest of the world. The age of paid professional singers, comedians or athletes was still to

*Women's hockey has deep roots in Canadian society. How "big" is hockey in your community?*

make dramatic strides forward in technology, communications, transportation and medicine. Our population would swell with new immigrants, and the country would become renowned for its rich, multicultural diversity by the end of the twentieth century. Aboriginal people would make great advances in the areas of **self-determination** and land rights. French Canadians would move to control their own destiny. Canadian astronauts would fly into space, while people at home would gain a global perspective. Natural resources would play a vital role in the country's economic and social growth, and Canada would develop its unique national character and heritage.

come. Most people provided their own entertainment. A singsong around the family piano or dancing to a treasured violin or accordion brought from the old country—these were high points of any family gathering. A night out meant watching local talent in a play or a concert at the church hall. Opera and music halls were very popular in some parts of the country.

## A New Century

The 1800s had been a period of gradual change. In 1900, most Canadians expected that the twentieth century would continue in the same way, but the years ahead would be stormy and fast-changing. Canada would take part in two world wars and the Korean War—though we are best known as peacekeepers. Canadian scientists and inventors would

Prime Minister Wilfrid Laurier once said: "The nineteenth century has been the century of the United States.... The twentieth century shall be the century of Canada." Perhaps this century did not develop quite as he expected. Canada at the end of the twentieth century was a very different place from the Canada Laurier knew.

*Dried cod was an important staple during the long winters in the Maritimes.*

# CANADIAN LIVES

(COGWAGEE, CYCLONE JACK)

**BORN:** 1887, Six Nations Reserve, Brantford, Ontario

**DIED:** 1949, Six Nations Reserve, Brantford, Ontario

**SIGNIFICANCE:** One of the best long-distance runners Canada has ever known.

**BRIEF BIOGRAPHY:** In 1905, after coming in second at a local 8-kilometre race, Longboat decided to train seriously for long-distance running. The following year, he won 4 spectacular races, including the important 30.5-kilometre race around Hamilton Bay. In 1906, Longboat entered the Boston Marathon. By this time, his fame had spread so widely that crowds flooded the track to cheer him forward for the last 6 kilometres of the race. Longboat not only won the marathon, but he broke the standing world record by a full 5 minutes.

In 1908, Longboat turned professional. Within months he had won 3 professional marathons. In 1909, however, Longboat's professional career turned sour. His promoters sold his contract without Longboat's permission. Not only was he given a new agent, but this agent received 50 percent of all Longboat's earnings and could register him in any race he wanted. Upset by these contract problems, Longboat began losing. The newspapers blamed "Indian laziness" and claimed he was drinking too much, inadvertently demonstrating that anti-Aboriginal sentiment still prevailed in turn-of-the-century Canada. In 1911, Longboat bought back his contract and, now that he had control over his own career, began to win again. In 1912, he broke his own world record twice for the 28-kilometre race.

The outbreak of the First World War cut short Longboat's career as a professional runner. He enlisted in 1916 and served as a dispatch runner for the Canadian Army. After the war, interest in professional running declined rapidly. Longboat took a job as a farm labourer in Alberta to support his family. From 1926-1945, he worked for the Toronto Streets Department. He died in 1949 at the Six Nations Reserve, where he was buried according to the Longhouse tradition. *What Canadian athletes are popular today?*

## Tom Longboat

## The Technical Edge

The world became a global village during the twentieth century, united by the invention and development of technologies that shrank the vast distances between the four corners of the globe. One of the most important of these new technologies was successfully tested on Newfoundland shores in 1901. Guglielmo Marconi, the Italian inventor of wireless telegraphy, received the first wireless message sent from England—more than 3,200 kilometres across the Atlantic Ocean—to Signal Hill, Newfoundland. Marconi had mastered the science of instantaneously sending a ray of electrical energy across the ocean. The Radio Age had begun.

From that point on, the world would become a smaller place as news, military commands, government instructions, and even stock market buy-and-sell orders could be beamed around the globe. The wireless was but one stop on a long path of technical innovation, which included radio, television, satellite communication and the Internet. Canadian companies, including BCE, RIM, Nortel, Corel, Mitel and many others, rank among the largest and most creative in the world in the complex field of telecommunications.

GUGLIELMO MARCONI

## Canadian Vision

*"We are, I believe, entering on an age of wonderful scientific development. We will do things that are hardly dreamed of as yet but we will not write great literature or paint great pictures. We can't have everything at the same time. We will fly around the world—and solve the secret of the atom—but there will be no Shakespeare or Homer. They went out with the gods."*

Do you agree or disagree with this quotation, penned in the 1920s by Lucy Maud Montgomery, author of *Anne of Green Gables*? Montgomery's novels about Anne, Emily, Rilla and Pat would establish her as one of Canada's most popular and widely-read authors. Montgomery's work would be translated into 16 languages. *Anne of Green Gables*, first published in 1908, would be turned into a stage play, several movies and a popular television series, as well as provide a reason for the annual Charlottetown (P.E.I.) Festival.

### FOCUS

1. List at least 10 ways in which living in Canada in 1900 was different from today.
2. Select 3 ways in which life was better in 1900, and 3 ways in which it is better today.
3. Explain the reasons behind the choices you made. What do you think was the most important invention of the twentieth century? Why?

# Settling the West

**2**

There were 16,835 immigrants to Canada in 1896. These people, like most of their predecessors, came from France or the United Kingdom. Many Québécois and Acadians were descended from French settlers who had come to Canada in the seventeenth and eighteenth centuries. The rest of Canada was mostly settled by the English, Irish and Scottish. There were also German, Pennsylvania Dutch and Mennonite settlements such as Lunenburg, Nova Scotia and Berlin (now Kitchener), Ontario.

Still, the largest part of Canada's landscape, the sparsely populated West, was a grave concern to the Canadian government. It feared American expansion into the lands south of the border might spill over into Canada. In 1872, Prime Minister John A. Macdonald commissioned the Canadian Pacific Railway to build a transcontinental railroad in order to join the West with central Canada. The railway was completed in 1885. The anticipated flood of settlers, however, remained a trickle.

In 1896, Prime Minister Wilfrid Laurier appointed Clifford Sifton Minister of the Interior. Sifton's job was to fill the "Last Best West" with settlers. He advertised free Canadian land throughout the United States, Britain and Europe. Sifton was looking for settlers with agricultural

*Many people immigrated to Canada to escape persecution and to give their children a better life.*

Today, Métis people are found all over North America, from Quebec to the southwestern United States, from New England to the Northwest Territories.

T I M E L I N E

1900  1910  1920  1930  1940  1950  1960  1970  1980  1990

experience. He knew that immigrants had to be strong and healthy. They would have to break new soil, put up buildings, and make it through the tough Canadian winters. "I think a stalwart peasant in a sheepskin coat, born on the soil, whose forefathers have been farmers for generations, with a stout wife and a half-dozen children is good quality," he said.

The government set aside large blocks of land where immigrant groups from the same country, or of the same religion, could settle together. This policy made Canada an attractive home for Ukrainians, Doukhobors, Scandinavians, Mennonites, Jews and others, because it helped ease the settlers' loneliness and fear of isolation. The policy succeeded.

In 1905, 131,252 immigrants came to Canada. Now that there were enough settlers in the West, two new provinces, Alberta and Saskatchewan, were created.

By 1913, the number of immigrants coming to Canada rose to 400,870. Alongside the Bourassas, Cartiers and Lafleurs, the

*Mr. and Mrs. Oldham—a seasoned farm couple pose on the Prairies.*

O'Keefes, Carrs, and Macdonalds, people with names such as Richler, Diefenbaker, Getty, Mazankowski, Filmon, Romanow, Laumen and Beck would take their places as citizens and future leaders of this country.

Not all immigrants to Canada were welcomed. While new settlers from Europe were breaking ground in the prairies, Chinese, Japanese and East Indians travelled across the Pacific from Asia to work in the fisheries, mines and lumber camps of British Columbia. These Asians were often resented by other Canadians. In 1886, Chinese immigrants were forced to pay a **Head Tax** in order to enter the country. This amount was raised to $500 per person in 1904—almost a full year's earnings. It was not until 1947 that all restrictions on Chinese immigration to Canada were removed.

However, the arrival of so many new people would mean new strength and energy for the young country. As well, the multicultural nature of Canadian society was being established early in the new century. Increasing immigration meant the nation-building work of Macdonald and Laurier was beginning to bear fruit.

BORN: 1841, St. Lin, Quebec

DIED: 1919, Ottawa, Ontario, while still leader of the Liberal Party

SIGNIFICANCE: Became Canada's first French Canadian prime minister. Oversaw the completion of the second transcontinental railway, brought Alberta and Saskatchewan into Confederation, established the Canadian Navy, and opened the door to immigrants who were neither French nor English.

BRIEF BIOGRAPHY: Laurier was first elected to the Legislative Assembly of Quebec in 1871. A charismatic, charming and intelligent man, it was not long before he made a name for himself in Canadian politics. In 1887, Laurier succeeded Edward Blake as leader of the Liberal Party. Nine years later, at the age of 56, he became prime minister of Canada. Laurier's tenure as head of Canada was not always easy. The Boer War (1899-1901) deeply divided the country.

Although Laurier sought compromise on the conscription issue, his position caused a bitter dispute between French and English Canadians. Despite the Boer War controversy, Laurier was elected for a second term in 1900. He began construction on the second transcontinental railway in 1903 and, in 1904, after being re-elected for a third term, Laurier brought Alberta and Saskatchewan into Confederation. Although elected for a fourth term in 1908, Laurier's success began to decline.

His Naval Service Bill in 1910 and his proposed 1911 reciprocity agreement with the United States caused bitter disagreement among Canadians. Laurier suffered a depressing defeat in the 1911 election. Though never to be prime minister again, Laurier remained in politics as Leader of the Opposition until his death in 1919.

*In your view, what characteristics are necessary for success as a prime minister?*

## Wilfrid Laurier

**The Métis:** Any history of the Canadian West is incomplete without a portrayal of the **Métis** people. These Canadians were usually settlers and fur trappers of French, Scottish and Aboriginal descent, many of whom had settled in communities along the Red River area of Rupert's Land or the North West Territories. Most Métis were Roman Catholic. Their culture was a unique combination of traditions inherited from their European and Aboriginal ancestors. Some Métis were skilled leather workers who fashioned intricately beaded clothing and accessories. Others were accomplished musicians, especially with the fiddle. The famous Métis anthem, *Chanson de la Grenouille,* was often sung at community gatherings.

The Métis were independent. When Canada purchased Rupert's Land from the Hudson's Bay Company in 1869 for $1.5 million, the Métis did not want to join Confederation until their land and cultural rights were recognized. They did not want to give up their homeland and their prairie hunting grounds. They did not want to lose their culture and way of life. The Métis chose Louis Riel as their leader. When the Canadian government sent surveyors to divide up the land, the Métis set up their own provisional government to negotiate a place for the Métis people within Confederation. As a result, the province of Manitoba was established in 1870.

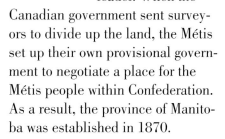

*Louis Riel*

More and more European settlers were attracted to the West. Many built farms in Manitoba. To preserve their way of life, the Métis people and their First Nations allies were forced to move farther west. They found new hunting grounds in Saskatchewan and Alberta, but still the Europeans came. Soon these lands, too, were filled with settlers. The Métis and their Native allies, such as Big Bear and Poundmaker, did not want to move again.

In 1885, they fought against the Canadian government. Louis Riel and Gabriel Dumont led the doomed uprising. Riel was put to death for treason. Dumont fled to the United States. The Métis were forced to give up their land. Many left; some decided to remain.

Today, Métis people are found all over North America, from Quebec to the southwestern United States, from New England to the Northwest Territories. Former Manitoba Premier, John Norquay, was a Métis; noted poet Pauline Johnson was a Métis; and so is award-winning architect, Douglas Cardinal. Métis have formed several organizations to help preserve their culture and history. These include the Métis Association of Alberta, the Ontario Métis Aboriginal Association, and the Canadian Métis Society.

### FOCUS

1. Why was the government concerned about the West?
2. What kinds of settlers were wanted for the West?
3. What evidence was there that some immigrants were not welcomed?
4. How did the Western settlement affect the Métis?

# Canadian Vision

My forest brave, my Red-skin love, farewell!
We may not meet tomorrow; who can tell
What mighty ills befall our little band,
Or what you'll suffer from the white man's hand?
Here is your knife! I thought 'twas sheathed from
    aye.
No roaming bison calls today;
No hide of Prairie cattle will it maim;
The plains are bare, it seeks a nobler game:
'Twill drink the life-blood of a soldier host.
Go; rise and strike, no matter what the cost.
Yet stay. Revolt not at the Union Jack,
Nor raise Thy hand against this stippling pack
Of white-faced warriors, marching West to quell
Our fallen tribe that rises to rebel.
They are all young and beautiful and good;
Curse to the war that drinks their harmless blood.
Curse to the fate that brought them from the East
To be our chiefs—to make our nation least
That breathes the air of this vast continent.
Still their new rule and council is well meant.
They but forget we Indians owned the land
From ocean unto ocean; that they stand
Upon a soil that centuries agone
Was our sole kingdom and our right alone.
They never think how they will feel today,
If some great nation came from far away,
Wresting their country from their hapless braves,
Giving what they gave us—but wars and graves.
Then go and strike for liberty and life,
And bring back honour to your Indian wife.
Your wife? Ah, what of that, who cares for me?
Who pities my poor love and agony?
What white-robed priest prays for your safety
    here,
As prayer is said for every volunteer
That swells the ranks that Canada sends out?
Who prays for vict'ry for the Indian scout?
Who prays for our poor nation lying low?

None—therefore take your tomahawk and go.
My heart may break and burn into its core,
But I am strong to bid you go to war.
Yet stay, my heart is not the only one
That grieves the loss of husband and of son;
Think of the mothers o'er the inland seas;
Think of the pale-faced maiden on her knees;
One pleads her God to guard some sweet-faced
    child
That marches on toward the North-West wild.
The other prays to shield her love from harm,
To strengthen his young, proud uplifted arm.
Ah, her white face quivers thus to think,
Your tomahawk his life's best blood will drink.
She never thinks of my wild aching breast,
Nor prays for your dark face and eagle crest
Endangered by a thousand rifle balls,
My heart the target if my warrior falls.
O! coward self I hesitate no more;
Go forth, and win the glories of the war.
Go forth, nor bend to greed of white men's hands,
By right, by birth we Indians own these lands,
Though starved, crushed, plundered, lies our
    nation low…
Perhaps the white man's God has willed it so.

Written by Pauline Johnson in 1885—one of Canada's most popular and successful entertainers at the turn of the century. This poem is a tribute to those who died during the Riel Rebellions. Born in Brantford, Ontario, in 1861 to an Aboriginal father and English mother, Johnson was the first Native-Canadian to be published in Canada. During her lifetime, she was considered one of the country's best poets, equal to such great Confederation Poets as Charles G.D. Roberts and Bliss Carmen. She spent her life travelling the country giving recitals. No town was too small or too big for Pauline Johnson. She was as comfortable performing in the drawing rooms of Toronto as she was in church basements of Canada's vast wilderness. Johnson died in 1913 in Vancouver. She was the only person ever buried in Stanley Park.

*What was Pauline Johnson's attitude towards war?*

and mentally. Many were even scarred for life. By the time the last residential schools were phased out in the 1980s, entire generations of Aboriginal peoples had lost much of their history, family ties and pride. These would be very diffcult things for future generations to replace. In 1998, the government of Canada apologized to Canada's Aboriginal peoples for the abuse suffered in many of the residential schools. *In your view, what would be the hardest thing about attending a residental school? Why?*

Late in the 1890s, Canada's Department of Indian Affairs established **residential** (boarding) **schools** for Aboriginal children, building on what the British government had established even before Confederation. The Department wanted to provide a "general and moral" education for the next generation of First Nation peoples. Officials believed that, once removed from their homes and from life on the reserves, these children would become **assimilated** into the European culture that dominated Canada at the time. The government wanted to eliminate family and tribal influences. Failing to understand the nature of the Aboriginal heritage, the government also failed to understand the negative effects of the assimilation process. It felt that First Nation peoples should learn to farm or ranch, and give up their hunting and gathering way of life. Residential schools were not well funded. They were often poorly equipped and poorly monitored. The quality of teaching was not always strong. Many Aboriginal students suffered physically, emotionally, spiritually

# 3 New Immigrants

The story of the first difficult years in the Canadian West is often best described by the people who were there at the time. In particular, **oral history** can provide an immediacy and level of detail, which may be missed by more academic historians writing at a later date. The following first-hand stories about settling the West show the hardship and

*Scottish Immigrants arrive in Quebec City.*

suffering, the back-breaking labour and drudgery, and the courage and determination shared by all our pioneer ancestors.

"At that time a person was only allowed to stay at the Immigration Hall for one week. At the end of the week one had to get out and find their own way in the world. I was fortunate in accepting a position as section hand on the C.P.R., working out of Morley, sixty miles west of Calgary. My pay if I worked a full month—no sickness, no wet days, fifty-four hours a week—was $18 and board. In the fall of 1905, I moved back to Edmonton. The average wage at that time was $1.00 per day for manual work, $10.00 per month for farm work."

Scottish settler, Alberta, 1905. Reprinted with permission from *The Last Best West* by Jean Bruce.

"When I left school, I went to Oxford University, but I had no training for a job. So I decided to emigrate to Canada. My uncle gave me $200 to help me get started.

I worked on a farm near Regina, and then another near Saskatoon. After 18 months, I had saved $1500. I was a wealthy young man. I bought a horse and buggy and spent a month driving around looking for land. I found a good farm of 128 ha. The land company

One of the worst things was the loneliness. You couldn't even see the light of the neighbour's house.

wanted $12.50 a hectare. I put $500 down. I hired a man to help me with the ploughing. As he turned that land over, those furrows rolled out like the waves of the sea. I had about 60 ha broken and ready for spring. That winter, I worked for a lumber yard in Regina. In spring I had moved onto my farm with a seeder and four good horses. I bought some lumber, a keg of nails, and tarpaper to build a shack. By this time I was pretty deep in debt but I knew what I was doing. I got that new Marquis wheat that everyone was talking about. That was the finest wheat I've ever seen. Hard and wonderful for milling and it made the finest bread in the world."

Adapted from *The Pioneer Years*
by Barry Broadfoot.

"In those days, you just had to make the most of what you had. We had no money at all, and if we wanted something, we'd just have to look around and see what we could make it from. The women on the prairies had to be able to do anything. I used to spin all my own wool, and knit all my family's sweaters, and their stockings, and their mitts, and all that. We had no deep-freeze, of course, so we canned all the vegetables and the fruit and all that. We canned the meat too. No matter how hard times were, we seemed to have enough to eat.

With the clothing, that was something else. I patched till my fingers were sore, and tried to make things different by remodeling

them. We just kept using and using things, over and over again, for one thing or another until it was gone! I mean really gone. Until it wasn't good for anything, except maybe a floor cloth or a duster. Even then, when a floor cloth was all falling apart, we used to dry it out and roll it into little balls, and use it in the fire, or to stuff up the cracks in the walls of the barn...

One of the worst things was the loneliness. You couldn't even see the light of the neighbour's house. The nights were very, very long in the wintertime and, of course, there were no radios or anything like that. I used to sing a lot. The harder I worked, the more I sang, and every night, I sang my children to sleep with the song about a lily that lived alone in the woods; and even today when they come to see me, they'll ask if I'll sing it again, and I always do."

Scandinavian settler, reprinted with permission from *Voice of the Pioneer* by Bill McNeil.

"Once we got our own homestead we all took part in the work: the threshing and stoking and milling. It was very hard work, real pioneering. That's what I remember most about my childhood—hard work.

I must say, though, it wasn't really good when I was young. I didn't know why at that time, but now I do know. The other children and even the teachers seemed to try and make us feel out of place. You see, my parents had no money at all, so we weren't *dressed as good as some of the kids, and the kids, along with some of the teachers, would look down on us. Our parents were looked down on too because they were Russian immigrants and had customs that the others didn't understand. We spoke Russian, of course, and we had no English at all when we started school. The teacher wouldn't look at us at all! She just couldn't be bothered. Our parents dressed different too, and because they only had time enough to work* *they couldn't, of course, know what the fashions for clothes were in this country. So Mother would just make us a dress the same way she had always done and we had to wear it even though it didn't look like the dresses the other children were wearing. And because she had no time for buttons and buttonholes, we just used safety pins."*

Doukhobor immigrant, Saskatchewan, reprinted with permission from *Voice of the Pioneer* by Bill McNeil.

*An average day on board the* Lake Huron *bringing the first Doukhobors to Canada.*

*"I cleared my land with a grub hoe and axe. You take a grub hoe and dig around the tree, then cut the roots, have a ladder, climb up and put a chain hook in the top of the tree and pull it over with horses. It takes a fellow two or three years to learn how to clear land."*

Black American settler, Alberta, early 1900s, reprinted with permission from *Last Best West*, by Jean Bruce

*"About 1905, the first Polish immigrants came to Manitoba. Up until then we'd had people from Ontario, and from the States, England, Germany, and Scandinavia. At the Immigration Hall in Winnipeg, they'd send them down to look at the land that was left. This was usually swampy and covered with poplar, but they usually took it. 64 ha of free land looked pretty good when all you needed was $10.00 for the registration fee. A peasant had about 2 ha of land in Poland or Russia if he had anything at all. But they worked hard and they learned….*

*At first they lived with their animals. This used to shock some of the old-timers. The houses were small. They cut poles out of the bush and laid them on top of one another for the walls. They laid smaller poles side by side for a roof. They plastered the walls with a guck of straw and mud and lime. The roof had straw on it and then a thick layer of dirt. You'd be surprised how cozy they were. They liked music. They made their own violins. You could buy a violin at Eaton's for $2-$5, but they'd spend a whole winter working on one. When they started coming to our dances, they could sure make the night lively. When they started coming out to the July 1 picnic, their children were the best-behaved kids of the lot. One word from Mother and that was it."*

Adapted from *The Pioneer Years* by Barry Broadfoot

**John Ware** was one of Canada's greatest cowboys. Born a slave in 1845 in Texas, Ware became a cowboy after the American Civil War. He arrived in Canada in 1882, working as a cow-hand and bronco rider until 1888, when he bought his own ranch. Renowned for his remarkable horsemanship, there was not a horse "running on the Prairie which John could not ride." Ware died in 1905 after a tragic riding accident.

**F O C U S**

1. What do you feel are the most important challenges presented in these personal narratives?
2. How do these experiences compare to the experiences of immigrants today?
3. Despite all the hard work when they arrived, why did so many people come to Canada?
4. Could you handle the workload of a Canadian pioneer at the turn-of-the-century? Explain.

**Chinese Canadians:** Racism against the Chinese began when the first group of Chinese settlers arrived in Canada. Between 1881-1885, 17,000 Chinese immigrants arrived to work on the railway for $1 a day, half the rate of pay given to white railway workers. The railway companies saved an estimated $3.5 million dollars by hiring Chinese workers.

Fifteen hundred Chinese workers died during the construction of Canada's transcontinental railway. Living conditions were inadequate, with regular shortages of food and lack of medical care. Landslides and careless dynamiting were also responsible for many deaths.

When the railway was completed in 1885, hundreds of Chinese workers were put out of work. Many stayed in Vancouver where they settled in Chinatown. A few

moved east to the Prairies and Ontario; others returned to China. In 1891, 8,910 Chinese lived in British Columbia while only 219 lived in the rest of Canada. By 1911, things had changed. The number of Chinese in Canada had reached 27,568—8,000 of whom lived outside British Columbia.

Despite the growing numbers, Chinese Canadians still endured racism and oppression. They could not vote. Their children could not attend public schools unless they were born in Canada or spoke English. This resulted in partial segregation. Children in grades 1 to 4 were still sent to separate schools. Mob violence was partic-

ularly common. In 1907, 7,000 whites in Vancouver went on a rampage through Chinatown, breaking every single store window.

Canada's government supported racist views against the Chinese. In 1923, it passed the Chinese Immigration Act, which prohibited any Chinese from entering the country. Family members of Chinese immigrants already here were not allowed entry into Canada. During the Depression, Chinese Canadians needing public relief were given half the amount allocated to white Canadians in the same circumstances.

It was not until World War II, when Canada and China became war time allies, that Canada's treatment of its own Chinese population changed for the better. Conscription was extended to include Chinese Canadians in 1944. All anti-Chinese legislation, including the Chinese Immigration Act, was repealed in 1947. That year, Chinese Canadians were allowed to vote for the first time in Canadian history.

*Describe three examples of unfair treatment endured by the Chinese-Canadian community.*

*Damage incurred during anti-Asian riots of 1907.*

# Votes for Women

**4**

At the turn of the century more than half of Canadian adults could not vote. "No woman, idiot, lunatic, or criminal shall vote," was the way the law was phrased. Women were not recognized as independent human beings under the Canadian legal system. Their fathers or husbands were legally responsible for them. Men controlled their property, their money, their children and their lives.

Some people began to realize how unfair and dangerous this inequality was for women. A woman had no legal protection in 1900. If her husband abused her, her property, or her children, the law could do nothing. Thus, the matter of votes for women was tied in with other social issues.

**Man voting for the first time in 15 years:**
"You bet I came out today to vote against giving these fool women a vote. What's the good of it? They wouldn't use it!"

## Temperance and Women's Rights

Alcoholism was a major concern in the late 1800s. The concern was justified. Pay envelopes were often handed out in taverns. Many workers would stay for a friendly drink. A man with a drinking problem could drink away his wages before starting home. If his wife also worked outside the family home, he could legally demand her earnings to spend on liquor as well. Because of the "demon drink," some families went without food, heat and clothing.

Many people felt that the only answer was Prohibition, or banning the sale of alcohol completely. Societies were set up to promote temperance, or moderation, in the use of liquor. The Women's Christian Temperance Union (WCTU), founded in 1874,

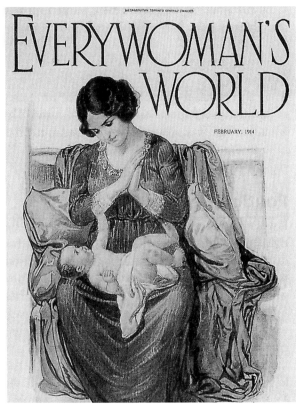

EVERYWOMAN'S WORLD

FEBRUARY, 1914

METROPOLITAN TORONTO CENTRAL LIBRARY

The Suffragette Movement really began on the Prairies. There, farmers knew the importance of women's work and felt it should be recognized, socially and legally.

became the leader in the battle for Prohibition. In 1878, the Canadian Temperance Act allowed local areas to vote on the issue.

Temperance workers were usually concerned with promoting good family life. It is not surprising that many of the same people were involved in the struggle to give women a fairer say in marriage. By the turn of the century nearly all provinces had passed Married Women's Property Acts to allow women at least some control over their own property.

Many politicians thought this was enough. The reformers wanted more. They wanted the abuse of alcohol to be stopped by total Prohibition, and they wanted votes for women.

## The Vote

The **Suffragette** Movement really began on the Prairies. There, farmers knew the importance of women's work and felt it should be recognized, socially and legally.

The most active suffragette struggles occurred in Manitoba, led by Nellie McClung, author, mother and temperance worker. In 1912, McClung joined a group of Manitoba women in the Political Equality League. Her keen mind and quick tongue soon made her the league's chief spokesperson.

Manitoba premier, Rodmond Roblin, was determined that women should not get the vote. "I don't want a hyena in petticoats talking politics to me. I want a nice gentle creature to bring me my slippers." The idea of women voting was "illogical and absurd. Making women equal to men would cause strife. It would break up the home. Women are too emotional," he told the Manitoba Legislature on January 27, 1914.

The next night, the Political Equality League held a "mock parliament" in a local theatre. All the members were women. They debated giving the vote to men. "Premier" Nellie McClung was against it: "If men start to vote, they will vote too much. Politics unsettles men. If men get into the habit of voting, who knows what might happen?"

Everyone thought it was a great joke, but it would take two more years of struggle and a change of government before Manitoba gave

---

### WOMEN GET THE VOTE

**1916** Manitoba and Saskatchewan

**1917** British Columbia, Ontario, and Canada (some women only)

**1918** Nova Scotia, and Canada* (all women)

**1919** New Brunswick

**1925** Dominion of Newfoundland

**1940** Quebec

**1960** Aboriginal women

*By 1918, Canadian women over 21 could vote in federal elections. Some provinces continued to restrict voting rights in provincial elections.

women the vote. In 1916, McClung's "bonny fight, knock-down fight, drag-out fight, uniting the women of Manitoba in a great cause" was finally over. Unfortunately, by then the McClungs had moved to Alberta, so she was not there to enjoy her triumph. Women got the vote in Alberta three months later.

McClung became a member of the Alberta Legislature in 1921. True to her convictions, she supported legislation for old age pensions, for mothers' allowances, for more liberal divorce legislation, for temperance, and for better factory conditions, no matter what party introduced it.

## In Their Own Words

### The following is a complaint from a young middle-class girl in 1855.

*"I want to know why it is that I, a well-brought-up lady-like...girl, am so utterly helpless and dependent. I have not been taught anything that is of the slightest earthly use to anybody in the whole world. Of course I can sing correctly; but have no special power or compass of voice.... As a pianist, I am a brilliant success, and yet a humbug as regards the science of music. ...I can sew—fancy work; but I could not cut out and 'build' a dress; even if I was never to have another. I can't make up a bonnet, nor even a hat; but I do know when the milliner has made a mess of either. I am self-conceited enough to think I have extremely good taste in such matters as a critic, yet I don't see how I could turn my good taste into a single solitary dollar if I had to. I just love parties, balls, concerts and—shall I confess it?—theatres, and yet, if I had to earn the money with which to gratify myself with these indulgences, I fancy I must perforce go amusementless for many a year."*

**What is this girl complaining about? How would learning to do the things she claims change her position in life? What type of life has she been trained to live?**

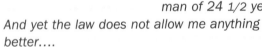

### A letter written to the Premier of Saskatchewan, 1915

*"I beg of you in the name of justice to women that you give them your most careful consideration and urge upon your Government the necessity of passing a law at this session to give a married women a legal and equal right to the property they have jointly accumulated... Why should a man have the legal right to will even half of their joint earnings to his friends, especially where there are no children?... That is what I get in return for my work, money and most of all my devotion to a man of 24 1/2 years. And yet the law does not allow me anything better....*

*Now you ask me why I did all this hard work? My reply is simple. I had no choice in the matter. I was forced to it. I had either to do it or walk out penniless and so I have just held on for the 6 years waiting patiently for the Government of Sask. to wake up and do justice to its women slaves. ..."*

**What is this woman concerned about? What are some of the similarities in these two women's lives? Are they seeking the same types of reforms? Why or why not?**

BORN: 1873, Chatsworth, Ontario

DIED: 1951, Victoria, B.C.

SIGNIFICANCE: Lecturer, teacher, author, suffragette, legislator and temperance worker, Nellie McClung fought tirelessly to make Canada a better place for women.

BRIEF BIOGRAPHY: A devoted Christian, Nellie McClung became involved in the Women's Christian Temperance Union in 1896, where she began her life-long fight against alcohol abuse. She published *Sowing Seeds in Danny* in 1908, the first of many books. In 1911, McClung and her family moved to Winnipeg, where she joined the Canadian Women's Press Club. McClung helped found the Political Equality League in 1912 and campaigned for women's right to vote. After moving to Alberta, McClung was elected a Liberal member of the Alberta Legislature in 1921. She was defeated in 1926, whereupon she joined Emily Murphy and three other Alberta women in their fight to establish that women were persons, and could therefore be appointed to the Senate. She became the first woman on the Board of Governors of the CBC in 1936. In 1938, she was appointed a Canadian delegate to the League of Nations.

*How do you think Nellie would view the lives of Canadian women today? Explain.*

## Nellie McClung

FOCUS
1. Why were many men and women concerned about "temperance?"
2. How did Nellie McClung help bring about better conditions for women?
3. In your view, do Canadian women and men have equal rights today? Explain your position.

# 5 The Land

Canada is an urban society today, with over three quarters of Canadians living in cities. Office towers, concrete parking lots, shopping malls and houses nestled together is what most of us recognize as Canada. Things were very different in 1900. More than half of all Canadians made their living on small family farms. One quarter lived in small villages and towns. Less than a quarter lived in cities. Farming families tried to raise as much of their own food as possible. Usually, they had a cow or two, some chickens and perhaps a pig. They would also grow their own vegetables and fruit. Most of the farm, however, was used to make money from cash crops.

The cash crop on the Prairies was wheat. In Ontario and Quebec, dairy farming was most common. Prince Edward Islanders found their clay soil grew great potatoes. Fruit orchards thrived in sheltered areas—Nova Scotia's Annapolis Valley, the Niagara Region of Ontario, and British Columbia's Okanagan Valley. When the cash crop was good, farmers could buy things they could not grow themselves. When it was not, farmers faced serious problems.

*Modern equipment made farm work easier by 1900. Horse-drawn mowers and binders replaced sickles and rakes.*

In 1900, more than half of all Canadians made their living on small family farms.

# FARM COSTS 1900–1910

## Costs to build

| | | | |
|---|---|---|---|
| a six room house | $700.00 | an implement shed | $100.00 |
| a stable to accommodate 6 horses | $200.00 | a granary for 2,000 bushels | $100.00 |
| a cow shed to accommodate 8 cattle | $400.00 | | |

## Cost of starting a farm in western Canada – 1910 – 1919

| | | | |
|---|---|---|---|
| 1 team of horses | $250.00-$400.00 | 1 mower & rake | $95.00 |
| 1 set of harness | $35.00-$40.00 | 1 reaper & binder | $170.00 |
| 1 wagon | $80.00-$90.00 | other implements | $50.00-$75.00 |
| 1 sleigh | $35.00 | 4 cows | $160.00 |
| 1 plough | $28.00 | 4 pigs | $15.00 |
| 1 set of harrows | $35.00 | 4 good sheep | $20.00 |
| 1 set of disk harrows | $35.00 | rooster and hens | $10.00 |
| 1 seeder | $85.00 | | |

# LAND VALUES 1900-1910

**Nova Scotia:** A 700-acre farm with 80 acres under cultivation, 150 in pasture, 470 woodland and 40 acres along a river sold for $3,500. Included in this real estate offer was a 6-room, 25 x 30 foot farmhouse, 2 new barns and all necessary out buildings.

**New Brunswick:** Crown land could be purchased in 100-acre parcels for $20.00 as long as the settler lived on the land for 3 years, worked on the roads to a value of $30.00, cleared 4 acres of land; and built a dwelling at least 16 x 20 feet in size.

**Quebec:** Existing farms went for around $20.00 - $30.00 an acre. Crown land sold for $.20 - $.50 an acre as long as the settler built a house at least 16 x 20 feet in size, remained on the land for a portion of each year for 4 years, and had cleared 10% of the lot.

**Ontario:** Crown land sold for about $.50 an acre and was sold in 160-acre parcels, as long as the purchaser built a house about 16 x 20 feet in size that he would occupy within 6 months of buying the land. He also had to cultivate 10% of the land and reside on the farm for at least 3 years.

**Manitoba:** Location of the land with respect to railways, towns and water greatly affected the price of land in Manitoba. Generally speaking, an acre of unimproved farmland cost about $3.00 - $12.00 an acre.

**Alberta:** Land prices ranged from $12.00 - $18.00 an acre, depending on location.

**British Columbia:** Farming land in British Columbia varied greatly, depending on location. First-class land cost about $5.00 per acre; second-class land $2.50 - $5.00 an acre, and third-class land $1.00 - $2.50 an acre. Minimum area sold was 160 acres.

Establishing a successful homestead was quite a challenge. Critical to a new family's success and survival was the harvesting of a good crop. Farmers soon found out that many strains of wheat were not up to the brutal Canadian winters and strong prairie winds. An early frost endangered lives and threatened the establishment of successful communities.

Fortunately, two scientific discoveries allowed our vast northern areas to be settled and produce rich yields of high quality grains.

The first was by Angus Mackay, a farmer from Alberta. In the spring of 1885, after Mackay and his hired help had cultivated the land, his men were called away by police to help during the Riel Rebellion.

*Charles Saunders surveys a field of wheat.*

Mackay was left with land ready to be planted, but no one to help with the seeding. So, he left half his land as it was—fallow. The following summer was a brutal one for Prairie farmers. Drought destroyed most crops. At Mackay's farm, however, something unusual happened. On the land that he had managed to cultivate the previous year, the wheat was dry and withered. On the land that had been fallow that year, by contrast, the wheat was healthy and thriving. Mackay had inadvertently discovered the concept of "summer fallow"—that leaving plowed land uncultivated for a year allows it to retain moisture and produce a good crop the next year, regardless of the amount of rainfall.

The second discovery was made by Charles Saunders (1867 – 1937), an Ontario farmer. Saunders had originally wanted to be a musician.

Instead, his father, William Saunders, director of Canada's Experimental Farms, appointed Charles as Dominion Cerealist, giving him the task of finding a wheat that would ripen rapidly in the short Canadian summers. By 1904, Saunders had developed a new strain of wheat, called Marquis, by crossbreeding a popular Canadian wheat, Red Fife, with wheats found in the colder climates of Asia. Marquis wheat was hardy, disease resistant, early-germinating, fast-ripening, and able to be made into large quantities of good quality flour.

Developed in 1904, tested across the Canadian prairies in 1907, Marquis wheat was commercially available by 1909. By 1920, it had been sown successfully on over 6 million hectares of what had formerly been inhospitable prairie. The price of wheat quadrupled from 1901 to 1921, and Prairie farmers were able to protect their farms and communities. Saunders went on to experiment with peas, beans, barley and oats. He retired in 1922, and was awarded a knighthood in 1934. Canadian technical ingenuity fostered settlement and agricultural development of Canada's western plains. Canadian wheat was eagerly sought after around the world.

*How did "summer fallow" and Marquis wheat open up Canada's northern prairies to successful farming?*

## Mechanized Farming

Modern inventions and technology made farm work easier by 1900. Horse-drawn mowers and binders were replacing sickles and rakes. Steam-powered tractors were available to break up the soil and plough the land. Many farmers could not afford to own these machines, so they rented. Sometimes they would hire a crew of workers along with the machines. Sometimes groups of neighbours would work together, collectively using the machines on each farmer's field in turn. This helped lead to the co-op movement.

There was still plenty of physical work to be done. Animals had to be cared for, eggs gathered, water hauled, firewood chopped, split and stacked.

Farming, especially wheat farming, was a booming business in Canada, which advertised the Prairies as "the bread basket of the world" and "the granary of the Empire." In 1904, the Canadian wheat crop was 54 million

bushels; by 1909, it had risen to 118 million bushels. Each bushel made about 60 pounds of flour, or 60 loaves of bread.

*A young boy feeding ducks on an Alberta farm. Does the farm lifestyle appeal to you today? Explain.*

FOCUS
1. What proportion of people lived on farms? In the cities?
2. Describe at least two technical developments that helped farmers increase their yields.
3. Why was Canada called "the bread basket of the world?"

**The Ukrainians** Among the many groups attracted to the Canadian West in the first years of the twentieth century were the Ukrainians. This community has played a significant role in the development of Canada, yet has also managed to maintain close ties with its homeland and traditions. Most Ukrainians found themselves subjects of the Russian Czar or the Emperor of Austria-Hungary at the turn of the century. Many suffered political oppression and economic hardship. European crop failures, overpopulation, and the threat of war drove them to seek a better future. Canadian agents in Europe offered 64 hectares of land for $10, plus religious and political freedom. Earlier Ukrainian visitors to this country, people such as Dr. Joseph Oleskow, pictured the Canadian West as a golden opportunity not to be missed.

The first large group of Ukrainians settled in the western prairies in 1891. From 1891-1914, 170,000 Ukrainian peasants came to Canada keen to embrace the challenge of building a life from scratch in this vast, free but, nonetheless, difficult land. Although poor and

unskilled in modern farming techniques, the settlers established solid communities in Alberta, Saskatchewan and Manitoba.

Unfortunately, during WWI, Canadian authorities treated many Ukrainians as enemy aliens, because they came from Austria-Hungary, with whom Canada was at war. Too many Canadians now turned on the same settlers they had eagerly enticed to our shores, treating them with hatred and prejudice. Thousands of Ukrainian men were rounded up, some with their families, and sent to internment camps in remote areas of the country. Authorities admitted later that these people had done nothing wrong. Today, the Ukrainian community is almost all native-born, and thrives in such urban centres as Edmonton, Winnipeg and Toronto. Well-known members of the community include former Governor-General Ray Hnatyshyn and comedian Luba Goy.

*What factors "pushed" Ukrainians from Europe to Canada? What factors "pulled" Ukrainians to settle in Canada?*

BORN: 1857, Brant County, Ontario

DIED: 1910, Toronto, Ontario

SIGNIFICANCE: Founded the Women's Institute, the National Council of Women, the Victorian Order of Nurses, and the YWCA.

BRIEF BIOGRAPHY: After an infant son died from drinking impure milk, Hoodless dedicated her life to educating women about motherhood and the domestic sciences. She campaigned for domestic science in the schools, and persuaded Ontario boards to start courses in home economics for girls and manual training for boys. Working with Lady Aberdeen, Hoodless helped found the YWCA, the National Council of Women and the Victorian Order of Nurses. In 1897, she founded the first Women's Institute in Stoney Creek, Ontario. Within a few years there were branches all over Canada and the world. Today there are Women's Institutes in 108 countries. Canada has 3,350 branches with over 72,000 members.

*What issues are of concern to Canadian women today?*

## Adelaide Hunter Hoodless

BORN: 1861, Toronto, Ontario

DIED: 1942, Winnipeg, Manitoba

SIGNIFICANCE: E. Cora Hind was the first woman journalist in Western Canada, and a tireless promoter of women's rights.

BRIEF BIOGRAPHY: After being denied a position at the Manitoba *Free Press* in 1881, Hind learned to use the type-writer—a recent invention—and worked as a secretary. In 1893, she set up her own stenographer's bureau and was appointed secretary to the Manitoba Dairy Association. She wrote regular articles for the Manitoba *Free Press.* In 1901, twenty years after her first application, Hind was offered a job with the *Free Press* as Agricultural Editor. She completed the first of what would become her annual crop predictions in 1904. These were so accurate that grain dealers around the world would not set wheat prices until E. Cora Hind's predictions were released each September.

After more than a decade at the *Free Press,* Hind turned her attention to women's rights. With Nellie McClung, Kennethe Haig and Lillian Beynon Thomas, she founded the Political Equality League in 1912. The group's main purpose was to obtain the vote for women, which they did in 1916. Hind promoted women's rights not just by words, but also by action. She was famous in Winnipeg for her philanthropic activities, often taking poor girls off the street to feed and house them until they were able to find a job. Her charitable acts were so famous around Winnipeg that when she finally had enough money to pay back the bank for the loan she took out to establish her stenography bureau, the bank manager would not accept it. Instead, he paid for her loan out of his own pocket, so that she could continue her charity.

E. Cora Hind received an honorary doctor of law degree from the University of Manitoba in 1935. When she died in 1942, the Winnipeg Grain Exchange stopped trading for 2 minutes in her honour.

**E. Cora Hind**

## In Their Own Words

**Read the following selections describing pioneer life at the beginning of the 20th century.**

*"We sure knew how to work. We were doing things around the yard before I was 5 or 6. I hunted up brooding hens and got them back to the henhouse. I went for the cows. I handed Dad things when he was fixing a piece of machinery, oiling it, or replacing a part he'd fixed. In the summer, I'd load up my wagon with a jar of water and one of lemonade, and sandwiches and cookies. I'd take afternoon lunch to the field where the men were working.*

*When I was 7, I milked my one cow, and then it got to be 2 cows. By the time I was 9, I was doing a man's job with the cows. When I was 11, I handled the team of four horses for ploughing. Other times I helped load the hay on the wagon.*

*If you were a boy, by the time you were 12, you'd pretty well given up the business of school. There didn't seem to be much sense in going anymore. Each year you stayed away, the harder it got to go. What 15-year-old fellow wanted to sit with a bunch of 11-year-olds. I don't think that there were any laws about when a fellow had to go to school or when he didn't. A lot of fellows never went beyond the third or fourth grade. I got to the sixth and I could read and write and do arithmetic. Usually a fellow married a girl who had gone through school. If it came to doing figures, she could do it. A lot of those farm wives did all the figuring and books in those days."*

Adapted from *The Pioneer Years* by Barry Broadfoot

**Which jobs might you enjoy doing? Why?**
**Which jobs would you prefer not to do? Why?**
**How is schooling different today?**

# City Life

Immigrants were pouring into Canada. Most were recruited to go to the rich farmlands of the West. Many never got there. They were too poor to buy the equipment and supplies they would need to set up a farm. Some tried farming but failed. Instead, these people found jobs in the lumber camps and the mines. They helped build the new railways. They also came to the cities looking for work in the expanding factories.

## The Cities Grow

With the country's population growing quickly, Canadian manufacturers did well.

*A busy Canadian city in the early part of the 1900s. How many methods of transportation do you see?*

There were plenty of jobs. Many people—immigrants, people raised on farms and people in small towns—moved to the cities to earn money.

*Middle class home in Toronto.*

more and more jobs: digging sewers, paving streets, building streetcar lines. Even unskilled workers with little knowledge of English or French could usually find some sort of work.

## Contrasts

Factory and storeowners lived in large homes on tree-lined streets, with the houses and grounds kept clean and tidy by servants. Most city dwellers were not so fortunate.

They made tractors and threshing machines for the new farms. They built buggies, bicycles and automobiles. Steel mills turned out nails, wire, pots and pans, railway tracks and locomotives. Flour, canned meats and vegetables, brooms, stoves, clothing—all the things people needed for everyday life—poured out of the factories.

There were plenty of jobs. Many people—immigrants, people raised on farms and people in small towns—moved to the cities to earn money. Cities across the country grew rapidly, creating

*"Instant Slum" in Winnipeg.*

## POPULATIONS
### (of Canadian cities)

| | 1901 | 1911 |
|---|---|---|
| HALIFAX | 40,832 | 46,619 |
| QUEBEC CITY | 68,840 | 78,710 |
| MONTREAL | 328,172 | 490,504 |
| TORONTO | 209,892 | 381,833 |
| OTTAWA | 59,928 | 87,062 |
| WINNIPEG | 42,340 | 136,035 |
| REGINA | 2,249 | 30,213 |
| EDMONTON | 4,176 | 31,064 |
| CALGARY | 4,392 | 43,704 |
| VANCOUVER | 29,432 | 120,847 |

Which city added the most people from 1901-1911? Which city had the largest percentage increase?

The housing supply did not keep up with the number of people streaming into the cities. Most people were very poorly paid, and could not afford decent homes even when they were available. The downtown areas of many cities became "instant slums." Sometimes immigrant families of ten would live in one run-down room. City water was not always safe to drink. Children were forced to play in the street.

City councils and concerned citizens knew such conditions were horrific, but they didn't know what to do. The concept of planning city growth to avoid these types of problems was still very new.

City councils did their best:
- they provided electric lights and a clean water supply
- they established public health clinics
- they improved public transportation
- they set up parks and playgrounds; so people could relax and play in pleasant surroundings

## THE TORONTO PLAYGROUND SYSTEM—EARLY 1900S

| | |
|---|---|
| 29 soccer fields | 8 bowling greens |
| 9 rugby fields | 2 croquet grounds |
| 98 tennis courts | 2 quoit grounds |
| 3 lacrosse fields | 33 hockey cushions (rinks) |
| 10 cricket creases | 39 skating rinks and toboggan slides |

Which of the above would still be found in cities today?

**Immigrant children found that where you came from didn't matter on the playground.**

**Poverty was an all too common aspect of the early twentieth century. Although government help and community services had not yet been established, some people began to notice the appalling living conditions of the poor.**

*"The health inspector rudely paid a midnight visit to a place...the other night....There he found thirty-two men living, where there should be seven, according to the laws of health. Scientists say that in a room where human beings live, there should be 400 cubic feet [122 cubic metres] of air space to each man. In...[this] house it worked out at 91 cubic feet [28 cubic metres] to each occupant, a fact which, not only being uncomfortable, was dangerous to the human health.*

*There were four rooms and each filled literally to the roof. The boarders were located in rooms as follows.*
*One room, 13 ft. by 8 ft. by 8 ft. [3.9m x 2.43m x 2.43m],—6 occupants, should be 2.*
*One room, 12 ft. by 8 ft. by 8 ft. [3.65m x 2.43m x 2.43m], —6 occupants, should be 2.*
*One room, 13 ft. by 8 ft. by 8 ft. [3.9m x 2.43m x 2.43m], —8 occupants, should be 2.*
*One room, 13 ft. by 12 ft. by 7 ft. [3.9m x 2.65m x 2.13m], —12 occupants, should be 2.*

*If these people had even kept the place decent at all, the case might not be quite so bad, but in the words of the health officer, it was 'filthy.' The bed-clothes, chairs and everything in the room was covered with dirt.*

*In handling this case, the magistrate addressed the [landlord] and said: 'People are supposed to live like human beings and not like hogs. In your house there was not space for a dog, let alone a man. Besides being overcrowded the place was abominably filthy....'*

J.S. Woodsworth, My Neighbour: *A Study of City Conditions, A Plea for Social Services* (Toronto, 1911), pp219-20.

**Is poverty still a major problem in your commmunity? Explain.**

---

**FOCUS**

1. Briefly describe Canadian cities in 1900.
2. Why did some cities grow faster than others?
3. List at least 3 differences between the lives of middle class people and working class people in the early 1900s. Are there great contrasts in living standards in your community? Explain.

# LET'S GO SHOPPING

## Eaton's Catalogue Price List

| | |
|---|---|
| Phonographs | $ 20.00 - $ 150.00 |
| Records | $ 5.00 - $ 15.00 per dozen |
| Cameras | $ 5.00 - $ 15.00 |
| Reading glasses | $ 0.25 - $ 1.25 |
| Arm chairs | $ 26.50 |
| Rocking chairs | $ 9.00 |
| Sleds | $ 0.20 - $ 1.25 |
| Wagons | $ 58.00 - $73.00 |
| Tea kettles | $ 0.55 - $ 2.00 |
| Baby carriages | $ 6.59 - $22.50 |
| Wood stoves | $ 21.50 - $ 35.50 |
| Men's summer coats | $ 0.75 - $ 5.00 |
| Men's fur coats | $ 17.50 - $ 47.50 |
| Men's wool sweaters | $ 0.75 - $ 2.50 |
| Men's boots | $ 1.00 - $ 4.00 |
| Women's boots | $ 2.00 - $ 4.00 |
| Women's cloaks | $ 3.00 - $ 11.00 |
| Women's blouses | $ 0.50 - $ 2.75 |
| Children's coats | $ 1.25 - $ 7.50 |
| Children's long pants | $ 1.75 - $ 2.50 |

Once one of Canada's most successful department store chains, Eaton's collapsed in 1999, and was sold off lock, stock and barrel.

# LET'S GO SHOPPING

## An example of grocery costs: 1900 – 1910

| | | | |
|---|---|---|---|
| **BEEF** | | Cheddar Cheese | $ .08 kg |
| Sirloin Steak | $ .08 kg | Bread | $ .06 to $ .08 a loaf |
| Chuck Roast | $ .05 kg | Flour | $ .01 kg |
| | | Rolled Oats | $ .02 kg |
| **PORK** | | Rice | $ .02 kg |
| Roast | $ .08 kg | Sugar, white | $ .02 kg |
| Bacon | $ .10 kg | Sugar, yellow | $ .02 kg |
| | | | |
| Eggs | $ .30 dozen | Tea | $ .06 to $ .18 kg |
| Milk | $ .08 litre | Coffee | $ .06 to $ .18 kg |
| Butter | $ .11 kg | Oranges, only in season | $ .40 dozen |

## POSTAL RATES: 1900 – 1910

FIRST CLASS LETTERS TO:

Canada, Mexico, United Kingdom & U.S.A.   $ .56 per gram or fraction thereof

Other Postal Union Countries   $ .56 per gram or fraction thereof

"Penny Post" – Local delivery in Canada   $ 1.41 per gram

PARCEL POST

| | |
|---|---|
| To Hong Kong | $.07 kilogram, $ .05 for each kilogram |
| To Newfoundland | $.06 kilogram, $ .05 for each kilogram |
| To New Zealand | $.10 kilogram, $ .05 for each kilogram |
| To United Kingdom | $.05 kilogram, $ .05 for each kilogram |
| Within Canada and to the U.S.A. | $.02 per gram or fraction thereof |

# 7 The Economy

## Forestry

Today forest products are one of Canada's largest industries. When Europeans first came to Canada, Quebec, Ontario and the Maritimes were covered with forests. Forestry was big business. Europe needed timber and, by 1900, the United States also needed to buy Canadian lumber. Demand was increasing in Canada as well. Cities and towns needed more and more lumber for new buildings. Prairie farmers also needed wood to build their homes and barns. Railway construction created a demand for wooden trestles and ties. The spread of electricity and

*This painting by H.J. Hughes, is called "Mill at Mesachie Lake," (1986).*

Fishing was a financial mainstay in the Maritimes and British Columbia throughout most of the twentieth century.

the telephone required wooden utility poles.

In the east, it soon became harder to find the big trees that produced the best timber. Lumberjacks began to move west to the cedar and Douglas fir forests of British Columbia. The timber they cut was sold to the Prairie provinces, the United States and Asia.

The end of the big trees in the east was not the end of the forest industry. There were still smaller trees left that were ideal for making pulp and paper. With increasing literacy, newspapers all over the world required more and more paper. Canadian forest companies moved to supply this need, but little was done to conserve the forests. When trees were cut, new trees were not planted. Waste branches and cuttings were left in the bush where they became fire hazards. With so much land and forest, it was easy to believe the resources would always be there. Canadians did not realize that our forests had to be looked after if this valuable resource were to survive until much later in the century.

## Mining

Four hundred years ago, when people thought of the "new world," they envisioned a land of gold and riches. The search for gold led to two Canadian gold rushes—the Cariboo in British Columbia during the 1860s and the 1898 Klondike gold rush, when hundreds of would-be miners swarmed to our northern territories in search of gold.

Coal, copper, iron and nickel, although less glamorous than gold, were far more useful. By 1900, industries all over the world needed these minerals. Both new ways of processing minerals and new uses were developed for them.

*Mining was an important industry in the early 1900s. How important is it today?*

The rocky Canadian Shield north of the St. Lawrence Lowlands proved to hold great wealth. In earlier days *coureurs de bois* ranged the forests of the Shield hunting furs. Later, lumberjacks felled its mighty trees. During the early 1900s, prospectors looked under the forest floor for minerals. New mining towns sprang up overnight, especially in northern Ontario. The development of our mineral wealth increased in other parts of the country too—Nova Scotia and southern British Columbia.

## Fishing

Fishing was a financial mainstay in the Maritimes and British Columbia throughout most of the twentieth century. Toward the end of the 1900s, however, serious depletion of fish stock as a result of over-fishing and the presence of foreign fishing fleets in Canadian waters led to laws restricting fishing.

*Frontier College was founded in 1899 as a way of making education accessible to labourers in the work camps of Canada. Teachers worked by day alongside the workers in mines, lumber camps, factories and on fishing ships, and taught reading and writing at night. Still operating today, Frontier College has changed its focus to include urban frontiers. Volunteers now teach reading and writing to prisoners, street kids and people with special needs. It won the UNESCO Award for literacy in 1976.*

Massive unemployment resulted; many fishing families faced uncertain and bleak futures.

Similarly, fur trapping flourished during the first half of the twentieth century. Fur coats and hats were considered very fashionable. However, anti-fur lobby groups launched a successful campaign against the use of furs during the later half of the century. By 2000, Canadian fur trapping was at an historic low, despite the fact that there are as many fur-bearing animals in Canada now as there were when European explorers first settled Canadian shores.

## RATES OF PAY PER DAY 1900-1910

| | | | | | |
|---|---|---|---|---|---|
| ASBESTOS & SLATE QUARRIES | Quebec | $1.50 – $2.00 | COAL MINERS | Nova Scotia | $3.00 – $5.00 |
| | Ontario | $3.00 – $3.50 | | Alberta | $75.00 – $180.00 |
| | | | | | |
| BRICKLAYERS | Montreal | $4.00 | GLASS BLOWERS | Hamilton | $6.00 – $10.00 |
| | Toronto | $4.50 | | | |
| | Ottawa | $4.50 | IRON WORKERS | Nova Scotia | $1.50 – $3.00 |
| | Winnipeg | $5.40 | BOILER MAKERS | New Brunswick | $1.50 – $3.00 |
| | Prince Albert | $2.50 – $3.50 | MACHINISTS | Quebec | $1.50 – $3.00 |
| | Calgary | $5.60 | BLACKSMITHS | Ontario | $1.50 – $3.00 |
| | Vancouver | $5.00 | SHEET METAL WORKERS | Manitoba | $2.00 – $3.00 |
| | | | | Saskatchewan | $3.00 – $4.00 |
| CARPENTERS | Halifax | $2.70 | | Alberta | $3.00 – $4.00 |
| | St. John | $2.50 | | British Columbia | $3.00 – $5.00 |
| | Montreal | $1.98 –$2.43 | | | |
| | Quebec City | $1.75 | PLASTERERS | Winnipeg | $5.00 |
| | Toronto | $2.97 | | Prince Albert | $2.50 – $3.50 |
| | Prince Albert | $2.00 – $2.50 | | | |
| | Regina | $3.60 – 4.05 | SILVER & GOLD MINERS | Nova Scotia | $1.50 – $2.00 |
| | Calgary | $4.05 | | British Columbia | $3.25 – $3.50 |
| | | | | Yukon | $4.50 – $6.00 |

FOCUS
1. Why were the following important?  a) pulp and paper in eastern Canada
                                       b) gold in the Cariboo and Klondike
                                       c) fishing in the Maritimes and British Columbia
                                       d) mining in Ontario and Quebec
2. How important are they today?

# Industry and Unions

During the first 10 years of the twentieth century, output from Canadian industry more than doubled. Some industries, iron and steel for example, produced 5 times as much in 1910 as they had in 1900.

| VALUE OF PRODUCTION (in thousands of dollars) | | |
|---|---|---|
| | **1900** | **1910** |
| Tobacco | 8,000 | 13,000 |
| Boots and shoes | 7,500 | 16,000 |
| Clothes | 20,000 | 44,000 |
| Furniture | 4,300 | 8,000 |
| Farm machinery | 5,000 | 11,000 |
| Iron and steel | 3,100 | 15,000 |
| Automobiles | — | 2,500 |
| Electric light and power | 2,000 | 13,000 |

## Electricity

One of the most important contributors to this monumental growth was electricity. Canadian rivers and waterfalls were first dammed in 1880 to produce electricity. Electric motors replaced the horses used to pull city streetcars. Electric lights made streets and homes brighter, effectively making days longer. Electric appliances—vacuum cleaners, irons—soon appeared, making life easier for the homemaker. Electricity's greatest impact, however, was in the factory. Electricity allowed the creation of ways to mass produce pulp and paper, sew clothes, and grind wheat into flour. Manufacturing could be done by machine rather than by hand.

## Mergers and Takeovers

The larger the factory, the more efficiently it could produce goods. This was called the "economy of scale." Large companies gradually started to dominate the scene. Some times several small companies banded together and "merged" into one. Other times one company would "buy out" its competitors or force them out of business.

Small local producers were losing business. Rural brewers found people preferred to buy from Molson in Montreal, O'Keefe in Toronto or Labatt in London. Instead of selling flour ground at the local mill, storekeepers would stock Ogilvie's Five Roses or Robin Hood. Companies like Burns, Swift and Canada Packers dominated the meat-packing business. Small-town stores were not able to carry the variety of goods available from an Eaton's or Simpson's catalogue.

Industry was changing. Profits were growing and, often, the last thing on the minds of many mill owners and factory bosses was their workers' quality of life. Factory machinery was designed for efficiency, not safety. Work places were often dark, uncomfortable and poorly ventilated. Workers' hours were long and their wages low. Work was often boring and monotonous.

During the first 10 years of the twentieth century, output from Canadian industries more than doubled.

*This Winnipeg factory in 1904 had electric light, but the sewing machines were probably still operated by foot treadles. Why might this be a difficult way to earn a living?*

*What will electricity do for you? To encourage the installation of electricity, Ontario Hydro loaded this truck with electric equipment. Among the items on display are a circular saw and a washing machine. This kind of advertising helped both manufacturers and the electric company sell their products.*

labour battles to be fought. So many people were working in factories by 1907 that the Federal Department of Labour was created to help regulate relations between employers and workers.

Big business did not take over completely. Many small companies survived and others started up. Some people wanted a more independent way of life than working for others gave them. They scraped and saved until they had enough to open their own restaurants, barber shops, laundries, grocery stores, clothing stores, bakeries or fruit stalls. Immigrants followed trades they had learned in the old country and worked as tailors, jewellers, music teachers or shoemakers. Often, they worked as hard or even harder than they would have in a factory. Their reward was that the profit, however small, was theirs and theirs alone.

## Unions

Canadian workers began to organize **unions** during the 1830s to demand better wages and working conditions. By 1900, there had been many advances. Some laws protecting workers and unions were passed, but most employers did not like dealing with unions. There were still many management and

*Opposite: A broom factory in 1896. Employers found they could pay children far less than adults for doing many tedious and unpleasant jobs. Unions fought to have laws passed to stop children working. Although they wanted to protect the children, they also wanted to make sure children did not take jobs away from adults. The first child labour law was passed in Ontario in 1908. Other provinces soon followed.*

### FOCUS

1. How did electricity change life for many Canadians?
2. If you worked in a factory in the early 1900s, why might you have wanted to join a trade union?
3. If you owned a factory in the early 1900s, why might you be against trade unions?
4. Why did many Canadians accept the hard work and long hours of running their own business?

# Railways and Automobiles

The completion of the Canadian Pacific Railway in 1885 was a great success. It carried settlers to the Canadian West and wheat crops from the prairies to the ports of Vancouver, Montreal, and Quebec City. New towns such as Regina grew up along its tracks.

*The railroad connected Canada from east to west. New towns, such as this one in Broadview, Alberta, sprang up along the railway tracks.*

The CPR did not have enough railway cars to ship grain at harvest time. Also, settlers were moving into areas of the West and North where the railway did not reach. Many farmers thought the CPR should have some competition, hoping this might bring down the freight rates they had to pay to ship out their grain and bring in farming machinery. Even today, shipping costs continue to be a thorny issue for prairie farmers.

## New Railways

In the early 1900s, the federal and provincial governments also believed Canada needed more railroads. Railway-building fever swept across the country. Investors saw an opportunity to make a fortune by putting money into new railways.

The Grand Trunk Railway in eastern Canada decided to build a western extension called the Grand Trunk Pacific. The Manitoba government, however, supported another railroad, the Canadian Northern Railway, as a western alternative to the CPR. Common sense said the two groups should cooperate, but greed got in the way.

Both groups had friends in Ottawa. Both asked the government for financial help. Instead of deciding which plan was better, the government gave each company money. Prime Minister Laurier believed more railways were necessary. He thought that both companies could survive.

The railway-building boom continued until the onset of World War I in 1914. The government could no longer afford to provide money for trains when so much was needed for the war effort.

In the early 1900s, railway-building fever swept across the country. Investors saw an opportunity to make a fortune.

## TRAVEL COSTS 1900-1910

### By train from TORONTO, Ontario to:

|  | First Class | Second Class | Return |
|---|---|---|---|
| CALGARY, Alberta | 47.45 | 37.20 | 85.00 |
| CHARLOTTETOWN, Prince Edward Island | 24.10 | 19.45 | 44.35 |
| COBALT, Ontario | 9.90 | 9.40 | 16.50 |
| EDMONTON, Alberta | 49.10 | 37.80 | 85.00 |
| HALIFAX, Nova Scotia | 24.85 | 18.95 | 44.40 |
| HAMILTON, Ontario | 1.15 | ......... | 1.95 |
| MONTREAL, Quebec | 10.00 | 6.65 | 16.70 |
| OTTAWA, Ontario | 7.70 | 6.40 | 12.85 |
| PRINCE ALBERT, Saskatchewan | 41.25 | 32.10 | ......... |
| REGINA, Saskatchewan | 34.20 | 27.50 | 67.95 |
| ST. JOHN, New Brunswick | 20.55 | 16.65 | 39.20 |
| ST. JOHN'S, Newfoundland | 42.35 | 27.15 | 73.25 |
| VANCOUVER, British Columbia | 64.95 | 56.05 | 120.40 |
| VERNON, British Columbia | 61.65 | 51.40 | ......... |
| VICTORIA, British Columbia | 64.95 | 56.05 | 120.40 |
| WINNIPEG, Manitoba | 26.05 | 21.00 | 50.00 |

## RAILWAY BUILDING (1902- 1914)

| | | |
|---|---|---|
| **Grand Trunk Pacific** | **National Transcontinental** | **Hudson Bay (Sask. and Man.)** |
| **Canadian Northern** | **Timiskaming and Northern** | **Canadian Pacific (branch lines)** |
| **Great Northern (B.C.)** | **(Ont.)** | |

Economic reality burst the investors' dreams. There was not enough grain or other freight to support three transcontinental railway systems. The Grand Trunk and Canadian Nothern Railways went bankrupt.

Others struggled to survive. In 1922, the federal government amalgamated several of the existing railways to form the Canadian National Railway (CNR).

about a new form of transportation—the automobile.

Sam McLaughlin worked for his father at the McLaughlin Carriage Company in Oshawa, Ontario—one of the biggest carriage making firms in the country. Sam saw "Russell

## The Automobile

The railway was the fastest and most comfortable way of travelling for Canadians at the turn of the century. Rich and poor alike used the train, but some Canadians were thinking

*Although cars became more widespread during the early twentieth century, they were a long way from being dependable. Winter driving was especially hazardous.*

Cars" built by the Canada Cycle and Motor Company (CCM) in Toronto and decided it was time for the McLaughlins to start making cars.

Since it would be too expensive to design his own engine, Sam arranged a deal with the Buick Company of Michigan. Buick supplied the engines and McLaughlin built the bodies. The McLaughlin, as the car was called, could reach speeds of 60 kilometres per hour and sold for $1,420—a considerable sum in those days. This tie with Buick proved to be good business. In 1907, the McLaughlin Carriage Company produced 193 cars. In 1915, the carriage-making business was sold in order to make room to build Chevrolets. An American company, General Motors, bought the entire company in 1918. Sam McLaughlin became president of the new Canadian branch plant. Big American companies purchasing smaller Canadian companies would be an important issue facing Canadians in the twentieth century.

SATURDAY AFTERNOON

McLaughlin Carriages and Automobiles as seen on a Saturday Afternoon, passing the "Rouge Hill," a popular driveway 12 miles east of Toronto. An historic piece

F O C U S

1. Why was there a railway-building boom in the 1900s?
2. Why were some new railways combined to form the CNR in 1922?
3. Describe the role of Sam McLaughlin in the early Canadian automobile industry.
4. Compare the speed and cost of McLaughlin's cars with cars today.

## In Their Own Words

"When they were old enough, my grandfather's sons Sam and George became very involved in the business. Colonel Sam, as they called him, was a very dynamic man and he was the engineer. My father, George, was the quieter one. He was the company salesman who travelled across Canada; in fact, he was the first man ever to drive a motor car across the Canadian prairies. Looking back now on when I was young, it seems that I was always waiting for my dad to come home from work. In those days people worked very long hours. They worked Saturday too, you know. Anyway, my dad would go to the factory at 7:00 and then at noon the whistles would blow. That meant the factory was closing for an hour. As soon as I heard the whistle blow, I would go to meet my dad on the wooden sidewalk. And I would wait until I figured out which man walking up the sidewalk was him and then I'd meet him and walk back home the rest of the way with him."

Dorothy McLaughlin Henderson reprinted from *Voice of the Pioneer* by Bill McNeil

*Alexander Graham Bell's* Silver Dart *takes off in Baddock Bay, Nova Scotia, signalling the dawn of the airplane as a new way to travel.*

Banff National Park, established in 1885 after a chance discovery of hot springs on Sulphur Mountain, is Canada's oldest park. Initially, only 26 square kilometres were set aside as a wildlife reserve. Today, Banff National Park is 6, 641 square kilometres of unparalleled beauty and wilderness. It is a haven for adventure seekers, old and young. Over 5 million people visit the park each year, hoping to glimpse a grizzly, climb the Rocky Mountains or hike through Banff's rugged backcountry. Thrill seekers, however, are not new to Banff. As early as 1896, an American tourist was killed while attempting to scale the Rockies. This promptly led the government to import skilled Swiss mountaineers to safely guide the tourists over the rough terrain.

Today, the park is part of the largest system of national parks in the world—the Rocky Mountain Parks System. Together with Kootenay, Yoho, Jasper and three national parks in BC, the 23,000 square kilometre system has been declared a UNESCO World Heritage Site.

At the turn of the century, Ontarians began to show concern over the seemingly endless exploitation of Canada's natural resources. In 1893, on the advice of a number of civil servants directly involved with Ontario forests, the provincial government established a royal commission to analyze the possibility of creating a national wildlife preserve. Many people supported this proposal, including the lumbering industry, which saw it as a way of guaranteeing a continued supply of timber. In 1893, the Ontario Government passed an Act creating Algonquin National Park, as it was called in those days. It was a 3,755 square kilometre wildlife preserve.

Algonquin Park soon grew. The northern railway was completed in 1896, making the park accessible to many city dwellers eager to experience Canada's great outdoors. Lodges, summer camps and cottages sprang up along the southern borders of the park. Today, the Park encompasses an area 7,700 square kilometres in size and has remained a favourite place for canoeing, hiking and camping.

*Which national or provincial parks have you visited? Describe your visit. Is it important for Canadians to protect and develop our park system? Explain.*

# Political Issues

# 10

Although Canada was booming by 1900, there were still deep divisions about what kind of country Canadians wanted. French and English Canadians clashed regularly over Canada's ties with Great Britain. All Canadians were concerned about the powerful neighbour to the south—the United States. The huge American economy presented both threats and opportunities. Even at this time Canadians were quick to enter into passionate debate about what kind of country Canada was to become—an issue that is still important to Canadians.

## Canada and the British Empire

English and French Canadians have often differed. In 1900, most English-speaking Canadians were descendants of people from the British Isles. The idea of loyalty to the British Crown and to the British Empire remained strong. French Canadians did not share this feeling. They had lived in Canada for many generations and viewed themselves as "Canadiens" not British or even French. Why should they be loyal to the British Empire? New France had been conquered by the English in 1759-60. To French Canadians, Britain was a foreign, dominating empire. Why should they take part in British wars? At the turn of the century, several issues revealed this deep division in Canadian society.

These differences became intense during the South African, or Boer War (1899-1902). Prospectors had discovered gold in Southern Africa and the British wanted control of it. The area had been settled by the Boers— Dutch pioneers— who did not want to be ruled by Britain. When war started, many

*Soldiers regroup during the Boer War.*

English Canadians wanted to send soldiers to help the British gain control over South Africa. Few cared to ask the existing Black South Africans what they thought about white European nations fighting for possession of their land.

Many French Canadians supported the Boers, because they felt the British were treating the Boers much as they had treated New France. They believed the Boer War had nothing to do with Canada. They were com-

Although Canada was booming by 1900, there was a deep division about what kind of country Canadians wanted.

pletely opposed to sending troops to fight in what they considered a British colonial adventure.

Prime Minister Laurier came up with a compromise. Canadians could volunteer to fight with the British in South Africa. Nobody would be forced to go. The 6,000 volunteers

would be paid by the British government. Laurier's attempt to bridge the gap between English and French Canadians was to prove frustrating indeed. Neither side was satisfied with Laurier's solution. English Canadians felt Canada had not done enough: French

Canadians felt Canada had done too much. For much of the twentieth century, English and French Canadians often found themselves on opposing sides of issues similar to this one.

### The Naval Question

Britain and Germany were competing European empires. Since the early 1800s, Britain had had the most powerful navy in the world. "Britannia ruled the waves," and the British wanted to keep it that way. By 1900, Germany was catching up quickly. The British asked Canada, Australia, and the other Dominions of their empire for help in keeping the British navy strong. Britain wanted money to build dreadnoughts (battleships). Britain argued that its powerful navy was also needed to defend its far-flung empire.

Most English Canadians thought this was the right thing to do. Many French Canadians did not. Henri Bourassa, editor of Montreal's influential newspaper, *Le Devoir,* had once been a prominent Liberal. Bourassa left the party over Laurier's Boer War policy. He believed that Canada should not help finance Britain's navy. To do so could involve Canada in future British wars. French Canadians wanted to stay out of European wars. They felt Canada would gain nothing from them.

H.M.S. Niobe, *one of Canada's early navy vessels.*

Once again, Laurier tried to compromise. He suggested Canada should have a navy of its own. Canada would build some small ships to protect Canadian shores. In case of war, this "Canadian navy" would fight alongside the British navy. The Naval Service Act of 1910 brought the Royal Canadian Navy into being.

Robert Borden, leader of the Conservative Party, wanted Canada to support the British navy directly with money. A small Canadian navy would be nothing but a "tin-pot" navy, he said, consisting of just two old British cruisers. Most English Canadians sided with Borden and the Conservatives. French Canadians felt that the English-Canadian majority had once again given in to Britain.

FOCUS

1. Why did French and English Canadians have different views about the British Empire in the early 1900s?
2. With which view do you most agree? Why?
3. Explain the different viewpoints of French and English Canadians to
   a) the Boer War b) a Canadian navy.

BORN: 1868, in Montreal, Quebec

DIED: 1952, in Montreal, Quebec

SIGNIFICANCE: Canadian national-ist, spokesperson for Quebec, Founder of *Le Devoir,* one of Canada's most influential French-language papers.

BRIEF BIOGRAPHY: Bourassa's early start in politics began in 1890, when, at the age of 22, he became the mayor of Montebello. He entered federal politics in 1896 as a member of Laurier's Liberal Party. In 1907, he split with Laurier over the Boer War, although he continued to support all other Liberal policies. Bourassa was elected to the Quebec Assembly in 1908, where he fought for more balanced immi-gration policies so French Canada would not be swamped by English-speaking immigrants. He also fought for the equal status for French and English languages. In 1910, Bourassa founded *Le Devoir,* one of Canada's most outspoken newspapers. Its first battle was over Reciprocity, which Bourassa claimed would lead to U.S. interference. Bourassa also attacked Laurier's Naval Policy. He did not want

Canada involved in foreign wars. During the First World War, Bourassa cam-paigned actively against conscription. He was labeled a traitor by most English-speaking Canadians. Feelings against him ran so high that a riot broke out at a speaking engagement, and Bourassa had to leave without giving his speech. In 1918, believ-ing that his vision of Canada was an impossible dream, Bourassa went into semi-retirement, and *Le Devoir* became less contro-versial. When he re-entered politics in 1925 as an Independent, Bourassa devoted himself to local issues. He was defeated in the 1935 election. At the same time, Bourassa became a supporter of J. S. Woodsworth's Co-operative Commonwealth Federation (CCF). *How do you feel about Bourassa's claim that Canada was too British oriented at the turn of the century? Explain fully.*

## Henri Bourassa

# The National Policy

John A. Macdonald and the Conservatives wanted to encourage Canadian industry. If people bought Canadian goods, money would stay in the country. Canadian manufacturers would make profits and there would be plenty of jobs for Canadians. In 1878, the Conservatives developed a plan they called the National Policy. All goods coming into the country would be charged a **tariff** or duty. This meant people would buy Canadian products because they would be cheaper than imported ones. The National Policy helped the Conservatives get elected in 1878.

| HOW THE TARIFF PROTECTED CANADIAN INDUSTRIES: | | | |
|---|---|---|---|
| Cost of imported stove | $40 | Cost of Canadian stove | $46 |
| Import duty or tariff | $12 | | — |
| Total price in Canada | $52 | Total price | $46 |

## High or Low Tariffs?

The tariff policy was popular in industrial areas. Factory owners and workers in Quebec, Ontario and Nova Scotia supported the tariff—it protected profits and jobs. Farmers and people in the West opposed the tariff. They wanted to purchase goods manufactured in the United States because they were cheaper than those made in eastern Canada. The tariff forced them to buy the more expensive Canadian products. Many farmers in eastern Canada also objected to the tariff.

By the 1890s, the country was split on the tariff issue. The Conservatives supported the tariff policy. The Liberals wanted freer trade. When the Liberals were elected in 1896, they kept the tariff. Many farmers and consumers urged them to change the policy, but Laurier was in a difficult position. He could not abolish the tariff without angering a large percentage of the country. The Americans offered a solution in 1910—free trade on certain items like farming, fishing, mining and forestry products in return for a lower tariff on many American goods. This type of compromise is called a **reciprocity agreement**—basically a free trade agreement where each side gives something to the other.

## The Election of 1911

Laurier called an election on the reciprocity issue early in 1911. His Liberals campaigned for lower tariffs with the United States. They hoped to win support from the farmers and workers in the East, as well as the settlers on the Prairies.

The Conservatives were strongly opposed to reciprocity. They argued that it would lead to cheaper American goods flooding the Canadian market, which would mean the end of many Canadian industries and lead to unemployment. They believed Canada would fall increasingly under American control. In the end, Canada might even have to join the United States.

Large Canadian companies did not want

Laurier called an election on the reciprocity issue early in 1911. Liberals campaigned for lower tariffs with the United States.

1900  1910  1920  1930  1940  1950  1960  1970  1980  1990

reciprocity either. They supported the Conservatives. They bought advertisements in newspapers across the country appealing to people's feelings of loyalty to the King and Empire. They claimed Canada would soon become totally American if there was freer trade.

These tactics made a great impression in Ontario, Manitoba and British Columbia—areas settled largely by British immigrants. In Quebec, however, the battle between Liberals and Conservatives had little to do with reciprocity. The Naval Question was the biggest issue there. Henri Bourassa joined the fight against the Liberals because he thought Laurier's "pro-British" policy betrayed Quebec's interests.

The Conservatives won the 1911 election with 133 seats to the Liberals' 86. Where the elected members came from, however, was more significant. Some regions—such as Ontario—had voted heavily Conservative, others—such as Quebec—heavily Liberal. This split caused anger and resentment. Similar regional differences would cause problems in the future.

| RESULTS OF THE ELECTION OF 1911 | | |
|---|---|---|
| | Con. | Lib. |
| B.C. | 7 | 0 |
| Alta. | 1 | 6 |
| Sask. | 1 | 9 |
| Man. | 7 | 2 |
| Ont. | 73 | 13 |
| Que. | 27 | 37 |
| N.B. | 5 | 8 |
| P.E.I. | 2 | 2 |
| N.S. | 9 | 9 |
| Yukon | 1 | 0 |
| TOTAL | 133 | 86 |

FOCUS

1. What is a) a protective tariff b) free trade c) reciprocity?
2. Why did Canadians from different regions disagree on the tariff policy?
3. Compare the attitudes towards free trade in 1911 with viewpoints in your province today.
4. Do you fear that the U.S. will one day absorb Canada? Explain.

# Questions & Activities

**Match the persons or groups in column A with the description in column B.**

| A | B |
|---|---|
| **1.** Tom Longboat | **a)** founded the first Women's Institute |
| **2.** Wilfrid Laurier | **b)** changed the family carriage factory into an automobile-making business |
| **3.** Clifford Sifton | **c)** fought for women's right to vote |
| **4.** Adelaide Hunter Hoodless | **d)** a world champion marathon runner |
| **5.** Robert Borden | **e)** was the minister in charge of immigration in the early 1900s. |
| **6.** Nellie McClung | **f)** wanted a separate Canadian navy |
| **7.** Sam McLaughlin | **g)** opposed the policy of reciprocity |
| **8.** Henri Bourassa | **h)** Quebec nationalist |

## Let's Discuss It

**1.** What sorts of problems did immigrants to Canada face in the early 1900s?

Which of these problems do immigrants still face today?

What different sorts of problems do they face today?

Discuss what the government should do to help immigrants today.

What can immigrants do to help themselves adjust to life in their new country?

**2.** What problems did women face in the early 1900s?

Which of these problems have been solved or reduced? Which still exist today?

Select one problem that women still face in today's society.

How would you solve or reduce this problem?

**3.** Why did workers join trade unions in the early 1900s?

Why do they join trade unions today?

Hold a debate on the topic: Resolve that trade unions are as necessary today as they were in the early 1900s.

## Let's Find Out

**1.** In the early 1900s, many immigrants settled in the same area as others of their national group or religious background. In this way they often formed their own communities. Do some research on one of the following groups and write your own "Community Snapshot" about that group.

**a)** Doukhobor    **b)** German

**c)** Jewish    **d)** Mennonite

**e)** Mormon    **f)** Polish

**g)** your own immigrant roots in Canada

Your "snapshot" should include: Origins in the Old Country, and Development in Canada.

**2.** Find out more about one of the following people. Write a brief biography, explaining his or her achievements and importance.

**a)** Clifford Sifton    **d)** Nellie McClung

**b)** Henri Bourassa    **e)** Tom Longboat

**c)** Sam McLaughlin    **f)** Lucy Maud Montgomery

**d)** E. Cora Hind

**3.** Interview a local businessperson or farmer. Find out what his or her views are on free trade today.

**4.** Interview a local trade union member. Find out why he or she thinks unions are still necessary.

## Be Creative

1. With a small group of other students, prepare a folder about settlement on the Prairies. Your folder should include:

   a) a map of Canada showing the ports where settlers arrived in Canada, the routes of the railways that took them to their new homes, and the location of settlements.

   b) a poster advertising free land in Canada

   c) a description of Canadian immigration policy under Clifford Sifton and its results

   d) a drawing of a settler's home or a typical farm around 1900

2. At the turn of the century, electricity greatly changed the way of life for many Canadians. Write a newspaper article describing how your life today would be without electricity. Your opening might be: "Our community has been without electricity for almost a week, and life is so different."

3. Find out more about life in the cities in the early 1900s. Present your findings in the form of a diary entry that might have been written by a teenager in a poor working class family or a wealthy family. Do you think that anything should have been done about the differences between the rich and the poor? If so, what and by whom?

4. Do further research about the Boer War. Should Canada have been involved? Assume you were living at the time and write a letter to your member of parliament explaining your point of view.

## Web sites

**Canadian Museum of Civilization:** www.cmcc.muse.digital.ca

**Canadian History Subject Guide:** www.mcgill.ca

**20th-Century Canadian History:** www.ualberta.ca/~slis/guides/canada/

**Canadian Navy:** www.dnd.ca

**Naval Museum of Manitoba:** www.naval-museum.mb.ca

# You Are There

It is 1911. A vigorous election campaign is being fought on the issue of reciprocity, or lower tariffs, with the United States. You attend meetings held by both the Liberal Party and the Conservative Party in your riding. The candidates make the speeches below. How will you vote? Why? Try to persuade other voters to agree with you. Write a letter to relatives living in another part of Canada explaining the attitude of people in your region.

## BORDEN IN ONTARIO
### THE CONSERVATIVE CANDIDATE

My Fellow Canadians,

In 1879, John A. Macdonald introduced a protective tariff. This was a customs duty, which was added to the cost of manufactured goods imported from the United States. We all know that because American manufacturers are producing goods for a larger market, these goods are often cheaper than Canadian goods. Without the tariff, American goods would flood into Canada. The entire farm implement industry—stove, shoes and clothing manufacturers—would go out of business. The cities of Hamilton, Winnipeg, Halifax, Montreal and Toronto would lose their main industries. Workers all across eastern Canada would lose their jobs. Without these industries, we would be a nation of farmers, fishermen, and lumberjacks— and a land of "hewers of wood and drawers of water" providing raw materials for others to process.

No, my friends, low tariffs, or "Reciprocity" would not only cause mass unemployment; it would be the first step towards Canada losing its existence. If you follow the Liberal policy, we will all soon not only buy our manufactured goods from the U.S., we will soon be part of the United States. We would lose our ties to Britain and the Empire.

If you want a prosperous, independent country, vote for the Conservative party. Vote to maintain the collective tariff.

## LAURIER IN ALBERTA
### THE LIBERAL CANDIDATE

People of Canada:

For many years we have had a protective tariff. This policy has helped the factory owners in the big cities like Toronto and Montreal. They have become wealthy selling their goods in a protected market. But at whose expense?

I say it is the farmers of the Prairie Provinces who have paid the price. I say it is the farmers and people of the small valleys of eastern Canada who are losing out. It is the fishermen of British Columbia and the Maritimes. It is the lumber workers of Ontario, Quebec, New Brunswick and Nova Scotia. These people have had to pay higher prices for Canadian goods. They could have bought less expensive goods from the United States. And the farmers of the West would not have had to pay those high freight costs to bring goods from Ontario and Quebec.

But this is only the beginning. Our tariffs have caused the Americans to place tariffs of their own against our grain, fish and lumber.

I say reduce the tariffs. If elected, the Liberal Party will arrange a treaty with the Americans. If we agree to reduce tariffs on manufactured goods from the U.S., they will reciprocate by reducing tariffs to let in our raw materials.

Fellow Canadians, we have a great future if we increase our trade. Join with the Liberal Party. Let us reduce the tariffs. Let us have a policy that benefits all Canadians, not just the wealthy factory owners in eastern Canada.

# Point
## Counterpoint

With which of the following statements do you most agree? Why?

With which of the following statements do you least agree? Why?

"We French Canadians belong to one country, Canada. Canada is, for us, the whole world. The English Canadians have two countries, one here and one across the seas."

Wilfrid Laurier, quoted in Montreal's *La Presse*

"Those who cut your fathers to pieces on the Plains of Abraham are asking you today to go and get killed for them."

Quebec politician, 1911

"There is Ontario patriotism, Quebec patriotism, and Western patriotism. Each hopes it may swallow up the others. But there is no Canadian patriotism. We can have no Canadian nation when we have no Canadian patriotism."

Henri Bourassa, 1907

"British Canadians will find a way, through the ballot box or otherwise, to rid themselves of the influence of this inferior and disloyal race."

Toronto News

"One Fleet, One Flag, One Throne."

Slogan of the Conservative party in the election of 1911, designed to appeal to feelings of loyalty to Britain.

"I am branded in Quebec as a traitor to the French, and in Ontario as a traitor to the English. In Quebec I am attacked as an imperialist, in Ontario as a separatist. I am neither. I am a Canadian."

Wilfrid Laurier, 1911

# Introduction
## War and Recognition

**C**ANADA'S SUNNY PROGRESS AT THE TURN OF THE TWENTIETH CENTURY was brutally shattered by the outbreak of one of the bloodiest wars in history. During the long, savage years of combat, Canadian troops found themselves in the thick of battle. Although "green" and inexperienced at the start of the war, they soon proved themselves to be among the toughest frontline troops in the British Empire.

At home, the Canadian economy boomed as orders for war supplies flooded in. Jobs formerly open to men alone were more than capably filled by a new generation of women eager to help, proud to earn a pay cheque, and ready to fight for greater political equality. Children helped by working in the fields, digging victory gardens at school and writing letters to the troops overseas.

War meant the tragedy of lost limbs and lost lives. The easy unity felt by all during the first few days of battle was tested by the long, brutal nature of the war. Canadian unity proved more fragile than imagined. Compulsory military service—conscription—nearly tore the nation apart and spawned divisions which have yet to heal in Canada. Many Canadians eagerly recruited from Europe to help populate the West found themselves "interned" as enemy aliens during the conflict. Some workers claimed that unscrupulous businesses were profiting from the war.

## METHODS OF HISTORICAL INQUIRY

### Analysis, Evaluation and Communication

Writing is a necessary part of modern life, and communicating ideas is a basic skill all Canadians must share. We need to be able to write a memo, fill out a job application or compose a letter to friends. History students use writing to communicate their ideas and findings to others. For them, it is important that these ideas be written clearly and precisely. One way to achieve clarity is to organize one's thoughts in a logical sequence, starting with the paragraph and moving on to a short essay.

# Chapter Two:
## War and Recognition

# Expectations

## General Expectations:
**By the end of this chapter, you will be able to:**

- understand Canada's participation and role in the First World War

- understand the impact of World War I on French-English relations and on Canadian identity

## Specific Expectations:
**By the end of this chapter, you will be able to:**

- recognize the causes, events and consequences of the First World War

- know Canada's role during the war

- understand the contribution of Canadian soldiers at Ypres and Vimy Ridge

- recognize the contribution made by a wide range of Canadians during the war

- identify the increased role played by the federal government during the war

- recognize how the First World War changed the lives of Canadian women

## WORD LIST

| | | | |
|---|---|---|---|
| Armaments | Convoy | Over-the-top | Trench |
| Armistice | Enemy aliens | Profiteering | Triple Alliance |
| Artillery | Income-tax | Regiment | Triple Entente |
| Conscription | No-man's land | Regulation | War Measures Act |

# Chapter 2

# *Advance* Organizer

## 1

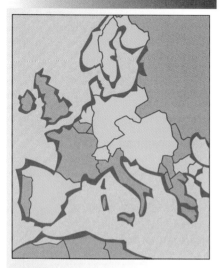

By the 1900s, Europe was divided into two armed camps. One consisted of Germany, Austria-Hungary and Italy — the Triple Alliance. The other was made up of the British Empire, France and Russia — the Triple Entente. Only a spark was needed to set off an explosion of war. It came on June 28, 1914, when the Crown Prince of Austria was assassinated. Within one month, the two alliances were at war.

## 2

Canadians volunteered to fight for the British Empire in 1914. Few knew what war would be like. Soldiers had little or no protection, except for the trenches that they dug on the battlefield. They lived in these night and day. For months on end they fended off the enemy while trying to gain a little territory. This went on for four years.

Often a long and bloody battle meant winning or losing only a few metres of ground. In battles like those at Ypres and Vimy Ridge, Canadians gained a new pride in their country.

## 3

At the beginning of the war, planes were used mainly to observe the movements of enemy troops. Then pilots began carrying rifles and firing upon enemy aircraft. Soon machine guns were mounted on the planes, bringing the war in the air to full force. Many Canadians were among the best fighter pilots of the war. The airplane changed the face of modern warfare forever.

## 4

Disasters at sea were not limited to the war front. One thousand passengers drowned when the British liner *Lusitania* was sunk by a German submarine. In Halifax harbour, two supply ships collided. One was laden with high explosives. The resulting explosion killed and maimed thousands.

## 6

The Canadian army was made up of volunteers. By 1917, so many soldiers were being killed and wounded, volunteers could not replace them. The Conservative government introduced conscription, forcing  young men to join the army. This policy caused one of Canada's major crises. Many English Canadians felt loyal to the British Empire, and were in favour of conscription. But almost all French Canadians were opposed to forcing people to fight in a foreign country. Conscription caused bitter hostility between French and English Canadians, and seriously threatened the unity of Canada.

## 5

With war came the need to produce military machinery and equipment. New factories were opened. Five-hundred-thousand soldiers were overseas, and workers were in short supply. Women served as munitions workers in the new war factories. They also replaced men in other important jobs in Canadian society. To pay for the war, the government issued Victory Bonds and introduced new taxes.

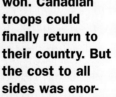

## 7

On 11 November 1918, the armistice was declared, ending the war. The Allies had won. Canadian troops could finally return to their country. But the cost to all sides was enormous. Over 66,000 Canadian soldiers were killed in the First World War. All told, more than 13 million soldiers lost their lives in the war.

# The Road to War

In August 1914, most major European countries became involved in the First World War. The previous 100 years had been a relatively peaceful time for Europe. True, Germany and Italy had expanded their territories, sometimes by warring on neighbouring states. Yet, from the end of the Napoleonic wars in 1815 to the outbreak of this conflict, there had been no major strife. All this ended in 1914. The remainder of the twentieth century was troubled with wars, revolutions, and international conflict.

A number of causes contributed to the outbreak of war in 1914:

**1 – Emergence of Germany as a major power**

By 1871, German Chancellor (Prime Minister) Otto von Bismarck, had united most German-speaking people into a new nation that wished to be recognized as a major power of Europe. German leaders increased Germany's power by expanding its army and navy.

**2 – Clash of Empires**

In the early 1900s, Britain, France, Spain and Portugal, in what was known as Imperialism, controlled large empires with colonies in Asia and Africa. By the 1890s, German political and industrial leaders demanded that Germany also acquire colonies, which would be sources of raw materials for expanding German industries. Because most accessible lands had already been conquered, this demand brought Germany into conflict with other European powers, particularly Britain and France.

**3 – Naval and Arms Race**

The British navy was the largest navy in the world in the early 1900s. Its main duty was to protect Britain's far-flung empire. If Germany were to have a colonial empire, it, too, would require a large navy. When Germany began to build a powerful, modern navy, Britain saw this as a challenge to its position of power. This led the two countries into a race to see who could build the biggest and strongest navy.

Similarly, Germany raced against France and Russia to develop the largest and best-equipped army. The resulting naval and arms races increased tension and hostility in Europe. The world was clearly drifting toward war.

**4 – Nationalism**

Wars are often caused, in part, by countries that prize national interests over anything else. This was certainly the case in the period immediately preceding World War I, as European countries wanted to assert themselves and their national identity.

## 5 – Alliance System

Rivalries in Europe led each country to seek friends—defensive alliances—for their protection. By the early 1900s, two rival alliances were established:

**The Triple Alliance**—Germany, Austria-Hungary and Italy agreed to support each other if attacked by France, Britain or Russia.

**The Triple Entente**—France, Russia, and Britain agreed to support each other if attacked by Germany, Italy or Austria-Hungary.

By 1914, Europe was divided into these two heavily-armed and hostile camps. All that was needed to cause an explosion was a political incident, a spark.

### The Spark

Archduke Franz Ferdinand, the heir to the Austrian throne, was killed on 28 June, 1914, by a Serbian terrorist group, the Black Hand, in Sarajevo, Bosnia-Herzegovina, a state within the Austro-Hungarian Empire. The Austrians sent Serbia an **ultimatum,** which the Serbs refused. Austria invaded. Russia came to the aid of its Serbian allies.

Within one month, most members of the rival alliances were drawn into the conflict. Germany and Austria-Hungary (Triple Alliance) were fighting against France, Russia, and Britain (Triple Entente). As Canada was a member of the British Empire, Canada was automatically involved. Most Canadians were enthusiastic in their support for Britain.

## TIMELINE

**WWI had both long and short-term causes. The short-term events are as follows. Given the events, do you think the war could have been avoided?**

### THE STEPS TO WAR—SUMMER OF 1914

| | |
|---|---|
| **28 June** | Archduke Ferdinand is assassinated at Sarajevo. |
| **23 July** | Austria sends ultimatum (a list of demands) to Serbia. |
| **25 July** | Serbia replies, rejecting one term. |
| **28 July** | Austria invades Serbia. |
| **29 July** | Russia mobilizes army along borders with Austria and Germany. Germany declares war on Russia. |
| **3 August** | France mobilizes forces to assist Russia. Germany declares war on France. |
| **4 August** | Germany invades Belgium, whose neutrality is guaranteed by Britain. Britain declares war on Germany. |
| **5 August** | Canada and the rest of the British Empire are at war. |

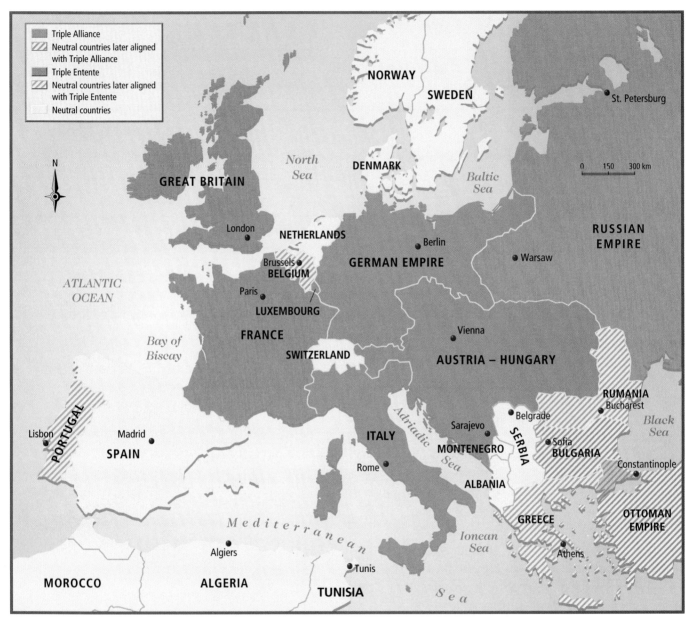

*Europe at the time of World War I.*

Although the common belief was that World War I would be over by Christmas, the shot fired in Sarajevo started a war that lasted four years and killed millions, including over 66,000 Canadians. World War I changed Canada and Canadians forever.

Italy left the Triple Alliance with Germany and Austria, and came into the war on the side of France and Britain. Japan also fought against Germany in World War I, taking over German colonies in China.

One of the new century's most impressive weapons was a battleship called the Dreadnought. Heavily armoured, speedy, and loaded with huge 30-centimetre guns able to fire 400–kilograms of shells a distance of 6,000 metres, the Dreadnought was designed to make all existing warships obsolete. Both Germany and Britain engaged in a furious race to build these powerful ships. This naval race fueled prewar tensions.

Machine guns and the tank were also major new weapons that played key roles during the war. The machine gun, firing at 600 rounds per minute, made it almost impossible for attacking armies to overrun an enemy's position. This led to the seemingly endless war in the trenches.

The tank was developed during the war, and helped to end the stalemate of trench warfare as it could be used to ram through enemy lines. The tank was particularly effective during the final year of the war (1918).

*A tank going into action.*

*Why would tanks be such an effective weapon of war?*

FOCUS

1. Briefly describe the major long-term causes of WWI.
2. What were the major short-term causes?
3. Why was Canada involved in the war?

# 2 The War Begins

Germany, during the late 1800s, tried to keep on friendly terms with Russia. Indeed, the German Kaiser (Emperor) and the Russian Tsar were cousins. If war came, Germany expected it to be with France, not Russia, which would mean battles to the west—a Western Front. If Russia joined France against Germany, it would mean battles to the east—an Eastern Front

When Germany allied with Austria in 1879, Russia's friendship was lost. Russia became France's ally. How could Germany avoid a war on two fronts at once?

## The Schlieffen Plan

German General Von Schlieffen developed a plan. He expected the Russians to take a long time to mobilize their army. He would move rapidly against the French and mislead their army as to the origin of the main attack. The French army would concentrate along the southern part of the Franco-German border, believing the German soldiers would cross over into France from their homeland.

Schlieffen's plan called for the majority of the German army to invade France from the north, sweeping across the flat lands of neutral Belgium and northern France to the English Channel. Then, they would turn toward Paris like a curved claw, falling on the capital from the west. All this would take about six weeks, Schlieffen estimated.

The French would be knocked out of the war, and the Germans could then turn their attention to the slower-moving Russians.

## Why the Schlieffen Plan Failed

Schlieffen based his plan on a gamble. Over 70 years before, France, Germany, and Britain had signed a treaty guaranteeing that Belgium should be neutral. Germany assumed wrongly that Britain would not object to the invasion of Belgium. But Britain did object; they used the invasion as a reason to enter the war.

General Von Schlieffen died in 1913. The new German

*The Schlieffen Plan*

"When the call comes our answer goes at once, and it goes in the classical language of the British answer to the call of duty: 'Ready, aye, ready.'"
Sir Wilfrid Laurier, 1914

**1900   1910   1920   1930   1940   1950   1960   1970   1980   1990**

generals continued with his plan, but made a few changes. Instead of approaching Paris from the west, they were forced to turn south too soon, which meant the French army from the Franco-German border could reach them. The Germans were also attacked by French troops moving out from Paris, and British troops from the Channel ports.

The German advance was halted on the Marne River. Both sides "dug in" extensive trench systems protected by artillery and machine guns. The Schlieffen Plan failed. Instead of knock-

*A group of Aboriginal soldiers have their picture taken before joining the Expeditionary Force.*

ing France out of the war, the Germans found themselves trapped on the Western Front, facing the combined armies of France, Britain, and their empires, including Canada.

Instead of a short, swift campaign as anticipated, Germany's attack on France became a long, costly—and horrible—war. Four years of trench warfare had begun.

## Canada Responds

"When the call comes, our answer goes at once, and it goes in the classical language of the British answer to the call of duty: 'Ready, aye, ready.'"

*Sir Wilfrid Laurier, 1914*

*One last embrace before going off to war.*

**Sam Hughes**

BORN: 1853, Darlington, Ontario

DIED: 1921, Lindsay, Ontario

SIGNIFICANCE: Rapidly organized the Canadian Expeditionary Force in a matter of weeks, and stubbornly fought to maintain it as an independent Canadian fighting unit.

BRIEF BIOGRAPHY: Before entering politics, Hughes was a teacher and newspaper owner-editor. He was appointed Minister of Militia and Defence in Robert Borden's new Conservative government in 1911. Hughes was one of the most energetic supporters of the war effort. Brushing aside the advice and experience of regular officers, Hughes pushed for rapid expansion of Canada's armed forces. Within months, the army had received 100,000 volunteers, and its first contingent of 3,000 left Canada for Britain with just two months of training. When British officers attempted to blend Canadian soldiers into British units, Hughes furiously refused. Although Hughes was energetic and tireless in his defence of Canada, he was also rash, made many enemies, created many foolish and unworkable schemes, and was not liked in French Canada. Eventually, Borden asked for his resignation. Interestingly, Hughes's niece, Laura, a peace activist, was an outspoken critic of the war.

*Describe the major strengths and weaknesses of Sam Hughes.*

*Volunteers are recruited.*

*Canadians were eager to join the fight.*

Most regions of Canada were soon caught up in war fever. Young men rushed to join the armed forces; many worried it would be over before they got there. Outside Quebec, few questioned the war, or whether Canada should participate.

All across the nation, citizens rushed along the road to war. Although Canada was automatically at war when Britain was at war, Canada was able to determine the extent of its participation. So keen were Canadians to fight that an expedi-tionary force was prepared even before the British requested one. The brutal savagery of the next four years, however, would test Canada's enthusiasm and unity.

*Uxbridge, Ontario: men march through town before joining the battle overseas.*

**FOCUS**

1. What was the main aim of the Schlieffen Plan?
2. Why did the plan fail?
3. Why did Britain declare war on Germany when Belgium, not France, was invaded?
4. Who was Sir Sam Hughes? What was his job?
5. How did most Canadians respond to the outbreak of war?

# 3 War in the Trenches

Mud. Barbed wire. Lice. Hardtack and bully beef. Rain, sleet and snow. Mud. Rats. Shell holes full of stagnant water. Bodies. Machine-gun bullets. Sandbags. More mud.

## Digging In

The Schlieffen Plan had failed. The Germans could not advance. The French and the British could not drive them back. Both sides set about **digging-in,** fortifying their positions on the Western Front.

They dug trenches (ditches) to protect their troops. Each **trench** was about 2 metres deep, topped with sandbags. Soldiers could stand in the trench without being seen by the enemy. A narrow strip, called **no-man's land**, lay between the Allies and their enemies. Rifle and machine gun fire spattered across no-man's land whenever a soldier detected movement in enemy territory. Shells flew from the **artillery** behind the front lines, spraying shrapnel everywhere.

*Trench living was often cramped and uncomfortable.*

*These soldiers are going "over-the-top" in an attempt to gain some distance in no man's land.*

"I have often wanted to see a fight. Never again. I remember the next morning, all the dead and dying lying around in twisted shapes. War is hell."

## Over the Top

Officers would sometimes order an advance, which meant **"going over the top"** of the trench and across no-man's-land fully exposed to the enemy's fire. Occasionally, the troops managed to capture the enemy's front line. The enemy would then retire to its reserve trenches a short distance away. Barbed wire stretched across the new patch of no-man's land. A few metres of land had been lost or won. Hundreds of thousands of soldiers were often killed in the process. Then the whole dreary business started all over again.

Soldiers fought, died, ate and slept in the trenches. Eventually they would be relieved for a few days by fresh troops. In winter, they froze in the snow and sleet. Spring rains sometimes filled the trenches waist deep with icy water. In summer, the rich farmlands of Belgium and northern France turned to mud.

## In Their Own Words

*"We are filthy. Our bodies are the color of the earth we have been living in these past months. We are alive with vermin and sit picking at ourselves like baboons. It is months since we have been out of our clothes."*
Source: *Charles Yale Harrison*, Generals Die in Bed.
*Potlach Publications, 1974*

foundland Regiment went over the top in an almost suicidal attack against German machine guns. The regiment was torn to pieces within minutes. Ninety-one percent of the Newfoundland Regiment died that day. Of the 840 who left their trenches, only 79 were able to answer roll-call the following morning. The war settled into a long slaughter of the Western world's youth.

### Battle of the Somme-Beaumont Hamel

The Battle of the Somme was one of the bloodiest, most wasteful battles of WWI. On the first day of the battle, 57,540 casualties were recorded. On one terrible day, July 1, 1915, the young men of the New-

*Trench warfare meant disease and death for millions.*

*The war turned rich farmland into a wasteland of mud and death.*

# In Their Own Words

## Two Letters Home

One of the best sources of information about the brutal reality of trench warfare is the letters of soldiers from the front lines. Read these two letters and note the major differences in their view of the war.

### Before heavy action:
### 24 March 1915

"We have been put in the trenches for a week with British troops. Then we'll be taken back for further training. Then we will be in the trenches for 5 weeks, and then we get a rest.

Our German friends opposite have a sense of humour. One day they stuck a toy horse up above their trench. Our chaps shot it down. They put it up again with a bandage round its neck.

They call out things like 'We no shoot, you no shoot.'

'If you come halfway, we'll give you cigarettes.'

'Hello B.C., how'd you like to be walking down Hastings Street?'

Our men are so light-hearted—full of life and ginger. Somebody is going to be badly hurt when these boys let loose."

### After heavy action:
### 15 May 1915

"We were called out from Ypres about 5 o'clock. The sky was a hell of bursting shrapnel. We lay in reserve until nearly midnight. Then they told us to take the wood. We charged across 500 m of open country. We lost many men during that charge.

I saw poor Charlie go down and stopped to help him, but he urged us on. Then Andy fell, shot right through the head. When we got to the edge of the wood we found a trench just dug by the Germans. This is when the hell began. They had 2 machine guns, and the fire was like hailstones on a tin roof. Somehow they missed a few of us, but the other fellows were cut in half by the stream of lead.

I have often wanted to see a fight. Never again. I remember the next morning, all the dead and dying lying around in twisted shapes. War is hell.

We are going back to the base to be reorganized. We had 26 officers before, and 2 after, so you can see it was pretty bad. I shall try to transfer, as most of my nerve has gone."

**FOCUS**

1. Carefully describe the reality of trench warfare.
2. Imagine you are a soldier fighting in the trenches and write a letter home describing your experiences.

# 4 A Tale of Two Battles

The first Canadian troops arrived in England in October, 1914. The British officers sneered: "These 'colonials' were sloppy. They couldn't even salute properly. The only way to lick them into shape would be to divide them among British units. They would be no use in their own regiment."

The Canadian minister of militia, Sam Hughes, was furious. He refused to let the Canadians be broken up. As a result, Canada had its own army. The Canadian Corps soon proved its worth.

## Ypres

The Canadians arrived in Europe in March, 1915, after four months of training in Britain. They were sent to Ypres, a city near the Belgium coast in order to stop the Germans from breaking through to the English Channel. Since the failure of the Schlieffen Plan the year before, there had been little fighting here.

The Germans wanted to break the stalemate. They decided to use a new weapon—poisonous chlorine gas. On April 22, a gentle breeze blew toward the Allied lines—perfect for a gas attack.

The Canadians had been assigned a section of the front-line trenches. To the left were troops from the French colony of Algeria. The Algerians saw a green cloud drifting across no-man's land. As it reached the trenches, they found themselves choking and gasping for breath. Those who were not suffocated fled.

*Soldiers injured by gas warfare.*

Although people had talked about gas warfare, the Allied commanders did not think it would be used, so they sent the Canadian soldiers to the front without gas masks. When the Germans used mustard gas, the soldiers had no protection. All they could do was

**In Flanders Fields**, the most memorized poem from WWI, was written by a Canadian, John McCrae.

*The stately 500-year old Cloth Hall and Cathedral in Ypres, destroyed by war.*

soak cotton pads in urine and hold them over their faces. The acid in the urine neutralized the chlorine. The soldiers then moved into the gap to prevent a German breakthrough. They miraculously held on for two whole days.

Finally British relief troops took over.

The Canadians had proved themselves. Nobody sneered at them after the battle of Ypres or "Wipers," as Canadian and British soldiers pronounced the name.

*Gas was often used as a weapon during the First World War, forcing the use of masks.*

## Vimy Ridge

"Zero hour will be 5:30 a.m."

The word spread through the Canadian Army on Easter Sunday, 1917. Every soldier was aware that Vimy Ridge was the key to the German lines. If the Allies were to break the stalemate of the war, Vimy Ridge would have to be taken. In two years of tough fighting, Canadians had done well. The dubious honour of storming Vimy Ridge would fall to them.

The soldiers looked across no-man's land. About 100 metres beyond lay the German trenches. It would be sheer hell to get across. That night they enjoyed one last hot meal and a shot of rum to heat their stomachs— and give them courage.

For the past two weeks the **artillery** had been firing shells into enemy lines. Easter Monday dawned cold, with sleet and snow falling. At 5:30 in the morning, the command was given to go over the top. Covered by more shellfire, 15,000 soldiers moved in the first wave of attack. They valiantly struggled across the mud and through what was left of the barbed wire. The return fire from German machine guns and artillery was murderous, but the Canadians wiped out the German front line. The soldiers had passed it in the snow without knowing. They surprised the second line of defence. Some Germans

## COMMUNITY SNAPSHOT

When the First World War broke out in 1914, the Canadian Red Cross Society, founded in 1876, had 156 local branches across Canada. By the end of the war, there were 1303 such branches. Staffed almost entirely by volunteers, the society made clothes, raised money, purchased medical supplies and packaged food to be sent overseas to Canadian soldiers in army hospitals. When Christmas arrived, these soldiers were often surprised to find stockings hanging by their beds. Provided by the Red Cross, the stockings contained clothes, food, candy and cigarettes, all of which were in short supply in Europe.

After the Second Battle of Ypres, when 1,500 Canadians were taken prisoner, the Red Cross Society set up a Prisoners of War Department. The department prepared parcels to be sent to the men in the P.O.W. camps. Nearly all of the one-half million parcels sent to the P.O.W.'s safely arrived at their destinations.

*Red Cross supplies stand ready to be sent to our soldiers in Europe.*

fled, but others surrendered to the Canadians. Despite massive losses, by midmorning the Canadians had seized the heights. Vimy Ridge was in Allied hands.

Nevertheless, the pride felt after such an accomplishment was dampened by the cost. In just a few hours, 3,598 brave Canadians had died.

*Canadian and German wounded help each other through the mud during the capture of Passchendaele.*

## CANADIAN SYMBOLS

Vimy Ridge was the first great Allied victory since the beginning of the war. Canadian pride received a great boost that cold morning in northern France. As one participant noted:

> From dugouts, shell holes and trenches men sprang into action, fell into artillery formations and advanced to the ridge, every division of the Corps moved forward together. It was Canada from the Atlantic to the Pacific on parade. I thought then and I think today, that in those few minutes I witnessed the birth of a nation.
>
> *Brigadier General Alex Ross*

### FOCUS

1. Explain the important role played by Canadians in the battles of Ypres and Vimy Ridge.
2. How did the Canadian Red Cross help in the war effort?

BORN: 1901, Middle Arm, Newfoundland

DIED: 1967, St. John's, Newfoundland

SIGNIFICANCE: Youngest recipient of the Victoria Cross—Britain's highest award for bravery—which he won at the age of 17.

BRIEF BIOGRAPHY: Newfoundland was still a British colony during the First World War (it did not join Confederation until 1949), and the rugged Islanders were quick to volunteer alongside Canadians in their eagerness to stand beside Britain. The soldiers of the Newfoundland Regiment took part in some of the bloodiest battles of the war. They were almost annihilated at the Battle of Beaumont-Hamel in 1916. One of their young fighters gained particular fame with his courageous actions during the terrible battles of Europe.

Ricketts lied about his age and enlisted in the Newfoundland Regiment when he was only 14. He soon saw action and was wounded in 1917. In 1918, under heavy fire, Ricketts displayed uncommon courage and raced across no-man's land, unarmed, to gather ammunition for his unit. He led an attack against a German battery with no artillery support, which resulted in the capture of German field and machine guns and eight prisoners.

After the war, Ricketts returned to Newfoundland, where he studied pharmacy at Memorial University in St. John's. When he died in 1967, he was awarded a state funeral.

**Tommy Ricketts**

**Here's an account taken from a newspaper death notice in 1992. It shows that there are other human costs in war, not just death or physical wounding:**

*"World War I, the Great War, the war to end all wars! What a price was paid in human lives and human misery. It was all so long ago but there are still a few souls left to remind us of those far oft times. My uncle…was such a one. Perhaps there are those who would say he was fortunate to escape with his life, but I wonder what kind of life it has been for him. Uncle Jim and his brother John were fighting in the trenches in Passchendaele, France, when the call came to pull back. Jim would not leave without his brother and waded through the bodies, wiping the mud from the faces of the wounded and dying soldiers until he saw the face of his brother. He picked him up and carried him back behind the lines. Upon reaching the Red Cross medical tent, Jim placed his brother's wounded body on the table. 'Here,' he said, 'this is my brother, look after him—you have to save him.' Jim then retreated outside into the darkness and collapsed. When he awoke hours later, he found himself lying on a pile of dead bodies. His brother was saved, but what of Jim? Uncle Jim was sent back home and made an effort to take up a normal semblance of his old life once more, but it was in vain. The ceaseless bombardment and the horror of the senseless slaughter of human lives had taken its toll. He retreated into a world where no war could reach him again.*

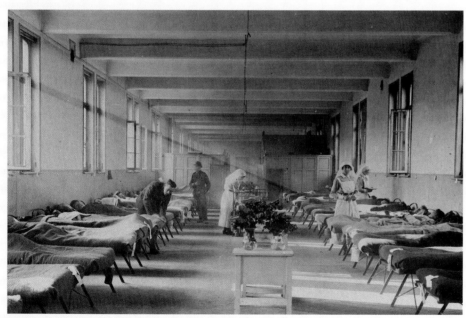

*Ward of soldiers' hospital in France.*

*Unfortunately, he also shut out the rest of the world. In 1931, Jim was admitted to the Veterans' Hospital where he remained until July 15, 1992. 'Shell shock,' they called it. No physical injury, just a damaged mind. His days passed in a twilight world where no one could reach him. Yet I must believe that his sacrifice was not in vain, and I also must believe that he is at peace…."*

### Canada's Aboriginal Fighters

Many Canadian communities supported Canada's efforts in WWI. Canada's First Nations, while small in number, were particularly effective. Although officials at first discouraged the recruitment of Aboriginal Canadians partly because of racist views and partly because they felt Aboriginals might be mistreated if captured, the need for men was so great and the willingness of Aboriginal Canadians so persistent that the Canadian Army soon had many volunteers. In total, about 4,000 Aboriginal Canadians fought in the war. They were particularly valued as scouts and snipers—two of the most dangerous and important combat positions in the war.

Scouts were expected to penetrate enemy positions and report back to headquarters. As well, they would create havoc behind enemy lines. Snipers were crack shots able to camouflage themselves and then fire into the ranks of the enemy. Canada's greatest snipers were Aboriginal Canadians such as Francis Pegahmagabow, an Ojibway from Parry Sound, Ontario. "Peg" is credited with 378 hits on enemy soldiers. Henry "Ducky" Norwest, a Cree, had the best sharp-shooting record in the British forces, with 115 observed "kills." A Métis relative of Louis Riel, Patrick Riel, was also a skilled marksman, and had 38 "kills." The legendary runner Tom Longboat was an excellent dispatch runner during WWI.

After the war, these soldiers returned to a Canada slow to recognize their efforts. Only recently, the Canadian government has promised a special war memorial in Ottawa dedicated to the memory and contributions of Canada's Aboriginal fighters.

# Canadian Vision

**In Flanders Fields,** the most memorized poem from WWI, was written by a Canadian, John McCrae. His vision of the devastation of war is often a key element in Remembrance Day services. Tragically, McCrae died a few weeks after penning this famous poem.

### In Flanders Fields

In Flanders Fields the poppies blow
Between the crosses, row on row,
That mark our place; and in the sky,
The larks, still bravely singing, fly
Scarce heard amid the guns below.

We are the Dead. Short days ago
We lived, felt dawn, saw sunset glow,
Loved, and were loved, and now we lie
In Flanders Fields.

To you from failing hands we throw
The torch; be yours to hold it high.
If ye break faith with us who die
We shall not sleep, though poppies grow
In Flanders Fields.

**Which lines are the most moving in your opinion? Why?**

FOCUS
1. What terrible price did "Uncle Jim" pay for his heroic efforts in WWI?
2. Why is Tommy Ricketts considered a hero?
3. Why were Aboriginal soldiers so valuable on the battle field?
4. Outline your personal reaction to *In Flanders Fields.*

# 5 Total War

### The War in the Air

The Wright brothers flew the first successful airplane at Kitty Hawk, North Carolina, in 1903. Six years later, John McCurdy flew the Silver Dart—designed by McCurdy and Alexander Graham Bell—at Baddeck, Nova Scotia. Airplanes were still regarded as "too

*Canadian Officers, Royal Flying Corps, Reading, England, 1916.*

expensive a luxury for Canada to indulge in," however. Consequently, at the outbreak of the First World War, Canada had no planes and no pilots.

This attitude did not appeal to young Canadian flying buffs. Many went to Britain to join the Royal Flying Corps. They were among the best fighter pilots of the war.

### Dogfights

Meetings between warring aircraft often became deadly "dogfights." Pilots tried to tailgate enemy planes so that the enemies could not return the gunfire. Being shot down usually meant instant death. Pilots were not allowed to carry parachutes because, if they did, they might bail out. Their officers wanted them to try to save planes instead. The average lifespan of a pilot was only three weeks long. They called their planes, "flying coffins."

One of the leading "aces" of the Royal Flying Corps was a Canadian, Billy Bishop. He shot down 72 enemy planes. The greatest flying ace of the war was Germany's Manfred von Richthofen, the famous "Red Baron." He shot down 80 planes.

**World War I** was the first war to involve all sections of society, and was, in fact, a total war.

## The Technical Edge

*A young Lester B. Pearson*

Aircraft design had not advanced greatly from 1903 to the onset of the First World War. Most planes flew at about 150 km/h. They had open, single-seat cockpits. Planes were used mainly to observe enemy troop movements. The thrill of flying united all pilots, regardless of nationality. British, German and French fighters would wave to each other as their planes passed above the lines of battle. Before long, some pilots started to bring rifles into the cockpit. They shot at enemy planes in order to stop information reaching enemy generals. The friendly camaraderie was over.

Soon, machine guns were mounted on planes. A major problem with this new design was that the guns often hit the plane's propellers. One British design mounted the gun behind the pilot. The French placed it above the propeller, on the top wing of the biplane. The Germans had a gun timed to fire through the propeller without hitting the blades. When the British tried this system, it did not always work perfectly. These guns had fixed mounts. The only way to aim the gun was to point the entire plane directly at the target. By war's end, many new designs had been built and bombers, zeppelins and fighters were a regular feature in the skies high above the trenches. WWI spurred the development of aircraft to a central role in modern warfare.

*How were airplanes used in WWI?*

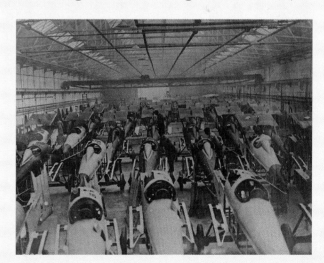

*Airplane factory during WWI.*

BORN: 1894, Owen Sound, Ontario

DIED: 1956, Palm Beach, Florida

SIGNIFICANCE: Canada's flying hero in WWI with 72 recorded "kills," which made him the greatest ace in the British Empire and earned him the Victoria Cross, the highest award for bravery under fire.

BRIEF BIOGRAPHY: A charming, rambunctious youth, Bishop did not do well at school, but was an excellent marksman. Bishop entered the war as a cavalry officer. Realizing that flying was where the action was, he became a gunner-observer and then a pilot. Bishop was a rebel who often found himself in trouble with authorities. He was also a brave and gifted fighter pilot. The average lifespan of a rookie pilot in combat was eleven days. Bishop was a natural and in his first month at the front downed 17 enemy aircraft. He duelled with the Red Baron, and both men limped home in shot-up aircraft.

Bishop shot down 5 enemy aircraft in one battle alone. He won the Victoria Cross for his daring solo attack on a German aerodrome, which resulted in three "kills." He was recalled to Canada to inspire recruiting and swell Victory Bond sales—a means of raising funds to support the war financially.

After the war, Bishop flew in air shows, gave lectures and dabbled in business. When the Second World War erupted in 1939, Bishop was made an Air Marshal to spur recruitment to the RCAF.

*Why is Billy Bishop considered a "hero?"*

## Billy Bishop

*Wilfrid May nearly perished under the guns of the "Red Baron."*

### The Red Baron's Last Flight

One day in April, 1918, Richthofen took his pilots on their usual daily patrol. They were met by a British squadron led by Roy Brown of Carleton Place, Ontario. Soon the two groups were in a fierce dogfight.

Wilfrid "Wop" May was on his first combat flight. The young Canadian realized his guns were jammed and drifted out of the battle. The Red Baron moved onto his tail. Preparing for the kill, he did not notice that Roy Brown had moved behind him. Brown got the German ace in his gun sights and knocked him out of the sky. A Canadian had downed the legendary Red Baron!

Recently, however, some Australian soldiers have disputed this claim as they maintain that they shot down the Red Baron when his plane was close to the ground chasing Brown's plane.

**FOCUS**
1. Define "dogfights" and "flying coffins."
2. Why is Billy Bishop considered such a great ace?

### The War at Sea

When the war began, Canada had only two mid-sized cruisers in its navy—the H.M.S. *Niobe* was based in Halifax and the H.M.S. *Rainbow* in Vancouver. Canada's navy did little fighting at sea. Nevertheless, by the end of the war, the Royal Canadian Navy had grown to about 100 ships, mostly small coastal vessels. Only one warship was lost at sea during the war.

### Atlantic Convoys

Canada's main role in the war at sea was in shipping Canadian troops, food and munitions to Europe. The United States remained neutral throughout most of the war. Although Americans sold goods to Britain, France and Germany, most Americans were sympathetic to the Allies. Britain tried to block goods being sent to Germany. The British navy mined the North Sea so that neutral ships could not reach German ports. The German navy wanted to stop goods reaching Britain. They declared a war zone in the waters around the British Isles.

The Germans used submarines to attack ships bound for Britain. A German submarine sank the *Lusitania*, a British passenger liner, in 1915. Over 1,000 people died, including 128 Americans. The *Lusitania* tragedy contributed to anti-German sentiment in the United States.

The British started to collect ships into large groups called **convoys**. Convoys would sail together from Quebec, Halifax or St. John's. They could be protected from submarines by warships. The convoy system greatly reduced the number of ships sunk. Because of its large harbour and excellent location, Halifax soon became the major assembly point for convoys to England.

### The Halifax Explosion

Thursday, December 6, 1917, dawned clear and mild in Halifax. At 7:30 that morning, the *Mont Blanc,* a French freighter loaded with benzene, picric acid and TNT, started to move through the Narrows to Bedford Basin, the city's inner harbour. It had come from New York to join the next convoy across the Atlantic. At about 8:00, the *Imo,* a Norwegian tramp steamer carrying relief supplies for

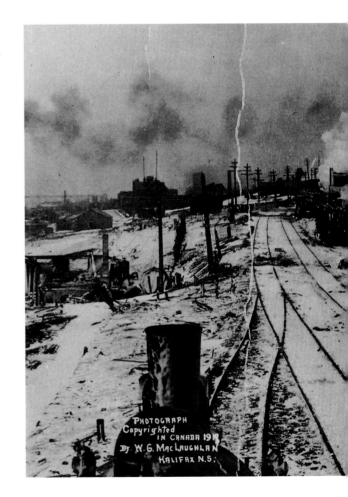

Belgium, headed out through the Narrows. Ships must take care as they pass in the Narrows.

In the city, factory workers were already at their jobs. Children were assembling in school playgrounds. Offices and stores were getting ready for the day's business. As the *Mont Blanc* and the *Imo* drew close to each other, they signalled their intentions.

*Haligonians pay tribute to those killed by the explosion.*

Suddenly, the *Mont Blanc* sailed right across the *Imo's* bow. At 8:43 the *Imo* rammed into it. The two ships drifted apart. People in the city out enjoying the winter sunshine watched as a wisp of smoke rose from the harbour. At 9:06 the *Mont Blanc's* cargo of high explosives blew up.

*The Halifax explosion destroyed Halifax, leaving 10,000 people homeless in the middle of the winter.*

*Central view of Halifax waterfront after the explosion.*

Schools, factories, stores and houses in a 5 kilometre area were completely destroyed. Part of the two-tonne anchor of the *Mont Blanc* was found 4 kilometres away. Over 2,000 people died and another 9,000 were injured. That night, with 10,000 people homeless, the temperature plunged to -8°C and a blizzard was on the way.

Within days, relief supplies began to pour in from other parts of Canada, and as far away as Jamaica and New Zealand. The state of Massachusetts sent a relief committee, for which reason Halifax still sends a Christmas tree annually to the city of Boston.

The Halifax explosion was the biggest man-made explosion the world had known until then, not to be surpassed until the dropping of the atomic bombs at the end of World War II in 1945. It brought the full savagery of war to Canada's shores

**FOCUS**
1. What important role did the Canadian navy play during World War I?
2. How did the Halifax Explosion bring the horror of the war home to Canadians?

## The War on the Home Front

Wars have traditionally been fought by soldiers in the front line. World War I was the first war to involve all sections of society, and was, in fact, a total war. In Canada, far from the battle lines, people made their contributions. The war put great stress and strain on Canadian society.

## Farming

The war disrupted farming in Europe, which caused major shortages of food. More than three-fifths of the soldiers fighting in Europe came from farms. Canada had been exporting wheat to Europe for many years, and Canadian farmers had to fill a large part of the shortages during the war. By the end of the war, "sod busters" in the West had doubled the land used for wheat farming. Cheese exports tripled. Pork and beef exports shot sky high.

*Women served on the battle front and on the home front.*

*Many women worked in factories to aid the war effort.*

## Industry

Canadian business also found new markets. Before the war, factories produced goods solely for the Canadian market. Few tried to compete outside the country. Most of our exports were raw materials— to be processed elsewhere.

Businessmen now saw new opportunities. Canadian companies started to make

**armaments** for the Allied forces. Steel companies turned out shell cases. Others made fuses and explosives. By 1917, Canada was making one-third of the shells used by the British during the war.

Canadians made guns, airplane parts, submarines and ships. Aluminum, nickel, railway track and timber were all sent to Europe. Uniforms, equipment and medical supplies were made for the Canadian Army.

Most Canadians worked hard to help the war effort. City workers gave up their free time to help farmers harvest the crops. Women entered the workforce to keep the soldiers supplied with essentials. Businessmen and government officials worked long hours without extra pay. All this activity created great opportunities for profit.

## Profiteering

Most businessmen were content to take a fair mark-up, but some tried to "corner the market" on a product. A few engaged in what is known as **profiteering.** They would not sell until they could get the best price. Others used cheap materials and did sloppy work. The boots the first Canadian troops were given wore out in less than two months. Canned meat for soldiers sometimes came from diseased animals. Some industrialists used bribery to get government contracts.

Ordinary people did both good and bad things. Some made up parcels for soldiers and planted "war gardens" with vegetables. Others hoarded supplies, wasted food, and tried to get around government **regulations.**

## The War Measures Act

At the outset of the war, some Canadians cast a disapproving eye at those who had recently entered Canada from enemy countries. The same people who were courted by Clifford Sifton and his agents to come to Canada were now seen as security risks. In response, Borden's government passed the **War Measures Act**, which gave it sweeping powers to arrest and detain "enemy aliens."

During the war, over 8,000 men were sent to toil in remote camps across Canada. Ukrainian Canadians were the most targeted group, because many had come from lands controlled by the Austrians. Often denied work, many Ukrainians had their newspapers suppressed by authorities. The attacks on newcomers revealed a Canada reacting to fear. No evidence was ever found that any of these people posed a threat to their adopted country. Democracy and freedom also became victims of the war.

## Victory Bonds

War is expensive. Canadians paid no income or profit tax in the early twentieth century. How could the government pay for the war?

To raise money, Canada issued Victory Bonds. Canadians were urged to buy bonds to help the war effort. After the war, they could cash in their bonds and get their money back with interest. Banks and large companies purchased most of the bonds, but ordinary citizens did their part as well.

Two new "temporary" taxes were introduced. The first was a business profits tax (now called Corporate Tax); the second, an **income tax**. Canadians still pay these taxes today.

*Victory Bonds were a necessary part of the war effort. These advertisements used propaganda to attract people.*

FOCUS
1. How did Canadian farmers and businesses help in the war effort?
2. How did Ukrainian-Canadians become victims of the war?
3. What is profiteering?

# 6 Wartime Issues

## Conscription

The Canadian army relied on volunteers for most of the war. Many young men were excited at first at the idea of fighting for their country. They rushed to volunteer in their enthusiasm to get overseas.

The horrors of the trenches soon changed this enthusiasm. From 1915 to 1917, Canadian soldiers gained a high reputation for courage. As a result, they were often chosen for the toughest and most dangerous assignments during battles.

Canadians fought at Vimy Ridge in April, 1917. That month over 10,000 Canadian soldiers died, but fewer than 5,000 volunteered to join the army. The volunteer system was not recruiting enough soldiers to replace the losses.

Prime Minister Borden had promised that his government would not introduce

*This poster says: Forward! For the King. For the Fatherland. For France. Your blood for humanity and freedom. To Arms! Sons of Montcalm and Chateauguay.*
*How does this poster try to drum up war fever in French Canadians? Is this an effective poster? Explain.*

---

### In Their Own Words

*"When the war broke out, the country went mad. People were singing in the streets. Everybody wanted to go to war. We hadn't had a war since the Boer War in 1899. Everybody was going to be a hero, and I wanted to be a hero too. But I wasn't big enough. I was only 150 cm tall and weighed 40 kg. I was 19 but looked 15. Finally a drill sergeant said, 'We need buglers!' So I joined the army as a bugler."*
　　　Bert Remington of Montreal,
　　　who had emigrated from Britain in 1910.

*"Me? I was probably as patriotic as most, but I was mainly restless. I joined up because it was a chance to see the world."*
　　　Robert Swan, Yarmouth, N.S.

conscription. It would not force men to join the army. Now he had to break that promise. He called an election to prove that conscription was the "will of the people." This campaign was one of the fiercest and angriest in Canadian history.

## People against Conscription

The largest group against conscription was French Canadians. When the war started, many volunteered to enter the army. The Royal 22nd Regiment, "the "VanDoos" (from vingt-deux), was a French-speaking unit. It had a great fighting record right through the war.

The minister of militia at the war's beginning was Sam Hughes, an Irish Protestant. Hughes did not try to understand the position of French-Canadians. He hated Roman Catholics. He sent Protestant clergymen as recruiting officers to Quebec. He insisted the French soldiers be trained in English. Borden fired Hughes in 1916, but it was too late to save the situation in Quebec.

French Canadians had not supported Britain during the Boer War. Some felt the same way now. They were being asked to defend Britain, not Canada. Former Prime Minister Wilfrid Laurier, Leader of the Opposition during the war, did not feel this way. He urged French Canadians to join the army, but he did not think that they should be forced to do so.

*(right) Many Canadians and business groups entered the conscription debate with enthusiasm.*

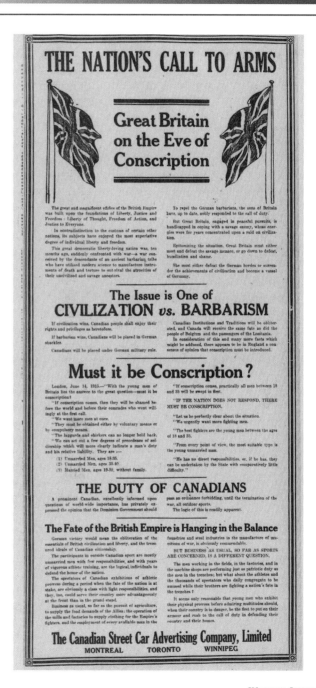

# THE NATION'S CALL TO ARMS

## Great Britain on the Eve of Conscription

The great and magnificent edifice of the British Empire was built upon the foundations of Liberty, Justice and Freedom : Liberty of Thought, Freedom of Action, and Justice to Everyone.

In contradistinction to the customs of certain other nations, its subjects have enjoyed the most superlative degree of individual liberty and freedom.

This great democratic liberty-loving nation was, ten months ago, suddenly confronted with war—a war conceived by the descendants of an ancient barbarian tribe who have utilized modern science to manufacture instruments of death and torture to out-rival the atrocities of their uncivilised and savage ancestors.

To repel the German barbarians, the sons of Britain have, up to date, nobly responded to the call of duty.

But Great Britain, engaged in peaceful pursuits, is handicapped in coping with a savage enemy, whose energies were for years concentrated upon a raid on civilization.

Epitomising the situation, Great Britain must either meet and defeat the savage menace, or go down to defeat, humiliation and shame.

She must either defeat the German hordes or surrender the achievements of civilization and become a vassal of Germany.

### The Issue is One of CIVILIZATION vs. BARBARISM

If civilization wins, Canadian people shall enjoy their rights and privileges as heretofore.

If barbarism wins, Canadians will be placed in German shackles.

Canadians will be placed under German military rule.

Canadian Institutions and Traditions will be obliterated, and Canada will receive the same fate as did the people of Belgium and the passengers of the Lusitania.

In consideration of this and many more facts which might be adduced, there appears to be in England a consensus of opinion that conscription must be introduced.

### Must it be Conscription?

London, June 14, 1915.—"With the young men of Britain lies the answer to the great question—must it be conscription?

"If conscription comes, then they will be shamed before the world and before their comrades who went willingly at the first call.

"We want more men at once.

"They must be obtained either by voluntary means or by compulsory means.

"The laggards and shirkers can no longer hold back.

"We can act out a few degrees of precedence of soldiership which will more clearly indicate a man's duty and his relative liability. They are :—

(1) Unmarried Men, ages 18-35.
(2) Unmarried Men, ages 35-40.
(3) Married Men, ages 18-35, without family.

"If conscription comes, practically all men between 18 and 35 will be swept in first.

"IF THE NATION DOES NOT RESPOND, THERE MUST BE CONSCRIPTION.

"Let us be perfectly clear about the situation.

"We urgently want more fighting men.

"The best fighters are the young men between the ages of 18 and 35.

"From every point of view, the most suitable type is the young unmarried man.

"He has no direct responsibilities, or, if he has, they can be undertaken by the State with comparatively little difficulty."

### THE DUTY OF CANADIANS

A prominent Canadian, excellently informed upon questions of world-wide importance, has privately expressed the opinion that the Dominion Government should pass an ordinance forbidding, until the termination of the war, all outdoor sports.

The logic of this is readily apparent.

#### The Fate of the British Empire is Hanging in the Balance

German victory would mean the obliteration of the essentials of British civilization and liberty, and the treasured ideals of Canadian citizenship.

The participants in outside Canadian sport are mostly unmarried men with few responsibilities, and with years of vigorous athletic training, are the logical individuals to defend the honor of the nation.

The spectators of Canadian exhibitions of athletic prowess during a period when the fate of the nation is at stake, are obviously a class with light responsibilities and they, too, could serve their country more advantageously at the front than in the grand stand.

Business as usual, so far as the pursuit of agriculture, to supply the food demands of the Allies ; the operation of the mills and factories to supply clothing for the Empire's fighters, and the employment of every available man in the foundries and steel industries in the manufacture of munitions of war, is obviously commendable.

BUT BUSINESS AS USUAL, SO FAR AS SPORTS ARE CONCERNED, IS A DIFFERENT QUESTION.

The men working in the fields, in the factories, and in the machine shops are performing just as patriotic duty as the men in the trenches ; but what about the athletes and the thousands of spectators who daily congregate to be amused while their brothers are fighting a nation's fate in the trenches ?

It seems only reasonable that young men who exhibit their physical prowess before admiring multitudes should, when their country is in danger, be the first to put on their armour and rush to the call of duty in defending their country and their homes.

## The Canadian Street Car Advertising Company, Limited

MONTREAL    TORONTO    WINNIPEG

# PATTERNS

By 1917, the war had grown even more desperate and bloody. People at home read the casualty lists and saw the wounded—often horribly maimed and disfigured—return home, some in baskets because they had no limbs. Few believed the war was glorious or that it would end soon. It became more difficult to find volunteers willing to risk their lives and future for a long, brutal struggle in a foreign land. Examine these statistics on enlistment and casualty figures.

| MONTH | ENLISTMENTS | CASUALTIES |
|---|---|---|
| January | 9 194 | 4 396 |
| February | 6 809 | 1 250 |
| March | 6 640 | 6 161 |
| April ( Vimy Ridge) | 5 530 | 13 477 |
| May | 6 407 | 13 457 |
| June | 6 348 | 7 931 |
| July | 3 882 | 7 906 |
| August (Hill 70) | 3 117 | 13 232 |
| September | 3 588 | 10 990 |
| October | 4 884 | 5 929 |
| November (Passchendaele) | 4 019 | 30 741 |
| December | 3 921 | 7 476 |

What pattern seemed to be emerging? What was happening to the Canadian army?
Why might these figures suggest a crisis?

In the West, many settlers objected to conscription. They had moved to Canada to get away from European wars. In many countries, governments could force men into the army. They thought they had escaped that way of life. Now it seemed to be coming to Canada.

Farmers everywhere objected to conscription. Their part in the war effort was to provide much-needed food. Who would work with them if their sons were taken away?

## What the Government Did

Prime Minister Borden was convinced that conscription was necessary. Those in favour of conscription had to win the election to justify breaking his earlier promise. First, Borden asked Laurier to join him in a coalition or union government. Laurier could not do this. Although he supported the war effort, he was against conscription. Borden then approached other Liberals. Some of them were for conscription. Several Liberals joined the Conservatives in a new party. They called it the Unionist Party.

## The Election of 1917

The Unionists won the election with 153 seats; the Liberals had 82. Only 20 of those 82 seats came from outside Quebec, but the results did not show the true feelings of the people. Many English-speaking Canadians did not want conscription either. In fact, if the soldiers' votes were omitted from the polls, nearly half the people voted against mandatory enlistment.

The conscription issue aroused many bitter feelings. In Quebec, there were bloody riots. Canadians were divided as they had not been since the execution of Louis Riel in 1885. Borden's wartime victory cost the nation dearly.

## A CLOSER LOOK AT PACIFISM

Canada is home to several religious communities for whom the waging of war is a mortal sin. These peoples were persecuted in other countries before immigrating to Canada, where they were promised religious freedom. Mennonites from Russia and Holland settled the Canadian prairies in the late 19th and early 20th centuries. Doukhobors from Russia settled first in Saskatchewan, and then in Southern British Columbia in 1908. The first Quaker immigrants to this country were fleeing the violence of the American Revolution, because of their refusal to join in military service. All of these people are pacifists. They oppose war or any kind of military activity. They believe violence is immoral, that the natural state of humankind is peace. Canada guaranteed all of these communities the right to live according to their belief in nonviolence, and exempted them from military service.

## FOCUS

1. What was conscription?
2. Who was opposed to conscription and why?
3. What was the Unionist Party?
4. What was the result of the 1917 election?

# Women at War

The conscription crisis helped Canadian women gain the right to vote. Before World War I, some women began breaking out of traditional roles. They stayed in school longer. Some went to university. A few even became doctors and lawyers, but these were special cases. It was still almost impossible for women to get hired for many jobs. They still could not vote.

## The Needs of Industry

The wartime industrial boom created a problem. The young men who would normally work in industry were in the army. Women filled the gap by working in the war factories. Over 20,000 women were employed making guns, shells and aircraft by the end of the war—these were skilled jobs. Before the war, women had only done unskilled work in the factories. Skilled jobs had been for men.

Women also replaced men in many civilian jobs. They became streetcar drivers, secretaries and office managers. More than anything else, they worked farms to help plant and harvest the crops.

Women without paying jobs also did their part. They knitted socks for soldiers, sent them letters and care packages, and visited the families of men who had been killed. Women supported the Canadian Red Cross and other volunteer organizations.

*Over 20,000 women went to work for the war effort, making guns, shells and aircraft.*

Women's efforts and achievements could not be ignored forever.

## In Their Own Words

"Things were bad for the war, for us, and we just felt we had to get our shoulder to the wheel and get down to business. When you're young, you do what everybody's doing….There was a kind of esprit de corps. Everybody wanted to be there; you were in the swim of things; everything was war, war, war. I think a lot of the girls….they were a wonderful bunch, and I see so many of them to this day. They enriched my life so.

There was everybody, every single class….I thought it was fascinating. You get in the canteen or up in that big rest room and hear them talking. It was very, very interesting…

In meeting these people that we had never had the opportunity to meet before, and finding they were just the same as we were, but they hadn't had the chances that we'd had for education and that kind of thing, we began to realize that we were all sisters under the skins.

Wars do bring every class together and I think we need to do a little bit more of that without war if we can."

From Daphne Read, ed. The Great War and Canadian Society: An Oral History (Toronto: New Hogtown Press, 1978),

**How was the war a positive experience for some women?**

### The Army Medical Corps

Wounded soldiers on the Western Front needed medical care. Over 3,000 women became army nurses and ambulance drivers. They were called "Bluebirds," because they

*Burial of Canadian Nurses killed in a German Air Raid, May 1918.*

wore blue cloaks. Most of them served overseas. They willingly shared the dangers of warfare with Canadian men.

As the war ground on, field hospitals and hospital ships became German targets. Forty-

six "Bluebirds" lost their lives, some from German bombs and torpedoes.

### Pacifists

Some Canadian women boldly championed peace. Seeing the senseless brutality of war and the total misery it brought to warring nations, they tried to ignite a peace movement. Laura Hughes, niece of Sir Sam Hughes, was a leading spokesperson of the Canadian Women's Peace Party, a small but significant group. While generally unheeded during their time, the peace movement gained strength after the full horrors of WWI were revealed.

### The Right to Vote

Women's efforts and achievements could not be ignored forever. Women wanted the right to vote. World War I helped them receive that right, even though the federal government granted it in a rather grudging way.

When Prime Minister Borden decided to call an election in 1917, he passed the Wartime Elections Act shortly before the election took place. This act took the vote away from citizens who had emigrated from "enemy" countries, since they might vote against conscription. It gave the vote to women—but not all women. Only army nurses and close relatives of soldiers were allowed to vote, since they would probably support conscription.

Obviously this act was unfair to other women. In 1918, all women were given the vote, but they still could not be elected to Parliament. That right did not come until 1920. In 1921, Agnes Macphail became the first woman elected to the House of Commons. The first steps had been taken, but the long struggle for real equality had just begun.

*Silver Cross Mothers—like this one—were women who had lost sons in battle.*

---

## TIME LINES —The Fight for the Vote

Canadian women faced a long, uphill struggle to win political equality with men in the twentieth century. One of the most important victories was gaining the right to vote. Here is a partial list of the most significant dates in that important battle.

**1916** Women in the Western provinces of Manitoba, Saskatchewan and Alberta won the right to vote in provincial elections.

**1917** The Military Voters Act granted the vote in federal elections for Canadian nurses serving in the war. The Wartime Elections Act gave the vote in federal elections to close female relatives of soldiers.

**1918** Prime Minister Borden's Union government gave the vote to Canadian women over 21 for federal elections.

**1920** Canadian women earned the right to run in federal elections and become members of Parliament.

---

FOCUS
1. What new and important roles were played by Canadian women during WWI?
2. How did women earn the right to vote?
3. Why might immigrants from "enemy" countries vote against conscription? Why would women whose husbands, fathers, sons and brothers were fighting in the war vote for conscription?

# The War Ends

The stalemate on the Western Front in France and Belgium continued into 1918. Neither side seemed capable of winning the decisive battle that would bring victory. Soldiers on all sides wondered why they were involved in this hell on earth. The fighting on the front offered little hope and, for many, certain death. People became desperate.

Brest-Litovsk. Germany then turned all of its armies against the Allies on the Western Front.

## The United States Enters the War

When Germany announced unrestricted warfare against neutral shipping in April, 1917, the United States entered the war on the side of Britain and France. Germany knew that a great new supply of American troops would arrive in France within the year. General Ludendorff decided on a final German offensive before the American forces arrived.

Germany's last offensive began in April, 1918. Over 3,000,000 soldiers attacked, supported by massive artillery barrages. The German forces advanced over 60 kilometres; it appeared that the breakthrough had been achieved.

*The Tower, St. Martin's Cathedral, Ypres (Belgium), damaged by the war.*
*(Right) A Canadian solider tends to a tiny victim of war.*

Russians revolted against the Emperor, Nicholas II, in 1917, demanding "Land, Bread, and Peace." Soldiers and sailors in Russia mutinied and refused to fight. In March, 1918, the Russians signed a separate peace treaty with Germany, the Treaty of

An armistice was signed on **November 11, 1918**. At 11 a.m. on the 11th day of the 11th month, the bloody war came to an end.

But, British, French and Canadian forces pulled back to new defensive lines; the German offensive slowed down.

Reinforcements were collected for the Allied counter-attack. For the first time these forces included thousands of American troops. The counter-attack began in July, 1918. This Allied advance forced the German army to retreat. By August, the German army was in total retreat.

In Germany, there were riots because of food shortages and protests against continuing the war. Some members of the German Navy mutinied and refused to go to sea. By October, it was obvious that Germany and its allies had lost the war. Negotiations for peace began.

An armistice was signed on

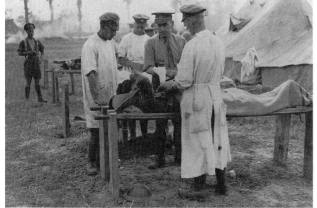

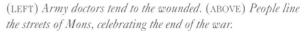

(LEFT) *Army doctors tend to the wounded.* (ABOVE) *People line the streets of Mons, celebrating the end of the war.*

November 11, 1918. At 11 a.m. on the 11th day of the 11th month, the bloody war came to an end.

Over 8 million soldiers had died. More than 20 million more would live out their lives with wounds, shell shock, gassed lungs, and lost limbs, sight, or hearing. An equal number of civilians were also victims of war.

BORN: 1875, Napperton, Ontario

DIED: 1933, Montreal, Quebec, while still vice-chancellor of McGill University

SIGNIFICANCE: As the first Commander of the Canadian Corps, **Currie successfully led the Canadian troops until** the end of the war.

BRIEF BIOGRAPHY: **Currie was an active member of the militia when the First World War broke out in 1914, and was appointed Brigade Commander of the 2nd Canadian Infantry Brigade. In 1915, he took over full com**mand of the entire Canadian Division. In 1917, Currie was appointed Commander of the Canadian Corps, where he excelled at planning for the attack at Vimy Ridge. He insisted on new tactics for the attack, such as careful training of soldiers, close support of artillery, the element of surprise and rehearsals on mock targets. Under Currie's careful control, Vimy Ridge fell to victorious Canadian forces. This victory is sometimes viewed as the birth of the Canadian nation because troops from all over Canada fought as a single unit. Currie was hailed as a modern general with new ideas. British Prime Minister Loyd George even considered him for Commander of all British forces.

After the war, Currie became the principal and vice-chancellor of McGill University. **Though he had no formal post-secondary** education himself, Currie was extremely successful at his administrative duties **at the university.**

*Why was Currie considered to be a "modern general?"*

## Sir Arthur Currie

"The great European War has introduced new and more deadly instruments of destruction, and has relegated to the background and the scrap heap many hitherto accepted tactics and weapons. The most effective of these new arms has been the submarine. Gunboats, cruisers, even superdreadnoughts, have been unable to withstand its onslaughts. Aeroplanes and airships have also definitely taken their permanent place as most effective arms of war. The former have literally been the eyes of the armies, and by their aid not only detection of the enemy's position is made possible, but range and direction of great gun fire is checked, corrected and in part conducted. Airships have struck terror in many besieged city as well as those outside the zone of fighting. Their effectiveness as absolute destructive agents has yet to be definitely shown, but their immense value as terror-inspiring agents has been fully demonstrated by their raids along the English coast cities."

*Source:* Collier's Photographic History of the European War, *by Francis Reynolds and C.W. Taylor, P.F. Collier and Sons, New York, 1916.*

# Canadian Vision

## The Canadian War Memorials Fund

One of the most remarkable Canadians of both world wars was Max Aitken, who moved to England after earning a fortune in the Canadian newspaper business. He was named a British peer and took the title Lord Beaverbrook. An enthusiastic supporter of the war, Beaverbrook organized a highly effective and secret propaganda effort on behalf of the British government. He created the Canadian War Memorials Fund, which commissioned artists to record the events of the war for posterity. This resulted in 800 works of art, many of great power and terrible beauty. You can see these paintings at the War Memorial Website: www.harrypalmergallery.ca.

### FOCUS
1. How did the following affect the stalemate on the Western Front?
   a) the Russian Revolution b) the United States' entry into the war
2. What is the origin of Remembrance Day?

# The Treaty of Versailles

**9**

The November 11 Armistice ended the fighting. As a first step, Germany agreed to withdraw its troops to within its own borders, to surrender its fleet to Great Britain, and to disarm its army.

The victorious powers in January met at Versailles, France, to draw up a permanent peace treaty. Strong differences of opinion existed among the Allied leaders. Georges Clemenceau, the French premier, was determined that Germany be punished for its invasions of France in 1870 and 1914. He demanded a harsh peace treaty.

President Woodrow Wilson of the United States, on the other hand, wanted a more generous peace settlement. Wilson had previously drawn up the "14 Points" as a basis for a settlement. These included such ideas as "national determination for all peoples," "freedom of the seas," and "open peace treaties rather than secret agreements." One major proposal was for a League of Nations to guarantee world peace.

Germany expected a treaty based on the idealism of the 14 Points. Instead, the Treaty of Versailles was a compromise agreement, including many of the harsher terms of Clemenceau and Prime Minister Lloyd George of Great Britain.

## Reaction to the Peace Treaty

The French and British considered the treaty to be, on the whole, fair and just. Both sides had lost hundreds of thousands of their youth in the horrible battles of the Western Front. Both were determined that the treaty should do everything possible to prevent the outbreak of another world war.

Most Germans, however, were shocked by what they considered to be the treaty's harsh and unfair terms. The

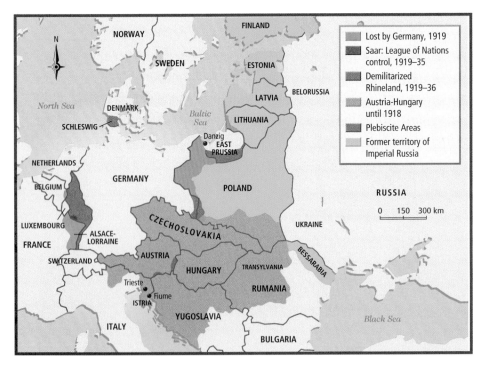

*Europe in 1919.*

Legend:
- Lost by Germany, 1919
- Saar: League of Nations control, 1919–35
- Demilitarized Rhineland, 1919–36
- Austria-Hungary until 1918
- Plebiscite Areas
- Former territory of Imperial Russia

War Guilt Clause (Article 231)
– Germany was forced to sign a
  statement that it had been the
  primary cause of the war

*Adolf Hitler, seen here in the 1920s, directly blamed the Treaty of Versailles for the economic hardship Germany faced after the War, and promised to avenge its treatment of Germany.*

BORN: 1854, Grand Pré, Nova Scotia

DIED: 1937, Ottawa, Ontario

SIGNIFICANCE: Borden led Canada through the long, difficult years of the First World War. As prime minister, he oversaw Canada's remarkable contribution of people, resources and finances. He encouraged the development of an independent Canadian identity and won Canada its own place on the world stage.

BRIEF BIOGRAPHY: Robert Borden often disliked serving as PM. He found the work tiring and depressing. Nevertheless, he soldiered on and, in the end, successfully led Canada through some of the most important and divisive issues the young nation had ever faced.

Born into a Liberal family, Borden was first elected as a Conservative in 1896. In 1901, he became party leader. In the brutal election of 1911, Borden skilfully organized the defeat of Wilfrid Laurier by working with both English-speaking Imperialists and French-Canadian nationalists.

Borden soon found himself leading Canada through the traumatic years of WWI. He insisted that Canadian soldiers fight as an independent unit. He demanded and won a larger voice for Canada in the direction of the war. Under his leadership, Canada provided vast quantities of soldiers and war materials. While prime minister, Borden introduced legislation giving the vote to Canadian women.

During the conscription crisis, Borden proved to be a shrewd and tough leader who was able to steam-roll over the opposition. When the war ended, he successfully insisted that Canada had earned its own place at the peace conference. When the League of Nations was formed, Canada joined on its own, separate from Great Britain.

The toll of the war years wore Borden down. In spite of his successes, Borden knew the country was also divided. French Canada turned away from the Conservative Party. Workers and farmers often thought the war only benefited rich manufacturers. Many Canadians were troubled by the price Canadians had paid for victory and recognition. Suffering from poor health and political fatigue, Borden resigned in 1920.

*In your view, what was Borden's greatest achievement? Why?*

## Sir Robert Borden

payment of reparations threatened to crush their struggling industries. The loss of key lands to France, Poland and Czechoslovakia offended their sense of nationality. The limitations on their armed forces offended their sense of national dignity. The War Guilt Clause offended their sense of justice.

In the years after 1919, the sense of injustice festered like an open wound. A myth developed that Germany had been "stabbed in the back" by civilians within the country and not defeated on the field of battle. Many waited for the arrival of a new leader to help them avenge their defeat.

Fifteen years later, in 1933, Adolf Hitler appeared to be that leader (fuhrer) who would lead Germany to avenge the Treaty of Versailles.

# TREATY OF VERSAILLES

**Geographical Terms**
- Germany lost control of all its colonies
- Alsace-Lorraine was transferred back from Germany to France
- the rich Saar coal region was to be run by France for 15 years
- part of eastern Germany was given to Poland

**Reparations**
- Germany was to pay money and goods to Great Britain, France and Belgium to repair damages of the war

**Military Controls**
- the German Army was restricted to 100,000 people and was to have no tanks or heavy guns
- Germany was not to have an air force
- the German Navy was to include only small ships

**War Guilt Clause (Article 231)**
- Germany was forced to sign a statement that it had been the primary cause of the war

FOCUS
1. What was the Treaty of Versailles? In your view, was the treaty fair? Explain.
2. How did the treaty help lead to World War II?

# Questions and Activities

**Match the persons or groups in column A with the definition in column B.**

| A | B |
|---|---|
| **1.** Archduke Ferdinand | **a)** opposed conscription for Canada during WWI |
| **2.** General Von Schlieffen | **b)** was the leading German air ace |
| **3.** Wilfrid Laurier | **c)** insisted Canadian soldiers fight together in their own army. |
| **4.** John McCrae | **d)** was assassinated in Sarajevo in an incident that sparked the outbreak of WWI |
| **5.** Sam Hughes | **e)** wrote a poem about soldiers on the Western Front |
| **6.** Billy Bishop | **f)** planned the German invasion of France |
| **7.** Manfred von Richthofen | **g)** was the leading Canadian air ace |

## Do Some Research

**1.** Find out more about the development of one of the following weapons during WWI. What different sorts of problems do soldiers face today?

    **a)** the fighter plane     **d)** the submarine
    **b)** the machine gun     **e)** the tank
    **c)** mustard gas     **f)** the dreadnought

**2.** Do further research on the changing role of women during World War I.

**3.** Find out more about the causes and effects of the Halifax explosion.

## Be Creative

**1.** Prepare a newspaper on the Canadian contribution to World War I. Your newspaper could include maps, interviews, letters, statistics, pictures, editorials. Try to cover as many aspects of the war as possible, including recruitment and training, providing supplies and equipment, volunteer work, as well as the actual fighting on land, sea and air.

**2.** What does your school do for Remembrance Day each year? Design a Remembrance Day program for your class or school.

**3.** With another student, choose a person who played a prominent role at the time of World War I. Conduct an interview, with one of you playing the interviewer and the other, the historical person. You will need to do further research in order to prepare questions and answers that will highlight the role the person played in the war.

## Ideas for Discussion

**1.** What role did the following groups play during the war? Rank these groups in order of importance. Compare your ranking with that of other members of your class.

   **a)** farming families    **d)** soldiers

   **b)** city families       **e)** nurses

   **c)** armament workers  **f)** politicians

**2.** It has been said that "war brings out the best in people and the worst in people." In small groups, compose two lists: The Best in People and The Worst in People. Compare your lists with those of other groups of students.

**3.** Here are two different opinions on the Treaty of Versailles. Read them and decide which you agree with most. Discuss the treaty with your classmates, giving reasons for your views.

*I think the Treaty of Versailles was fair. Germany had caused the war. It had invaded Belgium, a neutral country, without excuse. Germany had been try-ing to expand for 75 years. It had to be punished and it had to be weakened. When the new Soviet government in Russia wanted to withdraw from the war, Germany imposed much harsher terms in the Treaty of Brest-Litovsk than the Western Allies did in the Treaty of Versailles.*

*This kind of treaty was the only way to guarantee that a strong Germany would not cause another war. If the treaty was enforced, it would keep peace in Europe.*

*I think the Treaty of Versailles was too harsh. The war had not been caused by Germany alone; Austria-Hungary and Russia were just as guilty. Making Germany pay all that money for the war meant its economy could not recover. Germany should not have had its colonies and so much territory taken away. After the war, the Allies and the Germans would have to live together. The treaty was so unfair, the Germans were bound to be resentful. They would look for a chance to get back what they had lost. This might lead to another war.*

## Web sites

# You Are There

You Are There

**It is 1917. The country is about to vote in an election. The main issue is whether the government should introduce conscription. If you were one of the people described here, what would be your opinion? Why would you feel that way? Write a letter to a newspaper explaining how you feel conscription would affect the war effort, national unity, English Canadians, French Canadians and recent immigrants.**

**Mary Porter** was an army nurse in France. She was wounded during an air raid and has been sent home to Vancouver. She has two brothers with the Canadian Army. Jack is hoping for a transfer to the Royal Flying Corps. Ed had just been awarded a DSO (Distinguished Service Order) for saving the life of a companion, wounded while going over the top during the Battle of the Somme. Jack is engaged to Mary's best friend, Susan. Before she left for France, Mary was aware that Canadian regiments were not operating at full strength because there were not enough volunteers to replace those killed or wounded.

**André Savard**'s family have farmed on the shores of the St. Lawrence for nearly 300 years. He is one of nine children and has recently married. He and his wife are expecting a baby. When the war broke out, he did not even hear about it for over a month or so. He does not see how a war being fought over 5,000 km away can possible affect him. He knows that his cousin Pierre from Québec City has volunteered and is now a sergeant with the Royal 22nd Regiment. André, however, does not want to fight or kill people in a distant land. He is happy to let others fight if they believe in the cause. André sees his life in terms of his village, his farm and his family.

**Stefan Klemens** brought his family to Saskatchewan in 1901. They came from Austria to escape the almost constant warfare. Now, Stefan farms the 64 ha of land given to him by the government when he arrived. He is married with six children. It has been a struggle to provide for his large family, but now they are doing well. Last year they harvested a good crop, and got a good price for it. He does not know how he would manage without the help of his sons Kurt (22) and Hans (19). Last week, Greta (7) came home from school in tears because the kids called her a Hunky. It bothers Stefan that Canada is fighting a war against the land where his parents and siblings still live.

**Bill McAdam** was born and raised in Nova Scotia. His family came here from Scotland over a hundred years ago, and he thinks of himself as a loyal son of Nova Scotia. When the war broke out, many of his friends volunteered to join the army. He is still under the age limit of 18 and has not decided whether he will volunteer or not. He sometimes wonders what Canadians are doing fighting a war in France. His neighbours, Charlie Armstrong and George Macdonald, have already been killed, and nobody knows if Robert Cormier will ever recover from that gas attack. Yet he considers himself a good Canadian and Canada is at war. He has a strong sense of duty. He wonders what would happen if people didn't join up.

**Shirley Evans** lives in Hamilton and is the mother of three children—Karen (19), Timothy (16), and Daniel (9). Shirley does volunteer work for the Salvation Army. Her group serves refreshments to soldiers on the troop trains that pass through the city. Lately, they have helped tend the trainloads of wounded soldiers returning home. Karen's fiancé, Jim Lee from down the street, was killed in action at Vimy Ridge. The Evans family shares the grief with the Lees, who have lost their only son. Timothy had planned to join his father's automobile sales company, but he expects to be in uniform soon. Shirley hopes the war will end before he is old enough to fight.

# Point
## Counterpoint

The conscription issue brutally divided Canadians at a time when unity was vital for victory. Most volunteers were Canadians who were born in Britain. Native-born Canadians—English and French—were generally reluctant to fight overseas. Nonetheless, the debate quickly became a French-English battle, which only served to further separate Canada's two main language groups. Read the selections below and decide which one is the most/least accurate. Can you detect tones of racism? In your own view, would you have supported or rejected compulsory military service in WWI? Why? Should we have it today? Why? Why not?

"Conscription means national division and strife. It will hurt the cause of the Allies more than a few thousand extra soldiers will bring them help and comfort."

Henri Bourassa,
French Canadian nationalist

"All citizens are liable to military service for the defence of their country, and I conceive that the battle for Canadian liberty and autonomy is being fought today on the fields of France and Belgium. If the war should end in defeat, Canada, in all the years to come, would be under the shadow of German military domination."

Sir Robert Borden,
Prime Minister

"The trouble between the English and the French Canadians has become acute, because French Canadians have refused to play their part in this war—being the only known race of white men to quit."

J.W. Dafoe,
newspaper editor

# Introduction

## The Radio Age

**A**FTER THE FIRST WORLD WAR, CANADA FACED ECONOMIC HARDSHIP. During the great boom of the war years, demand for goods was high and prices rose accordingly. When the soldiers returned, they found that things cost nearly twice as much as they had before the war. To make matters worse, many industries fell into a slump. Factories that thrived during the war had to cut production significantly or close down altogether. For the war veterans, this meant that jobs were hard to find. Many turned to the labour movement, which gained the national spotlight as unions demanded the right to strike. The Winnipeg General Strike of 1919 came to symbolize workers' discontent.

Once the economy improved during the early part of the 1920s, Canada experienced one of the greatest economic booms in its history. American companies invested in Canada's natural resources and manufacturing industries. A seemingly endless supply of new products, such as vacuum cleaners, stoves and refrigerators, became available. Automobiles and radios had the greatest impact on the social and economic life of Canadians. The stock market boomed with new investors.

The 1929 stock market crash wiped out the huge stock market gains and signalled the beginning of the Great Depression. The successive governments of Mackenzie King and R. B. Bennett struggled to solve the social and economic problems of the Depression. Many Canadians began to look at alternative political parties such as the Cooperative Commonwealth Federation (CCF), the Social Credit Party and the Union Nationale.

The outbreak of the Second World War in 1939 brought back the war economy and the Depression came to an end.

## METHODS OF HISTORICAL INQUIRY

### Inquiry Process and Causation

Although the Great Depression was sparked by the stock market crash in 1929, it is an oversimplification to state that the crash caused the Depression. To understand why the Depression occurred, historians follow a process of inquiry similar to a detective's investigation. They ask themselves these simple questions: who, what, where, when, why and how. Answering these questions helps historians establish trends and patterns and determine the cause and effect relationship between the events leading up to the Depression and the events that followed.

# Chapter Three: The Radio Age

## Expectations

### Overall Expectations:

- describe the continuing impact of technological development on Canadian society
- demonstrate how Canadians adapted to the difficult economic conditions of the 1930s
- explain the economic factors which resulted in the boom and bust cycle of the 1920s and 1930s

### Specific Expectations:

- evaluate the role of labour unions after the First World War
- assess the role of government intervention in the Winnipeg General Strike
- identify the events of the Winnipeg General Strike
- describe contributions made by Canadian men and women during the 1920s and 1930s
- describe the "women are persons" case and the impact it had for Canadian women
- identify the causes of the Great Depression
- describe how Canadians coped during the Depression
- explain how and why different provincial governments intervened in Canada's economic and social life during the 1930s
- explain how Liberal and Conservative governments reacted to the Depression
- identify the social and political movements behind such new political parties as the Social Credit Party and the Cooperative Commonwealth Federation (CCF)

## WORD LIST

| | | | |
|---|---|---|---|
| Assembly line | Conspiracy | Laissez-faire | Stock market |
| Bootleggers | Deflation | Margin | Supply-and-demand |
| Collective Bargaining | Equalization of labour | Socialism | |
| Communism | Inflation | Specialization of Labour | |

# *Advance* Organizer

**1**

After the war, returning soldiers expected to find security and well-paying jobs. Instead, factories were closing or cutting back production. Prices had nearly doubled. With the war over, there was no longer a demand for wartime supplies. Workers had to be laid off until new markets were found.

Canadian unions were much stronger than they had been before the war. Workers were ready to demand higher wages and shorter working hours. The unions joined forces in a general strike in Winnipeg in 1919. Over 30,000 workers left their jobs. The city ground to a halt. The strike lasted over a month. A clash between mounted police and the strikers led to two deaths and many injuries. The strike itself failed, but Canadian unions had demonstrated their strength to industry and government.

**2**

Women continued their struggle for equal rights. Emily Murphy and Nellie McClung teamed up in a court case to prove women could be appointed to government positions, including the Senate. Women took greater part in business and industry, but still met with prejudice.

**3**

Business gradually recovered in the 1920s. Jobs became plentiful again and wages increased. For many Canadians. the 1920s was a decade of plenty. People could afford to enjoy the new luxuries of the period—movies, record players, radios and automobiles, for example. It seemed that the new prosperity would last forever.

**4**

Big businesses sold shares of their companies on the stock exchange. They needed new capital to grow. Prices were based on supply and demand. The excitement of buying and selling was intense, and shares were bought and sold at ever-increasing, unrealistic prices. In 1929, the bottom dropped out of the stock market. The Great Depression had begun.

The stock market crash affected the whole world. Workers were laid off, causing them to search desperately for jobs that did not exist. Sometimes they ended up in hobo camps outside the towns. The price of wheat fell to one quarter of what it was in 1929. The Prairies suffered a five-year drought. Life was bleak on the farm and in the city during the thirties.

**5**

During the twenties and thirties, Canada relied less on Britain to handle its world affairs. The Statute of Westminster was passed by the British Parliament in 1931 and confirmed Canada's independence. With the founding of the Canadian Broadcasting Corporation (CBC) and the National Film Board (NFB), Canada was developing its own voice as a nation. By 1939, the country was a respected member of the world community. In that year, World War II began. Airplane and armament factories opened up, creating jobs. The Great Depression was over. Amid all this activity, one lingering question remained: Is war the only way to end a Depression?

# 1 After the War

Canadian industry developed rapidly during the First World War. Canada supplied shells to the Western Front. The country built and maintained ships for the Atlantic convoys. The Canadian steel industry boomed. Soldiers needed boots, clothes and blankets. Many factory owners became very wealthy. Farmers grew more food. Demand was high and prices rose accordingly. The cost of necessities such as bread, milk, rent and housing increased. Returning soldiers found goods cost nearly twice as much as they had in 1913. Wages rose during the war as well, but only by about 18%. Canadians had a difficult time making ends meet because of **inflation**.

World War I ended on November 11, 1918, after four years of fighting. Many Canadian soldiers, sailors and airmen had not been home in a long time. Now they were returning to take up their lives again. What would they find? How would a grateful nation welcome them back? Canada's nine million people had reason to be proud of the country's war effort.

Troop ships tied up at the government docks in Halifax, and troop trains streamed west, loaded with returning heroes. Cheers greeted them at every station. Family and friends turned out in celebration. However, when Canada's ex-soldiers headed down Main Street, they were in for a big surprise. Prices all over the country had skyrocketed. The dollar did not buy as much as it had before the war.

## Worker's Unrest

When Canada's war veterans returned home in 1919, after fighting "the war to end all wars," they expected the country would be grateful, that they would find secure employment and live better

*These war veterans are protesting the lack of jobs.*

Employers had no room to hire ex-soldiers. As a result, unemployment increased, and many workers faced tough times.

lives. Instead they found widespread labour unrest and frustration. Many ex-soldiers could not even find a job.

1919 introduced a period of adjustment for Canada. The booming war economy ended with the war. Many industries fell into a slump, and factories closed or cut production as ammunitions, weapons and military equipment were no longer needed. There were no new jobs; jobs that remained were already filled with employees who had worked throughout the war. Employers had no room to hire ex-soldiers. As a result, unemployment increased and many workers faced tough times. This situation was made worse because there was no unemployment insurance in 1919.

What had happened? Who was to blame? Some blamed people who immigrated to Canada before the war. They believed immigrants were aliens who took jobs away from native-born Canadians. Many soldiers were also angry with the profiteers who, they believed, had made large amounts of money during the war.

The Canadian government set up a royal commission to study the labour situation, but it provided little relief. Discontented workers wanted to listen to people who offered solutions. Political parties and governments did not. In the late 1800s, workers began to band together to get what they wanted. Workers within the same trade organized as trade unions. After World War I, carpenters joined together to form their own union. Mechanics and electricians did the same. Each union elected representatives to represent all its members, and to negotiate with employers. This process, which we know now as **collective bargaining**, made it possible for unions to negotiate higher wages, better benefits and

## A CLOSER LOOK AT COMMUNISM

Communists follow the political and ideas of philosopher Karl Marx, whose **Communist Manifesto** was published in 1848. Marx explained how unregulated **capitalism** (business practices) take advantage of the working class. According to Marx, the only way workers could improve their lot in life was to overthrow the business classes (or bourgeoisie) and establish a worker or proletarian dictatorship. All citizens would benefit equally from society's industrial production, and a classless society—one in which everyone was financially equal—would be the result. Communist Parties were established in many countries to secure the goals Marx outlined. The Communist Party of Canada was labelled an unlawful association from 1931 to 1936. It was banned outright in 1939 after World War II was declared. Today, members are still actively engaged in social and labour issues. Compared to other political parties, however, the Communist Party of Canada does not have a large following, and therefore does not have candidates in all of Canada's 301 ridings.

BORN: 1888, Glasgow, Scotland

DIED: 1964, Winnipeg, Manitoba

SIGNIFICANCE: Dedicated to fighting what he saw as the exploitation of Canadian workers by rich factory and business owners, Russell spent his life championing the plight of the working class.

BRIEF BIOGRAPHY: Russell became an apprentice machinist in 1900 at the age of 12, and learned how to build machines and engines from engineers' drawings. He immigrated to Canada in 1911, settled in Winnipeg, and found a job in the CPR machine shop. He soon became involved in organizing a union at the CPR. During the First World War, Russell refused to support Canada's participation in the war. He believed that Canadian workers were being unfairly asked to bear the cost of the war on the battle lines, while their bosses sat back and made fat profits

at home. In 1919, at the close of the war, Russell became a central player in the One Big Union and helped organize the Winnipeg General Strike. He was arrested for sedition and spent 2 years in prison for his strike work. After serving time, Russell travelled widely in support of the OBU, but the ideal of a universal union was slowly losing ground. Workers left the OBU to return to their trade unions. In the 1930s, Russell supported the CCF Party with the platform that there be a single industrial union for all workers within an industry. He became the executive secretary of the Winnipeg Branch of the newly organized Canadian Labour Congress in 1956. He retired from political life in 1962 and died a few years later. Winnipeg's R.B Russell Vocational School was named in his honour in 1967.

## Robert Boyd Russell

The City of Winnipeg ground to a halt. Non-union members all left their jobs. Within three days, over 30,000 workers were on strike.

TIMELINE

1900   1910   1920   1930   1940   1950   1960   1970   1980   1990   2000

ensure essential city services were maintained. They wanted to make sure no lasting damage to the city's economy occurred. Some citizens feared workers wanted more than higher wages, and claimed the strike was part of a communist plot. Some union leaders seemed to speak in the same terms as the Russian Bolsheviks, which suggested that the strike was the beginning of a revolution in Canada. Feelings against immigrants and foreigners ran high. The Committee of One Thousand urged the federal government to step in.

When Winnipeg employers had not backed down by the middle of June, workers' enthusiasm for the strike began to wane. Many strikers could not afford to stay out any longer. Public opinion began to turn against unions. The Strike Committee seemed to be running the city. People began to drift back to work; many strikers were disappointed.

*Angry workers overturn a streetcar during the Winnipeg General Strike.*

### The Arrests

Then, on June 17, the government decided to act; it arrested strike leaders. The men were taken to Stony Mountain Penitentiary and charged with conspiracy and libel before being released on bail. Protests erupted all across Canada. A mass meeting and march was planned for Saturday, June 21. Winnipeg Mayor Gray forbade the rally and read the Riot Act. In protest, a group of ex-soldiers led thousands of people down Main Street. They were met by Mounties swinging clubs and firing pistols. Two people died in the riot that followed. The federal government sent troops into the city to patrol Winnipeg streets with machine guns. "Bloody Saturday" was a day many Canadians would never forget. The Strike Committee called off the strike a week later.

### A Communist Plot?

No one has ever proved the Winnipeg strikers planned a revolution. Most likely, the workers were merely trying to obtain higher wages and better working conditions. Nevertheless,

BORN: 1874, Etobicoke, Ontario

DIED: 1942, Vancouver, British Columbia

SIGNIFICANCE: Became the first leader of the Cooperative Commonwealth Federation (CCF) in 1933.

BRIEF BIOGRAPHY: Ordained as a minister at the age of 26, Woodsworth preached what is known as social gospel. He urged his followers to improve life for people on earth rather than worry about Heaven. In 1904, he moved from his middle-class church to a mission in Winnipeg's slums, where Woodsworth worked tirelessly to help the city's poverty-stricken immigrants. His experiences led him to write *Strangers Within Our Gate,* an analysis of Canada's immigration system that was highly critical of government policies. By 1914, Woodsworth had become a supporter of trade unions and pacifism. He was fired from his job as Director of Social Research in 1916 because of his opposition to the First World War and to conscription.

In 1918, to protest the church's support of the war, he resigned from the ministry. He took a longshoreman's position on the Vancouver docks. While on a speaking tour in Winnipeg in 1919, Woodsworth took over the newspaper of the strikers after its editor was arrested. His editorial position caused Woodsworth to be arrested, too, but charges were dropped when prosecutors realized he had been quoting from the Bible. In 1921, Woodsworth's democratic socialism got him elected as an Independent Labour MP for Winnipeg. As a politician, he continued his fight against workers' exploitation and the unfair treatment of immigrants. He also supported old age pensions and unemployment insurance. In 1933, Woodsworth was elected leader of the newly formed Cooperative Commonwealth Federation (CCF). By the outbreak of World War II, Woodsworth's belief in pacifism had not changed. He was the only MP to vote against Canada's entry in the Second World War.

## J.S. (James Shaver) Woodsworth

## CAPE BRETON MINERS' STRIKE

Winnipeg was not the only city engaged in violent strikes. From 1921 to 1925, Cape Breton miners went on strike 3 times against the Montreal-based British Empire Steel Corporation, demanding higher wages and better working conditions. Labour unrest lasted 4 years with over 2 million work days lost to striking miners. By far, the most violent and bloody battle occurred in 1925, when the miners went on strike for 5 months. At the company's request provincial police and federal troops were brought in to subdue the angry workers. Credit was cut off from company stores, so the workers could no longer afford groceries and clothing. During a particularly bloody battle at Waterford Lake, many miners were injured. One was killed by police. His death is still mourned by Cape Bretoners every June 11, Miners' Memorial Day.

In the end, the company was chastised by a royal commission that had been called in to analyze the situation. The British Empire Steel Corporation eventually went bankrupt.

their leaders did not talk that way. The angry strike speeches helped many people believe the Winnipeg Strike was a plot to overthrow the government. Seven of the strikers arrested were convicted of **conspiracy**; they received sentences of up to two years in prison. Five men were never brought to trial. Two strike leaders, J.S. Dixon and A.A. Heaps, were acquitted. Charges against J.S. Woodsworth were dropped. Four Slav immigrants who had nothing to do with the strike leadership were deported.

The Winnipeg General Strike had failed. Workers found other ways to solve their problems, and the public became more aware of these problems and concerns. The Canadian trade union movement gained support, although Manitoba's labour movement would be divided and crippled for many years. Heaps and Woodsworth turned to politics. Woodsworth founded the CCF Party in 1933 as one of the first major democratic socialist parties in this country.

> **FOCUS**
> 1. Why did the Trades and Labour Council call a general strike?
> 2. What was the goal of the Citizens' Committee of One Thousand?
> 3. Do you believe the strike was a communist plot? Why or why not?
> 4. Should government forces be employed to stop strikes? Why or why not?

# Women Are Persons Too

**3**

Canadian women's horizons were expanding in the early years of the twentieth century—in the workplace, on the social scene, in sports, and even at home. Alcohol, poverty and child welfare became important social issues. Many women's groups believed the country's widespread consumption of liquor contributed to financial problems, to crime, and often to physical and mental abuse within the family. The Women's Christian Temperance Union or WCTU (organized in Ontario in 1875) worked tirelessly to ban the sale of liquor in Canada. The WCTU was successful and Prohibition was officially introduced in March, 1918, as part of the war effort. The grain used in alcohol production would be used for food instead.

But Prohibition did not work. People who seriously wanted to drink found alcohol from sources outside the law. Bootlegging became big business as criminals devised ways to make, sell or import liquor illegally from the United States. By 1924, most provinces decided liquor control was better than Prohibition. Legalizing alcohol would force **bootleggers** out of business. The government would be able to regulate liquor sales and make money from liquor taxes. Bars and licensed beverage rooms would replace the illegal stills, blind pigs and speakeasies.

Canada's temperance movement was not successful, but it did make Canadians aware of alcohol abuse. Canadian alcohol consumption never again reached the same high levels of the late nineteenth century.

*In 1938, Prime Minister Mackenzie King unveils a plaque in memory of the Alberta Five. With him are (from left to right) back row: Senator Fallis and Senator Wilson. Front row: Mrs. Muir Edwards (daughter-in-law of Henrietta Muir Edwards), J.C. Kenwood and Nellie McClung.*

The Privy Council ruled on October 18, 1929, that women were indeed "persons," and that "the exclusion of women from all public offices is a relic of days more barbarous than ours."

T I M E L I N E

1900   1910   **1920**   1930   1940   1950   1960   1970   1980   1990   2000

## Women Are Persons Too

In 1916, the City of Edmonton appointed Emily Murphy as Judge of the Juvenile Court. Within a year, the province of Alberta would make her a provincial magistrate. Murphy was the first female judge in Canada. Her first day in court was eventful because a male lawyer challenged the legality of Murphy's appointment, claiming only a "qualified person" could preside on the bench. British law considered only men as persons; women were not even mentioned.

The persons issue refused to go away. Canada's constitution (the British North America Act) stated that Canadian Senators must be "qualified persons." Were women persons? Did the wording in the BNA Act mean women could not be Senators? In 1921, the Montreal Women's Club asked Prime Minister Borden to appoint Emily Murphy to the Canadian Senate. They wanted to test the law.

Murphy had given many years of public service to Canada. She worked for poor people, for new immigrants, for Aboriginal Canadians, for children, for women and for drug addicts. Murphy's comprehensive book about the drug trade, *The Black Candle,* was the first of its kind and it had an impact around the world. Many people felt its author would make an excellent Senator.

Prime Minister Borden thought not. He claimed it was impossible for him to appoint a female to the Canadian Senate. Women's

*Emily Murphy.*

groups believed Borden's decision was discriminatory.

By 1927, Emily Murphy had had enough of the government and its attitude toward women. She teamed up with Nellie McClung, Louise McKinney, Irene Parlby, and long-time women's rights worker Henrietta Muir Edwards—the Alberta Five—to fight the "persons case" in the courts. The government won round one when the Supreme Court ruled women were not persons. The court based its decision on social conditions

BORN: 1890, Owen Sound, Ontario

DIED: 1954, Toronto, Ontario

SIGNIFICANCE: In 1921, Macphail became the first woman in Canada to be elected to Parliament and was responsible for the first equal pay legislation in Canada (1951).

BRIEF BIOGRAPHY: Macphail became an MP for the United Farmers of Ontario in 1921, the first year women were able to vote in the province. Although primarily concerned with rural issues such as the tariff, Macphail was an ardent spokesperson for female equality and women's rights. She was the founder of the Elizabeth Fry Society of Canada and was an active participant in the Woman's International League for Peace and Freedom. Macphail championed the underdog—the powerless. Macphail fought tirelessly to improve the lot of farmers, workers, the elderly, and the physically and mentally challenged. She strongly supported prison reform, old age and disability pensions, and better health care. Her socialist and pacifist beliefs often led Macphail to support the politics of J.S. Woodsworth and, later, the CCF.

## Agnes Macphail

at the time of Confederation in 1867. No one expected women to hold office then. The BNA Act never even considered women when it referred to persons. By 1927, the Alberta Five were part of a new century, and times were different. The women appealed their case all the way to the Judicial Committee of the Privy Council in England, the final court of appeal for all members of the British Empire. The Privy Council ruled on October 18, 1929, that women were indeed "persons," and that "the exclusion of women from all public offices is a

*Cairine Wilson*

relic of days more barbarous than ours."

The Alberta Five had triumphed, but Emily Murphy never did become a Senator. Liberal Prime Minister Mackenzie King appointed another Liberal, Cairine Wilson from Montreal, as the first female representative to the Canadian Senate in 1930. Some people believed the Prime Minister passed over Murphy, not because she was a Conservative, but because she had caused too much trouble for the government.

## In Their Own Words

**Emily Murphy describes her first day in court:**
*"It was as pleasant an experience as running rapids without a guide. Besides, the lawyers and police officials looked so accustomed and so terribly sophisticated. Indeed, I have never seen brass buttons so bright and menacing as on this particular day. All the men became embarrassed and started to stammer over their manner of addressing me. One said 'Your Worship' and others 'Your Honour'...and the rest said 'Sir.'"*

**How did Emily Murphy feel on her first day in court? How did the rest of the court feel?**

## FOCUS

1. Who were the Alberta Five? How did they gain for women the right to be appointed to the Senate?
2. Who was Emily Murphy?
3. Who was Agnes Macphail? How did she help the "powerless?"

# 4 New Fields for Women

1920s Canadian society had many prejudices towards both minority groups and women. For instance, it was not respectable for a married woman to work. Many employers would automatically fire a woman who married.

Women were not encouraged to obtain university or college degrees. Society expected women to be teachers, clerks or nurses. People assumed these were the natural female occupations. Professions such as medicine, law and journalism were regarded as natural male occupations. Women who wanted to study and practise in these fields faced many hurdles, including discrimination, ridicule, financial hardship and loneliness. That some women succeeded was strong testimony to their determination.

*Canada's Bobbie Rosenfeld won a silver medal in the 100 m race at the 1928 Olympics.*

## Sports

Some women found new freedom in sports. They played basketball, hockey and baseball, often for company-sponsored teams. Women's basketball games were broadcast on the radio. Toronto's Sunnyside Stadium would fill with 6,000 spectators when women's baseball teams were playing. Crowds for the men's games were often nowhere near as large.

Canadian female athletes debuted at the summer Olympic games in 1928. Canada's track and field team won medals in nearly every event. Ethel Catherwood, "the Saskatoon lily," won a gold medal in the high jump. Bobbie Rosenfeld won a silver medal in a dead heat in the 100 m race, and led the Canadian women to gold in the 400 m relay.

The rise of male athletes put an end to the popularity of women's sports. Men and boys were seen as "real athletes," more important and more dynamic than their female counterparts. Company sponsorship of women's teams declined, and those women's teams remaining had trouble getting time in public sports arenas. Women were discouraged from active sports by the 1930s. Some doctors even claimed that sports harmed a woman's ability to have children. This attitude lasted well into the 1950s.

The new twentieth-century woman wanted the freedom of easy movement. Young flappers were not going to climb into the corsets and long skirts their mothers wore before the war. Female clothing in the 1920s was loose and comfortable.

# CANADA'S DREAM TEAM: THE EDMONTON GRADS

Canada's most successful basketball team ever was the Edmonton Grads—the Commercial Graduates Basketball Club at McDougall Commercial High School, as they were officially known. Coached by Page Percy, the Grads ruled Canadian basketball from 1915 to 1940—a stellar 25-year span. They never lost a series in the twenty-three years they competed in the International Underwood Championships. Indeed, they won that cup so consistently, they were given permanent possession of it in 1940. They won 96% of their games and 49 out of a possible 51 domestic titles. After losing the first North American Championship, the Grads came back with a vengeance—winning the next three years straight. They played in the 1924 Women's Olympics, and were declared World Champions by the Federation Sportive International in Paris

that year. In 1928, they won the French and European Championships. During their twenty-five-year career, the Edmonton Grads had only 48 players listed on the original game records. The turnover rate for this phenomenal dream team was fewer than 2 players a year. All team-members, with the exception of 2, attended McDougall Commercial High School. Playing against both men and women throughout their history, the Edmonton Grads held 108 local, provincial, national and international titles at the time of their retirement. Known simply as the "finest basketball team ever," by basketball's inventor, James Naismith, the Edmonton dream team played for the love of the sport. No member ever received payment for her skills on the basketball court.

## Clothing

Another aspect of women's lives that changed dramatically in the 1920s was clothing. The new twentieth-century woman wanted the freedom of easy movement. Young flappers were not going to climb into the corsets and long skirts their mothers wore before the war. Female clothing in the 1920s was loose and comfortable. Skirts barely covered the knees. Bobs and shingled haircuts replaced long hair and hairpins. Other freedoms followed. It was not uncommon to see young women smoking—and even drinking—in public.

BORN: 1905, Vancouver, British Columbia

DIED: 1980, Cambridge, Massachusetts

SIGNIFICANCE: Was the first woman to graduate from the University of Toronto with a degree in electrical engineering.

BRIEF BIOGRAPHY: Daughter of Helen MacGill, women's rights activist and journalist who was appointed a juvenile court judge one year after Emily Murphy's appointment, Elsie was raised in a strongly feminist environment. Excelling at science and mathematics, MacGill enrolled in the University of Toronto's Engineering Department in 1923. Four years later, she became the first woman to graduate with a degree in electrical engineering. She pursued her studies at the University of Michigan where, in 1928, she became the first woman to graduate with a degree in aeronautics. Determined to continue her studies, MacGill was accepted by the prestigious Massachu-

setts Institute of Technology (MIT) in 1933 to continue her work in aeronautical research. From 1934 to 1957, she helped test-fly the first Canadian-designed and built all-metal aircraft for Fairchild Aircraft Ltd, in Longeuil, Quebec, where she was employed. In 1939, MacGill left this job for another at the Canadian Car and Foundry in Fort William, Ontario, where she was in charge of engineering on the Canadian-built Hawker Hurricanes and the U.S. Navy Helldivers, which were launched by catapult from aircraft carriers. She married Eric Soulsby, an executive at the firm, and opened her own consulting business, which she ran well into the 1970s. In 1946, MacGill helped the International Civil Aviation Organization (ICAO) to establish air-worthiness regulations. In 1955, she published a biography of her mother entitled *My Mother the Judge* and, in 1967, continuing the legacy of her mother, she served on the Royal Commission on the Status of Women.

## Elsie MacGill

# NURSES

The first trained nurses arrived in Quebec in 1639 and were members of religious orders. Unlike present-day nurses, these nuns served as doctors, administering to the sick in the nunneries and religious buildings in and around Quebec. The Sisters of Charity, a non-cloistered order, arrived in 1737 and are considered Canada's first Public Health Nurses. They built hospitals—the first one opened in Montreal in 1737—and canoed to remote areas to provide care to the ill. Training was mostly on the job. It was not until 1874 that the first school of nursing opened in St. Catharines, Ontario, as part of the General and Marine Hospital. Toronto and Montreal soon followed when their major hospitals opened nursing programs

in 1881 and 1890, respectively. Nurses, however, were responsible for little more than making the hospitals look nice. They had no professional status. Their education was determined by the hospital and the doctors who ran it. Working hours were grueling—anywhere from 12-to-20 hour days with half a day off every week—and working conditions were cramped and primitive. All wages were taken by the hospital.

Most graduates from these institutions left the hospital for private nursing in the homes of the wealthy. The Victorian Order of Nurses was established in 1897 by Lady Aberdeen to try to close the gap between the nursing care the affluent could afford and that which the poor received in the hospitals. The VON built and operated over 40 hospitals.

During the early years of the twentieth century, a group of nurses began lobbying for professional status for nurses. They wanted to improve the education of nurses and protect the title of nurse. The Canadian National Association of Nurses was formed in 1907, as a result of their demands. The University of British Columbia instituted a university degree program for nurses in 1919, but most nursing schools remained under the control of the hospitals. It was not until the 1960s that nurses gained control of their education and professional degrees were widely available to those entering the profession. Today, there are over 250,000 registered nurses in Canada.

**FOCUS**

1. What gains did women make in the 1920s in employment and recreation?
2. How did the change in fashion mirror a change in social attitudes towards women?
3. Why were some of these gains lost in the 1930s?
4. Who was Elsie MacGill?

# 5 The Roaring Twenties

## Technology and Canadian Life in the 1920s

Canadians, today, take modern conveniences for granted. We flip a switch and turn on our lights, our TV, our appliances and even our cars. We enjoy the convenience of central heating and air conditioning. Our modern stereos feature digital sound, and our computers provide multi-media and satellite communication. Life was not always so. The early 1900s was a period of intense invention, a period which would have enormous impact on future generations—which made the inventions we use possible.

Electricity became part of everyday life in the 1920s. People could buy electric stoves, washing machines, irons, vacuum cleaners and toasters. These appliances may not have looked like those we use today—they had few automatic features—but they did work, and they helped take the drudgery and much of the time out of housework.

Improvements in technology made the telephone more prevalent in Canadian homes. By 1928, over 1 million Canadian homes had telephones—an average of 12.79 telephones per 100 people. The installation of new international lines in 1927 made it possible for Canadians to phone their relatives in Great Britain. At a rate of $75 for 3 minutes and $25 for any additional minutes, however, overseas calls were not cheap. In 1928, rates were reduced to $45 for the first 3 minutes plus $15 per extra minute.

*Announcer's booth at Station C.K.N.C., Toronto, 1933.*

The 1920s was a time of social and economic revolution in North America. More Canadians than ever before were able to afford the comforts of life.

1900 1910 **1920** 1930 1940 1950 1960 1970 1980 1990 2000

## Entertainment

Evenings in many homes were spent around the kitchen table building and adjusting the homemade crystal radio set. Crystal sets did not have amplification so listeners had to wear earphones. Big electric radios in fancy wooden cabinets were one of the major sources of family entertainment. Montreal's CFCF was Canada's first commercial radio station but, by 1929, all the major cities had radio stations. There was not much programming on the air during the day, but at night, the radio could pull in stations from halfway across the continent—Montreal, Calgary, Boston, Toronto, Salt Lake City and Winnipeg. Radio transformed the business and entertainment world. Farmers and small towns were no longer isolated from the cities. Businesses could advertise their products directly to consumers and politicians could speak directly to the public. The first radio broadcasts were live. Performers, dressed in tuxedos or long gowns, would sing or play their instruments right in the studio. Listeners often heard the broadcast unedited, complete with mistakes or bloopers.

## Investors

The 1920s was a time of social and economic revolution in North America. More Canadians than ever before were able to afford the comforts of life. One of every two Canadian families owned a car in 1928. By 1929, over 60 percent of Canadians had electricity in the home. The rich were not the only people speculating on the stock market. Investors, or capitalists, had a free hand. The government did not regulate investment. There were no laws protecting working conditions or wages. **Laissez-faire capitalism** (or free enterprise business without government interference) prevailed.

Many businesses were too large to be owned by one person or family. When these companies needed money, they would finance themselves by selling shares of company stock to the public through the **stock market**. Share prices were determined by **supply and demand.** If the stock was popular, its price rose. If more people wanted to sell

### In Their Own Words

*"I'll always remember the first time I listened to a radio. I was fourteen years old, so that would have been 1924.... Trembling with excitement I put the earphones on. Like magic, from the very air around, I heard the song 'Oranges and Lemons.' The music was in my ears, clear and melodic, as if the singers were actually in the room. How could they possibly be a hundred miles away? In a trance I listened, wishing I could listen forever. ...Papa tapped me on the shoulder when it was time for Esther and Thora to listen. I took off the earphones and returned to reality. The music was gone. But I could see it now in my sisters' smiles and in their faraway, unfocused eyes."*

Source: Five Pennies. *Irene Morck. Calgary: Fifth House, 1999.*

shares than buy, the stock price fell.

Careful investors bought wisely. They investigated a company's prospects before purchasing stock. Stock values increased dramatically during the 1920s, and the stock market rose. As the excitement of buying and selling took over, some people forgot what the whole business was about. Shares were traded at higher and higher prices. Investors made huge profits on paper. The price of a company's shares often bore no relation to the real value of its earnings and profit.

### Taking Risks

Compared to the general population, the number of actual investors was small, but everyone bought into the "get rich quick" philosophy of the time.

Daring investors took big risks. They bought on **margin**, paying the stockbroker 10-15% of the price of the shares. As the value of the stock rose, the shares would pay for themselves. Investors could sell, pay the broker what was owed and still make a profit.

Of course, if the stock fell, the broker could make a **margin call,** and the investor would have to pay all the money owed. No one worried about margin calls. The stock market was rising too fast to worry.

### Consumerism

Canadians learned to be "buy now, pay later" consumers. Retailers encouraged people to **buy on time.** Consumers could buy a car with a small down payment, and pay the balance (with interest) over a two to five year period. Consumer spending rose rapidly. People wanted to buy more and more products. Canada had entered a new era of consumerism as large department stores, such as Eaton's and Simpsons, carried the many items consumers wanted. The growing automotive industry created many new jobs. The 1920s seemed to be a period of endless prosperity.

Increased world demand forced the price of Canadian wheat up in 1924. Canada would export $352,000,000 worth of wheat by 1928. Many Canadian farmers on the prairies took advantage of the boom to buy expensive

*Tip Top Tailors, 1919.*

new equipment. Most borrowed the money from banks or bought the machinery on credit. Farmers organized into wheat pools or cooperatives, which allowed them to sell their product for the highest possible price. Farm co-op stores allowed farmers to buy their supplies and materials for the lowest possible price.

Not everyone in Canada thrived. Life was particularly hard on immigrants in the cities. They usually did not speak English, and had very few job skills. Employers took advantage, paying as little as possible. Women were paid much less than men for doing the same work. Wages for most factory workers stayed low. A company might be making huge profits, but workers did not share in them. Business owners priced goods as high as possible. Often the workers could not afford to buy the goods they helped produce. As a result, unsold merchandise began to pile up in warehouses and stores.

Most people thought the booming twenties would last forever, but some economists saw danger signals. They did not like the unequal distribution of wealth. The rich got richer, while workers, immigrants and farmers did not have enough money to buy their share of the goods.

## The Technical Edge

In 1912, at the age of 13, the radio-obsessed Edward Rogers won a prize for the best amateur radio in Ontario. Seven years later, at the age of 20, he won an American competition for low-power, transatlantic broadcasts. Rogers quit his job at the Independent Telephone Company in 1925 to develop the world's first alternating current (AC) radio tube, which allowed radios to run on a regular 110-volt household current. Up until that time, radios were run on rechargeable acid-filled batteries. The noise from these receivers was often louder than the actual radio signals, which made listening to the radio a frustrating experience. Roger's new invention eliminated this problem. In 1929, Rogers and his father founded Rogers Majestic Radio Company to sell batteryless radios. The following year, he established several broadcasting companies, including 9RB (named for Rogers Batteryless), which later became CFRB. In 1931, Rogers was awarded one of Canada's first experimental television licenses. He died in 1939 at the age of 38. His son Edward Jr., 5 years old at the time of Rogers' death, would go on to found Rogers Radio Broadcasting, pioneer FM broadcasting with Toronto radio station, CHFI (1962), and develop Rogers Communications, with interests in cable televison and the Internet.

FOCUS

1. Why did many  a) immigrants  b) women  c) factory workers not share in the prosperity of the 1920s?
2. Explain why buying on margin was so risky.
3. How did consumerism change the way Canadians purchased goods?

# Easy Street

## Cars in Canada

The automobile began life at the turn of the century as a motorized cart. One early design was a large tricycle with a small motor and hand bars. Henry Ford popularized the car in North America. He invented the assembly line, where many workers worked together using mass production to build a car piece-by-piece. One group of workers would add wheels, another the motor, others the gas tank, and still others the radiator. Each worker or group did a single job on many cars. This was called **specialization of labour**, and using it meant Ford's **assembly line** could produce cars very cheaply. In 1917, the "Tin Lizzie" cost $495. By 1925, so many cars were rolling off Ford's Canadian assembly line at Windsor, the price had dropped to $424.

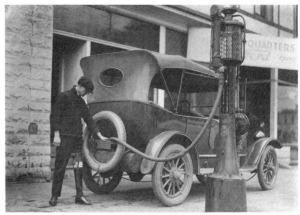

*Gas stations soon popped up all over the country.*

*Mud was a problem for cars in the 1920s. Roads were not yet paved.*

Most urban Canadians worked 9 to 10 hours a day, including a half day on Saturdays, but there was still plenty of time for pleasure on weekends.

T I M E L I N E

1900    1910    **1920**    1930    1940    1950    1960    1970    1980    1990    2000

The automobile changed the way Canadians lived. Families could drive 30-40 km to visit friends and still be home by dark. Weekend outings became popular. Farmers had faster access to market; they no longer needed to stockpile supplies to the same degree.

Soon the car became a status symbol. Exotic makes like the Auburn, Cadillac, Lincoln and Cord, many with 16 cylinder engines, could reach speeds of 160 km per hour. These expensive models shared the roads with lower priced Model Ts and Chevrolets.

The number of new cars increased from 838,672 in 1926 to 945,672 in 1927—an increase of 107,000. Of the 9,832 km of new roads constructed in 1927, 4,043 km were dirt roads, 4,481 km gravel, 388 km asphalt and 240 km concrete. Of course, the car was not much use in winter. Even if it started, roads were often too dangerous to travel. Many motorists put their automobiles up on blocks until the spring.

*Having automobiles enabled many Canadians to enjoy our vast wilderness.*

Driving during the other seasons could be a risky business too. Many farmers made extra money by lending their horses to haul motorists and their vehicles out of the mud. The Canadian Motor Vehicles Act of 1903 set speed limits of 16 kilometres per hour in the cities, and 22 kilometres per hour in the country (these speeds would be raised to 30 and 40 km in 1919). The limit on Ontario roads was 10 kilometres per hour whenever a horse-drawn carriage was near. Ontario drivers were not licensed until 1927, and even then, no one had to pass an exam. Any applicant who had driven 800 kilometres,

BORN: 1892, Toronto, Ontario

DIED: 1979, Hollywood, California

SIGNIFICANCE: Famous Hollywood actor—one of the first Canadians to go south of the border in order to pursue a career in entertainment.

BRIEF BIOGRAPHY: Mary Pickford began her acting career at the Princess Theatre in Toronto in 1900, shortly after the death of her father. In 1909, she auditioned for movie director D. W. Griffiths in New York. He hired her at $40 a week to act in silent movies. Pickford left Griffiths' studio in 1913 to work with Adolph Zukor, with whom she made *Tess of the Storm* in 1914. She left Zukor in 1917 for First National, where she gained creative approval over every aspect of her work, except distribution. Pickford reportedly earned 1-2 million dollars that year. In 1918, she left First International to found United Artists with Douglas Fairbanks, Charlie Chaplin and D.W. Griffiths. Pickford became the first female actor to produce, star in and distribute her own work. Although the most powerful woman in the business, Pickford's fans knew her as "America's Sweetheart."

Pickford and Fairbanks married in 1919, and built their famous Pickfair mansion in Hollywood. In 1929, Pickford won an Oscar for the film *Coquette,* her first talking film. She divorced Fairbanks in 1936. In 1956, Pickford sold her shares of United Artists. She received an honorary Oscar in 1976, not only for her work as an actress, but also for her determination to shape Hollywood's artistic community.

## Mary Pickford

who had no physical or mental impairments, and who paid the $1 fee could get a licence.

## Leisure Time Entertainment

Most urban Canadians worked 9 to 10 hours a day, including a half day on Saturdays, but there was still plenty of time for pleasure on weekends. As a result, the entertainment industry boomed. People looking for an afternoon or evening out on the town had lots of choice. Many Canadian cities and towns had theatres, which had been built during the early 1900s.

Travelling theatre companies used these locations to perform the latest plays from London or New York. Live variety shows for the whole family, known as vaudeville, were very popular. So were burlesque shows where, in between the stand-up comics and the skits, audiences would watch the ladies in the chorus line, or the exotic dancers, or even the strip-tease artists.

*Jazz became very popular during the 1920s. These members of Elks Jazz Band are in full swing.*

Many young people flocked to nightclubs, where they could listen to jazz music while having fun with their friends. Others went dancing. Live orchestras in the dance halls played the latest popular tunes. The tango, Charleston, and black bottom were all the rage.

But the most popular entertainment of all was the movies. There were movie houses in every city and town across the country. Many people felt a week was incomplete without an evening of laughing and crying with Charlie Chaplin, at falling in love with Rudolf Valentino, or waiting with bated breath as hero Douglas Fairbanks rescued a favourite actress from certain death.

In 1927, the first talking motion picture, *The Jazz Singer,* starring Al Jolson appeared. It would spell the end of silent films, and moviegoers became used to an even more powerful form of entertainment.

**FOCUS**
1. How did Canadians enjoy themselves during the 1920s?
2. How do Canadians enjoy themselves today?
3. What are the advantages of producing goods on an assembly line?
4. In what ways has the automobile changed our lives?

# 7 The Dirty Thirties

### The Stock Market Crash

Nobody knew on September 3, 1929 that the stock market had finally reached its peak. Prices began to slip, but they had slipped before. Most investors expected a turnaround soon. None came. Prices continued to plunge and brokers were forced to make margin calls. Investors could not pay up.

On Thursday, October 24, 1929, thousands of stock shares bought on margin were dumped onto the stock market. There were no buyers, however, so prices took a nosedive. When the news hit the newspapers, other investors panicked. Five days later, Black Tuesday, things were even worse. Small investors began dumping stock, rushing to sell out before they lost everything. The stock market bubble had finally crashed. Within days, stocks that were once valuable became worthless. Within months it became obvious that the economic downturn (recession) had turned into a worldwide **depression**. The price of raw materials collapsed: pulp dropped from $29.57 per ton in 1929 to $19.65 per ton in 1932. Copper prices fell from $19.75 to $7.02. Investors lost everything.

### The Great Depression

The panic that caused the stock market crash of 1929 began in the United States, but spread quickly to Canada and all other countries involved in trade. The stock market crash triggered the Great Depression of the 1930s. Canada suffered greatly while the whole world was in an economic slump. At first, many Canadians did

*Winnipeg Grain Exchange, 1930. What are the men in the upper half of the picture doing?*

By 1933, one in five Canadian workers had no job. There was no unemployment insurance. Two million people in this country were on relief.

| PROSPERITY | RECESSION | DEPRESSION | RECOVERY |
|---|---|---|---|
| • many jobs | • fewer sales/jobs | • very low sales | • jobs increase |
| • money to spend | • business cuts | • high unemployment | • production increases |
| • much production | • low profits | • businesses close | • demand increases |
| • much business expansion | • unemployment | • very low wages | • jobs are added |
| • high profits | • bankruptcies | • low demand for goods | • more $ to spend |
| • more jobs & spending | • more job cuts | • more unemployed | • business expands |

not realize the seriousness of the problem. Mackenzie King's Liberal government believed the economy would correct itself naturally. Many small investors thought they could survive the crash. After all, they still had jobs. Many more Canadians had never invested in the market at all. Why should its crash affect them?

## The Downward Spiral

Canada's economy was resource-based, because Canadian prosperity depended on the export of raw materials. Our natural resources—wheat, grains, lumber, fish and minerals—were sold to other countries, particularly the United States and Europe. After the crash, these countries bought much less and the decrease in demand resulted in lower prices. Canadian farmers were unable to sell their wheat. Mining companies were left with unsold coal, iron ore and copper. Lumbering companies had no buyers for their pulp and logs. In the meantime, they were unable to keep up payments for equipment bought on time. Many companies went bankrupt.

Canada's manufacturing industry fared no better. Many Canadian businesses had too much unsold inventory. They had been over-producing, churning out new products as fast as they could to meet consumer demand. Now, no one wanted to buy cars, boats, appliances or even clothing. With warehouses full of unsold goods, there was no point in making more. Factories and businesses closed down, or laid off workers until the backlog of goods was sold. Companies that stayed in business often made workers take pay cuts. Companies were forced to lower their prices in an effort to survive. With both prices and wages falling, the country was trapped in **deflation**.

Banks did not want to lose money. They called in their loans. Many businesses, and many people, could not repay their loans, so they went bankrupt. People no longer had money to buy luxuries like radios and vacuum cleaners. Workers who made these products were laid off too. Then the people who supplied the raw materials to build these products lost their jobs. Soon, many Canadians could not afford to buy coats, dresses or even shoes. And most consumers who had bought goods on the "buy now, pay later" plan could no longer make the payments. People lost their furniture, their cars and even their homes.

By 1933, one in five Canadian workers had no job. There was no unemployment insurance. Two million people in this country

## Learning to Survive

Perhaps the worst part of living through the Depression was the shame of being out of work. People had been taught that if they were poor, it was their own fault. Only lazy people failed. Every time Canada's homeless, hungry and unemployed lined up at a soup kitchen or accepted vouchers, their despair grew.

Women seeking well-paying jobs were frowned on because men "needed the jobs more." Many women accepted lower wages, and they sometimes found jobs when men could not. Some women left husbands at

*Soup kitchens seemed to spring up overnight during the Depression.*

were on relief. The area hardest hit was Canada's four western provinces. Canada's Atlantic provinces never had a chance to recover from the economic depression that floored them in the 1920s, but they were partially sustained by fishing and farming. Canada's young people, small business people and farmers were the true victims of the Depression. Many large businesses, property owners and people with jobs actually made money during this period.

home to keep house, while they went out to work long hours for $3 or $4 a week. Most Canadians believed males should be the family breadwinners. Every day that wives, sisters and mothers went out to work, their husbands, brothers and sons lost a little more self-respect.

But Canadians did not give up; they made do. People patched old clothes. When the clothes fell apart, they wore flour sacks. Wads of newspaper placed in worn-out shoes made

them last longer. Tea leaves, coffee grounds and soup bones were used over and over until there was no flavour left. People bartered services for goods. Many Canadians left the cities to return to the land. When there was nothing left at home on the land, they set off across the country, looking for work.

## Riding the Rails

With money scarce, some people rode in empty freight cars or rode on top of them. Others hitchhiked along the highways. Perhaps there would be work on the next farm or in the next town. A knock on the farmhouse door sometimes got them a meal, but rarely any work. Often, these transients worked for their food. Lines of unemployed gathered at factory gates only to find "No Help Wanted" signs and no work.

In summer, people slept beside open fires in hobo jungles on the edge of town. In winter, they might be allowed to sleep on

a jailhouse floor, or in barns or church basements. For many Canadians, this way of life went on for ten years. These were the Dirty Thirties.

**FOCUS**
1. Explain what happened to cause the stock market crash of October 1929.
2. Describe the upward economic spiral of the 1920s with the downward spiral of the 1930s.
3. How did people survive during the Dirty Thirties when there were few jobs and no unemployment insurance?

# The Drought and the Dustbowl

**8**

The worst place to be during the Depression was on the Prairies. In 1929, wheat sold for $1.60 a bushel. By 1932, farmers could hardly get rid of their crop at $.38. World economic conditions improved slightly in 1933; some factories in eastern Canada hired more workers. Mines started to reopen. For farmers in Manitoba and Saskatchewan, however, the real trouble was just beginning. The world's supply of grain was much higher than demand. Wheat prices remained low. Workers on the Prairies had no other jobs to go to, and many farmers abandoned their homes and their land. The weather brought more trouble.

Although parts of the Prairies had been experiencing droughts as early as 1927, the summer of 1931 was a particularly dry year. 1932 brought the rains again, but although the wheat crop of that year was one of the largest and most highly-ranked ever, its average price was only $.35 a bushel. Drought returned in 1933. It would be another five long years before Prairie farmers would see real rain again.

Crops grow in soil or topsoil on the land's surface. Topsoil contains the moisture and nutrients plants need to develop.

*Years of drought turned fertile soil into dust.*

The worst place to be during the Depression was on the Prairies. In 1929, wheat sold for $1.60 a bushel. By 1932, farmers could hardly get rid of their crop at $.38.

Subsoil contains no real nourishment. The 1930s drought caused topsoil in the Prairies to dry up and turn to dust. Strong winds whipped the dust into black blizzards, piling it high against fences and barns. Farmers stood by, watching helplessly as the land that fed them blew away. They watched as their once fertile farms turned to rocks and clay, and the few remaining wheat plants to survive the wind shriveled and died in the parched subsoil. Canadian wheat production decreased from 440,000,000 bushels in 1927 to a low 219,218,000 bushels in 1936.

*Dust storms were common on the Prairies during the drought and the Depression of the 1930s.*

Then the grasshoppers came. They hatched by the millions in the Prairie desert. Grasshoppers thrive under drought conditions. Farmers would look up to see dark

## In Their Own Words

*"Next to the farm home and the rural school the institution which shows most clearly the impact of depression and drought is the rural telephone. It may be assumed that ordinarily the farmer gives up telephone services with extreme reluctance. 'Consider,' writes Mrs. Telford of Pelly [Sask] 'a farmer's financial straits when for $10.50 a year he will do without a telephone. Perhaps he is 10 or 15 miles from town, perhaps a mile from his nearest neighbour, yet for the sake of that paltry sum, he will face the hazards of isolation, the social inconvenience of doing without his telephone. I think this more than anything else shows our western financial position."*

from A Submission by the Government of Saskatchewan to the Royal Commission on Dominion-Provincial Relations (Canada, 1937), reprinted from *Building a Province*, by David E. Smith, Fifth House, Publishers, Calgary, Alberta, 1976

clouds of these insects blotting out the sun. Little was left alive after the grasshoppers passed. One farmer reported they had even stripped the bristles from his broom—only the metal band and a chewed handle remained. Grasshopper damage to Saskatchewan wheat crops rose as high as 40% during the 1930s, and as high as 80% to other cereal crops.

Saskatchewan produced 8,750,000 tonnes of wheat or 1.6 tonnes per hectare in 1928. In 1937, the worst year of all during the Dirty Thirties, production was only 920,000 tonnes or .2 tonnes per hectare. It was no wonder the average Saskatchewan farmer was in debt $9,771 in 1936.

What did farming families do, hit by the double blows of Depression and the Dustbowl? They went barefoot, dressed in flour bags and burned wheat instead of wood—wheat was cheaper. They ate gopher stew. They gave up the telephone, the newspaper and the car. They fell behind on their mortgage payments and were forced off their land when the banks foreclosed. Some farmers moved to parkland areas north of Prince Albert where rain fell. Others gave up and headed for the cities of Ontario or west to British Columbia. Over one-quarter of the wheat farms on the Prairies were abandoned during the thirties.

Most families just hung on, hoping that the rains would come next year. Even if the crop was good, the price they were paid for it would often not cover the growing costs. The rains came again in 1938. So did the grasshoppers and hailstorms. It was not until 1939 that farmers on the Canadian Prairies began to recover. It took World War II to bring farming back to a profitable level.

## In Their Own Words

"Every year of the Depression was worse than the one before it. We were all short of money....One day, a neighbour came into [the] store for his mail. 'Oh good,' he said, 'this must be the cheque from the cattle I shipped to market last week. I sure need it. Me and my family are just plumb out of money.'

'Bet that cheque will hardly be worth cashing,' said one of the farmers, 'the way the price of cattle has been falling.'

'Yeah. You might get a couple of dollars per steer, or something ridiculous like that,' said another.

'Anything is better than nothing,' said the man, opening the envelope. His smile vanished, to be replaced by a look of horror. 'I don't believe it. This can't be true.'

'What's wrong?' We all rushed over to him.

'A bill. They say I owe them money.'

'For what?'

'For freight.' He looked ill. 'They say it cost more for the railway freight charges to ship my cattle than what they sold for at the market! Where am I going to get the money to pay this bill?'

In the weeks to come many more farmers had the same horrible experience, having to pay a bill when they sold cattle.

Soon no farmer dared send livestock away to sell. What family could take that chance?"

Source: Five Pennies, Irene Morck. Calgary: Fifth House, 1999

**Food for Thought** In our nutrition-conscious age, we often forget that it was not always easy finding nutritionally sound food. In the early part of the twentieth century, people tended to eat seasonally, which meant that during a large part of the year they ate mostly rutabaga, carrots and potatoes—vegetables they could store for the winter. Childhood diseases were rampant. Thousands of Canadian children died before reaching their fourth birthdays. Two innovative Canadian discoveries, however, helped to change all this.

*Hungry farmers line up for food. The Prairies were hit hard during the Depression.*

Fish was not a popular food for most Canadians, because there was no way to transport it without losing freshness. Dr. Archibald Huntsman, while working at the Biological Board in Halifax in 1926, set out to prove that if fresh fish was frozen at the height of its freshness, it would retain both its flavour and nutritional value and, more importantly, people would buy it. After three years in the laboratory, Huntsman finally had a product. Called Ice Fillets, his package of frozen fish went on sale in Hamilton, Ontario, in January 1929. Today, millions of Canadians enjoy the benefits of eating fish without having to live near an ocean.

Hospital for Sick Children doctor, Frederick Tisdall, along with two other prominent pediatricians, Dr. Alan Brown and Dr. T.G.H. Drake, turned their attention to solving Canada's high infant death rate. In their work at the hospital, the doctors were seeing a number of childhood ailments they believed were caused by poor nutrition. Many infant cereals of their day, for example, were based on refined flour and lacked enough vitamins, minerals and protein to ensure healthy growth in babies.

First, the doctors devised a vitamin-packed biscuit, but babies needed something that they didn't have to chew. In 1931, these three doctors from Toronto invented Pablum, the first scientifically engineered baby food. Instead of the usual refined flour—the base of most existing infant cereals—Pablum is made up of wheat meal, oatmeal, cornmeal, wheat germ, bone meal, brewer's yeast and alfalfa. It became an instant hit around the world. Now, all children were guaranteed a healthy, nutritional meal without a lot of fuss and bother.

**FOCUS**
1. Give 3 reasons why the Prairies were the worst place to be during the Depression.
2. How did families survive during this great economic slump?
3. What Canadian inventors improved health for Canadians?

# The On-To-Ottawa Trek

**9**

The Depression was probably hardest on young, single men. When employers were forced to cut staff, they let the young and single go first, assuming that older, married employees were more dependent on the work. Young women were often unemployed, but it was considered natural that their

*Men board trains during the On-to-Ottawa trek.*

families would support them.

Canada's young men set off to look for work in other cities across the country. Usually, there were no jobs anywhere. City relief officers worried about these drifters. Relief monies and goods were already being used up in support of regular city residents. There was nothing left for the newcomers.

The young men were asked to move on. There was no place to go. The drifters were desperate for food, for shelter and for work.

Authorities had many fears. What if the men turned violent? What if they organized together with the help of communist agitators? Canada could find itself in the middle of a revolution, just as Russia had in 1917. Canadian city officials demanded action from Ottawa.

## Relief Camps

The federal government decided to stop any possible revolution before it started. It set up Unemployment Relief Camps in remote areas of the country. It wanted to move the growing crowds of drifters off the roads, out of the cities, and out of trouble. Canada's relief camps were run by the Department of National Defence.

Camp inmates worked 8 hours a day, 6 days a week. They built roads, dug ditches and planted trees. In return, each worker received clothes, a bed, food, and $.20 a day. Most men were not happy. They felt they were living in a mixture of army and prison camps. They were cut off from the world, without a future. They were bored; there was nothing to do after work. Conditions were terrible. One bunkhouse measured 24 m by 7.3 m, and had no windows. The 88 men who lived there slept 2 to a bunk.

The Depression was probably hardest on young, single men. When employers were forced to cut staff, they let the young and single go first, assuming that older, married employees were more dependent on the work.

## Reaction

In April 1935, 1,500 men from British Columbia's relief camps went on strike. They made their way to Vancouver and took over the city library and the Hudson's Bay store. On May Day, 20,000 striking men and their supporters paraded through the city.

RP42-30 (AUG 1933)

Vancouver could not help them. It had very little relief money. Still, the strikers remained in the city for two months. When organizer Arthur "Slim" Evans of the Worker's Unity League (WUL) suggested the men travel to Ottawa to carry their message directly to Prime Minister Bennett, the response was enthusiastic. The On-To-Ottawa Trek was born.

The Trekkers had no money. They would have to ride the rods to Ottawa. On June 3, 1,000 strikers climbed on top of the boxcars of an eastbound CPR freight train. They would ride on the roof for free. First stop was Kamloops, after a long overnight ride through the mountains. Next came Golden, then Calgary after the terrifying trip through the long Connaught tunnel. Most Trekkers thought they would die, choking from the black engine smoke. Then it was on to Medicine Hat, Swift Current and Moose Jaw. The Trekkers were met by crowds bearing food and good wishes at every stop. There were Tag Sales to raise money. Other discontented workers joined the Trek. Even the train crews cooperated.

Prime Minister Bennett's government was terrified. It had set up the relief camps to avoid trouble. It had forbidden camp workers to form committees, and still a mass movement had begun. Crowds of workers waited in Winnipeg, Thunder Bay and Toronto to join the strikers. The On-to-Ottawa Trek had to be stopped. When 2,000 Trekkers arrived in Regina, Bennett ordered the railroads to refuse further transport. The Trekkers were rounded up and taken to the Regina Exhibition grounds. Eight leaders, including Evans, were allowed to continue to

*These men are at a relief camp in Ontario.*

Ottawa for a meeting with the prime minister on June 22.

The meeting was not a success. Both sides were angry. Bennett refused to listen to the Trekkers' demands. He believed the strikers were trying to start a revolution in Canada. Bennett called Evans a criminal, and Evans called Bennett a liar. The delegates returned to Regina determined that the Trek would continue. Bennett was equally determined it would not.

ON-TO-OTTAWA TREKKERS ARRESTED ON JULY 1st, 1935

FOR YOUTH AND DEMOCRACY

SECTION 98

## *The Regina Riots*

On July 1, Dominion Day, Trekkers and their supporters held a meeting in Regina's Market Square. They needed to raise money to continue. The government was worried the crowd would get out of hand. It stationed troops in large furniture vans at each of the four corners of the square. At the blast of a whistle, the van doors opened, and out poured RCMP and city police waving batons.

"We took it for a few minutes, and then we let go against them," one Trekker recalled. The riot lasted until late evening. One person was killed, several people injured and 130 were arrested. The On-To-Ottawa Trek was over. The Trekkers disbanded; many of them returned to Vancouver by train at government expense. The government would shut down the relief camps within a year, but the problems of the unemployed remained.

## Depression Across Canada

If one worker in five was out of a job, four people were still working. The hardship was great, but the country survived. How did people in each region cope? Everybody suffered to some degree, but those who produced goods for export had the biggest problems.

The factories of southern Ontario and Quebec produced products that were sold mainly in Canada. The products were protected by high tariffs, which kept foreign-made goods out of the country. Some factories remained in production, but produced much less than before. Tariff protection meant that prices could be high, even though high prices produced hardship for people who needed the goods.

Farmers in Central Canada and the Maritimes had mixed farms—growing a little wheat, some corn, a vegetable garden, raising some cattle, and some poultry. They could trade or barter their produce when they could not sell it. The local storekeeper knew

his customers had no cash. He or she would gladly accept a few dozen eggs and a barrel of

### TOTAL EXPENDITURE ON RELIEF 1930-1937*
#### * in millions of dollars

| Year | All Governments | Federal Goverments |
|------|-----------------|--------------------|
| 1930 | 18  | 4  |
| 1931 | 97  | 38 |
| 1932 | 95  | 37 |
| 1933 | 98  | 36 |
| 1934 | 159 | 61 |
| 1935 | 173 | 79 |
| 1936 | 159 | 81 |
| 1937 | 165 | 89 |

What year saw the greatest increase in government spending on relief?

apples for a pair of shoes. Maritimers were used to hardship. They had missed out on the boom of the 1920s, and although Depression conditions were worse, they'd had plenty of practice with adversity, and knew how to survive.

British Columbia was almost entirely dependent upon export. Lumbering, mining and salmon fishing were the major industries. There were no markets and no jobs.

The Prairies were the hardest hit. First, farmers could not sell their wheat. Then the Dustbowl meant they could not even grow it.

FOCUS
1. Why did the government set up relief camps?
2. Why did camp workers start the On-To-Ottawa Trek? What happened?
3. Describe the Regina Riots.
4. How did people cope with the Depression?

# 10 Bennett and King

William Lyon Mackenzie King, leader of Canada's Liberal party, was first elected prime minister in 1921. He remained prime minister for nine years as "people seemed to want what King gave them: a small government that did not tinker, a more or less well-run government that helped business exploit and develop the nation: above all a government that minded its own business..." With the difficult economic times of 1929 and 1930, Canadians lost confidence in his leadership.

They became impatient and expected their government to find solutions to the Depression. Canadians wanted to get back to work. Prime Minister Mackenzie King and his Liberals had no answers. "Prosperity is just around the corner," they said. The Liberals believed the best policy was to let the Depression run its course. When the provinces (most of whom had Conservative governments) asked Ottawa for monies to support unemployment relief, King refused. He would not give "a five-cent piece" to any Conservative. Relief was a provincial responsibility, King said. Voters were not impressed. The Liberals lost the 1930 election to Richard Bedford (R.B.) Bennett and his Conservatives.

Canada's new prime minister was a wealthy western lawyer. Bennett promised dynamic action to solve the nation's problems. He believed, like King

*R.B. Bennett*

The Great Depression was not ended by the policies of R. B. Bennett or those of Mackenzie King. It was ended by World War II.

1900   1910   1920   **1930**   1940   1950   1960   1970   1980   1990   2000

before him, that Canadian business needed to find its own level, free of government influence. Bennett moved to protect Canadian factory jobs by introducing high Canadian tariffs on imported goods. He introduced the Unemployment Relief Act, which promised $20,000,000 in relief aid during its first year to be administered by the provinces. He worked to develop a Commonwealth trading group, which would grant its members preferential treatment on tariffs. Most Canadians, however, felt little effect from these policies. They were still out of work. The lines outside the soup kitchens grew longer.

American President Franklin Delano Roosevelt announced his New Deal to the American people in 1933. Roosevelt decided that the Depression would not cure itself; he brought the government into the economic arena by spending money and creating jobs. Slowly things began to improve in the United States.

R.B. Bennett introduced his Canadian version of the New Deal in 1935, just before the federal election. Bennett proposed an 8-hour workday, a minimum wage, unemployment insurance, and price controls.

### "King or Chaos"

Mackenzie King poured scorn on Bennett's plans. The Liberals campaigned on the slogan "King or Chaos." Canadian voters wanted to know why the Conservatives took five long years to move forward while Canadians

*Mackenzie King*

BENNETT AND KING   **165**

# LETTERS TO PRIME MINISTER BENNETT

**R.B. Bennett was a rich man, but he could not solve the problems caused by the Depression from his private fortune. He received many, many letters from desperate Canadians, and often responded with gifts of clothing or money. Which of these letters is the most moving in your opinion? Why?**

**Chichester, Quebec**
March 13, 1935
Dear Mr. Bennett:
I am a little boy 11 years old I live in a very back wood place and I am very poor there is a bunch of us I am going to school My little Sister and I we have three miles to go and break our own path but we don't mind that if we were only able to buy our books, the Quebec books are very expensive so I just thought I would write you maybe you would give us enough to buy our books if you don't I guess we will have to stop and try and earn a little money to help out our father please excuse paper and pencil as I have no better. Hoping to hear from you real soon I am

> Yours Loving Friend
> Albert Drummond
> Please answer soon soon soon

**Murray Harbour, P.E.I.**
March 24, 1935
Dear Sir:
I am writing you to see if their is any help I could get. As I have a baby thirteen days old that only weighs One Pound and I have to keep it in Cotton Wool & Olive Oil, and I haven't the money to buy it, the people bought it so far and fed me when I was in Bed. if their is any help I could get I would like to get it as soon as possible. their is five of a family. Counting the baby. their will be two votes for you next Election. Hoping too hear from you soon

> Yours Truly
> Mrs. Jack O'Hannon

**Calgary**
June 18 1935
Dear Mr. Bennett,
   Do please raise the Old Age Pension to at least thirty dollar per month. So many of your very old friends, myself included, have really not enough to exist on.

> Very best wishes for your good health,
> Sincerely, Alma Ward

**Sudbury**
May 20, 1931
Mr. Bennette
   Since you have been elected, work has been impossible to get. We have decided that in a month from this date, if thing's are the same, We'll skin you alive, the first chance we get

> Starving Unemployed

**Regina Sask.**
May 24, 1935
Dear Sir:
You will. no doubt be surpriced to recived this requaist.
   I thought that you would have second hand clothing that would not be suitable for you to wear. as I am strapped for clothes fit to wear to Church I desided to write to you.
   My best suit is over 8 years old and pretty well frayed.
   Judging you by your picture I beleve you are about the same size as myself.
   I might say my people and I have allways been stunch Conservatives I wouldn't ask a Liberal part if I had to go naked.
   I was 69 years of age May 22/35.
   I voted as a farmer's son when I was 18 years old for Sir John A McDonald's Government and Im still on the list

> I am yours respectfuly
> J.A. Graydon

starved without jobs? Bennett's New Deal sounded like an election ploy to get votes.

King and the Liberals swept to victory in 1935. They offered few real policies, but Canadians were tired of Bennett. Everyone realized that government action was needed to help people out of the Depression. The situation was confused by conflict between federal and provincial politicians. Although the federal government could raise the most money through taxes, social policies such as unemployment relief, which cost money, were provincial responsibilities. It seemed an impossible situation.

In 1937, King set up a Royal Commission on Dominion-Provincial Relations. The **Rowell-Sirois Commission** recommended sweeping changes in the tax system, changes which were designed to remove the stumbling blocks to federal-provincial cooperation. The Commission suggested **equalization payments** to the less wealthy provinces. It said the federal government should be responsible for unemployment insurance.

The Rowell-Sirois Commission's report was not released until 1940. By that time, the Depression was over. World War II had begun. The Great Depression was not ended by the policies of R.B. Bennett or those of Mackenzie King. It was ended by World War II.

On September 10, 1939, the Canadian Parliament supported Britain by declaring war on Nazi Germany. Canada's unemployed were back to work—in the army and in the arms factories. The country was ready for another war-related economic boom.

## In Their Own Words

*"Though Depression and prairie drought had generated massive unemployment and widespread penury, there was no federal welfare department. Old age pensions of $20 a month were paid by the provincial government to paupers over 70, and to those pensions the federal treasury made a 75-percent contribution. The total federal budget was a half a billion dollars a year, including grants to provincial governments to assist in the relief of the unemployed and of destitute farmers in the Prairies."*
Source: Seeing Canada Whole: A Memoir. J.W. Pickersgill. Toronto: Fitzhenry & Whiteside, 1994.

FOCUS
1. Why was King defeated in 1930?
2. What was Bennett's New Deal?
3. Why did voters elect King in 1935?

# 11 The New Politics

The depths of the Depression gave rise to new political ideas. Canada's Liberal and Conservative parties both believed government should steer clear of the economy, that economic problems would solve themselves. Other people disagreed. They looked for government intervention. These people formed new political parties to carry their views forward into government.

Liberals and Conservatives dominated Canada's Parliament, but there were members from other political groups as well. United Farmers groups in Ontario and the Prairie Provinces joined together in the 1920s to form the Progressives Party. Agnes Macphail, the first female member of Parliament, was a Progressive. J.S. Woodsworth, one of the leaders of the Winnipeg General Strike, was elected as a Labour Member of Parliament. Other MPs were Independents who did not belong to any particular party.

*The first Cooperative Commonwealth Federation (CCF) convention, 1933.*

Aberhart's Social Credit party proposed to give each Alberta citizen a monthly social dividend of $25. Residents would use the money to purchase needed goods.

## Cooperative Commonwealth Federation

The Cooperative Commonwealth Federation (CCF) was founded in 1932 in Calgary. When Progressives, Labour Party members, middle-class intellectuals, labour leaders and supporters of the British socialist movement joined together to develop an alternative political voice. The CCF believed in **socialism**; it wanted government control of business and industry. It believed the economy should be run on a cooperative basis for the good of the Canadian people. The CCF platform, known as the Regina Manifesto, was drawn up in 1933 at the party's first annual convention in Regina. CCFers believed the private enterprise system (wherein owners run businesses to make profits for themselves) lacked controls. Private enterprise and greed, they felt, had cast the country into the Great Depression.

---

### THE REGINA MANIFESTO – Program of the CCF

1. **The people (the government) should own all the banks and financial institutions.**

2. **The people should own key industries such as railways, mines, lumbering, telephone systems, hydroelectric companies.**

3. **There should be a large-scale program of public works (housing, roads, public buildings) to provide jobs for the unemployed.**

4. **Laws should guarantee minimum living standards for all through programs like unemployment insurance, family allowances, old age pensions.**

5. **Farmers' land should be protected from mortgage foreclosures.**

6. **There should be a guaranteed minimum wage.**

---

Many Canadians confused the socialist CCF with the Communist Party. There were big differences. Communists believed that change could only come through violent revolution. The CCF believed that changes in the system should be made democratically. Communists did not feel individual rights and freedoms were important. The welfare of the state was all that mattered.

The CCF upheld the individual's civil rights. People must be allowed to vote freely. The CCF elected J.S. Woodsworth as their first leader. Woodsworth had worked hard to help immigrants, the elderly and his fellow trade unionists. He was highly respected by all political parties.

*William Aberhart swept into power in Alberta in 1935.*

## Poverty in the Midst of Plenty

Alberta stores were stocked with clothes, radios and tractors, but people had no money to buy them. Farmers had wheat and usually could not sell it. When and if they managed to sell, the price received was often less than the cost of sowing and harvesting. It was a vicious circle.

William Aberhart was well known in Alberta. In 1932, the high school principal from Calgary (also known as Bible Bill, the radio preacher of the Calgary Prophetic Bible Institute) began to talk about a new political idea. He called it Social Credit. The root of the Depression, Aberhart believed, was the fact that people did not have enough money to buy the goods being produced. If people had more money, they could buy more goods. More people would have jobs, and they would earn more money. The Depression would be over; the prosperity cycle would return. Aberhart's Social Credit party proposed to give each Alberta citizen a monthly social dividend of $25. Residents would use the money to purchase needed goods.

This idea made great sense to the farmers and workers of Alberta. They trusted Bible Bill Aberhart. In the 1935 provincial election, Social Credit won 56 of 63 seats and Aberhart became premier.

The federal government ruled that issuing money was a federal power. Aberhart's government had no right to print money. Many Albertans felt the federal government's response was just one more example of how Liberals and Conservatives favoured Ontario and Quebec. It seemed as if the older established political parties were more interested in talking about laws and the constitution than helping people in need.

New parties and new politics sprang up all over Canada during the Depression. In British Columbia, Liberal Premier Thomas Pattullo tried to move his government into

### In Their Own Words

"You can strip down the appeal of Social Credit to the $25 a month. All of us farmers were in desperate straits. Here was William Aberhart promising $25 a month, and he was a Minister of the Gospel. I asked him about that $25 after one of his meetings, and he told me I must have faith."

a farmer from central Alberta

regulating the economy with the introduction of a "work and wages" program. Maurice Duplessis swept to power in Quebec in 1936 as the leader of the Union Nationale, which he had founded. Mitch Hepburn, Liberal Premier of Ontario, adopted a number of policies from the Progressives, including auctioning off government limousines.

### FOCUS

1. Summarize the 6 main ideas of the Regina Manifesto.
2. Would you have voted for the CCF or Social Credit Party during the Depression? Explain.
3. What did Aberhart believe was the main cause of the Depression?
4. How did his Social Credit Party propose to end it?

# On the Sunny Side of the Street

**12**

Life in the thirties was not dull and drab all the time. People found their fun in many ways. If they could not afford to travel, they could still get together with friends and neighbours for a picnic. They could go swimming at community beaches. On Saturdays, there were often concerts in the bandstand at the local park.

Amos and Andy, Eddie Cantor, Bing Crosby, Fanny Brice, Jack Benny—these were the entertainers of the decade. If you had a radio, your pleasure was free. Soap operas ran daily. People could hardly wait to learn more of the loves, fears, disasters and joys of *Helen Trent, Our Gal Sunday* or *Ma Perkins*. Monday evenings, the Lux Radio Theatre presented radio versions of the latest movies. Other nights, people pushed aside the furniture and danced to the music of the big bands. Guy Lombardo and His Royal Canadians was one of the best known. Every year, millions of North Americans welcomed in the new year by listening to the Royal

*Radio announcer at KUKU.*

Canadians play *Auld Lang Syne.*

The Canadian Radio Broadcasting Corporation was established by the government in 1932. By 1936, when the CRBC became the CBC, it had 8 stations and 14 private affiliates. The first French station was added in 1937. Canadians from coast to coast could now listen to their own programs—Canadian entertainment provided by Canadian talent. CBC listeners would laugh at the antics of Vancouver's *Stag Party,* or hum along with the music of Toronto's *Happy Gang.* On Sunday mornings, boys and girls listened to the stories of *Just Mary* from the Maritimes. At Christmas, the whole family would gather round the radio for the King's Message. Farm news first appeared on the French station, and the programs were so popular that English farm broadcasts began shortly after. CBC's first on-the-spot news coverage was of the Moose River Mine disaster in Nova Scotia, reported by J. Frank Willis. When Ontario Premier Mitch Hepburn confronted striking

The nation would gather around the radio for Foster Hewitt's welcoming, "Hello Canada and hockey fans in the United States and Newfoundland," and listen throughout the live broadcast for his famous cry: "He shoots. He scores!"

1900   1910   1920   **1930**   1940   1950   1960   1970   1980   1990   2000

autoworkers at Oshawa's General Motors plant, Canadians heard about it through the CBC. Canadians followed the activities of British royalty via radio. Saturday night was *Hockey Night in Canada.* The nation would gather around the radio for Foster Hewitt's welcoming, "Hello Canada and hockey fans in the United States and Newfoundland," and listen throughout the live broadcast for his famous cry: "He shoots. He scores!"

Many towns had their own movie house. When there was $.15 to spare, children went to the Saturday afternoon show. The cartoons, the latest episode in the adventures of *The Shadow* or *Tom Mix,* a full-length movie, sometimes even a free comic book—all could be had for $.10. The extra nickel bought a chocolate bar or some jellybeans. A generation grew up on cowboy and Indian movies. These movies painted a distorted picture of the Aboriginal struggle for survival after European settlers came to North America. Today, Aboriginal peoples are still fighting the warped attitudes these movies created.

Most people wanted to escape real life during the Depression. The movies were a perfect solution. Canadians flocked to see the Marx Brothers, Laurel and Hardy, Charlie Chaplin, and W.C. Fields. Canadian movies? Impossible. Everyone knew movies were only made in Hollywood. There were plenty of movies about Canada. The fact that these movies painted a pretty strange picture of this country did not seem to bother anyone. Jeanette MacDonald's *Rose Marie* and Shirley Temple's *Susannah of the Mounties* were two popular movies supposedly set in Canada. Mountains and Mounties were what Hollywood thought Canada was all about. Add some snow, birch bark canoes, handsome lumberjacks and "wicked" French Canadians, and the picture was complete.

## HIT SONGS OF THE 1930s

**The music of the thirties reflected the spirit of the time. Some tunes reflected the struggles people faced. Others were more upbeat and hopeful. Everyone listened to the music on the radio.**

- I Can't Give You Anything But Love
- On the Sunny Side of the Street
- Brother, Can You Spare a Dime?
- I'm Getting Sentimental Over You
- Smoke Gets in Your Eyes
- Blue Moon
- I've Got You Under My Skin
- What a Difference a Day Makes
- The Lady Is a Tramp
- Pennies From Heaven
- They Can't Take That Away From Me
- Moonlight Serenade
- My Prayer
- I'll Never Smile Again
- Happy Days Are Here Again

**The automobile** had become quite a machine by the 1930s as manufacturers introduced new designs and options. Cars featured curved fenders with lots of chrome and more powerful engines. Ford intro-

duced its V-8 engine in 1932. Cadillac introduced its second V-16 engine in 1938. Chrysler developed a curved one-piece windshield. Automatic transmissions and power brakes were introduced for the first time. Canada's roads had also improved. Ontario's Queen Elizabeth Way, the first four-lane, limited access highway in North America, opened in 1939 and Canadians could motor from Toronto to Hamilton with ease.

## Sport

Professional sports became popular during the 1930s. The Montreal Royals and the Toronto Maple Leafs were the only professional sports teams. Football was beginning to attract attention, and each year the best Western team travelled east to meet the Eastern champions. Each year, the west was defeated. Finally in 1935, Fritz Hanson led the Winnipeg Blue Bombers to victory. National rivalry for the Grey Cup had begun.

Then, as now, hockey was the Canadian sport. The excitement was carried across the country by the magic of radio. Children who had never seen the Montreal Canadiens or the Toronto Maple Leafs play knew all the details of the latest game. If they missed it on radio, they picked up the story from the sports page of the newspaper the next day.

## The Dionne Quintuplets

The most publicized event of the decade was the birth of the Dionne Quintuplets in 1934. The five sisters, born to a poor Franco-Ontarian family near North Bay, Ontario, were the first quintuplets in the world to survive. This human interest, miracle-baby story

## MAPLE LEAF GARDENS

Maple Leaf Gardens, home of the Toronto Maple Leafs, opened for the public on November 12, 1931, as the Toronto Maple Leafs faced off against the Chicago Blackhawks before 15,000 spectators. Toronto lost the opener 2-1, but would go on to win the Stanley Cup that year. Maple Leaf Gardens was one of six "original" arenas commissioned by the newly created National Hockey League. Maple Leafs' owner Conn Smythe faced heavy odds financing a building of such size in the middle of the Depression, but construction workers took 20% of their salaries in Maple Leaf stock. The Gardens was finished in five months. It would be home to the Maple Leafs until February 13, 1999.

**Table-top Hockey** During the Depression, Don Munro was one of many Canadians out of work, with little spare cash to provide for his family. Wanting to entertain his children, but with little money to purchase toys and games, Munro decided to create a game. Using regular household items and recycling old materials instead of throwing them away, Munro created table-top hockey. The first model featured a four-man team of wooden players. One lever on the board controlled the goalie and another moved the remaining three men. The steel ball was kept moving by a slight bump in the center of the board. Munro's children were so happy with their new toy that Munro not only patented his invention, he paid a visit to the toy buyer at the local Eaton's store, armed with the board under his arm. The buyer, reluctant to purchase something new during a period of such widespread economic uncertainty, yet intrigued with the game, purchased 1 copy, just to see how things went. He sold that copy before Munro had returned home. Within hours he was on the phone ordering another 6 copies. Before long, the Munro family business became Munro Games Ltd., and table-top hockey a major part of growing up in Canada.

captured the hearts and minds of Canadians and Americans alike. The Ontario government removed the girls from their family, and raised them in a specially-built hospital, where tourists could pay to watch the quints (behind glass) during three daily visiting sessions. The quints generated millions of dollars for the government during the nine years they were on display. They were used in movies and in baby food advertisements. They were cut off from other people, and had no family life. Finally, in 1996, after a long legal battle, the Ontario government agreed to pay the three surviving sisters 2.8 million dollars for the suffering it had caused all of the Dionnes for so many years.

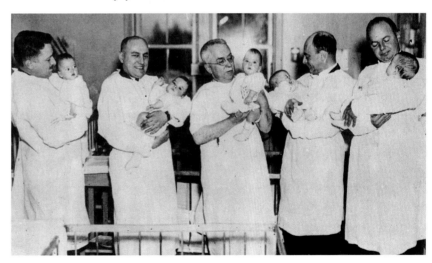

*The Dionne Quintuplets, born in 1934, were the first quintuplets in the world to survive.*

**FOCUS**
1. Which 1930s radio programs did Canadians enjoy?
2. Describe an afternoon at the movies during the 1930s.
3. How did sports fans find out about the achievements of their favourite stars and teams?

# 13 Changes Between the Wars

Even though Canada became a nation in 1867, Britain still made foreign policy decisions for Canada and the rest of the British Empire. At the outbreak of the First World War in 1914, for example, Canada did not declare war on Germany. Britain's declaration of war meant the whole British Empire was automatically at war, including Canada. Several important events after 1914 helped Canada achieve full independence from Britain.

Canada's contribution to World War I resulted in a more mature nation. Canada and the other Dominions of the British Empire sat as separate nations at the Paris Peace Conference. Later, Canada was an independent member of the new League of Nations.

In 1923, Canadians and Americans worked out a treaty to protect halibut on the Northwest coast. Canada announced that its own minister of fisheries would sign the treaty. This was the first time Canada signed a treaty on its own, and was symbolic of new independence.

## The British Commonwealth of Nations

It was obvious that the new relationship of countries within the British Empire had to be spelled out. Other groups—the Boers of South Africa and the Irish—were also unhappy. They had fought wars against Britain. The Imperial Conference of 1926 responded by issuing the Balfour Report. It stated that Dominions were free and equal, that they were united by the crown and associated as members of the British Commonwealth of Nations. In 1931, the British Parliament passed the Statute of Westminster. This act declared that the British Parliament had no power over the laws of the Dominions.

Canada's Constitution, the British North America Act, was an act of the British Parliament. When the Statute of Westminster was passed, Canadians had not yet worked out how they would make changes to the constitution. Britain kept the power to amend the BNA act until 1981.

## A Changing Identity

As British traditions faded through the 1900s, American influences on Canadian life became stronger. It was important that the people of Canada have a sense of their own country. The establishment of the CBC was one significant milestone in the development of a Canadian identity. The CBC provided news, entertainment and education services to tell Canadians about local and international events from a Canadian point of view.

The Canadian government established the National Research Council (NRC) in 1917 to "create, acquire and promote the application of scientific and engineering knowledge to meet Canadian needs for economic, regional and social development." The NRC's national laboratory in Ottawa was

As British traditions faded through the 1900s, American influences on Canadian life became stronger. It was important that the people of Canada have a sense of their own country.

not founded until the late 1920s, but it would play a crucial role in war research. Among the many fields of research conducted by NRC scientists were weapons development, fuels, packaging, aeronautics, mechanical engineering, space, medicine, food, energy and the biological sciences. By 1939, the staff at the Ottawa laboratory totalled 300 men and women.

In 1939, the Mackenzie King government set up the National Film Board (NFB) to make films for Canadians and to make films that would tell the rest of the world what Canada was all about. British documentary filmmaker John Grierson was Canada's first Government Film Commissioner. By 1945, the NFB employed over 700 people and was one of the largest film studios in the world.

*First passengers on Trans Canada Airline flight.*

## Transport by Air

The Trans Canada railways helped open the Canadian west and were important in establishing Canadian unity during the 1800s. In the 1920s and 1930s the airplane opened up Canada's north. World War I aces such as Punch Dickens and Wop May became bush pilots. They flew under incredible conditions into the Northwest and Yukon Territories. The airplane brought food, supplies, mail and medical assistance to Canadians in remote areas of the country. It also brought prospectors looking for gold and silver. Airline companies in the 20s and early 30s were small, often with only one or two single engine planes. Passenger service was just beginning and no single company was able to serve the whole country.

The federal government intervened in 1937 by forming Trans Canada Airlines as a Crown corporation (it later became Air Canada). Within two years, the company had 15 ten-passenger aircraft piloted by former bush pilots. To ensure the safety of passengers in the early days, flight attendants were all required to be registered nurses.

*The Canada Life building, seen here during the final stages of its construction, was the second largest building in the world at that time. What do you think was the largest? What proof is there that working conditions were unsafe?*

## The Government in Business

Canadian governments did not hesitate in intervening in some business aspect of the nation. For a variety of reasons, governments became involved in industries that provided important services to Canadians. The federal government operated a railway, an airline, a radio network, a research facility and even a film studio. Provincial governmentsran hydroelectric and telephone companies. Private companies handled these businesses in the United States. Why was Canada different?

Investors were not eager to invest in Canadian service industries. The distances were too vast. Sometimes the costs were too high and the risks too great. Canadians needed to communicate, and they needed transportation. Canadians needed to know about themselves and about each other. If private industry could not provide the proper support, then the government had to step in.

# Canadian Vision

The Canadian Author's Association established the Governor General's Literary Awards in 1937 for three categories—fiction, nonfiction and drama or poetry. Stephen Leacock, regarded by many as the funniest writer in the English language, won the 1937 nonfiction award for his book *My Discovery of the West*. Now run by the Canada Council, the Governor General's Awards are selected by two nine-member juries—one French speaking and one English—which are made up of experienced writers, academics and literary critics. As one of Canada's most prestigious awards, the GG's have attracted some of Canada's most pre-eminent authors. Margaret Atwood, Margaret Laurence and Al Purdy are three notable winners.

## Achievements

Canada was no longer a colony. It was an independent nation, proud of its citizens and their achievements. Canadian researchers contributed much in the field of medicine. Diabetics all over the world were given a new lease on life with the discovery of insulin by Doctors Frederick Banting and Charles Best. Although not a cure for diabetes, insulin stabilizes the blood sugar level for patients who suffer from the disease. In 1934, the Quebec government, in conjunction with the Rockefeller Institute, established the Montreal Neurological Hospital under the direction of Canadian surgeon Wilder Penfield. It would become world famous as an institution devoted to the teaching, research and treatment of nervous system diseases like epilepsy. Medical missionary Wilfred Grenfell opened his modern hospital at St. Anthony, Newfoundland in 1928, capping his years of work with the deep-sea fishermen, permanent settlers and Inuit of Newfoundland and Labrador.

Literary and visual arts in Canada flourished in the period between the wars. The Group of Seven, painters of Canada's rugged north, were active from 1920 – 1933, as Franklin Carmichael, A.Y. Jackson, Franz Johnston, Lawren Harris, Arthur Lismer, J.E.H. MacDonald, and F.H. Varley portrayed Canada as a land of "wilderness and stark beauty." Emily Carr's striking paintings of west coast scenery and Aboriginal life added a new dimension to the Canadian character.

---

**FOCUS**

1. How did the Statute of Westminster of 1931 describe Canada's position within the Commonwealth?
2. Name 3 organizations in Canada established by government.
3. List major Canadian achievements in art, medicine and literature.

# Canadian Vision

Tom Thomson, though never an official member of the Group of Seven, inspired the Group's break with traditional landscape painting.

## The Group of Seven

Perhaps best known of all Canada's artists, the Group of Seven came together in 1920 as an organization of "modern" painters. The original members included Frank Carmichael, Lawren Harris, A.Y. Jackson, Franz Johnston, Arthur Lismer, J.E.H. Macdonald and F.H. Varley. Although influenced greatly by Tom Thompson, whose love of the outdoors and daring portraits of the land in and around Georgian Bay inspired the Group of Seven to break with the traditional ways of landscape painting, Thompson never became an official member of the group because he died in 1917.

Above anything else, the Group of Seven were landscape painters. Unlike traditional landscape painters of the time, who painted a realistic likeness of their environment, the Group of Seven's art was an expression of their feelings about nature. Rather than depict what a particular scene looked like, they wanted to show how it made them feel. Thus, they used bold, striking colours and brush strokes to capture the magnificance and beauty of Ontario geography, particularly in the north.

Although people were critical of their style and paintings at first, the Group of Seven eventually became extremely popular. Franz Johnston retired from the Group in 1926 to pursue other interests, and A.J. Casson took his place. The Group disbanded in 1933 but, by then, they had experienced massive success both abroad in Europe and the United States, and at home. Most members became art teachers, influencing the next generation of Canadian artists.

BORN: 1891, Alliston, Ontario

DIED: 1941, in a plane crash

SIGNIFICANCE: Discovered insulin.

BRIEF BIOGRAPHY: Banting graduated from medical school in 1916 and joined the army in France as a doctor. In 1921, he began research on diabetes with Charles Best at the University of Toronto. Banting and Best knew that diabetes was a result of pancreatic malfunction. While experimenting with diabetic dogs, they found that an extract of the pancreas (later called insulin) controlled sugar buildup in the blood. The only known treatment for diabetes at the time was starvation as a means of slowing blood sugar buildup. In 1922, Banting tested insulin on Leonard Thompson, a 14-year-old diabetic who had lost so much weight he was close to death.

Within a few weeks, the boy had regained normal health. Banting sold the insulin patent to the University of Toronto for one dollar, as long as any profits went to medical research. In 1923, Banting was awarded the Nobel Prize for Medicine. Upset because fellow researcher, Best, was not similarly honoured, Banting shared the prize money with his colleague. From 1923 until 1929, Banting served as Director of the Banting and Best Department of Medical Research at the University of Toronto, where he supervised work on cancer, lead poisoning and silicosis, among other things. A good amateur painter, Banting befriended A. Y. Jackson from the Group of Seven. In 1939, he investigated the effects of high altitudes on pilots for the Royal Canadian Air Force. He died in 1941 in a plane crash on route to England while on a "mission of high importance" for the government.

## Fredrick Banting

# Questions and Activities

## Match the items in column A with the description in column B.

| A | B |
|---|---|
| **1.** One Big Union (OBU) | **a)** states the original program of the CCF. |
| **2.** Social Credit Party | **b)** granted Canada full independence within the Commonwealth. |
| **3.** Regina Manifesto | **c)** fought for the right of women to be made Senators. |
| **4.** Alberta Five | **d)** wanted to give each citizen $25 a month. |
| **5.** Statute of Westminster | **e)** sought bargaining power by uniting all workers. |

## Ideas for Discussion

**1.** If a general strike like the one in Winnipeg was organized in your community, what industries and services would be closed down? How would you personally be affected? Do you think workers should have the right to organize general strikes? Why or why not?

**2.** Summarize some of the main advances in rights and freedoms made by women between 1919 and 1930. Compare these to advances made since 1960.

**3.** Discuss the impact of the automobile on:
   **a)** shopping patterns
   **b)** city and community planning
   **c)** convenience and leisure
   **d)** travel and vacations
   **e)** jobs and industry
   **f)** social life

**4.** During the 1930s, the government set up work camps for unemployed young men. Some people suggest that a similar system, but with more freedom, should be established for the unemployed today. There would be a choice of:
   **a)** Working in local parks, public building, etc.
   **b)** Helping the aged or handicapped
   **c)** Replanting forest land
   **d)** Joining the armed forces
   What do you think?

**5.** How involved should the government be in running industries and providing services? Here is a list of organizations started by the federal government. What does each one do? Why did the government become involved in these areas? Which are no longer run by the government?
   **a)** CNR
   **b)** CBC
   **c)** NFB
   **d)** TCA (Trans Canada Airline)
   **e)** Petro Canada
   List other industries and services run by the federal and provincial government. Do you think the government should continue to be involved in these areas? Are there other industries or services that you think the government should run? Why or why not?

## Do Some Research

**1.** Do any members of your family belong to a trade union? Compile a list of unions that people in your community belong to. Name other unions in Canada today. What are their objectives? How have union aims changed since the Winnipeg General Strike? How have they remained the same?

**2.** Find out more about one of the following:
   **a)** J.S. Woodsworth
   **b)** Agnes Macphail
   **c)** Lionel Conacher
   **d)** Banting and Best
   **e)** The Alberta Five
   **f)** The Group of Seven
   **g)** The Saskatoon Lily
   **h)** Bobbie Rosenfeld

**3.** Write a report about an outstanding woman in Canada today in one of the following areas:
   **a)** industry and commerce
   **b)** politics and law
   **c)** science and technology
   **d)** sports
   **e)** entertainment

**4.** Do some research on automobiles of the 1920s. Describe the basic features and options that were available. How have automobiles changed since the 1920s? What features have disappeared? What new features have been introduced? What "options" of the 1920s are now standard features?

**5.** Find out more about one of the following:
   **a)** movies of the 1920s   **c)** the early days of radio
   **b)** movies of the 1930s   **d)** records and record players
   Write a paragraph describing their main features and importance.

**6.** Find out more about the success of Canadians during the 1928 Olympics. Compare their record to that of Canadian athletes in more recent Olympics. Can you draw any conclusions from this comparison?

**7.** The Edmonton Grads were one of the most successful sports teams ever. Do further research on the Grads or another Canadian sports team of the 1920s and 1930s. Your report should have some information under the following headings:
   **a)** Beginnings        **c)** Star Players
   **b)** Coaches          **d)** Win-and-loss records

## Creative

**1.** Write a letter from a soldier who has just returned home at the end of the war. Your opening might be: "I'm so pleased to see my family and friends again, but the town sure has changed."

**2.** With a group of other students, prepare a folder on the role of women from 1914 to 1930. Your folder should include:
   **a)** a poster advertising a women's rights rally
   **b)** a speech by a supporter of women's rights

   **c)** a picture of women's fashions and hairstyles during the 1920s with an explanation of how these gave women new freedom
   **d)** an editorial favouring or opposing the right of women to be Senators
   **e)** a letter to the editor disagreeing with the editorial

**3.** Design an advertisement for a product or appliance that became available during the 1920s. Let your ad explain how buying the item will make life easier, more convenient, or more entertaining. Compile a class brochure called Advertisements of the Roaring Twenties.

**4.** Make a mural or picture map of Canada showing industries across the country in the 1920s.

**5.** Write a letter to Prime Minister Bennett asking for help for you and your family. Write Bennett's reply.

**6.** Prepare an edition of a newspaper in your community for a specific date in the 1920s or 30s. Your newspaper should include:
   **a)** reports on local, provincial, national and international events
   **b)** entertainment and sports news
   **c)** information on new inventions and scientific discoveries
   **d)** human interest stories
   **e)** editorials
   **f)** letters to the editor
   **g)** political cartoons
   **h)** business news on local industries and job opportunities
   **i)** advertisements for new products
   **j)** fashion news
   **k)** want ads
   For some items you will need to do additional research.

Starting a company—a store, a factory, an industry, a mine—takes a lot of money. Most companies get this money by asking people to invest in the business by buying shares or portions of the company's stock. If the company does well and makes a profit, the shares will pay the investors dividends. More importantly, the value of the shares themselves will go up. If the company does not make a profit, there will be no dividends and the value of the shares will go down. Shares are bought and sold on the stock market.

## You're are a big investor.

Your Uncle Fred has died and left you with $10,000 on condition that you invest it in the stock market.

1. Start by consulting the business section of the daily paper or use the Internet over several days in order to establish the trends in the value of stock shares.
   Identify:
   a) a stock that has gone up in value
   b) a stock that has gone down

2. Invest Uncle Fred's $10,000 in stocks of your choice.

3. Record the value of your stocks each day. Remember that if you think your stock has "peaked," or if you don't like its performance, you can sell it at the going price and re-invest in another stock.

4. At the end of a month, calculate the current value of your shares. Did you make a profit? Compare results with other members of the class.

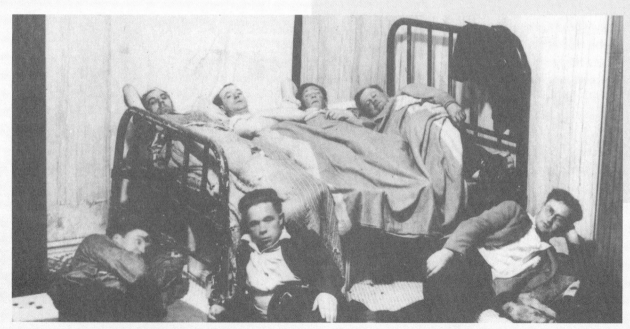

*Flophouses, where men could sleep for the night, were a temporary answer to homelessness. Are there any modern "flophouses" in your community today?*

# Point
## Counterpoint

With which of the following statements do you most agree? Why?

With which of the following statements do you least agree? Why?

"A wise man once said that the best way to survive a Depression is to become a politician. He was wrong. The best way to survive was to become a successful politician. Few did."

Barry Broadfoot, author

"The Dirty Thirties! Just put in your book that you met Harry Jacobson and he's seventy-eight years old. Might I say I never took a backward step in my life until the Depression whipped me, took my wife, my home, a section of good land back in Saskatchewan. Left me with nothing."

Barry Broadfoot, author

"One of the greatest assets any man can have on entering life's struggle is poverty."

Prime Minister Bennett

"What is needed more than a change of economic structure is a change of heart."

Mackenzie King

"Its wealth is endless, its possibilities boundless, opportunities are here for the taking. Any man who is not afraid of hard work can succeed in Canada."

Governor-General Lord Willingdon

# Introduction
## The World on Trial

IN 1939, CANADIANS ONCE AGAIN WENT OFF TO FIGHT ON FOREIGN SOIL. This time, the slaughter would go on for six long years and span the globe. Those who thought they had reached the depths of human tragedy in the First World War were to be proved wrong. During the Second World War, terrible weapons and brutal strategies resulted in the deaths of tens of millions of people.

Canada provided vital support to an isolated Britain in the dark, early years of the war. An energetic government and a willing population harnessed Canada's full military potential. Canadians tasted bitter defeats at Hong Kong and Dieppe. They gained costly victories at Ortona and Normandy. Canadians earned the endearing respect and affection of people enslaved by Hitler's armies. Our soldiers helped liberate the infamous death camps and revealed the full horrors of the Holocaust to the world. By the end of the war, Canada's armed forces were among the largest and most accomplished in the world.

At home, Canadians provided much-needed weapons and supplies. The United States became a close ally and economic partner. Thousands of Allied aircrews received their training in Canada. Canadians also faced serious divisions. Once again, conscription threatened to tear the country apart when unity was required for victory. Canadians turned on their fellow citizens, Japanese Canadians, and forced them from their homes, stripped them of their property and denied them the basic rights enjoyed by others.

## METHODS OF HISTORICAL INQUIRY
### The Inquiry Process and the Research Essay

Historians communicate their findings in **argumentative** essays. Unlike **expository** essays, which describe a topic, argumentative essays prove a point. After gathering information from primary and secondary sources, historians must analyze trends and patterns in their research. They often speculate or hypothesize about these findings, using their research to support these claims. Once they have established an hypothesis, historians must compose a **thesis statement,** a sentence that tells the reader what will be proven in the essay. Writing a research essay is like being a lawyer arguing in a courtroom. You must prove your point with solid evidence.

# Chapter Four:
## The World on Trial

## Expectations

### Overall Expectations:

**By the end of this chapter, you will be able to:**

- understand how outside forces and events shaped Canada's involvement in the Second World War

- assess Canada's role during the Second World War

- explain the changes in Canada's international policy because of the war

### Specific Expectations:

**By the end of this chapter, you will be able to:**

- understand the causes of the Second World War and why Canada became involved

- describe Canada's role at the home front and at the battle front

- identify the massive role played by the Canadian government during the war

- describe the impact of the war on Japanese Canadians

- compare conscription during the First and the Second World Wars

- describe the tragedy of the Holocaust and its impact on Canada

- trace Canada's changing relationship with the United States through the Second World War

## WORD LIST

| | | | |
|---|---|---|---|
| Anti-Semitism | Death Camps | Gestapo | Kristallnacht |
| Black-market | Dictator | Ghetto | Nazi |
| Blitzkrieg | Fascism | Glulag | Pogrom |
| | | | Ratio |

# *Advance* **Organizer**

## 1

**After the First World War, life was not easy in Europe. The war had destroyed economies and left many countries heavily in debt. Some people resented the new borders that had been drawn at the end of the war, and distrusted the new democratic forms of government that had been set up. The Depression intensified these problems. In all this uncertainty, dictators easily gained control. They offered simple solutions and promised glory for their country. They silenced all who spoke against them. In Italy and Spain, Mussolini and Franco came to power. In the Soviet Union, Stalin ruled.**

## 2

Most dangerous of all was Adolf Hitler, who gained power in Germany in 1933. He told Germans they were the "master race." He blamed all Germany's problems on scapegoats, "non-German traitors" within the country, and the unfair terms of the treaty that ended World War I. Hitler's sweeping racism became government policy. Fear of his secret police gripped the country while Hitler urged Germans to dream of ruling the world.

## 3

Other nations knew Germany had real causes for complaint. They hoped that if they let Hitler take a little, Germany would be satisfied.

In 1938, Hitler's armies swept into Austria and Czechoslovakia. When Poland fell to German tanks and dive-bombers in 1939, world leaders knew they had to fight back. Their resistance came too late: soon most of Europe was under Nazi rule.

**4**

Canadians figured prominently in World War II. The Royal Canadian Navy organized huge supply convoys to Britain. Canadian pilots helped stop Hitler in the Battle of Britain and other air battles. Canadian soldiers fought bravely on the battlefields of Europe and Asia. They suffered a tragic defeat at Dieppe, France. They played a valiant part in the slow advance through Italy and the final invasion of Western Europe after D-Day.

**5**

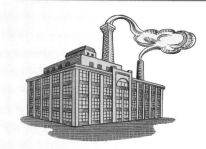

During the war, Canadians at home produced airplanes, ships, and armaments. They bought Victory bonds to help pay for the war. Food and gasoline were rationed so more supplies could go to Europe. Women entered the factories and joined the armed forces. Young people ploughed up their schoolyards to plant "victory gardens."

**6**

Japanese army leaders also dreamed of a vast empire. They attacked China, American colonies in the Pacific, and British and French colonies in Asia. Many Canadians feared and hated the Japanese who had moved to Canada. Japanese Canadians were taken from their homes on the Pacific coast and held in camps until the end of the war.

**7**

The war ended with the dropping of atomic bombs on two Japanese cities, Hiroshima and Nagaski. This was the final horror in a war marked by crimes against humanity. Millions of Jews and other minorities had been murdered under Hitler's rule. Too many powers had been willing to prove their might through warfare. The United Nations was founded in the hope of maintaining peace for all in the future.

# Dictators in a Changing World

Change, insecurity and frustration defined the 1920s for most people in Europe. They had expected the Treaty of Versailles to straighten out the chaos caused by the First World War. Instead, it created as many problems as it solved. The losers of the war felt unfairly treated; the winners felt they had gained nothing. Both felt cheated.

## A New Map of Europe

Some diplomats at the conference in Versailles believed every national group should have its own country. As a result, they gave lands that had been part of Germany back to Poland and France. (Alsace and Lorraine had been French territory before 1870.) They divided the Turkish and Austrian Empires into a number of independent countries. It was impossible, however, to draw a neat line and put all Germans or Slavs on one side, all Poles or Italians on the other. Many minority groups remained within the new borders. They resented being part of these countries. Majority groups feared the smaller nationalities might cause trouble.

## Rise of Fascist Dictators

Most countries in Europe had elected assemblies before the First World War, but these assemblies rarely had much power. Princes, kings, emperors and their advisors made most of the important decisions. After the war, Europeans lost faith in their old leaders, since it was this system that had led to the useless war. Under the leadership of U.S. President Woodrow Wilson, diplomats at Versailles attempted to set up democratic governments for the "new" countries. Since few people knew how to run a country in a democratic way, voters had difficulty judging the new politicians.

Then came the Depression during the 1930s, which caused huge social, economic and political problems in stable democracies like Canada, the United States and Britain. In unsettled Europe, the effects were disastrous.

Legend:
- Borders 1914
- Borders after the 1919 peace treaties
- Territory lost by Germany
- Territory lost by Austro-Hungary
- Territory lost by Bulgaria
- Territory lost by USSR
- Demilitarized zones

Fascism blossomed in these kinds of conditions. Benito Mussolini, Adolf Hitler and Francisco Franco rose to power on the backs of hopelessness, fear, poverty and hatred.

People wanted a way out of the hopelessness, the frustration and the insecurity that surrounded their lives.

They were ready to follow any leader who promised better things. They wanted to be told their country was great. They were prepared to believe their problems were somebody else's fault—foreigners, communists, democrats, Jews. **Fascism** blossomed in these kinds of conditions. Benito Mussolini, Adolf Hitler and Francisco Franco rose to power on the backs of hopelessness, fear, poverty and hatred.

High-ranking officials of the Nazi and Fascist Parties, 1936, including Benito Mussolini and Adolf Hitler (centre).

## Fascism in Italy

Benito Mussolini formed the Fascist Party to fight communism and democratic socialism in Italy. Fascists in black shirts gathered to listen to their leader. These "Blackshirts" broke up trade union meetings and communist rallies with clubs and fists. They conducted a campaign of terror against their opponents.

Italian Fascist symbol

There was widespread poverty and unemployment in Italy after the First World War. Workers formed unions and called for a general strike in 1922. Mussolini said that if the government didn't stop the strike, the Fascists would. Fascists from all over Italy marched on Rome. In a panic, the King asked Mussolini to form a new government. Soon, Mussolini was the **dictator** of Italy. No opposition was allowed, and only Fascists could run for office.

## Lenin's and Stalin's Russia

In 1917, after more than a decade of civil

unrest throughout Russia, a radical party led by Vladimir Lenin—the Bolsheviks—staged a revolution to overthrow the Russian Emperor (Tsar) Nicholas II. Lenin's new communist government launched a series of reforms aimed at turning the newly created Soviet Union into a classless society. Lenin died in 1924, however, before achieving many of his goals.

Joseph Stalin, Lenin's successor, was far more brutal in his methods. He was an able, yet ruthless, dictator. Under a series of "five year plans," Stalin dramatically transformed Soviet society. Using the army, terror, labour camps called **"Gulags"** and his secret police, Stalin created an industrial giant. Millions of Soviet citizens died as he drove the Soviet Union toward greater power.

*Soviet Communist symbol*

## The Army in Japan

Meanwhile, on the other side of the world, army officers prepared Japan for conquest and empire. Japan had begun to modernize in the late 1800s, had made gains as a result of the First World War, and had developed a strong relationship with both the United States and China. In the late 1920s, a group of young army officers—dreaming of a vast empire—took control of the armed forces. Businessmen who wanted raw materials and guaranteed markets for Japanese industry supported them. The civilian government was weak and divided. Those who opposed the army were often assassinated. By the 1930s, the Japanese military forces had gained control over the government and dictated Japanese policies.

## The Spanish Civil War

In 1936, General Francisco Franco led a military revolt against the elected government of Spain. The Spanish government was made up of many political groups, including the Communist Party, and Franco wanted to stamp out communism. The army, rich landowners, the Roman Catholic Church and the Falange (the Spanish Fascist Party) all supported Franco. Hitler and Mussolini sent military and financial aid. Stalin, on the other hand, sided with the government. The world looked the other way as Franco brutally destroyed Spain's democratic government. The Spanish civil war lasted three years, leaving a million dead. By 1939, yet another Fascist was in power in Europe. Franco ruled until his death in 1975, when Spain became a democratic constitutional monarchy.

*Spanish Fascist symbol*

## Fascism in Canada

Canada was not immune to the virus of fascism. Several small parties copied the racism and brutality of Mussolini's and Hitler's regimes. The most successful of the Canadian Fascists was Adrien Arcand, a Quebec racist who hated Jews and anyone who was not English or French. Arcand organized a private army dressed in navy blue uniforms, and freely employed the Nazi swastika alongside the maple leaf. He published numerous papers and brochures.

Arcand claimed a huge membership of 80,000, but most observers believe his following numbered only a few thousand. As Hitler and Mussolini became more aggressive and the world drifted toward yet another global conflict, Arcand lost support. Canadian authorities became more active in restraining him. When the Second World War broke out, the RCMP arrested Arcand and other Fascists, and kept them interned until 1944.

Arcand never recaptured his following after the war. He remained, however, an unrepentant racist and anti-Semite until his death in 1967. Unfortunately, people like Arcand still preach their hate in Canada today. It seems that each new generation of Canadians has to be prepared to fight racist views.

*Adrien Arcand, the one in the middle row with a beret, interned during WWII.*

## The Mac-Paps in Spain

Not all Canadians were willing to stand idly while Fascist dictators took control of the world. When the Spanish civil war exploded in 1936, people from all over the world volunteered to fight the Fascists. These "International Brigades" numbered 40,000. About 1,500 Canadians went to Spain to fight for the Republic. They formed the Mackenzie-Papineau Battalion (named after the leaders of the 1837 Rebellions), the Mac-Paps, as they were called. Half never returned. They were outgunned and outnumbered. The Canadian government disowned them, partly because some had been active in the "On-to-Ottawa" Trek of 1935, and partly because Canada wanted to avoid another terrible world war. However, thousands of Canadians lined up to see them return, even in defeat. In hindsight, these civilian soldiers were right about the eventual outcome of Fascist victories in Europe. Soon, regular soldiers would head to Europe once again to fight in a long, bloody war.

> ## FOCUS
> 1. Why did many people not accept the new national boundaries of Europe?
> 2. Why were so many people attracted to dictators?
> 3. Who took power in Russia, Italy, Japan and Spain?
> 4. How did Canadians respond to the rise of European fascism?

# 2 Adolf Hitler

In Germany, the leader of the **National Socialist German Workers' Party** (**Nazi** for short) watched Mussolini's rise to power with admiration. Adolf Hitler was born in Austria in 1889. After an unhappy childhood, he became a homeless drifter. At the outbreak of the First World War, Hitler eagerly joined the German army. He proved an able and courageous soldier, even though he never rose above the rank of corporal.

When Germany surrendered in 1918, soldiers everywhere cheered because the war was over. Hitler, on the other hand, cried because Germany had been beaten. He swore revenge on the "socialists and Jewish traitors who," he later claimed, "had stabbed Germany in the back." He joined the **Nazi** Party in its infancy. Its aim was to rebuild Ger-

*Before WWII erupted, Hitler was very popular among Germans and world leaders, such as Canada's Prime Minister Mackenzie King, who paid a state visit to the "new Germany."*

Hitler made being a Nazi exciting. He organized the party along military lines.

**TIMELINE**

1900    1910    1920    1930    1940    1950    1960    1970    1980

many and defeat its enemies. Hitler's passionate speeches and organizational skills soon made him the party leader.

Hitler made being a Nazi exciting. He organized the party along military lines. It had its own salute, its own uniform, its own songs, and its own symbol—the swastika. The Nazis listened to stirring speeches from their leader. They marched through the streets of German towns. The brown-shirted "storm troopers" broke up Communist Party meetings, attacked the homes and businesses of Jews, and struck terror into the hearts of other "traitors," people who did not view the world as they did.

By 1933, the Nazis were the largest party in the German parliament, but they had never won a majority in a free election. As leader, Hitler was asked to be chancellor of Germany. He accepted on condition that he be given dictatorial powers. That evening, the Nazis held torchlight parades. Swept along by excitement, the crowds roared "Sieg Heil! SIEG HEIL!" (Hail victory).

*All Germans soldiers swore an oath of personal loyalty to Hitler. Under Hitler, the army was expanded rapidly.*

## Why Germans Supported Hitler

Even people who had not voted for Hitler were glad to see a strong man in charge. They thought he would solve the country's problems. Few realized his real intentions, even though he had written of them in his book, *Mein Kampf (My Struggle)*.

Many saw Hitler as an inspiring leader. He was certainly a brilliant and hypnotizing speaker. Nazi rallies were full of colourful

**Percent of Unemployment**
- 0–15%
- 15–25%
- 25–35%
- Not known

*Unemployment rates were high in Europe during the 1930s. This map shows unemployment conditions across Europe shortly before the outbreak of the Second World War.*

parades and rousing marching songs. People who attended felt they were part of a great movement. Paul Joseph Goebbels, Hitler's propaganda minister, used these rallies to preach and spread hatred, especially against Jews.

The Depression hit Germany hard with widespread unemployment, and many Germans blamed the new democratic government for the economic hardships. It had never really worked. Perhaps the Nazis could put Germans back to work. Hitler promised a return to strong government. His private army of storm troopers paraded through the streets. They broke up the meetings of other political parties. Many people supported the Nazis out of fear.

Hitler gave the Germans targets to blame for all their problems. His favourite scapegoats were communists and Jews. The Nazis preached "racial purity." They claimed Germans were the "master race." Jews, Slavs and other minorities were to be regarded as "impure aliens."

Hitler blamed Germany's troubles on the Treaty of Versailles. The treaty demanded that Germany pay for the First World War with money and goods, which made life difficult for Germans during the 1920s. With the treaty's infamous "war guilt" clause, they were forced to accept full responsibility for causing World War I. Hitler, his face red with rage, tore the treaty to shreds before cheering crowds.

Once in power, Hitler delivered on his promises as Germans were put back to work. New roads and bridges were built all over the country. Guns, tanks, warships and planes—all forbidden by the Treaty of Versailles—started to pour from German factories. Young men flocked into the army and, in 1936, rode the new tanks down the new highways, across the bridges and into the Rhineland. The Versailles Treaty had declared this part of Germany to be demilitarized forever, but Germany was on the way back to glory as Hitler was prepared to challenge the terms of this despised treaty. The Allies protested mildly, but essentially did nothing to stop Hitler.

Meanwhile, all traces of democracy in Germany were destroyed. Socialists, democrats, communists, religious leaders, teachers and scientists—anyone who spoke out against the Nazis—found themselves in concentration camps. Jews lost their jobs and were persecuted in many ways. Newspapers printed Nazi propaganda; radios blared it forth. Unions, schools, churches and the army were under Nazi control. The **Gestapo**, Hitler's secret police, was everywhere.

---

**FOCUS**

1. List 5 reasons why many Germans were willing to support Hitler.
2. What actions did Hitler take once in power?
3. Why might young people have been attracted to Hitler?

# The Gathering Storm

**3**

Many countries of the world came together to form the League of Nations shortly after World War I, with a plan to prevent any future wars. The League was to settle international arguments through diplomacy. The United States, as a result of a dispute

*Lorne Green, the Voice of Doom, was a radio announcer for the CBC during the War.*

between President Wilson and the Senate, never did join, which created a serious weakness in the League. During the 1920s, the League managed to settle a number of disputes between nations, but by the 1930s things were not working as well. Some countries had learned they could defy the League and get away with it.

## Manchuria

In 1931, the Japanese army invaded the Chinese province of Manchuria. Within weeks, Manchuria was torn from China. The League of Nations was not prepared to act. Asia seemed so far away. All the League did to support China was to refuse to recognize the new government of the province. In defiance, Japan simply withdrew from the League.

Japan set out to conquer the rest of China and to build its empire in the Pacific. In a sense, by 1937, World War II had already begun in Asia.

## Ethiopia and the Rhineland

Mussolini's economic program was not working in Italy. To take people's minds off the problems of the Depression, Mussolini decided to go to war. He wanted to rebuild the Roman Empire. He saw himself as Italy's "Duce," a leader greater than Julius Caesar.

All through the summer of 1935, Italian troops gathered in Italy's colonies on the borders of the ancient African kingdom of Ethiopia. In October, they attacked. The Ethiopians fought bravely, but spears and old guns were no match for modern machine guns, planes, tanks and poison gas.

Haile Selassie, the emperor of Ethiopia, appealed to the League of Nations. The League members agreed that Italy was wrong. They said they would cut off Italy's oil supplies. "Oil means war!" replied Mussolini. The League backed down. In any case, it was

With the failure of the League to stop them, Hitler and Mussolini soon realized they served each other well.

more worried about the consequences of Hitler's march into the Rhineland. Would France declare war? France, at the urging of Britain, decided not to press the issue.

With the failure of the League to stop them, Hitler and Mussolini soon realized they served each other well. They had kept the League from acting against either of them. With the military rulers in Japan, they formed the Rome-Tokyo-Berlin Axis. This was an agreement to support each other against communist Russia. Now Hitler had allies. He was ready to gamble that the leaders of Europe would agree to anything to avoid war.

Germany's domain in 1938.

## The Appeasement of Germany

Hitler's vision of the "master race" required that Germans everywhere belong to one united Germany. In 1938, he announced that Austria, which had a mainly German-speaking population, was to be part of Germany. The German army marched in. The Austrians had no way of defending themselves. France and Britain did nothing. Seven million Austrians were now Germans. Hitler had his next target almost surrounded.

The rich industrialized Sudetenland area of Czechoslovakia was home to 3 million German-speaking Czechs. Hitler claimed they were oppressed and he threatened to occupy the area. France, Britain and Russia promised to stand by the Czechs. The leaders of Britain, France, Italy and Germany met at Munich. They gave in to Hitler's demands, however, because they wanted to avoid another war. British Prime Minister Neville Chamberlain went home to cheering crowds claiming he had achieved "peace with honour, peace in our time." Many people in Canada and elsewhere heaved a sigh of relief. Others, such as Britain's future prime minister, Winston Churchill, warned of greater threats to come.

Within months, the German army swallowed up the rest of Czechoslovakia.

BORN: 1890, Gravenhurst, Ontario

DIED: 1939, China

SIGNIFICANCE: Established the world's first mobile blood transfusion unit to aid injured soldiers.

BRIEF BIOGRAPHY: Bethune entered the University of Toronto in 1909, but interrupted his studies to take a teaching position with Frontier College. He returned to university in 1911, where he enrolled in medical school. His education was once again interrupted in 1914, when Bethune joined the Royal Canadian Army Corps and served as a stretcher bearer during the First World War. After returning to Canada in 1915, he finally completed his medical degree. Bethune contacted tuberculosis (TB) in 1926. While ill, he forced his doctor to perform a radical and dangerous surgery to help cure the disease. Between 1929 and 1936, Bethune devoted himself to other TB victims and to thoracic (lung) surgery.

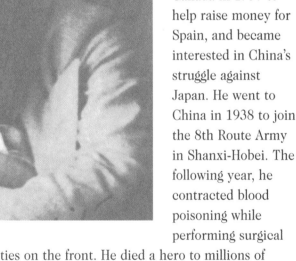

During this time, he invented 12 medical/surgical instruments. After becoming increasingly disillusioned with the medical establishment and with the social and economic aspects of the disease, Bethune joined the Communist Party. In 1936, he went to Spain with the Mac-Paps to fight in the Spanish civil war. While there, he organized the world's first mobile blood-transfusion service on the front lines. Bethune returned to Canada in 1937 to help raise money for Spain, and became interested in China's struggle against Japan. He went to China in 1938 to join the 8th Route Army in Shanxi-Hobei. The following year, he contracted blood poisoning while performing surgical duties on the front. He died a hero to millions of Chinese. Canadian authorities declared him a national hero in 1971.

*In your opinion, does Bethune deserve "hero" status? Explain.*

## Doctor Norman Bethune

Hitler now demanded the German-speaking areas of Poland. Finally, the leaders of France and Britain realized they had to take a stand. They declared that they would guarantee Poland's borders.

The Soviet Union decided it could not rely on the Western democracies for help against Hitler. Look at what had happened to Austria and Czechoslovakia. So, the Soviet Union and Germany signed a non-aggression pact in August, 1939, agreeing not to fight each other. A secret agreement was also made to divide Poland between them. With the Soviet Union out of his way, Hitler was now ready.

## Canada and Aggression

Most Canadians were not interested in forcing another war by standing up to Hitler and Mussolini. When the Canadian ambassador to the League of Nations spoke out against Mussolini's invasion of Ethiopia, his government said he did not speak for Canada. Canada's prime minister, Mackenzie King, had met Hitler and felt he was not a threat to world peace. He even had an autographed photo of the dictator. Canada and Canadians were still clawing their way out of the Depression and had sad memories of the last war—the "war to end all wars."

On September 1, 1939, German tanks thundered across the Polish border and bombers flattened the great city of Warsaw. On September 3, France and Britain declared

*One last good-bye before Canadian soldiers left for war.*

war against Germany. One week later, a hastily assembled Canadian Parliament voted to declare war on Germany. Tragically, the first Canadian victim of the Second World War was a ten-year-old girl, Margaret Hayworth of Hamilton, Ontario. She perished when a German submarine torpedoed the *Athenia,* an unarmed passenger ship, on the first day of war. Hayworth's state funeral encouraged Canadians to fight.

**FOCUS**
1. Why did the League of Nations fail to act against Japan, Italy and Germany?
2. Why were nations eager to appease Germany?
3. What was Canada's reaction to German aggression?

# 4 Blitzkrieg

Nazi armies crushed Poland in less than a month. By October 19, the Polish armed forces collapsed under the relentless attack by German tanks and Stuka dive-bombers. Hitler taught the world a new word—**blitzkrieg** (lightning war). After the defeat

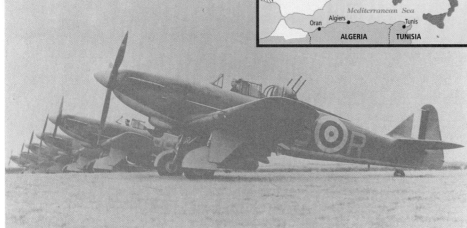

*Fighter pilots ready to take off on a night-flying mission.*

of Poland came a lull in the fighting. Some people called this the "phony war" or "sitzkrieg," but most knew it was a time of careful preparation before the bloody struggles to come. While the Allies scrambled to mobilize their armed forces, Germany used this time to move its forces from defeated Poland to staging areas for its next invasion.

Germany struck again during the spring of 1940. Denmark fell in one day; Norway in two. The Netherlands was smashed in five days. Belgium took eighteen. Even mighty France was shattered in six weeks. Hitler was master of Europe.

## The Miracle at Dunkirk

As the advancing German army swung south into France from the Netherlands, British and French troops were pinned against the English Channel near the tiny French port of Dunkirk. If British ships could reach Dunkirk

The Battle of Britain was won by a few hundred pilots. They included 80 Canadians, as well as Britons, Poles, Australians, New Zealanders and South Africans.

in time, the soldiers could be rescued. But the navy had few ships to spare. Instead, English fishermen, weekend-pleasure sailors and ferry captains all took their boats across the channel. Canal boats and river tugs towed rowboats and empty coal barges out to sea to rescue Allied soldiers. The volunteer fleet brought back 350,000 men—ten times what the government had hoped to save. The Germans had been unable to get to Dunkirk in time to prevent this heroic rescue.

Britain stood alone in Europe. The new prime minister, Winston Churchill, promised nothing but "blood, toil, tears, and sweat." It seemed that the war would soon be over. German forces began preparing for the invasion of Britain.

In the distant port of Halifax, Nova Scotia, ships were assembling to steam in convoy across the Atlantic. They carried the food and weapons, as well as soldiers, needed for one of the most important battles in the war—the Battle of Britain.

### The Battle of Britain

The British navy and air force controlled the 50 kilometres of water, the English Channel, separating Britain from Europe. Germany

*Ships waiting for a convoy in Bedford Basin, Nova Scotia.*

BORN: 1879, Maple Ontario

DIED: 1964, United Kingdom

SIGNIFICANCE: Canadian Max Aitken had a varied career as a millionaire businessman, British politician and successful author. As a member of the House of Lords, Lord Beaverbrook was a key figure in the Allied successes in two world wars.

BRIEF BIOGRAPHY: Although born to poor parents, and an early school leaver, this energetic and clever Canadian found fabulous success in business, and was a millionaire before he was thirty. He was behind the creation of enterprises such as Stelco and Canada Cement. While on his honeymoon, he even found time to purchase a hydroelectric company and a streetcar company.

Beaverbrook moved to England to pursue business interests, and soon became part of the social and political upper class. He was elected as an MP and later appointed to the British House of Lords. As Minister of Information (wartime propaganda), he kept morale high and worked to get the U.S. into the war on the side of the Allies. He established the Canadian War Memorials Fund, which paid artists to create 800 works of art to preserve memories of the war and inspire others to support the cause.

Between the wars, Beaverbrook returned to business and built a publishing empire. His papers regularly warned readers of the rise of Hitler in Germany. When the Second World War broke out, Prime Minister Churchill called on his friend to oversee the production of aircraft so vital to Britain's survival. He was ruthlessly efficient and boosted production from 183 to 471 aircraft per month. As Minister of Supply, Beaverbrook worked closely with Allies such as Russia and the U.S. to defeat the Nazi war machine. Winston Churchill said of his superb effort: "He did not fail. This was his hour."

After the war, Beaverbrook returned to his business interests and authored several best-selling books. Near the end of his life, he spent more time in his native land, Canada, and gave millions of dollars to establish an art gallery in Fredericton, N.B.

## Max Aitken, Lord Beaverbrook

needed to control the skies over the Channel before its planned invasion fleet could sail.

The German air force, or Luftwaffe, set out to clear the Royal Air Force (RAF) from the skies on July 10, 1940. Wave after wave of German *Messerschmitts* and *Heinkels* streamed across the channel. They spread out over Britain to their bombing targets—radar stations, airfields, ports and factories. Slowly the first RAF planes were wiped out. At one point, every fighter plane Britain owned was in the air. Had the Germans launched another attack, no planes would have been available to respond.

Suddenly, the German tactics changed. In August, the RAF made a surprise bombing raid on Berlin. The commander of the German air force, Herman Goering, was furious because he had promised Germans that no Allied plane would ever bomb a German city. The Germans decided to "blitz" the cities in revenge. They planned to terrorize the civilian population into surrender, but the plan backfired. Bombs rained on London, night and day. Londoners moved into air-raid shelters and subway stations. Each day they set about repairing homes, reopening stores—carrying on. British resistance grew stronger, not weaker.

The German raids on London enabled the few remaining RAF *Spitfires* and *Hurricanes* to regroup. Newly-trained pilots joined those who had been flying almost constantly since the battles began. New planes came off the assembly lines at the rate of almost 500 a month.

On September 15, German planes almost blackened the skies, but the RAF was ready for them. When the day was over, the Luftwaffe was decidedly beaten. Hitler called off the attack two days later. If he could not wipe out Britain, he would turn against the Soviet Union.

The Battle of Britain was won by a few hundred pilots. They included 80 Canadians as well as Britons, Poles, Australians, New Zealanders and South Africans. The *Luftwaffe* lost 1,722 planes, the RAF 915. Canadian pilots accounted for 60 definite and 50 probable "kills."

*After serving in the Second World War, Fred Savard became a renowned Canadian war artist. This is his self-portrait.*

**FOCUS**

1. What is the meaning of the term "blitzkrieg?"
2. Why was Dunkirk so important to Britain?
3. How did Canadians help win the Battle of Britain?
4. What was Lord Beaverbrook's contribution to the British war effort?

# 5 Dieppe

As France fell to Hitler's armies, Mussolini decided Italy was ready to join in. Nearly all of Europe was under German or Italian control by 1941. British and Australian troops were fighting Germans and Italians in North Africa. Germany turned against the Soviet Union by violating the 1939 Non-Aggression

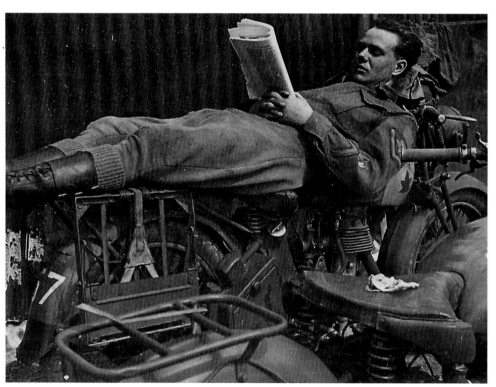

*This soldier patiently waits for the call to go to France.*

Pact. The Japanese attacked American and British positions in the Pacific in December. Hong Kong, a British colony, fell to Japan on Christmas Day.

## Why the Dieppe Raid?

The Soviet Union was bearing almost the full weight of German attack by the fall of 1941. Stalin pressed his Western Allies to open a second front. If they would attack France, the Soviet Union might get a little relief.

The British knew they were not ready to start a second front. But the whole Commonwealth was enraged at the fall of Hong Kong. The Americans, Britain's new allies, wanted to get moving. Canadian soldiers were also restless. They had been waiting in Britain since the start of the war three years ago. A large raid might satisfy the Soviets, the Americans and the Canadians. It might be useful too. It could test German coastal defences. It could help plan a full-scale invasion. It might also deceive Germany as to the location of the ultimate invasion of Europe in 1944.

## The Raid

On the morning of August 19, 1942, 5,000 Canadian soldiers crouched in landing crafts off the heavily fortified French port of

The Americans, Britain's new allies, wanted to get moving. Canadian soldiers were also restless. They had been waiting in Britain since the start of the war three years ago.

Dieppe. They intended to seize the town, destroy the port facilities and airport, take prisoners and return to England. The key to their victory was surprise.

When the first Canadians hit the beach, the Germans were ready and waiting. They had spotted the enemy ships during the night. Some Allied ships had gone off course and arrived late. The raid did not start until broad daylight.

*This painting by Charles Comfort shows the grim slaughter Allied soldiers experienced at Dieppe.*

The Canadians were facing a boulder beach in front of a town fortified with cannon, barbed wire, tanks, traps and mines. Many landing craft were blown right out of the water. In one boat of 80 men, 40 were killed and 20 wounded within minutes of landing. One regiment had 96% casualties. Only a few soldiers ever reached the town.

When the smoke cleared, 900 men lay dead. Nearly 2,000 had been taken prisoner. The men from Winnipeg, Hamilton, Montreal, Calgary, Windsor, Regina and Toronto had been savagely defeated.

A British military committee examined the causes of the failure. They noted the foolishness of attacking a fortified beach in broad daylight and the failure to pulverize defence positions by aerial and naval bombardment before landing.

The report concluded that, although from a purely military point of view the results (of the Dieppe raid) were disappointing, and the heavy casualties regrettable, the operation could be worthwhile if its lessons were carefully applied when the time came to re-enter France on a larger scale.

The principal lessons of the Dieppe tragedy were that much stronger military forces were required to break through the German coastal defences, and that a much higher proportion of military forces should be held in reserve until the progress of the initial assault is known. Unless this was done, there was no guarantee that any of the beaches would be secured. To satisfy these requirements, the invasion date was moved from 1943 to 1944.

The next time the Allied forces landed in Europe, they benefited from these earlier mistakes. D-Day occurred on June 6, 1944, the day Allied forces invaded Europe. Many of the disastrous errors of the Dieppe raid were avoided. The sacrifices made by Canadian soldiers on the beaches of Dieppe in 1942 helped reduce the casualties of Canadian, British and American forces in 1944.

## In Their Own Words

**Those who fought on the Dieppe beaches left a harrowing account of the slaughter.**

*First thing I remember after I left the boat, I got hit in the eye. I got to the wall, and then again I was hit in the leg. And after that—all hell had let loose, of course—I put the bandage on my leg. And my eye, it was gone. And I got hit in the head when I was trying to fix up my eye. Shrapnel in the eye and the head, and a bullet in the leg.*

> Source: *Private Peter Macleod, Royal Regiment of Canada, quoted in Dancocks, Daniel G. In Enemy Hands, (Toronto, McClelland & Stewart, Toronto, 1990)*

*The landing craft I was in was hit as we were coming in about a quarter mile off shore....I was shot in the eye at that point, and later, the eye completely closed up, but there was so much to do in a situation like that, you don't really notice these things. It wasn't until later in the action, around 11:00 in the morning, that I realized I was badly wounded and that my eye was gone. When there's so much excitement around you though, you have a tendency to keep going.*

*I think that everyone who landed on that beach that day deserved credit for doing the best possible job that could be done. I don't*

*believe in medals, but if there has to be such a thing, they should be awarded to anyone and everyone who was there.*

*No doubt Dieppe did teach the military planners a lot of lessons, but I think those lessons could have been learned without such a great loss of life...*

> Source: *Ed Bennett. From Voices of a War Remembered. Bill McNeil. Toronto: Doubleday Canada Ltd, 1991. p 271*

**Do you agree that all who were at Dieppe deserved a medal? Explain.**

# Canadian Vision

## A SISTER'S POEM FOR A BROTHER KILLED AT DIEPPE

**THIS WAS MY BROTHER**
*(For Lt-Col. Howard McTavish, killed in action at Dieppe)*

This was my brother
At Dieppe
Quietly a hero
Who gave his life like a gift,
Withholding nothing.

His youth, his love,
His enjoyment of being alive,
His future, like a book
With half the pages still uncut—

This was my brother
At Dieppe,
The one who built me a doll house
When I was seven,
Complete to the last small picture frame,
Nothing forgotten.

He was awfully good at fixing things,
At stepping into the breach when he was needed.

That's what he did at Dieppe;
He was needed.
And even Death must have been a little shamed
By his eagerness.

By Mona McTavish Gould, poet and broadcaster (1908-1999). *Tasting the Earth*, Macmillan, 1943.

**FOCUS**
1. How did the war expand in 1941?
2. Provide 3 reasons for the raid on Dieppe.
3. Why were the Canadians chosen for the raid?
4. What were the results of the raid?
5. In your view, was the lesson learned at Dieppe worth the cost of the lives? Explain.

# 6 Canada at War

There is more to war than sending soldiers to the battlefield. How could Canada, Canadians and our resources best be used to fight the Second World War?

## The War Plan

The Canadian government drew up a war plan, which covered the areas that were most important to Canadians, and the ones where Canada could make the biggest contribution to the Allied war effort. The Canadian government carefully coordinated its plan with the war plans of other countries. The plan included:

- the defence and security of Canada
- the production of food supplies for Britain
- the production of weapons and ammunition for Allied forces
- training for Allied pilots
- development of the Royal Canadian Air Force (RCAF) for home defence and overseas duty
- development of the Royal Canadian Navy (RCN) for home defence and convoy duty
- development of the Canadian Army for home defence and overseas duty
- development of the Merchant Marine to transport troops and war materials overseas

## Weapons of War

One thousand ships, 15,000 aircraft, 700,000 trucks, countless guns, bombs and bullets—under C.D. Howe, the no-nonsense Minister of Munitions and Supply, war products poured from Canadian factories.

Howe wanted to avoid the profiteering that had soured the war effort during the First World War. A Wartime Prices Trade Board limited prices to "cost plus 10%." Even with these controls, the government paid close to $65 million a week for war supplies.

Where did the money come from? The federal government borrowed heavily by selling Victo-

*Prime Minister Mackenzie King and Minister of Munitions and Supply, C.D. Howe discuss war strategy.*

If people had any money left after paying taxes and buying bonds, there was little to spend it on.

1900  1910  1920  1930  1940  1950  1960  1970  1980

ry Bonds to the people. There was so much money trying to buy the few goods available that prices would go up drastically. By buying bonds, Canadians gave the government their extra money. Income taxes soaked up more money. At the end of the war, Canada's government owed a large debt to Canadians.

*Blind munitions inspector Omer Auger works in a war plant.*

## Rationing

If people had any money left after paying taxes and buying bonds, there was little to spend it on. In 1942, all Canadians received a **ration** book. When they bought sugar, butter, meat, tea or coffee, they had to hand over some coupons from their book. When their coupons were gone they couldn't buy any rationed items— except on the **"black market."** If they were caught shopping on the black market, they had to pay stiff fines.

*Rationing was an important part of the war effort.*

Gas was rationed. Canadians could fill up once a month. They couldn't buy a new car because the last car was produced in 1942.

Canadians had good jobs. They could afford good food, new cars, clothes and appliances. Why did they go without?

Anything Canadians could spare went to the war effort. The butter and cheese they didn't eat went to Britain, where rationing was much more severe. The steel that had once made washing machines, now made bombers. Even the common nickel change— it was made of zinc instead. Nickel was needed for the armour coating on tanks.

## Canada and the U.S.A.: A Growing Partnership

One of the most important and long-lasting results of the Second World War was the growing partnership between Canada and the United States. Prime Minister William Lyon

*At a conference in Quebec, Prime Minister King hosted a meeting with Allied leaders, President Roosevelt and British Prime Minister Winston Churchill.*

Mackenzie King and President Franklin Roosevelt were on close personal terms. At one point, Roosevelt pledged American help if Canada was "threatened by any other empire." The President even took his summer holidays at Campobello Island in New Brunswick.

As the war went on, Canadian-American economic, political and military cooperation grew rapidly through such measures as:

• the building of the Alaska highway, most of which was built by Americans, but on Canadian territory

• the Ogdensburg Agreement, which created a Permanent Joint Board of Defence

• the Lend-Lease Act and the Hyde Park Declaration, which promoted closer military and economic relations among Great Britain, Canada and the United States

During the war, the Canadian economy

*Canadian students were prepared for gas attacks.*

boomed because the U.S. and Britain purchased war materials.

### The Children's War Effort

Children collected paper, metal, rags, rubber and bones. Contests were held to see who could make the biggest ball of aluminum foil. All these things could be recycled into war materials.

Students knitted during lunch hour, making socks and scarves for soldiers. Letter writing campaigns cheered up lonely prisoners of war. Children planted "victory gardens" in school baseball diamonds to produce food for the war. Boys drilled as cadets. Teenagers were let off school to help bring in the harvest.

### Volunteers

Canadians volunteered to be air-raid wardens. They patrolled the coasts to guard against an invasion that never came. They studied aircraft to serve as "spotters" in a bombing raid. They built public air-raid shelters. Wealthy Canadians worked for the government for a dollar a year. The war drew Canadians together in a spirit of cooperation.

## LEND-LEASE ACT AND HYDE PARK DECLARATION

The Lend-Lease Act, passed by the U.S. Congress just before the Americans entered the war, was a way for the United States to help Britain and its Allies during WWII without getting directly involved in the conflict. It gave the U.S. the power to send military supplies, including ships and weapons, to any country deemed vital to U.S. economic and military stability; it allowed countries receiving U.S. goods to postpone payment; and it gave the U.S. permission to use a number of British-owned military bases

The Lend-Lease Act, while beneficial to Britain, was detrimental to Canada's economic stability. Britain could now buy war materials from the U.S. rather than from Canada. Prime Minister King met with U.S. President Roosevelt soon after the Lend-Lease Act was passed to see if the two could come up with some sort of agreement. The two leaders amended the act and saved Canada from economic hardship during the war. The Hyde Park Declaration, as it was called, enabled Britain to spend Lend-Lease money on Canadian-manufactured goods, and the U.S. agreed to purchase more military goods from Canada.

### FOCUS

1. In your view, what was the most important part of the Canadian war plan? Why?
2. Describe 5 ways in which ordinary Canadians helped the war effort.
3. How did the war affect Canadian-American relations?

# 7 Behind the Scenes

## The British Commonwealth Air Training Plan

Military leaders knew that air power would be vital during the Second World War. Crews must be trained before they can go into action but, to do this, they need a safe place

*British Commonwealth Air Training Plan, trained fighters like this one.*

to train. Canada provided the bases for the British Commonwealth Air Training Plan.

Trainees came from all over the Commonwealth—Australia, South Africa, Britain, the West Indies and New Zealand. Volunteers who had escaped when Poland, France and Norway fell to the Germans also trained in Canada.

Courses were short and often inadequate. The rush to get pilots and service crews ready to fight caused many accidents. In one horrible month, 500 aircraft were put out of service by inexperienced fliers. All told, there were 850 deaths during training. On the other hand, 130,000 graduates, over half of them Canadian, went on to fight the battle of the skies.

## The Secret War

On the shores of Lake Ontario near Oshawa was Camp X. Few knew of its existence. Those who did, said nothing. Directed by Canadian master spy, William Stephenson, Camp X was a top-secret training post for spies, secret agents and sabotage experts. Agents from Camp X were dropped behind enemy lines to spy and report back by radio. They connected with underground movements in occupied countries to disrupt enemy activities.

Station M was a vital part of Camp X. It was staffed by forgers, safecrackers, chemists, movie set designers and costume experts. Station M provided agents with false passports and money, battered suitcases and shabby suits, and European-style toothpaste and underwear. Everything an agent carried had to look right to enemy eyes.

During World War II, Canada operated the fourth-largest merchant navy in the world, almost all of which was built in Canadian shipyards.

## Canadian Agents

"Set Europe ablaze," Churchill told the special agents who parachuted into enemy territory. Among the 28 Canadian agents sent into Europe, 8 died. Even today, little is known of what they did.

Guy Bieler was born in Montreal. His spine was badly injured when he parachuted into France. Even so, he organized a sabotage group. They derailed and blew up trains carrying troops and arms. In the end, Bieler was captured and shot.

Joe Gelleny was trained as an elite espionage agent and parachuted into Nazi-held Yugoslavia. Later, in Hungary, Joe was captured and tortured. He lost 170 pounds (77kg). He escaped and, while hiding out in Budapest, helped forge travel documents for fellow spies and Jews facing Nazi persecution. When the Russians arrived, they took him into custody but he was eventually freed. He felt he had aged two decades in his two-year stint as a secret agent.

Henry Fung was a nineteen-year-old Chinese-Canadian who was parachuted into Malaya. He was effective at destroying Japanese communications and transportation systems. When the war ended, Fung helped receive the surrender of Japanese forces in their jungle garrisons.

Frank Pickersgill of Winnipeg was captured when he landed in France. Nazi double agents had given him away. He refused to

*Camp X was a training post for secret agents.*

break under brutal questioning. When his captors switched from threats to bribery, he broke a bottle on his interrogator's desk, slashed the throat of an SS guard, and jumped out of a second floor window before being stopped by four bullets. In prison camp, he organized resistance, helping prisoners regain lost pride. The Nazis finally executed Pickersgill and 15 other agents by hanging them from meat hooks in 1944.

## The Sheepdog Navy

Far from land, on the chilly north Atlantic, Canadians also showed courage and endurance. Some were sailors in the merchant navy, the cargo ships that carried food, fuel and weapons to Britain. Others were part of the Royal Canadian Navy (RCN),

## The Man Known as "Intrepid"

BORN: 1896, Winnipeg, Manitoba

DIED: 1989, Bermuda

SIGNIFICANCE: WWI Ace, Inventor, and WWII Intelligence Agent.

BRIEF BIOGRAPHY: As a teenager, Stephenson showed an early skill for the world of spying when he developed his own secret "Morse Code." From 1914 until 1918, he fought in the First World War. After barely surviving two gas attacks, he falsified his medical records and joined the Royal Flying Corps. He quickly became an ace and recorded 26 "kills," including the brother of the Red Baron. He was later shot down and captured, but he escaped, ending the war as a decorated Canadian hero.

Back in Canada, he invented a new process for transmitting pictures without telephone or telegraph wires. He moved to Britain to earn his fortune. There, he helped organize the BBC, set up a film studio and

explored ideas such as laser beams and splitting the atom.

He became involved in intelligence work during the thirties. During WWII, he ran British Security Co-ordination in the Western Hemisphere. Located in New York with the code-name Intrepid, he led an army of code-breakers, spies, robbers, assassins and sabotage experts. Stephenson was very active in making sure that the U.S. dropped its neutrality and joined in the fight against Hitler. For his efforts in the "secret war," he was decorated by King George VI of Britain. In 1979 he was made a Companion of the Order of Canada, the country's highest civilian honour.

Although some historians believe Stephenson's legendary exploits are partly "hype," he remains one of Canada's most creative and exciting figures.

## William Stephenson

which shepherded the convoys. The RCN's job was to find and sink the German U boats before those submarines found and sank the ships of the convoys.

By the middle of 1943, U boats were on the run. They were being destroyed by weapons, sonar equipment and shore-based aircraft. At the end of the war, the RCN had 400 fighting ships, the third largest navy in the world. It had shepherded 25,000 ships across the ocean to keep the Atlantic lifeline open.

## Canada's Merchant Navy

During World War II, Canada operated the fourth-largest merchant navy in the world, almost all of which was built in Canadian shipyards. Indeed, wartime spending in the ship-building industry was larger than that of the aircraft industry. The ship building industry was so huge that Park Company—Canada's major supplier—was producing almost two 10-tonne ships a week by 1944.

The 12,000 seamen in Canada's merchant navy were responsible for transporting cargo and soldiers across the vast oceans between Canada and Europe. Their contribution to victory was critical because the Battle of the Atlantic was the longest battle of the Second World War.

Unfortunately, the importance of the merchant navy has largely been ignored. During the Second World War, official casualty lists did not include merchant seamen,

*The war at sea was an important step in Canada's development. By the end of WWII, the Royal Canadian Navy had 400 fighting ships and was the third largest navy in the world.*

although their losses were disproportionately higher than those of the Canadian Navy. One in eight merchant sailors died keeping the sea open. A total of 1,629 Canadians and Newfoundlanders perished keeping the vital sea open while serving in the merchant navy.

One continuing result of WWII has been the struggle of civilian sailors in Canada's merchant navy to receive the same benefits and recognition as their counterparts in the Royal Canadian Navy. In 1992, pensions and benefits were finally awarded to the sailors of the merchant navy. Some continued to fight for benefits not received from 1945-1992. Most of these long-overdue claims were finally recognized and honoured by the federal government in 1999.

**FOCUS**
1. How did Canada contribute to the war in the air and on the sea?
2. What was the secret war?
3. Who was "Intrepid," and what did he do?
4. What was the role of Canada's merchant navy?

# Japanese Canadians

## The Pacific War

War had been raging in Asia since 1937. With China weak and divided, Japan decided to expand its empire. When France fell to the Germans in 1940, Japan moved into the French colony of Indochina. Once Hitler attacked the Soviet Union, the Japanese

and Malaya, and swept through the islands of the Pacific.

## Pearl Harbor

At the important American naval base of Pearl Harbor, Hawaii, sailors were sleeping in their bunks. Most looked forward to a lazy day off on that pleasant Sunday morning of December 7, 1941. Suddenly, waves of Japanese bombers and fighter planes came out of the western skies. In just two hours, much of the American Pacific fleet lay at the bottom of the harbour. The United States had been brought into the war.

*Japanese Canadians were forcibly removed from the West Coast to camps further inland.*

## Hong Kong

On December 8, 1941, the Japanese laid siege to the British colony of Hong Kong. Just weeks before, 2,000 inexperienced Canadian troops had been rushed to Hong Kong with little training. Some had never fired their rifles. Some didn't even know how to throw a grenade.

knew they had nothing to fear from the North. They attacked Hong Kong, Indonesia

Japan's entry into the war caused near panic for many Canadians. To Canada's east, Hitler ruled in Europe. Now Japan was sweeping through Asia to the west.

T I M E L I N E

**1900 1910 1920 1930 1940 1950 1960 1970 1980**

These inexperienced, outnumbered troops fought bravely alongside British forces. After 17 hopeless days of battle, Hong Kong surrendered on Christmas Day, 1941. The survivors spent the rest of the war in Japanese prison camps. While 290 Canadians perished in the defence of Hong Kong, another 264 would die in the brutal Japanese prisoner of war camps.

Japan's entry into the war caused near panic for many Canadians. To Canada's east, Hitler ruled in Europe. Now

*These children's faces reveal the fear and pain of forced evacuation.*

## In Their Own Words

*Nothing affects me much just now except rather distractedly. Everything is like a bad dream. I keep telling myself to wake up. There's no sadness when friends of long standing disappear overnight—either to camp or to somewhere in the Interior. No farewells—no promise of future meetings or correspondence—or anything. We just disperse. It's as if we never existed. We're hit so many ways at one time that if I wasn't past feeling I think I would crumble.*

*This curfew business is horrible. At sundown we scuttle into our holes like furtive creatures. We look in the papers for the time of next morning's sunrise when we may venture forth.*

Source: *Obasan*. Joy Kogawa. Penguin Books, 1981.

BORN: 1936, Vancouver, B.C.

SIGNIFICANCE: David Suzuki is Canada's best known scientist. His work on television has raised concerns for the environment. He is a passionate fighter against racism and discrimination.

BRIEF BIOGRAPHY: Although of Japanese descent, Suzuki's parents were born in Canada and spoke English at home. His father encouraged his life-long interest in the natural environment. Suzuki and his family were rounded up during the Second World War and placed in an internment camp near Slocan, B.C. Japanese-Canadian kids jeered at him because he spoke no Japanese. Other kids treated him as an "enemy." After the war, the family moved to Leamington, Ontario, where his father told him: "You have to be ten times better than a white, because if you are just as good as a white, you'll lose out every time."

Suzuki was a brilliant student, winning schol-arships to pay for his education. He had a promis-ing career as a teacher of genetics, but in the 1970s, Suzuki left the academic world to popular-ize science on radio and television. His television productions are seen all over the world. Suzuki's concern for the planet's environment has made Suzuki a powerful spokesman against pollution. While he is best known as an influential defender of the environment, Suzuki continues to speak out against racism and discrimination.

**David Suzuki**

Japan was sweeping through Asia to the west. The fall of Hong Kong and the unprovoked attack on Pearl Harbor seemed like the end of the world. Some Canadians wanted revenge and struck out at the handiest target—Japanese Canadians.

## Canadian or Japanese?

Canadians had never been really welcoming to Asian immigrants. Few Asians were even allowed to enter the country after 1913. By 1942, more than half of the 23,000 "Japanese" living in Canada had been born here; they were Canadian citizens. Few had any sympathy for Japan's ambitions to take over the Pacific. Many had fought for Canada during the First World War.

Many Canadians paid no attention to these facts. They decided that Japanese Canadians were dangerous. They might be spies who would help Japan attack North America. In 1942, the government ordered that they be moved away from the coastal regions of British Columbia to isolated camps in the B.C. interior, such as the town of New Denver. Often, families were separated. Men were sent to one camp, women and children to another. Some men were sent as labourers to farms on the prairies and in Ontario.

The government held auctions to sell these people's personal possessions, homes and businesses. Many made their living by fishing, but their boats were confiscated and sold. These were great bargains for the buyers. Japanese Canadians never received a fair price for the things they had lost. There was not a single documented case of any Japanese Canadian who acted as a spy for Japan. In spite of this, the Canadian government refused any compensation for their losses.

## Partial Compensation for Japanese Canadians

Finally, in September 1988, Prime Minister Brian Mulroney announced that the government would partially repay Japanese-Canadian survivors for their losses. The terms were:

- a public apology for past injustices against Japanese Canadians, their families and their heritage
- $21,000 for each surviving Japanese-Canadian born before 1949
- $24 million to establish a Canadian Race Relations Foundation
- $12 million to the Japanese-Canadian Association for low-cost housing for elderly Japanese Canadians

**FOCUS**

1. How did Japanese aggression affect Canada and the United States?
2. What led the Canadian government to take action against Japanese Canadians?
3. What specific measures were taken against Japanese Canadians?
4. Do you support the 1988 policy to compensate Japanese Canadians for their losses during the Second World War? Explain.

# 9 Women Go to War

*Firefighting demonstration by women of the Canadian Women's Army Corps, 1943.*

Canadian women were eager to defend their country. Unfortunately, Canadian leaders saw little room for women in the war effort. As more and more men left for the battle front, however, the roles women could play became more obvious.

Industrial strength was the key to success in the war, and Canada had vast resources. Canada's women put their brains and muscles to turning raw materials into tanks, planes and ships. Over one million women worked in Canadian industry by 1943.

Managers had to change some of their ideas about workers and how to run a factory. Day care centres were set up in many plants. Production rose as workers donated free time to produce another tank or bomber. Men were often outnumbered; they sometimes had to endure female wolf whistles, just as women previously had endured male

During the war, women succeeded in a society dominated by men. Initially, many men had doubted their worth. Now women gained freedom and self-respect.

T I M E L I N E

1900    1910    1920    1930    1940    1950    1960    1970    1980    1990    2000

taunts. They learned that, in the right circumstances, women could swear as well as men.

In rural Canada, women took over all the farming jobs vacated by men who went overseas. The food supply, at home and abroad, had to be maintained. Women handled the added responsibilities to assist in the overall war effort.

Women volunteered to visit wounded soldiers. They sent packages to prisoners of war. They made dressings for the wounded. The family garbage shrank as housewives saved paper, scraps, fat and bones for recycling.

*These women in the WAC were positioned in Halifax to aid the war effort in that vulnerable port.*

## Women in Uniform

Society had initially wanted to keep women out of the factory. Now it was determined to keep them out of the armed forces. When women couldn't register with the armed forces, they set up their own volunteer units such as the CATS (Canadian Auxiliary

| Canada's Servicewomen | Total | Posted Overseas |
|---|---|---|
| Canadian Women's Army Corps (CWAC) | 21,624 | 2,900 |
| RCAF Women's Division (WDs) | 17,018 | 1,400 |
| Women's Royal Canadian Naval Service (WRENS) | 6,781 | 1,000 |
| Nursing Sisters | 4,172 | 4,172 |

*Molly Lamb's "Gas Drill" depicts some of the mundane aspects of war.*

**Molly Lamb Bobak:** First female official war artist.

**Gudrun Bjening:** War propaganda filmmaker for the National Film Board of Canada.

**Fern Blodgett:** First female wireless operator on a wartime ship. She crossed the Atlantic 78 times during the war.

**Margaret Brooke:** While crossing from Nova Scotia to Newfoundland, the ferry Brooke was aboard was torpedoed by a U boat deep in Canadian waters. She held a fellow nurse, Agnes Wilkie, up in the icy water all night. At dawn, a giant breaker forced them apart. Wilkie drowned, but Brooke, now unconscious, was rescued.

**Kathleen Christie and Maye Waters:** Stationed in Hong Kong, these two nurses aided the troops during the battle for Hong Kong and continued to help them during two years of imprisonment by the Japanese.

**Marion Orr:** One of Canada's first female bush pilots, Orr ferried military aircraft from factories to military bases overseas.

**Helen-Marie Stevens:** An army nurse who was the heroine at a bombing raid during the London "blitz." She worked for hours aiding customers in a bombed-out restaurant, using champagne as an anaesthetic. "I did what any Canadian nurse would do."

Territorial Service), which provided technical and first-aid training to women.

By 1941, the armed forces were in desperate need of recruits. Women were finally allowed to enlist. One young woman walked 30 kilometres to a recruiting station. Ultimately, Canada had 45,000 servicewomen, many of them posted overseas. They served in a wide variety of non-combat roles, such as radar operators, truck and ambulance drivers, nurses, secretaries and mechanics.

These women often found themselves in the heat of battle. They were bombed, shelled and torpedoed. Some were made prisoners of war. Two hundred and forty-four won medals for bravery. Sadly, 73 were killed and 19 wounded.

## Women Prove Themselves

During the war, women succeeded in a society dominated by men. Initially, many men had doubted their worth. Now, women gained freedom and self-respect. They knew the satisfaction of earning their own money. They also knew the injustice of getting less pay than a man for doing the same work.

After the war, many women returned to more traditional roles. For the young couples who had postponed marriage and babies during the war, peace meant it was time to start a family. Many women became housewives

*This young soldier in the CWAC was an expert marksman.*

and mothers. It was not until the 1960s and 1970s that women began to build on the gains they had made during wartime.

**FOCUS**
1. List 5 ways in which women contributed to the war effort.
2. In your opinion, were women treated equally? Explain.
3. How did the Second World War affect women's lives?

# 10 Conscription—Again

Should a person be forced to fight during war? This question almost split the country during World War I. Prime Minister Mackenzie King did not want that to happen again. He promised his government would not introduce conscription for overseas service.

*The conscription referendum split the nation.*

In October 1939, Quebec's premier, Maurice Duplessis, called a provincial election. A bitter critic of the war policy, Duplessis believed that the federal government wanted to use the war to take power away from Quebec. If Canada was to remain united through the war, Duplessis' Union Nationale party had to be defeated.

The federal Liberals threw their support behind the provincial Liberal Party in the election. Three Quebec federal cabinet ministers campaigned vigorously against Duplessis. They told the Quebec people that the federal government would not introduce conscription for overseas service. They would resign first. They also threatened to resign if Duplessis was re-elected, which would leave Quebec without any influence in the federal cabinet. The provincial Liberals were swept into office.

Meanwhile, Premier Mitch Hepburn of Ontario wanted to see more Canadians go to war. He accused his fellow Liberal, Prime Minister King, of being weak on the issue of conscription. King called a federal election in the early part of 1940. The Liberals won an overwhelming victory in all regions of Canada. Hepburn's political career was over.

## Home Defence

Volunteers filled Canada's fighting forces overseas. Many people felt this might not be enough. In the dark days of 1940, Parliament approved conscription for home defence only. Men drafted into this army were often jeered at because they hadn't volunteered to go overseas. They were later called "zombies" by those who thought every young man should want to fight.

## Conscription If Necessary

King had promised not to introduce conscription but, in 1942, he asked the country to release him from his pledge. At that time, it

King had promised not to introduce conscription but, in 1942, he asked the country to release him from his pledge.

did not look as if the government would need to force men into the armed services. The Canadian army was sitting in Britain waiting to go into action, but King knew the situation might change. If it did, he wanted to be ready.

The government organized a vote on the question. Across the country, 65% voted to let the government decide. Ontario, Manitoba and British Columbia were 80% in favour of conscription. In Quebec, 72% were against. Many French Canadians felt they had been betrayed. Mackenzie King tried to cool the issue. He used the slogan "Conscription if necessary, but not necessarily conscription."

## The War Heats Up

While the Canadian Army stayed in Britain, there was no need for conscription. The issue was avoided for two years, but after the Italian campaign and the invasion of France, things changed. The battle for Europe had begun and the losses were high. The Canadian government tried its best to recruit men voluntarily. Only a few joined up. Reluctantly, in November, 1944, King ordered 16,000 soldiers conscripted for Home Defence to go overseas.

There was an uproar. One Quebec cabinet minister resigned, but other French Canadians stood by King. Louis St. Laurent, King's "Quebec lieutenant," told Quebecers that the decision was necessary. Fortunately, the war ended soon after. Only 2,500 conscripts actually fought.

Unlike the conscription crisis of 1917, all Canadians had been consulted before conscription was introduced. This time Canadian unity was strained but not broken.

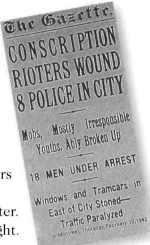

The Gazette.

**CONSCRIPTION RIOTERS WOUND 8 POLICE IN CITY**

Mobs, Mostly Irresponsible Youths, Ably Broken Up

18 MEN UNDER ARREST

Windows and Tramcars in East of City Stoned— Traffic Paralyzed
— Montreal, Thursday, February 12, 1942

---

**F O C U S**

1. What is conscription?
2. Why is it a sensitive issue in Canada?
3. How well did Prime Minister King handle the conscription issue? Explain.
4. Would you have supported or rejected conscription? Why?

# The Italian Campaign

**11**

### The Tide Turns

The tide of war began to turn in favour of Canada and its Allies in 1942. British and American troops drove back Italian and German forces in North Africa under Field Marshal Rommel, "the Desert Fox."

In the freezing Russian winter, German troops faced disaster. The decisive battle was fought at Stalingrad. In February, 1943, the once proud German Sixth Army surrendered. The Russians took 90,000 prisoners. Soviet forces started down the road to Berlin. They had suffered starvation, torture and atrocities at the hands of German troops. The Soviet forces prepared to take revenge on the German people.

The Americans recovered quickly after Pearl Harbor. They raised, refitted and put back in action most ships sunk on that fateful December morning. In June, American aircraft carriers decisively defeated the Japanese navy at Midway Island. Island by island, they moved closer to Japan. In China, communist and nationalist armies fought against the Japanese invaders. British and Commonwealth forces began to drive the Japanese from Southeast Asia.

Each Allied victory was paid for in blood.

*In June 1944, Allied Forces hit Normandy's beaches.*

Canadian soldiers had seen no action since the disastrous raid on Dieppe. Now the 1st Canadian Division took part in the invasion of Sicily under General Montgomery.

Winning the war had become a matter of time and of lives. In May, 1943, General Montgomery's British army and General Eisenhower's American army forced the German and Italian troops in North Africa to surrender. It was time to cross the Mediterranean Sea to Europe.

## The Invasion of Sicily

Canadian soldiers had seen no action since the disastrous raid on Dieppe. Now the 1st Canadian Division took part in the invasion of Sicily under General Montgomery.

The battle for Sicily was fought under the blazing July sun. Within 38 days, the victorious Allied troops prepared to invade the Italian mainland. Mussolini's dream of a new Roman Empire was shattered. His own people rebelled and threw him out of power. Hitler swiftly moved German troops into Italy. He would not be deterred by Italy's surrender.

## The Liberation of Italy

The Italian campaign was long and difficult. Ninety-one thousand Canadians fought in Italy, with 30,000 wounded or killed. A few snipers in the rugged mountains could slow an army to a crawl, and the German forces fought brilliantly. Even with the help of Ital-

*The Italian campaign was a long and difficult battle. Over 91,000 Canadians fought in Italy.*

ian partisans, the Allies paid heavily for each kilometre they won.

The battle for Ortona was a terrible lesson for Canadian troops. The Germans turned it into a series of house-to-house fights. It took a month to capture the town. The Canadians became experts at street fighting.

On June 4, 1944, the Allied armies entered Rome. Canadian soldiers marched with their British, American, New Zealand,

*The battle of Ortona was grueling. It took the Allies a month to capture the town.*

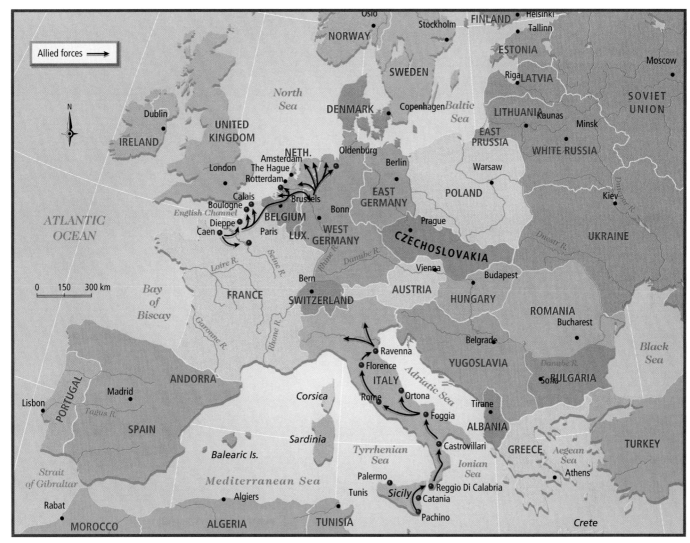

*Some allied forces during the Second World War.*

Indian, South African, French and Polish comrades to the cheers of the Italian people.

While one Canadian force crept up the boot of Italy, another had prepared for the greatest land-sea invasion in history. Two days later came D-Day—the long awaited Allied invasion of France.

**F O C U S**
1. In what way did the tide turn in 1942?
2. What made the battle for Italy so difficult?
3. What reputation did the Canadians get for their fighting in Ortona?

# 12 D-Day to V-E Day

Everything had been carefully planned. The tide was right. The moon was right. Would the weather be right for D-Day, the big invasion planned for June 5, 1944? Would it have to be put off for a month and kept a secret? The south of England was one big army camp. Everybody knew the invasion of France was about to begin, but only a few knew when and where the landing would be made.

On June 4, troops were ordered into the ships. Some ships set out. Suddenly, reports indicated the weather was deteriorating. The landing was postponed and the ships recalled. By the following morning, violent winds were battering the coast of northern France. The troops stayed crammed aboard the ships, awaiting further orders. Then, the weather forecasters said there would be a lull in the storm. General Eisenhower made the decision. D-Day would be June 6, a day later than planned.

*When Allied soldiers finally entered Germany, the end of WWII was near.*

## The Normandy Beaches

Across the English Channel, the Germans were waiting at Calais. German pilots returning from bombing raids had told them that the main buildup of troops and equipment was at Dover. What they had really seen were empty tents, dummy ships, plywood gliders and inflated rubber tanks.One of the great hoaxes of all time had succeeded.

The Allies actually struck 200 kilometres to the southwest on the beaches of Normandy. Bombers struck at the German defences all night long. Just before dawn, paratroopers dropped

It took 11 long months before Western troops met their Soviet Allies near the Elbe River in central Germany.

T I M E L I N E

1900   1910   1920   1930   1940   1950   1960   1970   1980   1990   200

behind enemy lines. The main force hit the beaches. The liberation of Europe had begun.

The Dieppe raid had taught the Allies that the Germans could defend any ports they tried to capture. So, they wouldn't use the ports. Two complete harbours were built in Britain, towed across and assembled in Normandy. Fuel for trucks and tanks flowed through "Pluto," an underwater pipeline, from ships to shore.

## The Push to Berlin

It took 11 long months before Western troops met their Soviet Allies near the Elbe River in central Germany. Hitler was determined to fight to the bitter end. He would rather destroy Germany and the German people than surrender.

*Canadian forces drove German soldiers from occupied Europe.*

Canadians were given the task of clearing German forces from the French, Belgian and Dutch ports during the push towards Berlin. This was slow, dangerous work. Enemy forces fought from behind strong fortifications. Every port taken meant more Allied ships could unload tanks, weapons—and troops.

The ports fell, one by one. On September 8, 1944, Canadian forces entered Dieppe. This time they came by land and as conquerors. The stain of defeat was erased as they marched into the port.

## Liberation of Holland

In 1945, the Canadian Army liberated the Netherlands. The Germans had opened the dykes that held back the water from the low-lying fields. Canadian troops found boats and kept moving. As the Germans retreated, grateful Dutch families poured out of their homes to welcome their liberators. Even today, Canadians are warmly received in the Netherlands.

BORN: 1891, Beeton, Ontario

DIED: 1971, Streetsville, Ontario

SIGNIFICANCE: Broadcaster, cook and author, Aitken was Canada's best-known woman during the 1940s and 1950s.

BRIEF BIOGRAPHY: Credited with being the first broadcaster to take women seriously, Aitken began her radio career in 1934. During the Second World War, she was appointed Conservation Director for the Federal Wartime Prices and Trade Board, where she worked tirelessly to aid in the war effort. Aitken's job was to help women conserve and stretch scarce food and clothing supplies. During her broadcasts, she taught her female audience how to make the most of the food in short supply, how to substitute unavailable ingredients with available ones, and how to can and preserve the food grown in wartime gardens. Aitken encouraged women to remake old clothes to get the most possible wear from them, and to send supplies to England. It is estimated that over $250,000 worth of clothing was sent

to children's homes and maternity hospitals in England at Aitken's encouragement. Although not a war correspondent, Aitken travelled to war torn Europe on a number of occasions, reporting back to her listeners on how the people were faring, how they were living and how they appreciated what Canadians at home were doing for them. Aitken's audiences had a tremendous effect on war torn Europe. They performed prodigious feats of conservation and organization to collect supplies and get them to where they were needed. By 1944, these volunteers had assembled over 10 million packages for prisoners of war, had collected more than 28 million kilograms of salvage, and had sent innumerable amounts of clothing, food and books to servicemen and servicewomen overseas. Aitken was there through it all: encouraging, teaching and exhorting these unsung heroes.

After the war, Aitken continued her broadcasting and writing career. She retired from radio in 1957 and served on the CBC's Board of Directors from 1957 until 1962.

## Kate Aitken

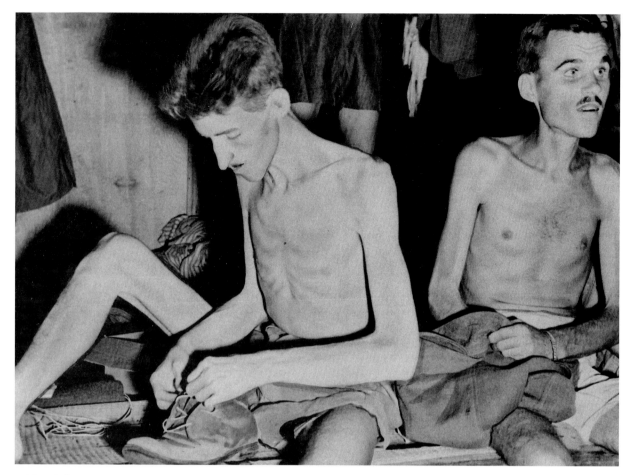

*Although the War had ended in Europe, it was still being fought in the Pacific. These Canadians were held at a Japanese prisoner of war camp.*

## The End of the Dictators

On April 27, 1945, Mussolini was captured and shot by his own people. They hanged his body upside down on a meat hook and displayed it in Milan. Three days later in his underground bunker, Hitler listened to Soviet guns bombarding Berlin. He placed a revolver in his mouth and pulled the trigger. His body was burned so that it could not be displayed by his enemies. On May 8, 1945, Germany surrendered unconditionally. This was V-E Day—Victory in Europe Day.

FOCUS
1. Why was the weather such an important factor in the planning of D-Day?
2. What preparations did the Allies make to ensure success for the invasion?
3. What role did the Canadians play after D-Day?

# 13 The Holocaust

When Hitler came to power in 1933 he began his war on the Jews. He ordered Germans to boycott Jewish stores. He forbade Jewish lawyers and doctors to practise freely. Jews lost the right to vote. In many places, they were not allowed to use public parks, swimming pools or sports fields. Jewish children had to attend segregated schools for Jews only. Western nations

*Toward the end of the war, Aba Bayefsky, a Canadian war artist, visited Nazi concentration camps. Those terrible scenes of human suffering so moved him that he spent the next 40 years trying to capture the tragedy and meaning of the camps in his art work. These brilliant, but deeply disturbing images, haunt the viewer long after the war has ended.*

made feeble protests against the German treatment of Jews, but took no concrete action.

In May of 1939, the passenger liner *St. Louis* sailed from Hamburg, Germany, with 907 Jews aboard. They were looking for a safe home far from the persecution of Nazi Germany. They tried to land in Cuba but were turned away. They headed for the United Sates but were forbidden to enter the country. They came north to Canada but Canadians, too, turned them away. The Canadian prime minister, Mackenzie King, showed a strong **anti-Semitic** attitude when he supported the Deputy Minister of Immigration's comment about allowing Jewish immigrants to enter Canada. Canada's official response to Jewish refugee applicants was: "At present, Canada is not admitting Jews. Please try some other country."

Most countries tried to keep all immigrants out during the Depression years. Many people were particularly prejudiced against Jews. In Canada, over 100,000 people signed a petition to stop Jewish immigration. Attitudes like these kept Jews from escaping Europe during the 1930s. When Hitler overran the continent, they were caught in a death trap.

The *St. Louis* returned to Europe where the Dutch, the French and the British agreed to give its passengers a home. A year later the Germans occupied the Netherlands. The Dutch were powerless to save these and other Jews. Most of the passengers of the *St. Louis* later perished in Nazi death camps.

The Nazis wanted a more systematic way of killing the Jews. They set up death camps, such as Dachau, Auschwitz and Treblinka, to quickly and scientifically kill Jews.

| 1900 | 1910 | 1920 | 1930 | 1940 | 1950 | 1960 | 1970 | 1980 | | |

## Kristallnacht

On November 7, 1938, Polish-Jewish student, Herschel Grynszpan, shot a German diplomat, Ernst von Rath. When news of Von Rath's death reached Hitler, he ordered his storm troopers to wreak havoc on Jewish communities in revenge. **Pogroms** occurred throughout Germany and Austria during the night of November 9. Ninety-one Jews were killed, hundreds were seriously injured and many more were terrorized and humiliated.

Almost 7,500 businesses were destroyed and roughly 177 synagogues were burned to the ground. Police were ordered not to interfere. The Gestapo arrested 30,000 wealthy Jews, who were only released on condition that they leave the country and that they surrender their wealth to the authorities. Insurance payments to owners of businesses destroyed during the night were confiscated by police. The state levied a 1,000,000,000 mark fine against the Jewish community and prohibited Jews from using public parks. **Kristallnacht**—the night of broken glass— marked a major escalation in the Nazi persecution of the Jews.

## Concentration Camps

By 1941, the German policy was becoming clear—the outright extermination of all Jews in areas under German control. It was referred to as the "Final Solution." When Germany conquered Russia, large numbers of Jews were forced into slave labour camps.

The Nazis wanted a more systematic way of killing the Jews. They set up **death camps,** such as Dachau, Auschwitz and Treblinka, to quickly and scientifically kill Jews. Men, women and children were herded into "showers" and murdered by clouds of poison gas. Later the bodies were burned in huge ovens.

### Ghetto

Formerly a section of a city set apart as a legally enforced residence for Jews, **ghettos** were particularly prevalent during the Middle Ages. Customarily, ghettos were enclosed within walls or gates, which were kept locked at night. Inside, Jews had complete freedom. They had their own places of worship, schools, courts and recreation centres. Outside, however, they were in constant danger of being assaulted. Although most ghettos were abolished during the nineteenth century, they were revived by the Nazis during World War II.

By 1945, over 6,000,000 innocent Jews had died in Nazi death camps—one-third of them children. Several million other enemies of the German government also lost their lives—French, Dutch, Russians, Poles, Romas, communists, homosexuals, and Germans who opposed the Nazi regime.

## Who Bears the Guilt?

Many war criminals were hunted down and punished after the war. Hitler committed suicide in Berlin in 1945. Adolph Eichmann, the person in charge of the "Final Solution," was captured in 1961 in Argentina by Israeli agents, tried as a war criminal, found guilty, and executed. The infamous Dr. Josef Mengele, who carried out medical experiments on live Jews, was never captured. He died in South America many years later in 1979. Some Nazis who had participated in the Holocaust were given forged identity papers by Allied authorities after the war in return for giving information and services. Some continued to live with new names in countries such as Canada and the United States.

But who bears the guilt?

Was it just Hitler and his fellow Nazis who gave the orders? What of the guards who ran the camps, chemical workers who made the poison gas, railway workers who carried thousands to the camps, ordinary citizens who watched their neighbours disappear and said or did nothing, those who claimed that they were innocent because they simply did what they were told, the nations who looked the other way before and during the war, or Canada, which refused to admit Jewish refugees in the 1930s?

Who bears the guilt?

## Criminals in Canada

In 1987, the Canadian Parliament passed a law allowing the arrest and trial of war criminals living in Canada. While officials attempt to locate, try or deport these people, little success has been achieved. These crimes are over fifty years old and it is difficult to find witnesses. People change a great deal in half a century. Legal proceedings move very slowly and suspects are often too old or infirm to be investigated properly.

A Canadian, Edgar Bronfman, has fought long and hard to recapture for Jewish families their wealth, which was stolen by the Nazis and hidden away in secret Swiss bank accounts. As head of the World Jewish Congress, Bronfman forced the Swiss banks to drop their famous wall of secrecy concerning bank accounts. The Swiss have agreed to search for all money deposited in their accounts that was stolen from European Jews. The initial fund was established at $300 million and the banks are combing the world to find owners or their heirs. Bronfman has also taken his campaign to other nations holding funds originally stolen from the Jewish community: "As long as I draw breath, I will see to it that nobody profits from the ashes of the Holocaust."

## The State of Israel

After the war, many Jews who survived the Holocaust wanted to escape from the persecution and destruction of Europe. Some wanted to return to what they believed was their ancestral homeland in Palestine. The State of Israel was created as a national home for the Jews in 1948. Although many survivors moved to Israel, it was not to be the land of peace they had expected. The creation of the State of Israel greatly offended the Palestinians and neighbouring Arab countries. The resentment and conflict from this dispute has continued to the present. The progress toward peace has been long and difficult.

## In Their Own Words

Some Canadian POWs (prisoners of war) found themselves in the infamous Nazi death camps of Buchenwald rather than the normal POW camps. They spent a few devastating weeks in nightmarish conditions. Here is one moving account of what they saw:

*The trip to Buchenwald was very scary. I didn't know what Buchenwald was. I don't think any of us knew what a concentration camp was at that time. When we arrived at Buchenwald, I don't think we were off the train five seconds when the fellow next to me got hit in the face with a rifle butt. The SS guard hit him because he didn't move fast enough.*

*First of all, they shaved us, our heads and our whole body. And then they gave us a pair of pants and a shirt and a little tiny hat. And we slept on the bare ground. This is the latter part of August, and Buchenwald is on a mountain, so it gets pretty cold. And we were there for I don't know how many nights. Quite a few, I know, and it was awful cold and uncomfortable.*

*I think the thing that frightened me most about it was the deaths every day. Because people would die and they would keep them in the huts to get the extra rations. And then the bodies were just thrown out on the street and a wagon came along each morning and they piled the bodies on and took them to a crematorium....The guards were maniacs. They would think nothing of setting the dogs on a prisoner, and that would be it.*

*We were suffering from malnutrition, because all we got to eat was a little bowl of soup made from grass or cabbage leaves and an inch of bread and three little potatoes a day.*

> Source: Pilot Officer Bill Gibson, 419 Squadron, RCAF, quoted in *Enemy Hands: Canadian Prisoners of War 1939-45* by Daniel G. Dancocks. McClelland & Stewart, Toronto,1990.

On December 10, 1945, Canada began the first war crimes trial in its history. Charged was German General Kurt (Panzer) Meyer. The crime, murders of Canadian POWs, Meyer was later convicted and sentenced to death; however, the sentence was never carried out.

### JEWISH IMMIGRATION DURING THE 1930s

| Country | Jewish Immigrants |
| --- | --- |
| United States | 150,000 |
| Palestine | 100,000 |
| United Kingdom | 85,000 |
| Argentina | 20,000 |
| Columbia | 20,000 |
| Mexico | 20,000 |
| Canada | 4,000 |

### FOCUS

1. What actions did the Nazis take against the Jews after 1933?
2. What is the significance of the *St. Louis*?
3. What was "the Final Solution?"
4. In your opinion, who was guilty for the mass slaughter of the Holocaust?
5. How should Canada deal with war criminals?

# 14 The Mushroom-Shaped Cloud

*Devastation was total in the Japanese city of Hiroshima.*

On August 6, 1945, a lone American bomber, the "Enola Gay," flew high over the Japanese city of Hiroshima. The plane dropped a single bomb, nicknamed "Little Boy." For the first time in history, an atomic bomb was unleashed on the world. By the end of the day, 173,000 people were dead or dying.

Hanging from a small parachute, the

For the first time in history, an atomic bomb was unleashed on the world. By the end of the day 173,000 people were dead or dying.

1900    1910    1920    1930    1940    1950    1960    1970    1980    1990

## The Technical Edge

The creation of the atomic bomb ushered in a period of great fear and uncertainty. This wartime technical development threatened the very existence of humankind. Although Canada has never manufactured or possessed nuclear weapons, it has played a major role in both the peaceful and wartime use of nuclear energy. The bombs which exploded over Japan contained uranium mined in Canada. One of the young scientists deeply involved in the creation of the nuclear bomb was Louis Slotin of Winnipeg. Slotin was an expert at

*A model shows what remained of the city after the bomb.*

assembling the firing mechanisms for atomic bombs. In fact, he completed the assembly of the first test bomb in 1945. Slotin prided himself on his nerves of steel as he finished putting together the firing mechanism by hand. He called the dangerous operation, "tickling the dragon's tail." Unfortunately, as he performed the procedure one last time in 1946, before moving to Chicago for a new job, something went wrong. His screwdriver slipped and a deadly chain reaction took place. The lab was flooded in a bluish glow. Fearing an explosion, Slotin separated the materials with his bare hands. Slotin suffered a massive dose of radiation and died within nine days.

bomb drifted over the city. It exploded with a burning white flash "brighter than a thousand suns." Shock waves destroyed buildings. Fireballs burned through the streets. Pieces of the city tore through the air. Finally, a huge mushroom-shaped cloud billowed over the city.

People who looked up at the sound of the explosion had their bodies melt from the heat of the blast. Skin turned black and flesh

*Robbie Engels survived the Holocaust before moving to Canada, after being liberated from a Dutch concentration camp by Canadian troops. Engels spent his life administering to the needy and underprivileged. Seen here delivering presents for* The Toronto Star's Santa Claus fund, *Engels worked for that organization for over 14 years.*

was ripped from bones. Those who died at once were lucky. Many more suffered slow, painful deaths from radiation poisoning. Decades later, deformed babies were still being born to the survivors of Hiroshima.

The Americans demanded that the Japanese surrender. There was no reply. Three days later the same horror was repeated at Nagasaki. Eighty-thousand more people were cremated in a nuclear inferno. Japan surrendered unconditionally on August 14, 1945—V-J Day.

## The United Nations

Even before V-E Day, the leaders of the world were looking for a way to maintain peace in the future. The old League of Nations had failed. They would learn from its mistakes and build a better, stronger organization, the United Nations.

It was not going to be easy. The war had created new borders, and new hatreds. The "old" world powers—Britain, Germany, France and Japan—lay shattered and exhausted. Two new rival superpowers—the United States and the Soviet Union—had gained strength and influence.

World War II left a bitter, confused and divided world. The shadow of the atomic bomb and a new arms race lay across it. Could the United Nations keep the peace? What role would Canada play in the new world order?

# The Technical Edge

Many people feel that Canada's role in the development of radar (radio detection and ranging) contributed as much to the end of the war as the invention of the atomic bomb. In 1935, A.G.L. McNaughton, an electrical engineer, became president of the NRC. Eleven years earlier, McNaughton and a colleague, W.A. Steel, had patented a cathode ray tube detection finder. A forerunner of radar, the cathode ray tube detector detected the position of radio signals. When he became president of the NRC, McNaughton saw the military potential of his earlier invention, but the NRC had little funding to pursue the development of radar at that time. When Canada entered the war in 1939, however, the army and the RCAF asked the NRC to develop coastal defence and airborne radar. The Navy also requested radar. They were concerned about Halifax's vulnerability. This time, the government allocated substantial funds to the NRC for its research, and established a secret Crown corporation, Research Enterprises Ltd. (REL), to manufacture any products designed or invented by scientists at the NRC. By 1940, the "Night Watchman," the first operational radar in North America, was installed in Nova Scotia.

Scientists at the NRC made another important contribution to radar development in 1943, when they invented a radar unit that worked with wavelengths of 10 cm, rather than the existing 60 metres. This new system could identify very small objects. Developed by William Crocker Brown, the CDX proved remarkable during testing and, by 1943, it was available for coastal defence. The timing could not have been better. German submarines had become a major threat to Canada's safety by 1943. Indeed, when the CDX radar was being installed on the coast of British Columbia, a submarine periscope was sighted in Canadian waters. The group hastily completed the finishing touches of installation, turned on the radar unit and, sure enough, picked up the submarine's signal. They quickly alerted the military and, after verifying that the submarine was definitely not a friendly one, the officers opened fire. The German submarine soon went out of the radar's range of detection.

FOCUS
1. What kind of weapon is the atomic bomb?
2. How was Canada connected to the atomic bomb?
3. What was the chief aim of the new United Nations?
4. What new superpowers arose out of the ashes of the Second World War?

# Questions & Activities

## Match the items in column A with the description in column B.

| A | | B |
|---|---|---|
| **1.** Blitzkrieg | **a)** | spy training centre near Oshawa |
| **2.** Little Boy | **b)** | allied retreat from France |
| **3.** The Axis | **c)** | city in Italy |
| **4.** The St. Louis | **d)** | conscripted soldiers |
| **5.** Pearl Harbor | **e)** | an atomic bomb |
| **6.** Camp X | **f)** | Jewish refugee ship |
| **7.** Ortona | **g)** | Canadian Fascist |
| **8.** Adrien Arcand | **h)** | alliance led by Germany |
| **9.** Dunkirk | **i)** | allied invasion of France |
| **10.** Zombies | **j)** | lightning war |
| **11.** D-Day | **k)** | American naval base in Hawaii |
| **12.** Holocaust | **l)** | the Nazi war against the Jews |

## Who Am I?
### Identify the following people from the clues

**1.** I served as British prime minister during the Second World War. I promised the British nothing but "blood, toil, tears, and sweat." Who am I?

**2.** I am a scientist of Asian ancestry. My people suffered greatly in Canada during the war. Who am I?

**3.** I ran a brilliant spy organization during the war. In 1979, I was honoured by the government of Canada. Who am I?

**4.** I led Canada during the Second World War. I engineered a solution to the conscription crisis. Who am I?

**5.** I grew up in New Brunswick but moved to Britain. I was in charge of British aircraft production during the Battle of Britain. Who am I?

**6.** I was a Canadian doctor who helped the Chinese in their struggle against invasion by the Japanese. Who am I?

## Ideas for Discussion

**1.** The conscription issue divided Canadians during two World Wars. Arrange the classroom to look like the House of Commons. Have each student be a member of Parliament for a different constituency in Canada. Be prepared to give a speech in favour of, or against, conscription during World War II. After the debate, hold a vote on the issue. If your class had been the House of Commons, would conscription have been introduced?

**2.** The decision to drop the atomic bomb on Japanese cities has often been criticized. Imagine you are an advisor to U.S. President Truman. Write a memo either supporting or attacking the plan to drop the A-bomb on Hiroshima and Nagasaki. Then hold a meeting of the president's advisors. Be prepared to defend your views.

**3.** Many Nazi supporters were tried for war crimes at Nuremberg after the war. Hitler, however, had committed suicide and could not be brought to trial. Imagine that Hitler had been captured alive. Organize his trial with judges and defence and prosecution lawyers. Select students to play the parts of witnesses, members of the jury, court reporters, guards, etc.

## Do Some Research

**1.** Find out about one of the following and write a brief report on:
   **a)** a famous Canadian soldier of World War II;
   **b)** a famous Canadian general of World War II;
   **c)** some new weapons invented during the Second World War;
   **d)** a Canadian winner of the Victoria Cross in World War II.

**2.** People's memories often tell historians a different story from the one recorded in books, papers and reports. Interview someone who remembers the

Second World War. Find out about his or her experiences at home in Canada and/or at the battle fronts of Europe, Africa, or the Pacific. Assemble a class booklet or tape of memories of World War II.

3. With a small group of other students, prepare a folder on life on the Canadian home front during World War II. Your folder should include:
   a) Posters               b) Pictures
   c) Songs                 d) Slogans
   e) Brief Biographies     f) Advertisements
   g) Wartime Regulations   h) Rations Card

4. Find out about one of the following war heroes. Write a "biocard" like the ones that appear in this book:
   a) Buzz Beurling         b) Anne Frank
   c) Winston Churchill     d) Osar Schindler
   e) Tommy Prince

5. Design a wall chart comparing Canada's involvement in World War I and in World War II. You may wish to compare some of the following items:
   a) Length of the war (dates)
   b) Number of soldiers fighting
   c) Number of people killed
   d) Important battles
   e) Types of weapons
   f) Activities on the home front

6. Governments often ask artists to paint pictures of wartime scenes. What can be shown in a painting that might not appear in a photograph? Go to the library and find out more on war artists. Report to the class, explaining which war artists you feel best convey the atmosphere of the war and why.

## Be Creative

1. Reporting the news as it happens is always an exciting job. During wartime, it is also very dangerous. Reporters from all nations risk their lives to bring you news from the battlefront. Imagine you are a Canadian war correspondent. Give an on-the-spot news report about one of the following:
   a) The fall of Hong Kong
   b) The Battle of Britain
   c) The Battle of Ortona
   d) The Normandy beaches on D-Day
   e) The liberation of the Netherlands
   Make your report as authentic as possible. You could present it as a newspaper article, a radio report, or a commentary to the news film that will be shown in a movie theatre before the main feature.

2. In a group of four or five students, prepare a brief play showing a scene from the life of some Japanese Canadians during the war. Present your play to the class and watch the plays of the other groups. Discuss your reactions to the plays.

3. Make a model or draw a diagram of a ship or plane used in World War II. Write a brief paragraph on its role in the war.

4. Design posters to point out the horrors of the war and to promote world peace.

## Web sites
**Department of National Defence:** www.dnd.org
**Japanese-Canadian Internment:** www.lib.washington.edu/subject/canadian/internment/
**United States Holocaust Museum:** www.ushmn.org
**Dieppe Raid Gallery:** www.harrypalmergallery.ab.ca
**Imperial War Museum:** www.iwm.org.uk

# You Are There You Are There

The Dieppe raid was a stunning disaster for the Canadian troops that took part. Today, the debate still rages over the real military worth of the operation. Your class has been appointed to conduct an investigation into the Dieppe raid. Some of you are investigators, whose job is to prepare questions, analyze documents, interview witnesses and report your conclusions. Others among you are witnesses. You may be called upon to testify on the raid in your role as:

a) citizens of Dieppe who saw the raid
b) German officers and soldiers
c) Canadian officers and soldiers who were captured
d) Canadian officers and soldiers who escaped
e) the Canadian and British officers who planned the raid.

Still others are reporters. Your job is to report on the proceedings on a day-to-day basis.

# Point

**Counterpoint**

With which of the following statements do you most agree? Why?

With which of the following statements do you least agree? Why?

Although the fight over conscription during World War II was less divisive than during the First World War, it nevertheless strained Canadian unity. Whether government should be able to force its citizens to go to war to kill and be killed is a difficult issue.

**"Parliament, according to my belief, has no mandate to vote conscription. I do not myself believe that I am held to conform to the law and I have no intention of doing so."**

> Camillien Houde,
> Mayor of Montreal, interned during the war
> for his views on conscription.

**"Not necessarily conscription, but conscription if necessary."**

> Prime Minister King
> trying to avoid splitting the country over
> this divisive issue.

**"Germany must be defeated, even if we all have to live like the Germans."**

> *Saturday Night* magazine suggesting a loss of
> freedom was necessary in an all-out war.

**"Conscript wealth as well as men."**

> Campaign slogan of CCF political party
> in 1942 election campaign.

# Introduction

## The Baby Boom

IN CONTRAST TO THE DIFFICULTY EXPERIENCED BY SOLDIERS RETURNING from the First World War, Canadian soldiers made a smooth transition after World War II. They were ready to settle down, get married and raise families. For the next 20 years, Canada experienced the biggest baby boom of its history. As Canadian families continued to grow, they moved out of the cities into surrounding areas, into what we now call suburbs. Cars, freeways and shopping malls were built to accommodate this growth.

American investment in Canada's natural resources increased greatly during the 1950s and provided many jobs for Canadians. The construction of the St. Lawrence Seaway was symbolic of the economic and political partnership between the United States and Canada. Some Canadians, however, were concerned about the extent of America's control over our economy.

The 1950s and 1960s saw the rise of the teenager. By the mid 1960s, more than 25% of Canada's population was under the age of 25. Social and political protests became typical of the time as Canada's young questioned the values and morals of their elders.

## METHODS OF HISTORICAL ANALYSIS

### Research, Record and Organize

The research process is closely connected to the organizational process. Historians must learn to distinguish between **relevant information** and **irrelevant facts**. Often, this distinction is determined by the topic in question. Some facts and information may be suitable to one topic, but unsuitable to another. Having a good—i.e., specific and focused—**thesis statement** also helps determine what is appropriate information and what is not.

# Chapter Five:
## The Baby Boom

# Expectations

## General Expectations
**By the end of this chapter, you will be able to:**
- describe the impact of technological development on Canadian society
- explain how Canadians adapted to challenges of the "Cold War"
- describe the economic factors that resulted in prosperous economic times after 1945

## Specific Expectations
**By the end of this chapter, you will be able to:**
- explain how cars and television impacted Canadian society during the 1950s and 1960s
- describe how the life of a teenager changed because of the increase in consumerism and leisure during the 1950s
- analyze how American investment affected the lives of Canadians
- identify the different groups of immigrants that came to Canada after the Second World War
- explain the challenges faced by different prime ministers of the period
- describe how the Cold War affected the lives of ordinary Canadians

## WORD LIST

| | | |
|---|---|---|
| Closure | Minority Government | Refugee |
| Cold War | Naturalized citizen | Suburbs |
| Commuter Age | Nuclear age | Urban planning |
| Democratic Socialism | Referendum | War Bride |

# *Advance* Organizer

## 1

In 1949, Newfoundland entered Confederation as the tenth province. Joey Smallwood spearheaded the movement for union with Canada. He became Newfoundland's first premier. The province has since progressed rapidly in many areas. Once solely dependent upon the fishing industry for

its economy, Newfoundland developed the industries of mining and forestry. The province now faces the prospect of new wealth in the form of deposits of oil and natural gas.

## 2

A wave of prosperity swept Canada in the fifties. Western oil and natural gas reserves yielded new sources of power for Canadian industry. Pipelines for oil and gas were built. Large bodies of water were harnessed to generate electricity. Uranium deposits were found, promising future benefits from nuclear power. As new resources were discovered, new industries developed. The St. Lawrence Seaway was constructed to aid in the transport of materials.

This economic growth was largely due to foreign investment, much of it American. Such investment brought Canada a much-desired prosperity during the 1950s and 1960s. Unfortunately, it also led to future conflicts over the ownership and financial control of Canada's resources.

## 3

With the end of the Second World War, the future looked bright for Canada. Returning soldiers and their brides were ready to raise families in these peaceful and prosperous times. Over four million babies were born in Canada during the 1950s.

The educational system had to accommodate the unexpected youth explosion. For the first time, teenagers became a driving force in Canadian society. Business began looking to the new teenage market. There arose a new "pop culture," one that often rebelled against society's traditional values. It found its greatest voice in a new form of popular music: rock 'n' roll.

**4**

The era of the postwar boom saw Mackenzie King's resignation as prime minister. His successor, Louis St. Laurent, was defeated by John Diefenbaker's Conservatives. Diefenbaker in turn was defeated by Lester Pearson's Liberals. Labour union leaders and members of the CCF party saw the need for a strong third voice, one that would uphold workers' rights. The two groups banded together and in 1961 formed the New Democratic Party. NDP ideas have found their way into important policies such as Medicare.

**5**

The rebellious streak of the 1950s came into full bloom in the 1960s. The youth culture was now accompanied by more concrete ideas. Social and political protest was typical of the times. The new patterns of lifestyle, music and dress reflected a desire for tolerance and peace in the world. Much of the rebellion was focused on the hopelessness of the Vietnam War.

**6**

Canada celebrated its 100th year of Confederation on July 1, 1967. This was a year that Canadians gloried in their country. People from all over the world attended Expo '67, held in Montreal. The election the next year of the new prime minister, Pierre Trudeau, gave people hope for a bright future.

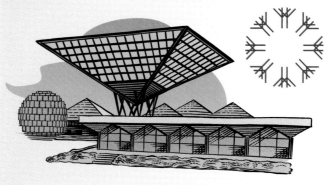

# Adjusting to Peace

**1**

In the fall of 1945, Canada once again faced a period of postwar adjustment as soldiers, sailors, pilots, nurses and mechanics returned home from the war. Could the Canadian economy provide jobs for the million people returning to civilian life?

*Barbara Ann Scott opened the postwar era by dazzling the world at the 1948 Winter Olympic Games, where she won a gold medal.*

Would it make a smooth transition from a war economy to a consumer-based one? Those who remembered the slump after the First World War and the Great Depression of the 1930s shuddered at what might happen.

The end of the Second World War introduced the world to the **nuclear age**. The United States had been the first country to develop and use atomic weapons. It had emerged from the Second World War as the world's strongest military power. The war also caused friction between the powerful communist Soviet Union and the equally powerful Western democracies. Each side searched for ways to secure its control over lands and to extend its political influence. The **Cold War** that resulted caused worldwide fear and tension. Not a fighting war in the usual sense, the Cold War was a war of words, propaganda and threats between the Soviet Union and the United States, and their respective allies.

This underlying insecurity made postwar adjustment a challenging task. Unlike the First World War, revenge on Germany was not an issue. The Allies agreed that global economic prosperity was necessary for lasting world peace. They thought that a prosperous Europe and Japan would not be tempted by communist ideas. By helping Japan and Europe rebuild their economies, they hoped to spread democracy throughout the world.

Economic recovery after the war was spectacular. Canadians shared in the general prosperity.

*Business boomed after the war. This barbershop circa 1950 looks a lot different than barbershops do today. What are some of the differences?*

America gave Europe billions of dollars to rebuild the devastation the war had caused. The economic renewal of Europe, however, would also help North America. Europeans would be able to buy North American products. World trade would then increase and more jobs would be created.

Canada's participation in the war had brought the country closer to the United States. Part of the Canadian war effort was coordinated with that of the Americans. After the war, American investments in Canada's resource sector increased.

Economic recovery after the war was spectacular. Canadians shared in the general prosperity. Manufacturing in Canada greatly increased as the war economy quickly became a consumer economy. People spent a lot of money on consumer goods. They bought cars, homes and electric appliances at an impressive rate. Overall, Canadians enjoyed a good life after the war.

BORN: 1874, Berlin (Kitchener), Ontario

DIED: 1950, Ottawa, Ontario

SIGNIFICANCE: Prime minister for almost 22 years, King introduced old-age pensions, unemployment insurance and family allowances.

BRIEF BIOGRAPHY: Grandson of William Lyon Mackenzie, the famed radical who led the Upper Canada Rebellions, Mackenzie King was prime minister more than two decades. After graduating from the University of Toronto in 1895, King studied economics at Harvard University and the University of Chicago. He entered politics shortly thereafter, becoming Canada's first deputy minister of labour in 1900. In 1909, he entered Laurier's Liberal Cabinet as minister of labour. When Laurier retired in 1919, King was appointed his successor.

During his time as leader of Canada, King's political views changed quite drastically. At first, he believed that government intervention was bad for the country. As a result, he did very little to lessen people's financial problems or worries during the Depression. By 1940, however, King's views began to change. He realized that some government intervention was necessary to keep the country strong and secure. In 1940, he introduced unemployment insurance and, after the war, family allowance.

King was a curious mixture of opposites. He never married and had few close friends. Outsiders regarded him as a practical, down-to-earth and ruthless politician. Yet his diary shows that this tough political realist wept for hours at the death of his pet dog. He also believed he received messages from the spirit of his dead mother.

King had recognized the abilities and dedication of two of his members of Parliament, C.D. Howe and Louis St. Laurent. St. Laurent became minister of justice in 1941. His support in Quebec was important for King when the conscription issue came to the forefront. When King retired, St. Laurent became the new leader of the Liberal Party. C.D. Howe held several Cabinet positions in King's government. He was referred to as the "minister of everything."

## William Lyon Mackenzie King

BORN: 1882, Compton, Quebec

DIED: 1973, Quebec City, Quebec

SIGNIFICANCE: As Canada's second French Canadian prime minister, St. Laurent began construction of the Trans-Canada Highway and the St. Lawrence Seaway. He also lead the country through a period of tremendous growth.

BRIEF BIOGRAPHY: Born to a French Canadian father and an Irish mother, St. Laurent believed that all children spoke French to one parent and English to another. It was not until he entered school at the age of 6 that St. Laurent realized the uniqueness of his bi-cultural family. He graduated from Laval University in 1905 with a law degree. In 1941, Prime Minster King asked St. Laurent to become minister of justice in King's Liberal government. St. Laurent accepted and was elected to the House of Commons the following year. He supported King's position on conscription—the only Quebec Liberal MP to do so—and represented Canada at the meeting to establish the United

Nations. In 1946, however, King made St. Laurent secretary of state for external affairs. St Laurent was a strong believer in Canada's membership in NATO, as he believed that Canadians must fight communism alongside our democratic allies. In 1948, when Mackenzie King retired from politics, St. Laurent became the new Liberal leader. He won sweeping victories in the 1949 and 1953 elections. As prime minister, he was responsible for making the Supreme Court of Canada the final court of appeal instead of the British Privy Council. He started construction of the St. Lawrence Seaway and the Trans-Canada Highway. In 1957, however, in response to the problems associated with the Trans-Canada pipeline, St. Laurent was narrowly defeated by Diefenbaker's Conservatives. At the age of 74, he retired from politics and returned to law. He died in 1973. For someone who once said, "I know nothing of politics and never had anything to do with politicians," St. Laurent successfully led the country through a period of tremendous change and prosperity.

## Louis St. Laurent

**The de Havilland Beaver** As a successor of the Noorduyn Norseman, this all-purpose bush plane of the Canadian North first flew on August 16, 1947. The specifications of the de Havilland Beaver were based on the results of a questionnaire sent out by "Punch" Dickens—Canada's aviation pioneer. Dickens first started flying in during the First World War, where he received the Distinguished Flying Cross for bravery. In 1927, he joined Western Canada Airways and demonstrated the value of the bush plane—a small plane able to fly over the vast distances of the North. After running 6 British Commonwealth Air Training Plan schools during the Second World War, Dickens joined de Havilland Aircraft as director in 1947. The de Havilland Beaver, Dickens first airplane, was a marvel in the industry. It was able to take off in 181 metres. It could carry 6 passengers, a pilot and heavy loads. The Beaver saw service in the Arctic, the Antarctic, Africa and the Andes. Indeed, its service in Antarctica was so valuable that a lake, glacier and island were named after it. By 1965, 1,600 Beavers were in operation in 63 countries. Its biggest customer was the United States' Army.

BORN: 1886, Waltham, Massachusetts

DIED: 1960, Montreal, Quebec

SIGNIFICANCE: This "American by birth, Canadian by choice," has been called the minister of everything. Howe was responsible for mobilizing Canada during the Second World War so that we produced enough goods for the soldiers overseas.

BRIEF BIOGRAPHY: After graduating from Boston Tech in 1907, C.D. Howe went on to teach civil engineering at Dalhousie University in Halifax, Nova Scotia. In 1913, he moved to Thunder Bay, Ontario to build grain elevators. "I've never seen one of these things in my life," he admitted, "but I'll take the job." From 1913 until 1929, Howe built grain elevators across Canada—from Prince Rupert B.C. to Prescott, Quebec. When his business collapsed during the Depression, he decided to enter politics. In 1935, Howe was elected as a Liberal and made minister of transport. By 1936, he had reorganized the harbour system and the CNR, and had set up the CBC. The following year, Howe created Trans-Canada Airlines, our first national airline. As minister of munitions and supply during the Second World War, Howe harnessed government industry and entire work forces to support the war effort. Under his expert command, tanks, planes and ships rolled out of factories to be used overseas in Europe. Despite being torpedoed by a German U boat and spending 8 hours clinging to a lifeboat before being rescued, Howe survived the war and, in 1945, became minister of trade and commerce, and minister of reconstruction and supply. During the Korean War in 1951, Howe was made minister of defence production. In 1954, Howe organized the route for the Trans-Canada pipeline, which ran from Alberta to central Canada. To get the pipeline construction started, Howe arranged a huge government loan, which he forced through parliament by using "closure." Howe was defeated in the 1957 election mostly over the closure issue, and retired from politics.

## C.D. Howe

FOCUS

1. Give three examples of the way Canada boomed after the war.
2. How did Mackenzie King's policies change during the period he was in power?
3. In what way did American influence in Canada grow after the war?
4. What contributions were made by St. Laurent while he was prime minister?

# 2 Newfoundland and Labrador Join Canada

*Canada cannot be considered
complete without Newfoundland.
It has the key to our front door.*

Sir John A. Macdonald

The vastness of Canada's land mass is impressive. The island of Newfoundland thrusts out from the east coast of Canada into the Atlantic. Its capital, St. John's, is 5,050 kilometres from Victoria, B.C. and only 3,800 kilometres (by airplane) from London, England. Over the centuries, Newfoundlanders remained isolated from mainland Canada, adapting, instead, to a maritime life and developing their own dialect and culture. It is no wonder that they retained strong ties to Britain and did not join Canada in 1867.

*Hart's Cove, Newfoundland*

Indeed, the island remained a British colony until 1949.

For centuries, Newfoundlanders fished for cod and hunted seal. The island's rugged interior offered a variety of natural resources. Lumbering provided most of the wood islanders needed. Deposits of iron ore, copper, lead and zinc created a vibrant mining industry. These resources were sold to Britain and the West Indies. In return, Newfoundland imported the manufactured and agricultural products the people needed.

## The Great Depression and Newfoundland

The Depression of the 1930s hit Newfoundland and Labrador very hard. By 1934, one third of its workers were out of work as world trade decreased and the demand for natural resources slumped. The average family income sank to $150 a year. The island's accumulated debt was so high that the government was unable to pay interest on its loans. The Dominion of Newfoundland was bankrupt.

The islanders asked Britain for help and, in 1933, an investigation of the island's political and economic condition was carried out. Britain established a government by a commission, and took control of Newfoundland's finances. The commission, made up of 6 appointed representatives, 3 from Newfoundland and 3 from Britain.It was responsible solely to Britain, not to Newfoundland.

**March 31, 1949.** Joe Smallwood, Canada's last "Father of Confederation," became the first Premier of Canada's tenth province.

## Strategic Position During the Second World War

During the Second World War, Newfoundland's isolation came to an end. Its location between North America and Europe made it a vital part of the sea and air wars against Germany. American and Canadian money and technology poured into the island. St. John's became a headquarters for ships on convoy duty. New airport facilities were built at Goose Bay in Labrador and at Gander on the island. These were important refueling stations for North American aircraft on the way to the battles of Europe. American military bases were built near Quidi Vidi Lake (Fort Pepperell), Stephenville (Ernest Harmon Field) and at Argentia. These military investments brought economic benefits to many communities on the island. Several military bases remained functional until the 1990s. Indeed, Gander still serves as an international airport today, although some of its functions are no longer operating.

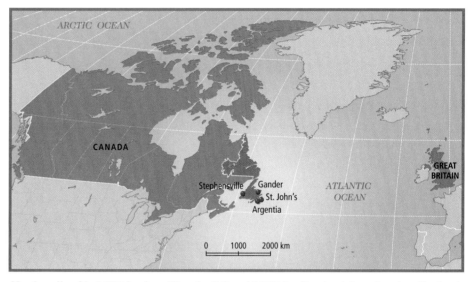

*Newfoundland is 5,050 km from Victoria, BC and 3,800 km (by plane) from London, England.*

## Referendum

After the war, Britain was burdened with the challenging task of re-building its own country and economy, and wanted less responsibility for its colonies. It was time to establish a more democratic form of government in Newfoundland and Labrador, and give the islanders more independence.

Newfoundlanders debated the options available to them. Should the island go back to "responsible self-government" and run its own affairs? Should it stay with the appointed commission responsible to Britain? Or, as some residents suggested, should it join Canada?

The people of Newfoundland voted on the three options in a **referendum**. The initial result was inconclusive—no single option received a majority of the votes. A second referendum was held on the two most popular options: responsible government or Confederation with Canada.

Pro- and anti-Confederation leaders made passionate speeches to convince voters. Gov-

# CANADIAN LIVES

BORN: 1900, Gambo, Newfoundland

DIED: 1991, St. John's, Newfoundland

SIGNIFICANCE: As Canada's last Father of Confederation, he brought Newfoundland into Confederation in 1949.

BRIEF BIOGRAPHY: Born into a poor family, Smallwood started his career as a journalist. He moved to New York City in 1920—where he wrote for a left-wing paper. When Smallwood returned to Newfoundland in 1925, he continued his socialist activities by becoming a union organizer, and his journalism career by becoming a radio broadcaster. In 1946, Smallwood was elected to a convention to advise the British government on what to do with Newfoundland. The British government wanted to hold a referendum on Newfoundland's political future and wanted these delegates to advise on what choices they should put forth on the referendum. Smallwood favoured Confederation. Newfoundlanders voted in 2 referendums (the first was inconclusive) and, in 1948, they voted in favour of Confederation. Smallwood—a Liberal by that time—was appointed leader of an "interim" government and, in 1949, was elected premier in Newfoundland's first provincial election. Although not seriously challenged for 20 years, Smallwood's government was plagued with problems and embarrassments. His attempt at forced industrialization ended in bankruptcy for most of the manufacturing plants involved, and his economic advisor was jailed for stealing money. Smallwood lost the 1971 election and resigned from politics in 1979. He published 2 volumes of a planned 4-volume *Encyclopedia of Newfoundland* and was made a Companion to the Order of Canada in 1986.

## Joey Smallwood

ernment workers thought they would lose some of their power if Newfoundland joined Canada. Merchants were afraid Canadians would move in on their markets. Fishery workers, loggers and miners were attracted to the economic security Confederation would bring. Joining Canada would give them long-term benefits and stability, such as unemployment insurance and old age pensions. Joey Smallwood, a popular broadcaster, led the campaign for union with Canada.

When the final votes were tallied, 52% of the islanders were in favour of joining Canada and 48% for responsible self-government. The people of Newfoundland had spoken. Newfoundland and Labrador entered Confederation on March 31, 1949. Joey Smallwood became the first Premier of Canada's tenth province and, arguably, Canada's last "Father of Confederation."

## A CLOSER LOOK AT LABRADOR

In 1763, when France gave up its colonies to Britain, Labrador was one of them. But, even then, the dispute over who should govern Labrador was a complex one. Newfoundland wanted to govern it because the Labrador coast was part of its fishing territory. Quebec, on the other hand, laid claim to Labrador because it was part of the mainland—physically closer to Quebec than Newfoundland. The British tried to please both parties. In 1809, they decided to grant part of Labrador to Newfoundland, particularly its coastal areas, and to allow the few who used it the right to the western part of the vast territory.

In 1902, the Newfoundland government granted a lumber licence to a company who wanted to log some trees in Labrador's interior — an area south of Hamilton River. This angered Quebec officials because they said the land south of the river belonged to Quebec. Neither side could reach an agreement, so Canada, on behalf of Quebec and Newfoundland took the matter to the Privy Council in 1904. Canada claimed all the land south of the Hamilton River for Quebec. Newfoundland, claimed all the land where rivers drained into the Atlantic Ocean. The argument continued for years, but the Privy Council eventually reached a verdict. In 1927, it voted in favour of Newfoundland.

When Newfoundland joined Confederation in 1949, it made sure that Labrador remained under its control. The province of Quebec, however, has never felt that the Privy Council's decision was fair. Although the land dispute is not considered settled for the moment, it appears to be dormant.

FOCUS
1. What jobs did the people of Newfoundland depend on?
2. What happened to Newfoundland during the Depression?
3. Who led the campaign for Newfoundland to join Canada?
4. Why did Newfoundlanders decide to enter Confederation?

# The Boom in Resources

**3**

February 13, 1947 was an important day in the history of Alberta oil exploration. After drilling 133 dry wells and spending $23 million, Imperial Oil struck "black gold." Its drilling of "Leduc Number 1" was the first major hit in Alberta's oil fields. The discovery of oil transformed Alberta's economy and the standard of living of its residents.

Other American oil companies invested money in searching for oil deposits. Additional fields were discovered in Redwater, Pembina and Joffre in Alberta. In Saskatchewan, too, oil was discovered near Steelman and Weyburn. Natural gas was another important resource found in various areas of the West.

Canada developed an ample supply of fuel for its industrial and domestic needs. These fuels powered Canada's factories and transportation systems. They also provided heat for homes, schools and businesses. Over 20,000 oil and gas wells had been drilled in Canada by 1960. This new petroleum industry created thousands of direct and indirect jobs for Canadians. Once in production, governments received **royalties** from oil companies.

## Energy and Minerals

Canada was also developing massive hydroelectric projects. Canada's rivers were ideal for damming to produce hydroelectric power. Several generating stations were constructed in British Columbia, Labrador, Manitoba, Northern Quebec and along the St. Lawrence River. Power lines were constructed to deliver electric power to remote farming areas and rural towns. Many Canadians had access to electrical

The fabulous fifties brought considerable prosperity to parts of Canada. Unfortunately, they also sowed the seeds for major problems in the future.

| 1900 | 1910 | 1920 | 1930 | 1940 | 1950 | 1960 | 1970 | 1980 | 1990 |

power for the first time.

Prospectors found uranium deposits in several areas of Canada. The increased knowledge about radiation had encouraged research into the peaceful use of atomic energy. Canada became a world leader in the study of atomic energy throughout the post-war era. This research resulted in the design and production of the CANDU nuclear reactor to produce electricity. Canada exported the rights to the CANDU technology to several countries, including Romania, Argentina, the Republic of Korea and China.

The booming American economy created a huge demand for Canadian natural resources. Wood, coal, iron ore, aluminum and copper were demanded by American manufacturers. Many American companies invested in Canada's natural resource industries in order to make money. This investment provided many jobs for Canadians. Towns sprang up in what seemed to be pure wilderness. People had to be served, and roads, airports and railways were quickly built. Additional jobs were created with the construction of schools and health care facilities.

Not all Canadians shared in the economic boom. Most of

*Mining in Canada was big business after the war. Here, trucks climb a roadway from an open pit mine in Sault Ste. Marie.*

*This map shows some of Canada's vast mineral resources in the 1950s.*

the Atlantic region was barely touched by the new wealth. The Prairies still relied mainly on wheat farming. They were rich one year and poor the next because of supply and demand in world markets. Although an age of prosperity, poverty was still a reality in many areas of Canada during the 1950s.

Central Canada benefited most from the economic boom. Most of the manufacturing, commercial and financial centres were located there. Many of the resource developments in other provinces were owned by corporations with headquarters in Toronto, Montreal and New York.

The Canadian landscape was often treated with little respect. Developers simply tore the wealth from the earth. They left permanent scars behind them, from open pit mines and clear-cut logging operations. They poured pollution into the rivers and into the air, with little or no concern about possible environmental effects.

Prosperity had a price. Much of the natural resource industry was American-owned and controlled as investment dollars originated in the United States. By 1956, American companies controlled over half of the manufacturing companies in Canada. Of the sixty

largest firms in Canada, less than thirty were Canadian-owned. It was a trend that was increasing rapidly. Were Canadians losing control of their economy?

The fabulous fifties brought considerable prosperity to parts of Canada. Unfortunately, they also sowed the seeds for major problems in the future.

### The Pipeline Debate

Oil and gas from western Canada had to be transported to Ontario and Quebec. Although Canada had relied on rail transportation for minerals and grain, this was not a practical way to transport large amounts of oil. The best way seemed to be by pipeline. The construction of a Trans-Canada pipeline would involve massive amounts of money and long-term construction.

The first oil pipeline was routed, in part, through the United States. St. Laurent's Liberal government preferred an all-Canadian

route, but the Canadian route would increase construction costs. C.D. Howe, minister of trade and commerce, agreed to lend tax dollars to construction companies to cover the extra costs. The Conservatives and the CCF objected. They claimed that Canadian money was financing American construction companies. An emotional debate followed in Parliament. St. Laurent's Liberal government cut the debate short by using a controversial procedure known as **closure**. In the end, the loan was approved by Parliament and, in 1956, the construction of the Trans-Canada pipeline resumed. By 1960, the 3,600-kilometre pipeline connected Alberta oil fields to Ontario and Quebec consumers.

Conservatives and CCF politicians were concerned about foreign control. Canadians, too, were concerned with the Liberal approach. As a general rule, voters do not like to see closure used because it limits democratic debate. People saw it as a heavy-handed approach. In the election of 1957, Canadians expressed their dislike of the Liberals' use of closure, and elected Diefenbaker's Conservatives. The political careers of C.D. Howe and St. Laurent had come to an end. Ironically, the pipeline loans were repaid not only in full, but also ahead of schedule.

**FOCUS**

1. Name 3 sources of energy that helped create the economic boom.
2. What regions of Canada did best from the boom? Why?
3. What regions gained little from the boom? Why?
4. What problems grew from the resource development of the 1950s?

*Deep River, Ontario*

**Deep River** Established in 1945 to serve scientists hired by the Chalk River Nuclear Laboratories (CRNL), Deep River, one of the few government-manufactured communities in Canada, once boasted the highest per-capita Ph.D. level and the highest birth rate in Canada. Not surprisingly, CRNL tried to keep its educated, high calibre staff by ensuring that schools, clubs, hospitals and community services maintained levels of excellence unsurpassed by many northern Ontario towns. By 1955, there were over 50 clubs active in Deep River, including a chess club, a theatre troupe and a Symphony Orchestra. Outdoor activities, however, were a mainstay for Deep River residents. The north part of Algonquin Park is only minutes away, as are the sandy beaches of the Ottawa River. Hiking, fishing, cross-country skiing and camping are just a few of the activities enjoyed by residents. While never a densely populated town, Deep River's population peaked in 1966 at 5,700, most of whom were employed at the NCRL. Today, government cutbacks have seriously limited job opportunities for the families of the Chalk River scientists. Many must leave to find work in urban centres, such as Ottawa, Montreal and Toronto. Although still a vibrant community, Deep River's population is now about 4,700.

**Nuclear Energy**  As part of the war effort, a group of Canadian, British and some French scientists working out of McGill University, began to research nuclear reactors. In 1945, they opened the ZEEP (Zero Energy Experimental Pile) in Chalk River, Ontario, the first nuclear reactor outside the United States. Concerned with peaceful ways to use nuclear power, Canada's nuclear research teams have been world-renowned for their discoveries. Six years after it was established, the nuclear reactor in Chalk River produced the world's first cobalt radiotherapy treatment for cancer. In 1962, the Nuclear Power Demonstration Plant—Canada's first nuclear power plant—was opened in Rolphton, Ontario. This generator was based on the CANDU design, a unique power plant system invented in Canada. What makes CANDU reactors unique is that they can be refueled without being shut down, which makes them highly efficient.

*Inside a CANDU reactor*

# The St. Lawrence Seaway

The St. Lawrence River proved to be too challenging and rugged to be conquered. For 400 years, from Jacques Cartier in 1535 until the 1950s, the turbulent Lachine rapids prevented travel upstream from Montreal.

*Ships waiting for the opening of the St. Lawrence Seaway.*

The opening of the St. Lawrence Seaway in 1959, however, finally allowed ships to travel from Lake Superior to the Gulf of the St. Lawrence.

Construction of the St. Lawrence Seaway in the 1950s was an example of economic cooperation between Canada and the United States. Historically, the Great Lakes provided a waterway for both countries. Both nations needed access to their hinterland. Grains, minerals and manufactured products had to find a way to their markets. The Great Lakes were deep enough to accommodate seagoing vessels, but their geography provided challenges.

Throughout the 1800s, investors on both sides of the border realized the benefits of canals. Between 1855 and 1900, canals were built between Lakes Superior and Huron in the Sault Ste. Marie area.

In 1824, construction of the first Welland Canal began in Ontario. The 42-kilometre water route connected Lakes Erie and Ontario, bypassing Niagara Falls. As commerce increased, the canal was rebuilt several times. By 1932, the Welland Canal was large enough to accommodate ocean going vessels. It could handle vessels 23 metres wide and 225 metres long.

Although, Americans and Canadians had discussed the possibility of a

Construction of the St. Lawrence Seaway in the 1950s was an example of economic cooperation between Canada and the United States.

joint venture on several occasions, an agreement to build a seaway was defeated in the American Senate in 1932. The idea was revived again in 1940, however, when Canada and the United States signed another agreement. Pressure from American railway and mining companies in the eastern States opposed the tentative agreement.

Canada needed the seaway. The Canadian west needed to get its agricultural products to eastern markets. New mines in Quebec and Labrador needed a way to get the minerals to smelters and factories in Hamilton, Toronto and Chicago.

Since heavy equipment was going to be on site, planners decided to build new power generating stations at the same time. New hydro stations planned in Ontario and Quebec would be cost effective and would provide economic and social benefits to Canadians living along the St. Lawrence River.

Canada decided to build the seaway on its own. This caused the United States to reconsider negotiations and an agreement was reached in 1954. Each country would pay and build sections of the seaway that were located in its territory. Costs of common sections on the St. Lawrence River would be shared.

*Queen Elizabeth II officially opened the St. Lawrence Seaway in 1959.*

Construction of the project was a difficult one as rapids had to be overcome. Lands were flooded and 6,500 Canadians were relocated. Construction costs were enormous. Nevertheless, the project was completed and, in 1959, the St. Lawrence Seaway was officially opened by Queen Elizabeth II and the American president, Dwight Eisenhower.

FOCUS
1. Give 3 reasons why Canada needed the St. Lawrence Seaway.
2. How did Canadians and Americans divide the work of building the seaway?
3. How did the seaway affect people in towns that were in its path?

### War Brides

The Depression and the Second World War had restricted immigration into Canada. Many soldiers serving in Great Britain, Holland and Belgium had married European women. When the war ended, these **war brides** joined their husbands in Canada. About 48,000 war brides and 21,000 children came to Canada. This represented the first large wave of postwar immigration.

*War brides sometime had a difficult time adjusting to life in their new country.*

### Immigration

In the postwar period, more immigrants came to Canada than at any time since 1913. Many were from the British Isles and Western Europe; some were **refugees** (displaced persons) from Communist-controlled countries in Eastern Europe.

Prime Minister King had stated that Canada's immigration policy would preserve "the fundamental character of the population." He meant that it would remain mainly European and white. Very few questioned that immigrants would come from Europe, and would exclude groups from Asia or the West Indies.

Gradually, the numbers of immigrants from Italy, Greece, the Ukraine and other parts of southern and eastern Europe increased, which changed the character of cities such as Toronto and Montreal. Canada began to lose its largely British and French nature. By the late 1960s, Prime Minister Trudeau recognized that Canada would be not only a bilingual country, but a multicultural society as well. Immigrants from the West Indies, Asia, Africa, the Middle East and Latin America were welcomed, without reference to race, colour, or religion, as long as they qualified under Canada's immigration laws.

**Canadian Citizenship** Before 1947, there was no such thing as a Canadian citizen. Native-born Canadians and **naturalized immigrants**—immigrants living in Canada for at least 5 years without criminal records—were considered British subjects. The Citizenship Act of 1947, however, conferred Canadian citizenship on all Canadian-born residents and naturalized immigrants. Women's citizenship status also changed. For the first time in history, their status was not dependent on that of their husbands'. Some say that the Citizenship Act helped establish a Canadian identity.

About 48,000 war brides and 21,000 children came to Canada. This represented the first large wave of postwar immigration.

## Refugees

Since 1948, a basic part of Canada's immigration policy has been to accept **refugees** fleeing from political oppression.

During the past 20 years, a number of large groups of immigrants have mysteriously arrived off the shores of Canada by boat, claiming to be refugees. Some Canadians felt that their claims were an abuse of the refugee policy. Yet, in spite of these potential abuses, Canadian policy is still to provide a home for legitimate refugees from oppression. The problem remains of distinguishing legitimate refugees from those seeking to abuse the system.

*These Hungarian refugees were one of the first Eastern Europeans to seek asylum in Canada after the Second World War.*

| IMMIGRATION PATTERNS TO CANADA BY YEAR | | | | | | | |
|---|---|---|---|---|---|---|---|
| 1901 | 55,747 | 1919 | 107,698 | 1948 | 125,414 | 1974 | 218,465 |
| 1906 | 211,653 | 1929 | 164,993 | 1951 | 194,391 | 1980 | 143,117 |
| 1913 | 400,870 | 1934 | 12,476 | 1957 | 282,164 | 1994 | 216 988 |
| 1914 | 150,484 | 1942 | 7,576 | 1964 | 112,606 | 1996 | 194,451 |

FOCUS
1. Explain the term war brides.
2. Why was the refugee issue a concern fo Canadians?
3. How did postwar immigration change the nature of the Canadian population and society?

# The Baby Boom

The Second World War had interrupted the normal pattern for Canadians who had served their country. When the war ended, they were eager to return home, find a job, get married and start a family. As the country's economic situation began to grow, so

did the size of Canadian families. During the **baby boom** our annual birthrate soared from an estimated 300,000 in 1945 to more than 400,00 by 1952. Babies were everywhere. In 1941, children under 5 made up 9.1% of the population. By 1951, they made up 12%. Indeed, by the mid-60s, more than half of Canada's population was under the age of 25.

Women's roles changed dramatically during this period. Although society had allowed them into the work force during the war, social attitudes toward women had really changed very little. When Canadian soldiers returned home from overseas, Canadian women were expected to return to the home. They were seen as the natural guardians of the family. They took that job very seriously, working an average 99 hours a week keeping the home well tended and their children safe. Babies became a popular topic of conversation. Child-rearing advice appeared regularly in magazines and newspapers. Discipline was more relaxed. Play was seen as an important step in a child's physical and intellectual development. Building blocks, trucks and dolls had an educational as

The car came to symbolize one's personal space. One could go to a drive-in movie theatre or restaurants with drive through services.

well as recreational value. Small hands manipulating wooden blocks into castles and buildings helped fine-tune the child's motor coordination. The toy industry blossomed.

## Education

The very large number of children in Canada gave way to radically changed ideas about education. Beginning in 1952 and continuing into the 1960s, baby boomers pushed school enroll-ment levels sky high. Enrollment increased by 668,000 students between 1951 and 1955. By 1961, it increased another 1,200,000. More and more schools had to be built and teachers

During the baby boom, school enrollments soared.

had to be hired to accommodate the mass-es of children attending Canadian schools. When the grandparents of these youngsters

---

## FEW MOTHERS IN STORK DERBY

*This article appeared in a Toronto newspaper in 1961. Thomas Foster was an eccentric former Toronto mayor who set up the baby competition. Could something like that happen today? Why or why not?*

A Toronto Trust Company has $2,500 waiting for three city mothers but few applicants for the money.

All the women have to do is prove they bore the most number of children in wedlock from Dec 10, 1951, to Dec. 10, this year [1961]. Winners in other years had 10 and 9 children respectively.

Deadline for entries in the Foster Stork Derby is Jan. 10. But the Canada Permanent Toronto General Trust Company has had only a handful of tentative inquiries thus far.

The award is set up under the will of Toronto eccen-tric and former mayor Thomas Foster, who lived much of his life alone but revered motherhood...

He revered it so much that he left $10,000 to be distributed to the winners of the four competitions...The $10,000 was to be divided between lawfully wedded Toronto mothers who produced the greatest number of children over 10-year periods, ending in 1955, 1958, 1961 and 1964.

The winner of the present competition—who must have resided within the city of Toronto from a year prior to the first birth claimed—will collect $1,250. The second-place mother will get $800 and the third $450...

had attended school in 1900, most stayed in school for an average of 6 years. Education was a luxury few could afford, especially when crops needed harvesting or parents needed help. For the baby boomers, however, education became a right. Children began to stay in school longer. High school and even university were no longer something only the wealthy could afford to attend.

The **commuter age** had begun as residents might drive as much as one to two hours to and from work. The **suburbs** offered residents single-family homes with more space and less congestion. Construction of new subdivisions created thousands of jobs. Roads, schools, stores, hospitals, utilities and recreation facilities had to be provided.

American influences on Canadian life

*By the 1950s, a car was often a necessity, and many times, it was a family's most valuable possession.*

### Suburbia

The 1950s saw other important changes in Canadian lifestyles. As the population increased because of the baby boom, new subdivisions were constructed outside major cities in what we now call suburbia.

continued to increase in the 1950s. The American car was the perfect example as no Canadian-owned automobile companies existed. Automobiles became the focal point of life in North America—even **urban planning** focused on the car. A national road-building boom took place. Local highways connected suburbs to cities and to new shopping malls. Expressways connected major cities to each other. Road construction created many

Today, people worldwide take plastic products for granted. Plastic was invented before the 1950s, but postwar research made it possible to use this new substance in consumer products. Many toys and industrial products were made available to the public. Perhaps the most important symbol of plastic was the newly developed 1953 Chevrolet Corvette. This American roadster had, and still has today, a fiberglass body on a steel chassis (frame).

jobs and contributed to the general prosperity. The Trans-Canada highway, opened in 1962, helped to link the entire country.

The car came to symbolize one's personal space. One could go to a drive-in movie theatre or restaurants with drive through services. There was no need to get out of the car. Society became "car friendly" during the 1950s as public transit declined in most cities and towns.

**FOCUS**

1. Explain the term "baby boom."
2. How did the baby boom alter Canada's education system?
3. How did it alter the nature of Canadian society?

## Television

In the 1950s, friends dropped in to see a marvelous new invention—television. Families purchased black and white sets in ever-increasing numbers. Adults and children spent countless hours watching TV. For the first time, entertainment, sports, politics and news could be seen by a wide audience on a daily basis. At last, Canadian sports fans could actually see hockey games described earlier on radio by Foster Hewitt on *Hockey Night in Canada*.

Programming reflected family values of the times. American shows such as *Ozzie and Harriet, I Love Lucy* and *My Three Sons* attracted millions of viewers. These programs portrayed ideal, white, middle-class families where everyone got along. They did not reflect all elements of life. Sex, racism, poverty and violence were notably absent from television shows. Many programs targeted children. *Howdy Doody,* Disney's *Mickey Mouse Club, The Flintstones* and Saturday morning cartoons were popular. For Canadians, television also represented a cultural threat. Could Canadian programs compete with American shows? Would Canadian children be influenced by American ideas and values?

Despite the constant fear of American invasion, the 1950s saw Canadian television begin to take hold of our imaginations. A number of programs produced in that decade were tremendously popular with Canadian audiences. *Front Page Challenge,* Canada's longest-running television show ever, debuted in 1957. Intended as a 13-week replacement for another show, *Front Page Challenge* aired for almost 40 years. In a curious mixture of current event subject matter and game show format, a group of panelists were asked to

Front Page Challenge *was a Canadian favourite for almost 40 years. Here Malcolm X is the "mystery guest."*

identify a "mystery guest," usually someone in the news at the time, by asking the guest a series of questions. Over the years guests included Indira Gandhi, Sir Edmond Hillary, Martin Luther King and Gordie Howe. The panelists all became prominent Canadian figures and included Pierre Berton, Betty Kennedy, Gordon Sinclair and Charles Templeton. When it finally went off the air in 1995, a Canadian institution was lost.

*La Famille Plouffe,* written by Roger Lemelin, made its debut on CBC in 1953, as the first serial show on Canadian TV. Essentially a television drama, this French Canadian program kept its viewers tuning in week after week as the tragedies and triumphs of this all-Canadian family unfolded.

Our Pet, Juliette.

Another popular favourite during the 1950s was *Our Pet, Juliette,* a variety show hosted by Manitoba singer, Juliette Augustina Sysak. Perhaps one of Canada's first superstars, Juliette entertained audiences for over 20 years. David Suzuki's *The Nature of Things* first aired on CBC in 1960. Still running 40 years later, *The Nature of Things* probes environmental and scientific concerns.

Some Canadian entertainers enjoyed huge success south of the border. Wayne and Shuster, for example, had performed on the *Ed Sullivan Show* a record-breaking 67 times by 1970. This comedy duo, composed of John Wayne and Frank Shuster, had met years earlier while both were attending the University of Toronto. During the Second World War, Wayne and Shuster met up again, this time writing and performing for the *Army Show.* Knowing a good professional relationship when they saw one, the duo continued performing together after the war, first on radio and later on TV, delighting Canadian and American audiences for years with their zany, slapstick comedy routines.

La Famille Plouffe *was a popular CBC family drama.*

*Wayne and Shuster are perhaps Canada's best remembered comedy duo.*

### Music and Teens

The prosperous 1950s redefined the teenager. The new affluence allowed many teens to stay in school longer, thus postponing entrance into the working world. In the mid-50s, only 5% of students studied beyond high school. Today, over 50% attend college or university. Teenagers developed an attitude and culture of their own. Boys either wore their

**Television** became a powerful advertising medium and it entrenched the age of consumerism. Most advertising was aimed at the young. Play-Doh, Frisbees and Hula Hoops became popular with boys and girls. In 1959, the first Barbie doll was sold. This American icon turned 41-years old with the new millennium. Symbolic of an American beach girl, the Barbie doll was also popular with Canadian children. Most of these products were made from the new wonder product—plastic.

hair in crew-cuts (short and bristly) or duck-tails (long and greasy). Girls wore bobby sox, sweater sets and ruby-red lipstick. Fitting in with the crowd was all-important.

This was the time when portable radios became available. Teens could carry the radio with them as they walked to school or to the mall. The conservative music of the early fifties was replaced by the sounds of Rock and Roll in the mid fifties. The voices of Elvis Presley, Buddy Holly, Canadian Paul Anka and others were recorded on plastic records featuring stereophonic sound. Dancing to Rock and Roll was seen as unnatural or evil by some. Several American and Canadian religious and conservative groups wanted this new music banned. In the 1950s, most popular music was American.

Teenagers of the 1950s demonstrated the same idealism and energy as teens today. Sometimes friction between the adult and teenage worlds developed. The generation gap became, and remains, a matter of concern to some adults.

*Paul Anka was a 1950s teen idol.*

# Canadian Vision

## The Music Industry

Although music during the 1950s and 1960s was mainly imported from Britain and the United States, Canada produced a number of major players who received international acclaim. Neil Young, son of journalist Scott Young, was a founding member of the popular 60s band, Buffalo Springfield. After the band's demise in 1968, Young went solo. Alone, Neil Young had an extremely successful career. His numerous albums have sold in the millions, and he has remained popular for over 30 years. Known recently as the Godfather of Grunge, Young recorded *Mirror Ball* with Pearl Jam in 1995.

Joni Mitchell, born in Macleod, Alberta, in 1943, has had an influential career in the music industry. Her 4th album, *Blue*, recorded in 1971, is still considered one of the best albums of its time. Indeed, it's hard to think of a contemporary female rock star who doesn't have some trace of Mitchell in her music. Alanis Morisette, Courtney Love, P.J. Harvey and Sarah McLachlan owe a great debt to Canada's original folk star.

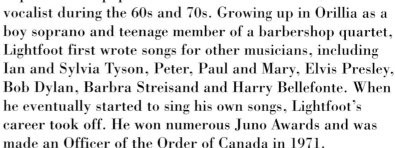

Gordon Lightfoot was perhaps our most popular male vocalist during the 60s and 70s. Growing up in Orillia as a boy soprano and teenage member of a barbershop quartet, Lightfoot first wrote songs for other musicians, including Ian and Sylvia Tyson, Peter, Paul and Mary, Elvis Presley, Bob Dylan, Barbra Streisand and Harry Bellefonte. When he eventually started to sing his own songs, Lightfoot's career took off. He won numerous Juno Awards and was made an Officer of the Order of Canada in 1971.

FOCUS

1. List some popular television shows of the 1950s.
2. Describe teen culture in the 1950s. How does it compare with teen culture today?
3. What Canadian bands and individual performers remain popular today?

# 7 Canada and The Cold War

The 1950s was an exciting decade as modern inventions and general prosperity changed Canadians' lives. It was also a decade of fear. The Cold War between the USSR and the United States made Canadians nervous and fearful. Most noticeable immediately after the war (1947-1953), the Cold War was a war of words, propaganda, espionage and economic pressure between western democracies and the Soviet Union. After the Second World War, Western democracies became concerned about what they saw as the aggressive military expansion of the Soviet Union. At that time, there was a great fear that Italy and France would become communist.

Although our allies during the war, after the Second World War, the Soviets felt that the only way to help war torn countries of Europe was for the Soviets to gain economic and military control over them. The United States disagreed. It felt that Soviet control in eastern Europe would mean a rise in communism—something a capitalist country such as the United States did not want to happen.

The tensions of the Cold War continued throughout the 1950s. Americans and Soviets raced to develop new weapons of mass destruction, with each country desperately trying to outdo the other. In 1952, the U.S. exploded the first hydrogen bomb. After the Soviets successfully launched the world's first spaceship to leave the earth's atmosphere in 1957, the Americans countered by quickly developing spacecraft of their own and intercontinental missiles with nuclear warheads. This nuclear arms race left many fearing that the world was on the verge of nuclear war at any given moment.

## KOREAN WAR

Soviet-American tension grew to a head in 1950, when Soviet-controlled North Korea invaded American-supported South Korea. Many believed this was the first step to a world war between communism and capitalism. Although the Canadian government was somewhat reluctant to send troops after the con-

scription crisis of the Second World War, they eventually sided with the Americans and sent a brigade to serve with UN forces in Korea. The Korean War lasted until 1953. Twenty-two thousand Canadians fought in that war. Three hundred and nine were killed, 1,202 were injured and 32 became POWs.

The Cold War between the United States and the USSR made Canadians nervous and fearful.

Espionage was also a real threat. Igor Gouzenko's unbelieveable tales of Soviet spy infiltration in Canada and, by extension, the United States, convinced many of the seriousness of the Cold War. When the Americans arrested Ethel and Julius Rosen- berg for supposedly passing atomic secrets to the Soviet Union, they were executed for their espionage activities. The threat of nuclear war was not taken lightly. Bomb shelters became the talk of the day for many Canadians.

## COLD WAR DEFENCES

### NATO

In 1949, Canada and the Unites States joined with 10 western European countries to form the North Atlantic Treaty Organization (NATO). Its purpose was to defend Europe and the North Atlantic from Soviet aggression. Although primarily a defensive alliance, NATO had an economic advantage for Canada as well, since such an arrangement binds together all of Canada's trading partners.

NATO was a real threat to the Soviets. In 1955, they formed their own alliance, the Warsaw Pact, with the Soviet satellite countries of Eastern Europe. In the event of attack by NATO countries, the Warsaw Pact members agreed to come to each other's defence.

### NORAD

In 1957, Canada signed a treaty with the United States that created the North American Air Defence System (NORAD). Aimed at protecting North America from Soviet attack—particularly nuclear attack—NORAD joined Canadian and American fighter, missile and radar units under a single command center. NORAD headquarters are located deep inside a mountain in Colorado. The commander in chief is an American general. A Canadian general serves as deputy commander. Both are always in direct contact with the Ameri- can president and the Canadian prime minister, whose approval would be necessary for an attack or counterattack.

### DEW

Canada's geographical position between the Unit- ed States and the Soviet Union makes it vital to North America's defence. Canada worked closely with the U.S. to monitor northern airspace and warn off aircraft that intruded there. In 1957, the United States and Canada built a line of long- range warning stations, known as Distant Early Warning (DEW) stations, to monitor airspace activity. If any station—there were 50 in total— detected missiles or aircraft of unknown origin, it sent a message to NORAD headquarters in Col- orado. Although both Canada and the U.S. were involved in the creation of DEW stations, the $250 million cost of building these radar stations was paid for solely by the United States.

BORN: 1919, Rogachov, Russia

DIED: 1982, Toronto, Ontario

SIGNIFICANCE: Told Canadian government of a widespread espionage activity in Canada, where Russians, among other things, were trying to get their hands on the secrets of the atomic bomb.

BRIEF BIOGRAPHY: While a cipher clerk at the Soviet legation in Ottawa in 1943, Gouzenko discovered that Soviet intelligence operated several spy rings in Canada.

In 1945, he also discovered that he and his family were going to be sent back to Russia. Gouzenko decided to defect. He left the embassy with several documents showing Soviet spy activity in Canada. At first no one believed him, but a few days later, when Soviet officials tried to capture Gouzenko and send him back to Russia, Canadian officials took notice. The government arrested 12 suspects and, after a royal commission, many others were also arrested. Gouzenko was given a new identity and police protection for the rest of his life. He wrote 2 books: a memoir called *This Was My Choice*, published in 1948, and a novel, *The Fall of a Titan*, which won the Governor General's Award for fiction in 1954.

*Fearful for his life, Igor Gouzenko never revealed his face in public.*

## Igor Gouzenko

# Canadian Vision

### THE DIEFENBUNKER

In 1959, fear of a nuclear war prompted the Canadian government to order a massive underground "bomb shelter." The secret project was the focus of speculation by local residents and the media simply because of its size. The government maintained that it was a communications centre and nothing out of the ordinary.

Construction took 2 years. The site was a farm in the town of Carp, near Ottawa. The massive Diefenbunker is a huge four-story structure built totally underground. It is surrounded by 1.5 metres of shock-absorbing gravel on all its sides including top and bottom. All machinery in the bunker (from simple fans to its huge diesel generators), was positioned on specially designed springs to cushion it from the concrete floor.

The underground structure did not require heating or air conditioning. A sophisticated fan and filtered circulation system provided the necessary air. Fresh water was obtained from deep well pipes. Garbage was a problem, so special garburators—crushers and compactors—were designed.

The Diefenbunker was equipped to handle 300 to 500 people for 30 plus consecutive days. It had its own hospital, morgue, cafeteria and bedrooms. The prime minister had a private room with a bath nearby. The CBC had a communication facility to broadcast to Canadians.

In the event of a nuclear emergency, Canada's prime minister, cabinet ministers and the nation's top military officials would be flown by helicopter to the site. These leaders would then carry out emergency communication to the rest of the country from the safety of the shelter.

The Diefenbunker was manned and maintained from 1961 until 1994. It is now a National historic site and it remains open as a tourist attraction. Its name originated from the name of the prime minister of the day—John Diefenbaker.

*You can visit the Diefenbunker website at www.diefenbunker.com*

## FOCUS

1. What was the Cold War?
2. What is NATO?
3. Why is Canada so important to the safety of the United States?
4. How were NORAD and the DEW station's connected?

# The Diefenbaker Years, 1957-1963

**8**

It seemed to Canadians that the Liberal party had been in power forever. From 1935 to 1957, Liberal Prime Ministers King and St. Laurent governed Canada. In 1956, the Conservatives chose a new leader, John Diefenbaker, a small-town lawyer from Prince Albert, Saskatchewan. A fiery orator and passionate Canadian, Diefenbaker brought new life to his party. His leadership coincided with the downfall of the Liberals, as they seemed to be tired and out of ideas. Canadians remembered the Liberals' use of closure during the pipeline debate. It was time for a change.

In the election of 1957, Diefenbaker's Conservatives won 111 seats to the Liberals 105 seats. The CCF won 25 seats and the Social Credit 19. Shortly after the defeat, St. Laurent resigned, and Lester Pearson became the new leader of the Liberal Party and Leader of the Opposition.

Because the Conservatives had a **minority government**, they were forced to negotiate with the opposition parties when legislation was proposed. Claiming that he could not govern this way, Diefenbaker called another election in 1958.

His fiery speeches energized Canadians and resulted in a landslide victory for the Conservatives—the greatest in Canadian history. The Conservatives won 208 seats, while the Liberals and rest of the opposition had only 57 seats combined.

*John Diefenbaker was a tireless campaigner and an excellent public speaker.*

A fiery orator and passionate Canadian, John Diefenbaker brought new life to his party

Diefenbaker tried hard to accommodate all Canadians. He appointed Ellen Fairclough, the first female cabinet minister. James Gladstone's appointment to the Senate made him the first Aboriginal member of the Upper House.

## Bill of Rights

One of Diefenbaker's most lasting contributions to Canadian society was his Bill of Rights, a bill that reflected his dedication to furthering the cause of human rights. For the first time in our history, the freedoms and rights Canadians enjoyed were written into law. They included:

- Freedom of speech, religion and of the press
- Protection of the law without discrimination because of race, colour, religion, sex or national origin
- Right of the individual to life, liberty, and security of the person

The Bill, however, had its limitations as it applied to federal law only. Moreover, the Canadian Parliament retained the right to change the Bill of Rights and to override it in times of national security.

## Disappointments

As the 1950s came to an end, so did the economic boom enjoyed by so many Canadians. Unemployment increased and Diefenbaker's government tried to fix our economy by devaluing the Canadian dollar to 92.5 cents against the U.S. dollar. This made exports cheaper and imports more expensive. Canadians did not favour this move and nicknamed our dollar the "Diefendollar."

Additional controversy followed in 1959, when Diefenbaker and his government cancelled the AVRO ARROW project. Canadian-owned A.V. Roe Company had developed a new jet fighter, the Arrow. Unfortunately, the estimated 12 million dollar cost per plane was a large sum of money back then.

The Arrow was a technological marvel. Some engineers claimed that it was 20 years ahead of its time. Its huge costs, however, would have drained Canada's military budget. Also, the introduction of the "missile age" by the Soviet Sputnik made fighter aircraft seem less important in 1959, although the United States, Great Britain and France continued to build them.

Over 15,000 people lost their jobs in the Toronto area. Many were highly skilled engi-

BORN: 1888, Montreal, Quebec

DIED: 1967, Ottawa, Ontario

SIGNIFICANCE: Governor General of Canada from 1959 until 1967, Georges Vanier emphasised the importance of the family, and did a lot of work for the poor and the young.

BRIEF BIOGRAPHY: After becoming a lawyer in Quebec, Vanier started the 22nd Regiment, the famed Van Doos of the First World War, and served overseas, distinguishing himself with acts of bravery and heroism. He was awarded both the Military Cross and the Distinguished Service Order, two of Canada's highest military decorations, for his outstanding service during the war,

After the war, Vanier served in the Canadian diplomatic corps at the League of Nations and as Canadian ambassador to France from 1944 to 1953. In 1959, John Diefenbaker appointed him to be Canada's first

*Georges and Pauline Vanier*

French-Canadian Governor-General. During his nearly eight years in this vice-regal post, Vanier served with distinction. One of his most noteworthy achievements was the creation, along with his wife Pauline, of the Vanier Institute of the Family in 1965, which still operates as a national charitable organization and focuses on issues such as childhood poverty, family violence and child-care.

After Vanier's death in 1967, his wife, Pauline, continued with the institute's work until her death in 1991. It is not surprising that the Roman Catholic Church is now considering whether these two distinguished Canadians should be declared saints. Their son, Jean, has continued his parents' humanitarian work. In 1964, Jean Vanier established the world's first "L'Arche" in France as a home for the disabled. Today, there are 13 homes in France, 26 in Canada, 9 in the U.S., as well as in many other countries.

## Georges Vanier

neers who specialized in different areas of aviation. Most went to the United States to work for NASA. Canadians blamed Diefenbaker for dealing a crippling blow to the Canadian aircraft industry and for the resulting brain drain.

## BOMARC

Enemy missiles could only be stopped by surface-to-air missiles. To protect Canada from possible missile attack, American BOMARC missiles were purchased and set up in Ontario and Quebec sites. However, more controversy followed Diefenbaker when his government was indecisive about the use of nuclear warheads on the BOMARC missiles in Canada and in Canadian NATO bases in Europe. Canada had no Arrow fighter planes and the BOMARC missiles were worthless to the military without nuclear warheads. Diefenbaker's own party was split over this issue and several members left the party. Lester Pearson, the Liberal Party leader, criticized the government. He stressed that Canada had an obligation to meet its international duties. Canadians had accepted the missiles. They should accept the nuclear warheads, Pearson insisted. Most Canadians agreed. Pearson came

*The Cold War threat of nuclear war prompted many such as Térèse Casgrain (ABOVE) to push for a ban on nuclear weapons.*

across as a decisive leader. In early 1963, Diefenbaker was forced to call an election over the issue. Pearson won his first election with a minority government.

FOCUS
1. Give 3 reasons why voters chose the Conservatives over the Liberals in the election of 1957.
2. How did Diefenbaker try to protect the rights of all Canadians?
3. What problems led to Diefenbaker's defeat in 1963?

# Canadian Vision

## Theatre

Canada has a wide array of popular and critically-acclaimed theatre companies. The Stratford Festival was founded in 1953 when Tom Patterson asked world-renowned theatre director Tyrone Guthrie to head a Shakespearean theatre in Canada. Performed in a tent beside the Avon River in Stratford, Ontario, *Richard III*, starring Alec Guinness, received rave reviews by all in attendance. After realizing that the audience quickly exceeded the existing tent's capabilities, the tent was replaced by a Festival Theatre in 1957. Designed by Canadian architect, Robert Fairfield, for over $2 million, the new theatre was revolutionary for its time. Although the theatre sits 2,262, no audience member is more than 19.8 metres from the stage.

Winnipeg's Manitoba Theatre Centre was created in 1958 as the first of Canada's regional theatres. Founded by Tom Henry and John Hirsch, later artistic director of the Stratford Festival and drama teacher at Yale University, the Manitoba Theatre Centre was applauded by critics worldwide. In 1962, the Canada Council cited it as the model that others should follow. The theatre continues to be widely influential throughout North America.

Halifax's Neptune Theatre was established in 1963 by Tom Patterson (founder of the Stratford Festival) and Leon Major, and was the first theatre in Canada to adopt the repertory system and to perform year round. Neptune's artistic integrity and high standards attracted a number of well-known directors, including Mavor Moore. In 1978, John Neville was appointed artistic director. Although at

*The Stratford Theatre was founded in 1953. Today it is a leading producer of Shakespearean theatre.*

that time the Neptune was experiencing severe financial problems, Neville not only sorted out the difficulties within 5 years, but he also doubled the number of season ticket-holders. In 1983, Neville retired from his position at the Neptune and made his acting debut in the Stratford Festival's *Love's Labour's Lost*. He became artistic director of Stratford in 1985.

**Avro Arrow** Perhaps the most advanced twin engine, supersonic jet of its time, the Arrow was commissioned by the government in 1949 at a cost of $2 million each, because of concern about the threat of Soviet bombers over the Canadian North. At that time, the RCAF was looking for a replacement for their fighter plane—something that would still be used in 10 years, something, in other words, that was years ahead of its time. On October 4, 1957, the first Avro Arrow was unveiled to the public. When it was test flown a few months later, the Arrow exceeded everyone's expectations. The Air Force had requested a plane capable of Mach 2—twice the speed of sound—and the Arrow reached that speed while still climbing and accelerating. Leading-edge technology, however, is not cheap. Canada had to develop the Arrow's engine, and fire-control and missile systems, and the cost rose accordingly. By 1957, each plane

cost the government $12.5 million. The government balked at the prohibitive cost, and orders for the Arrow began to decline from an anticipated 600 in 1953 to only 100 by 1957. Financial problems continued, until, in 1958, the new Conservative government cut the missile and fire-control parts of the development. By this time the United States was beginning to lose interest in the Arrow. It had just come out with the BOMARC missile and the USSR had just launched the ICBM missile, which suggested that Soviet bomber threats were no longer an issue. In 1959, the Diefenbaker government cancelled all orders, and A. V. Roe—the plane's manufacturers—fired 15,000 employees. The planes themselves were completely destroyed on command from the government, as were all plans, drawings, photographs, negatives and films associated with the planes.

# 9

# Lester B. Pearson: The Diplomat

Lester Pearson was a successful Canadian diplomat before becoming prime minister. Here, he is speaking at the United Nations in 1957.

Lester Pearson had been a career diplomat. He held several posts representing Canada in different countries. As Canadian Ambassador to the U.S., he was involved in the formation of the United Nations and oversaw Canada's joining The North Atlantic Treaty Organization (NATO).

In 1948, Pearson entered politics and was elected to the House of Commons. He served as St. Laurent's minister of external affairs. In this capacity, he achieved world attention when he played an important role in ending the Suez Crisis of 1956. He was instrumental in suggesting that the United Nations send troops to keep peace in the area. Canadian troops were included in the UN force, and Pearson was awarded the Nobel Peace Price in 1957 for his leadership. His efforts reinforced Canada's role as peacekeeper and a "middle power."

## Pearson as Prime Minister, 1963-1968

Leading a minority government is not an easy task. The ruling party must obtain some support

The Red Maple Leaf was proudly displayed and came to represent Canada's unique identity.

from opposition parties to stay in power. Pearson did this by introducing policies advocated by the NDP. During Pearson's term in office, Canadians received universal health care and the Canada Pension Plan. In response to women's demands for equality, his government established the Royal Commission on the Status of Women in 1957.

## The Flag and Canadian Identity

Canadian Confederation in 1867 came about in a peaceful way. After much discussion, Nova Scotia, New Brunswick, and Upper and Lower Canada asked the British Parliament to pass the British North America Act, Canada's Constitution. After 1867, Canada was still an extension of Britain and part of the British Empire. In 1931, the Statute of Westminster made Canada an independent country, but it still kept the British flag. Internationally, the Red

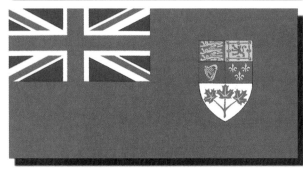

*The new Canadian flag was finally adopted in 1965 after much debate.*

Ensign, a British naval flag with Canada's coat of arms, was flown to represent Canada at such events as the Olympics, international conferences and at our embassies abroad.

Canadians whose background was not British did not share this enthusiasm for the British flag. Many French Canadians did not like the British flag because, for many, it symbolized the English Conquest of 1759-1760. In a way, the flag divided Canadians instead of uniting them.

In 1964, Pearson announced that Canada would choose a new flag. He established a committee to examine more than 2,000 designs. The choice was narrowed to just a few and, after 33 days of bitter debate, the present red maple leaf design was finally chosen. The majority of Canadians quickly identified with the new design. The Red Maple Leaf was proudly displayed and came to represent Canada's unique identity.

*Not all Canadians were happy with the new flag. These supporters of the Red Ensign were protesting on Parliament Hill, 1964.*

### Shadows for the Future

Canadians were concerned about French-English relations in Canada. Quebec's demand for more provincial powers in the 1960s created a unity crisis in Canada. The challenge for the Pearson government was to keep the country united.

Pearson established the Royal Commission on Bilingualism and Biculturalism in 1963 to investigate the relations between French and English Canadians. The commission did an exhaustive investigation into the complaints of the English and French, and made many recommendations in its report. Not all the recommendations were adopted, but the government agreed that the federal civil service should be bilingual. French and English Canadians were to have equal opportunities for promotions in the federal civil service.

Pearson remained prime minister until his retirement in 1968. The Liberal Party then elected a new leader—Pierre Elliot Trudeau.

# PROVINCIAL FLAGS

ONTARIO

QUEBEC

NOVA SCOTIA

NEW BRUNSWICK

MANITOBA

BRITISH COLUMBIA

PRINCE EDWARD ISLAND

SASKATCHEWAN

ALBERTA

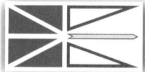

NEWFOUNDLAND

NORTHWEST TERRITORIES

YUKON

Canada's provincial flags are as diverse as Canada's history, and tell of a country made up of many different peoples. Ontario's flag, for example, adopts Britain's Union Jack as its predominant image.

NUNAVUT

Quebec's, on the other hand, celebrates the distinctly French fleur-de-lis. Nunavut's flag features the Inuksuk, a stone monument which guides people on land and marks sacred places.

FOCUS
1.  Why was Lester B. Pearson awarded the Nobel Peace Prize in 1957?
2. Construct a chart of his achievements. Explain in each case whether you think they were positive or negative for Canada.

# 10

# The New Democratic Party

Capitalism in Canada dates back to the fur trade. The Conservatives and the Liberals have dominated power in Canada since 1867, and both parties supported a capitalist economy. In 1933, the new Cooperative Commonwealth Federation (CCF) offered voters the choice of **democratic socialism**.

There is no single definition of democratic socialism. The idea originated over two hundred years ago in Europe and, like other political ideas, has changed over the years. Socialists believe governments must ensure that profits from natural resources and business enterprises should benefit all people, not just investors and owners.

Socialism also encourages regulating **minimum standards** for the social and economic life of the people by setting up pension plans, passing minimum wage laws and establishing welfare programs for the needy.

## Workers' Movements and Labour Unions

In 1956, a number of unions came together to form the Canadian Labour Congress (CLC). This was an umbrella organization that worked to strengthen the workers' movement on a national scale. It had many members, and therefore much more political influence than a single union.

The 1950s also saw a decline in support for the CCF. Canadian Labour Congress and CCF members got together to revive the socialist movement in Canada by forming a new party. In 1961, the New Democratic Party (NDP) was formed, giving Canada's labour movement a political voice. Like the CCF before it, the NDP presented socialist ideals to Canadians.

*NDP rally, 1963*

Today, Canadians are proud of universal health care, old age pensions, family benefits, workers compensation and workplace safety laws. The "social security safety net" policies Canadians enjoy began as social democratic ideas of the CCF and later, the NDP.

**TIMELINE**

1900 1910 1920 1930 1940 1950 1960 1970 1980

Historically, the CCF and NDP have fought for social security programs. Tommy Douglas, the provincial CCF leader in Saskatchewan (1944-61) introduced a government hospital plan and Medicare for his province. The Liberal governments of King, Pearson and Trudeau "borrowed" popular socialist ideas. King's Old Age Pension plan of 1927 was established because of the influence of J.S. Woodsworth. The Pearson Liberals introduced Medicare for all Canadians in the sixties. PetroCanada, the Foreign Investment Review Agency and the National Energy Program were created because of the NDP influence during minority Trudeau governments in the 1970s.

Today, Canadians are proud of universal health care, old age pensions, family benefits, workers compensation and workplace safety laws. The "social security safety net" programs Canadians enjoy began as social democratic ideas of the CCF and later, the NDP.

Provincial NDP candidates have formed governments in several Canadian provinces from the 1970s to the present. On the federal level, however, the NDP has not been as successful. Nevertheless, the party has had considerable influence. There is no doubt that the socialist democrats will fight to try to preserve "the safety net" in the free trade global economy of the new millennium.

## A CLOSER LOOK AT THE CANADIAN LEGION

After the First World War, returning soldiers faced economic hardship because jobs were difficult to find, and the cost of living had risen so much while they had been fighting overseas. Both the federal government and various lobby groups wanted to prevent these problems from happening again. The Canadian Legion of the British Empire Service League was founded in 1926 as Canadian veterans' associations sought to make sure soldiers returning from war would receive all available government benefits. The Legion lobbied for more financial assistance, for educational benefits, insurance and medical assistance. The 1930 War Veterans Allowance was one of the Legion's early achievements. Clothing allowances, pensions, vocational training and preference in civil service employment are other areas in which the Legion has been active. In the 1940s, the Legion founded the "Foster Fathers Program" for boys who had lost fathers in the war. The National Poppy Remembrance Campaign commemorates the memory of those Canadians who died in the military, merchant marine and ferry command services of this country. The Royal Canadian Legion (the name was changed in 1960) has more than 1600 branches in Canada, and contributes millions of dollars annually to community projects across the country.

BORN: 1904, Falkirk, Scotland

DIED: 1986, Ottawa, Ontario

SIGNIFICANCE: Founder of Canada's "social safety" net and the NDP.

BRIEF BIOGRAPHY: Tommy Douglas moved with his family to Manitoba in 1919. He attended the ministry program at Brandon College and was introduced to social gospel—a form of Christianity concerned as much with improving life on earth as with life in the hereafter. He graduated in 1930 as an ordained Baptist preacher and went to Weyburn, Saskatchewan just as the Depression hit. True to his belief that political action was a necessary part of religious life, Douglas joined the CCF Party shortly after. He ran in the 1934 provincial election but lost. The following year, he ran in the federal election and won. For 9 years he was the CCF's agricultural specialist. Renowned for his funny, sarcastic and self-deprecating style, Douglas quickly earned the reputation as one of the best speakers in the House of Commons. He returned to Saskatchewan in 1944, where he became the first social democrat

premier in Canada. His first budget gave 70% to social services, including giving medical and dental care to old-age pensioners, and taking over the cost of all cancer treatment. In 1947, Douglas introduced universal hospital insurance to all Saskatchewan residents. Health care was very important to Douglas, because as a child he had suffered from a serious bone disease. Since his family was poor, they could not afford the proper treatment for the boy and, if it had not been for some lucky coincidences and charitable people, Douglas would have lost his leg to the disease. He did not want others similarly dependent on the generosity of strangers. Douglas believed everyone should have the right to proper medical care, a revolutionary idea to Canadians at the time. In 1960, Douglas decided to put a universal medical care plan into effect that would satisfy both doctors and patients. Although he resigned as premier shortly before the universal medical bill went into effect, he was still in politics when the federal government made Medicare a national program at the end of the decade. Douglas was made a Companion to the Order of Canada in 1980.

## T.C. Douglas

BORN: 1921, Calgary, Alberta

SIGNIFICANCE: Writer, editor and journalist, Doris Anderson has long been one of Canada's leading spokespersons for women's rights.

BRIEF BIOGRAPHY: After returning to Toronto in 1951 from a year of writing in London and Paris, Anderson took a job at *Chatelaine* magazine as an editorial assistant. Within 7 years she was running the magazine. Before Anderson, *Chatelaine* was typical of its time. Countless pages were devoted to the art of domesticity: recipes for feeding a hungry family; tips on being the perfect hostess; and advice for raising the perfect child were all common features of this women's glossy. Anderson, however, had a radically different view of what a woman's periodical should be. She completely revamped the magazine. Not only did she change its physical makeup, but she intro-

duced a feminist slant to her editorials and the stories she commissioned. Women loved it. Under Anderson's leadership, *Chatelaine's* circulation rose from 460,000 to over 1 million readers. Soon, it became Maclean-Hunter's most lucrative magazine.

Anderson left *Chatelaine* in 1977 after a dispute with the publisher. She was appointed to the Canadian Advisory Council on the Status of Women and, in 1982, became president of the National Action Committee on the Status of Women (NAC). She has since published numerous books, including *Rebel Daughter* (1996), *The Unfinished Revolution: Status of Women in Twelve Countries* (1991) and *Affairs of State* (1988). Anderson was made an Officer of the Order of Canada. She won the Person's Award in 1991, and received the YWCA Award for Woman of Distinction in 1983.

## Doris Anderson

FOCUS
1. Why did the CCF lose support after the Second World War?
2. Which two groups formed the New Democratic Party?
3. What is Medicare? Do you think it has been successful in fulfilling its aims?
4. What are some of the NDP's major contributions to Canadian society. Why has our federal government adopted some of its chief policies?

# 11 The Rebellious '60s

The 1960s were a decade of rebellion, excitement and creativity. Some North American teens questioned existing values and rebelled against the social and economic inequalities that existed. Some organized strikes and sit-ins at schools and universities. Others dropped out and entered the "drug culture."

*St. Mary's Church in Red Deer, Alberta, was designed by Canadian architect Douglas Cardinal in 1967. Its design was so complex that, without the aid of computers, ten architects would have taken 100 years to map out the blueprint plans for construction.*

A few turned to communes to redefine community and family. The majority went to school, played loud music their parents hated, and wore new styles of clothing. Shoulder-length hair for both sexes, granny glasses, jeans and sandals replaced the bobby sox, sweater sets and coiffed hair of the 1950s.

Television influenced Canadian and American ways of thinking. The Cuban Missile Crisis was the first world crisis to receive widespread TV coverage. People saw first-hand the American naval blockade of Cuba. American and Russian viewpoints were reported in the nightly news. Television allowed people to see how close the world came to a nuclear war.

The extensive television coverage of the Vietnam War made it "a real TV war." Nightly news telecasts showed bombs exploding and American soldiers killed. Americans and Canadians were disturbed by images of bloody faces and body bags. Reporters told disturbing stories about American atrocities against Vietnamese civilians.

It was as if viewers were actually there. Everyone became a "television witness" to the war and the assassinations. The impact of these events was enormous. The baby boom generation had grown up with TV, which made them more aware of what was going on in the world. Television contributed to the anti-Vietnam War movement of the 1960s and to the general rebelliousness of the time.

The 1960s were a decade of rebellion, excitement and creativity.

Some young Americans and Canadians questioned existing ways. They wanted major changes in society. They wanted an end to the war in Vietnam. They supported the American civil rights movement and equal opportunities for non-whites. They protested and held demonstrations to support their belief in equality for all.

## A Changing Time

Canada's Aboriginal people fought against racism and neglect. Native and Métis leaders such as Harold Cardinal, Howard Adams, Buffy Sainte Marie and Kahn Tineta Horn called attention to the plight of their people. They demanded justice and equality from the Canadian government.

More women became aware of their disadvantaged status in Canadian society. The women's liberation movement became a powerful force. Women challenged their traditional roles as homemakers. They protested and marched for legalized abortions, simpler divorce laws and fairer employment practices. They wanted

contraception to be legal. Even though the birth control pill was available in the early '60s, women could not legally buy it. Taking contraceptive pills was a criminal offence in

*Protesters demonstrating against the war in Vietnam.*

Canada until 1969. More and more women entered the work force. Some needed the pay cheque; others were eager for a career and identity of their own. All wanted equal opportunity with men and equal pay for equal work.

## FOCUS

1. Why do you think the 1960s were termed the rebellious sixties?
2. How have teenagers changed since the 1960s? In your opinion, are teens more rebellious now or then? Are they more political now or then?
3. What concerns were raised by Aboriginal leaders and by women?

# 1967: A Year of Contrast

The decade came to an end in Canada on a positive note. In 1967, Canadians celebrated their centennial. The city of Montreal hosted the world's fair, EXPO '67. A world fair is an advertising display. Each country wants to show itself at its best. The last world fair had been held in 1956 in Brussels, Belgium. Since then, there had been great progress in such fields as film, architecture and science. These developments had grown behind the walls of studios and laboratories. Many were on show at Expo '67 for the first time.

Montreal's theme was "Man and His World." Expo '67 was held on three islands in the St. Lawrence River. One island was completely created for the event.

Many nations and private corporations sponsored pavilions showing their products and achievements. Expo '67 represented the optimistic view that Canada's century had arrived. Regional conflicts between east and west, and between French and English, would shatter that optimism in the decade to follow.

Montreal's theme was "Man and His World." Expo '67 was held on three islands in the St. Lawrence River.

## The Innu
### Relocation—Solution or Mistake

Some 16,000 Innu (formerly known as the Montagnais or Naskapi First Nations) live in Nitassinan on Canada's Ungava peninsula, which includes parts of Quebec, Labrador and Newfoundland. The Innu are a nomadic people with a long history of hunting and fishing. Anthropologists have discovered Innu camp sites dating back 5,000 years, and it is estimated that there were 4,000 Innu alive when Columbus first sighted the Americas. The Innu (the word means people) speak a dialect of the Cree language and, today, they live in thirteen villages—eleven in Quebec, and two—Sheshatshiu and Utshimassits (Davis Inlet)—in Labrador.

In 1967, Canada and Newfoundland established the village of Utshimassits or Davis Inlet on an island off the Labrador Coast. Five-hundred Innu settled in the new community, giving up their nomadic lifestyle. The move had tragic consequences. The new community had insufficient water; there were no sewers. Health care was almost non-existent, and the island was cut off from the mainland every year for almost four months. When six young Innu tried to commit suicide in 1993, the problems of Davis Inlet became world news.

In 1996, the people of Utshimassits signed an agreement with the government to relocate to a new 2,000-hectare settlement, Little Sango Pond (Natuashish), on the Labrador mainland. "The relocation agreement is a great achievement for all our people, but especially for the Elders who have been struggling for 30 years to build our future," said Innu Chief Katie Rich. "The key to our healing is for us to take back power and responsibility for ourselves. The relocation is not an end in itself—it is a vital tool for our re-empowerment."

## FOCUS

1. What sort of things did Canadians do to celebrate Canada's first 100 years?
2. Do you think there will be an independent Canada to celebrate its 200th birthday? Explain?
3. What does "Man and His World" suggest about Canadians?
4. Why do you think Canada and Newfoundland tried to resettle the Innu?

# Questions & Activities

Questions and Activities

## Who Am I?

1. I led Newfoundland into Confederation with Canada. I became known as the "last Father of Confederation." Who am I?
2. As prime minister, I gave Canadians their first Bill of Rights. My political supporters knew me as "the Chief." Who am I?
3. I won the Nobel Peace Prize in 1957. I was prime minister when Canadians received their own national flag. Who am I?
4. I was premier of Saskatchewan from 1955 to 1961. I brought Medicare to the Saskatchewan people. Later, I became the first leader of the NDP. Who am I?
5. I was a popular musician during the 1960s. Although I have been in the industry for over 30 years, I have recently gained new popularity as the "Godfather of Grunge." Who am I?

## Ideas for Discussion

1. What would have happened to Newfoundland if Newfoundlanders had voted not to enter Confederation in 1949? Write your thoughts down in a brief paragraph. Be prepared to read your paragraph aloud during class discussion.
2. List the good and the bad results of the economic boom of the early 1950s. Hold a class debate on the topic: Resolved that the economic boom of the 1950s created more problems than it solved.
3. With a group of other students, discuss the statement: "Parents rarely understand teenagers—and teenagers rarely understand adults.
4. Canada underwent a baby boom in the 1950s. Today, Canadians are having fewer children or none at all.
   a) Suggest reasons for this drop in the birth rate.
   b) What does the drop mean for the future of our country? Some possible areas of discussion are schools, the labour force, immigration and supporting the elderly.

## Do Some Research

1. Visit the library to find out more about the province of Newfoundland since it joined Canada in 1949. You might use the following headings:
   a) Geography
   b) Culture and Traditions
   c) Transportation
   d) Towns, Villages and Outports
   e) Political Leaders
   f) Economic Development
2. Research the recent history of a "boomtown" in your area. Why was the town established? Has the town continued to develop? What do you think the future will bring to your boomtown?
3. Find out more about the cancellation of the Avro Arrow project by the Diefenbaker government. Make a list of the reasons for the decision and the reasons against it. State your personal conclusions clearly and firmly
4. Write a brief biocard on an important Canadian of the 1950s or 1960s. Here are a few suggestions:
   a) Paul Anka
   b) Marshall McLuhan
   c) Maurice Richard
   d) Jacques Plante
   e) Tommy Douglas
   f) Margaret Laurence
   g) Marilyn Bell
   h) Celia Franca
5. Summarize the achievements and changes won by the protest movement of the 1960s.
6. Find out what projects your community undertook to celebrate Canada's 100th birthday. Were these projects a good idea?
7. Research the history of plastic. How has it changed life since the 1960s? What are some of the advantages of plastic? What are some of its disadvantages
8. Research the women's movement of the 1960s. What were women protesting against? How did it differ from the suffragette movement of the early 1900s? How did the women's movement change life for Canadian women? Can you see any changes in your own life that could be attributed to the women's movement?

**9.** Find out about the civil rights movement in the United States. How did Canada differ from the U.S. in terms of its racial views?

## Be Creative

**1.** Divide into groups and prepare a time capsule for the 1950s or 1960s. Include photo records, magazines, records, souvenirs, fashions and news statements. You might celebrate the end of your project with a theme party.

**2.** Compare the hit songs of the 1950s and 1960s with each other, and the hit songs of today. What differences do the songs reveal about attitudes to:
a) values      b) technology
c) teenagers      d) love

**3.** What role did folk music play during the baby boom?

**4.** Can you identify which term comes from what decade?

| | |
|---|---|
| Acid wash | Adidas |
| Afro | Bell-bottoms |
| Bermuda shorts | Bomber jacket |
| Beehive | Bouffant |
| Cargo pant | Caesar |
| Crushed velvet | Doc Martins |
| Drainpipes | Glam |
| Grunge | Hot pants |
| Kickers | Leisure suit |
| Micro-mini | Mods |
| Muttonchops | Nehru jacket |
| Peddle pushers | Penny loafers |
| Platform shoes | Preppie |
| Polo shirt | Punk |
| Rave | Rockers |
| Rugby pants | Scrunchy |
| Sneakers | Stone wash |
| Techno | Trainers |
| Topsiders | Welfare chic |

## Web sites

**St. Lawrence Seaway:** www.stlawrenceseaway.com
**The Baby Boom:** www.babyboomers.org
**The Diefenbunker:** www.diefenbunker.ca
**Innu Nation:** www.innu.ca
**Avro Arrow Alliance:** www.arrow-alliance.com
**Canadian Labour Congress:** www.clc-ctc.ca\

**In periods like the 1950s, Canadians regarded all economic development as progress. In the 1960s, people began to look at some of the side effects of development. They wondered if it all was worth it. Certainly, development in some form is necessary for the economic health of a nation. When we examine the question of development today, how do we count for the cost?**

**A major issue is confronting you—the people who care about the future of River Rock. You are going to a public meeting to discuss it. On a piece of paper, jot down the concerns you want raised at the meeting. Be prepared to make a statement, ask questions, or add comments to make sure these concerns are discussed. Keep an open mind. Others may have points that you have not yet considered.**

**What is the future of River Rock?**

## A Pulp and Paper Mill at River Rock

River Rock is in northern Canada. In the early years of the century, copper was discovered nearby. Miners and their families soon created a small town on the banks of the Rocky River. Merchants moved in to open stores. Teachers, lawyers, restaurant owners and doctors came to offer their services to the community.

River Rock is a pleasant place, surrounded by rich forests. Rushing streams tumble into still lakes that teem with fish. People enjoy living here.

Three years ago, the mine closed because the ore had run out. Now young people are leaving town in order to find work in the big cities to the south. Stores have closed because business is poor. The town council cannot raise the money to provide the services a modern community needs. Many residents rely on unemployment insurance and provincial welfare benefits. It seems that for the last three years the town has been limping along from one government grant to the next.

Recently U.S. Conglomerate Inc. has shown interest in River Rock. The company plans to develop a giant pulp and paper mill. The forests in the valley can be harvested. The Rocky River can be dammed to provide power. All that is needed is the go-ahead from the town council. Then the company will build the mill, provide jobs for local residents, and make profits for its shareholders. River Rock could boom again.

For weeks, all of you—citizens of River Rock, representatives of U.S. Conglomerate, town councillors and others—have been discussing the proposal.

Tonight, a public meeting is being held in the school auditorium. A number of groups with special concerns have asked to speak at the meeting:

**a)** The town council, led by Mayor Irene Nadeau: You know the town desperately needs jobs. The taxes paid by the company will help provide new roads, schools, recreation centres, libraries and a new hospital.

**b)** Young people in town: You are eager to get jobs in a highly-skilled industry. You also love your valley and fear that its beauty may be destroyed

**c)** Senior citizens: You want the valley to stay as it was when you were young. Yet you want your children and grandchildren to be able to live and work in River Rock.

**d)** First Nations people on the reserve nearby. You are afraid the company will ruin your traditional hunting and fishing grounds

**e)** Recently-arrived residents: You have recently moved to River Rock because of its beauty and isolation. You mistrust big business, especially American corporations. You fear the company will be out for profit at any cost.

**f)** U.S. Conglomerate's managers: You feel there is a great future for an operation in River Rock. But millions of dollars will have to be spent in start-up costs. There will be no profits for several years. You are prepared to comply with reasonable requests on the way you set up the mill. But you do not want expensive interference from local government. If you feel citizens are not behind the idea, you are prepared to invest elsewhere.

# Point
## Counterpoint

With which of the following statements do you most agree? Why?

With which of the following statements do you least agree? Why?

"The besetting disease of Canadian public life for almost a decade has been Diefenbakerism: the belief that promises were politics, that rhetoric was action, and that the electorate believed in Santa Claus."

Ramsey Cook,
Historian, 1971

"It has been said that Canada is the most difficult country in the world to govern."

Lester Pearson,
Prime Minister, 1965

"I am opposed to nationalism in all its forms, whether it be French Canadian, Jewish, Irish, or any other."

Pierre Elliot Trudeau,
1965

"We don't intend to use Canada as a dumping ground for nuclear warheads."

John Diefenbaker,
Prime Minister, 1963

# Introduction

**D**URING THE 1970s, PIERRE ELLIOT TRUDEAU REJUVENATED Canadians' interest in politics. His policy of multiculturalism changed the face of Canada. For the first time in history, minorities were welcomed. Our cities became more multicultural. Canadians discovered the advantages of living with people from other nations. We enjoyed diverse food, different dress and new celebrations.

During the 1980s and 1990s, Prime Ministers Mulroney and Chrétien encouraged Canada's participation in the global economy, with the signing of the North American Free Trade Agreement (NAFTA). Our economy boomed once more. Aboriginal Canadians began to demand their land back and the freedom of self-government. The creation of Nunavut suggested that our government was more friendly to these requests.

At home, Canada faced a serious unity crisis with the failed constitutional reform. Our Parliament began to reflect strong regionalism. Quebec called a referendum in 1995, asking its residents if they were prepared to separate from the rest of Canada. Although the country remained united, the threat of separatism was still as strong as ever. Other provinces also voiced their concern over Confederation. Small grassroots parties from the West—such as Alberta's Reform Party— were elected to the House of Commons, which forced the federal government to negotiate the needs of a varying and diverse population.

## METHODS OF HISTORICAL INQUIRY

### Notation

Historians use information to formulate theories and generalizations. Because they often use the work of others, historians must be rigorous that they don't **plagiarize;** that is, use someone else's thoughts as if they were their own. When historians use information from other sources, they must acknowledge this information using **footnotes** or **endnotes,** and by including a **bibliography** of sources used. Students learning history and writing research papers must learn to recognize what information needs to be cited and what information does not. Generally, information found in a variety of sources is considered common knowledge and does not need to be footnoted. Anything else, however, must be cited.

# Chapter Six: Canada Comes of Age: 1968–2000

## Expectations

### General Expectations:
By the end of this chapter, you will be able to:

- demonstrate an understanding of the Canadian identity
- describe the demographic and social patterns since the 1960s
- describe how Canadian values developed and changed

### Specific Expectations:
By the end of this chapter, you will be able to:

- understand the advantages of multiculturalism, as well as some of its disadvantages
- identify and describe problems and solutions faced by the Trudeau administration
- explain changing immigration policies and patterns after 1970
- describe the changing relationship between the First Nations and government after 1960
- outline the impact of free trade on Canada's economy
- identify values which Canadians deemed important
- explain the process of privatization and the concerns it created for Canadians

## WORD LIST

| | | | |
|---|---|---|---|
| Apartheid | Debt | Land Claims | Royalties |
| Coming of Age | Deficit | Melting Pot | Tokenism |
| Crown Corporation | Indian Act | Pay Equity | Trudeaumania |
| Cultural Identity | Just Society | Privatization | Wage-Price Cycle |

# *Advance* Organizer

**1**

**In late 1968, Pierre Trudeau offered a youthful approach to government affairs. His fresh ideas and moral strength appealed to the young, and gave new hope to the older generation of voters. World leaders were impressed with his ideas on foreign policy. Trudeau's main objective was a unified Canada. He sometimes achieved his aims by tightening federal controls, which often angered the provinces.**

**2**

In 1984, Canadians elected Conservative leader, Brian Mulroney, as their prime minister. Mulroney was determined to reduce the national debt and to provide more jobs for Canadians. He worked hard to get Quebec's approval on new constitutional proposals, but did not succeed. During his second term as prime minister, he implemented a free trade agreement with the United States.

**3**

The immigration policies of the 1960s and 1970s attracted people of many nationalities and cultures to Canada. These people brought with them their own traditions, values and approaches to day-to-day living. Most were accepted, but some faced hostility and prejudice in their new communities. Although multiculturalism was encouraged by Canadians and their government, racism remained a problem in some Canadian communities.

## 4

Canadian industry's desire for natural resources—furs, timber, oil and minerals—displaced Canada's Aboriginal communities from their land. Throughout the last 30 years, First Nations peoples fought hard to maintain their way of life and looked to the courts to regain control of their land.

A number of court decisions recognized Aboriginal rights and land claims. In 1999, the Nisga'a of British Columbia won a court decision for self-government of their lands near the Nass River. That same year, the Northwest Territories was divided to create Nunavut, giving the Innu of the area control over their land and their government.

## 5

The Liberals defeated the Conservatives in 1993, and Jean Chrétien became the new prime minister of Canada. Chrétien continued a number of policies implemented by Mulroney. He accepted Mexico into the free trade agreement with the United States (NAFTA) and travelled the globe encouraging world trade. He succeeded in reducing the national deficit, but Chrétien's attempts at addressing Quebec separatism have not been as successful.

## 6

The women's rights movement of the 1960s continued to gain momentum during the 1970s. The report of the Royal Commission on the Status of Women, released in the early 1970s, made the Canadian public aware of the issues faced by many women. Pay equity, child welfare programs and an end to poverty were some of the causes supported by Canadian women. Today, even though many Canadians believe in social equality, women are still fighting for equal pay and for an end to poverty.

# 1 Proudly Canadian

Who are you? What is your identity? Think about it for a moment. Where did your identity come from? How and when did it develop?

Describe yourself. It can be easy to give a physical description—height, build, eye and hair colour. But what's underneath? What is *inside* you that makes you the special person you are? How do we describe the things that make us unique? How do we recognize the

*The Canadian women's curling team under Sandra Schmirler won gold during the 1998 Winter Olympics in Nagano, Japan. Why do Canadians feel a strong sense of unity and national pride during the Olympics?*

things that make each of us proud to be who we are? How do we know those inner qualities that make up our individual identity?

Every identity has many features, all of which, taken together, make each individual person different from everyone else. Your individual identity makes you, you. It makes you feel good; it makes you feel valued. Features of your identity can include upbringing, family background, religion, life experiences, both good and bad, the area where you live, the sports and activities you take part in, your school, your friends, clothing, music, what you watch on TV, the movies you go to, the books you read and even your Internet time.

A country's identity develops in much the same way.

Some people believe a country's identity can be easily defined because it combines the identities of its residents. People, however, often behave differently in large groups than in small groups. They can act in one way when they are alone, and in another when at home among family.

A country's identity will often change in the same way as the identities of its peoples change.

Most students develop their identities—those unique characteristics that define them as individuals—by the time they leave school. We call this process **coming of age**.

Canada began its coming of age in 1968 as the country drew from past experiences and began to develop a national sense of identity.

Canadian achievements were recognized both at home and on the international scene.

Before the 1960s, some Canadians based their identity largely on regional loyalties, on family or on country of origin. We considered ourselves Maritimers, Québécois, Upper Canadians, Cree, Mi'kmaq, Blackfoot, English, Italian, Ukrainian or Chinese Canadians. Some had not yet developed a sense that all of us as Canadians shared a common identity.

The 1950s and 1960s were one of the most prosperous eras in Canadian history. The country's wealth increased dramatically. Canadians became confident they could achieve whatever they set out to do. The country was not involved in major wars. Baby boomers were the first generation to grow up in a world no longer dominated by global conflict. War, for many, was something to be watched on television.

Canada's years of peace gave birth to an outburst of cultural achievement. People began to believe that there might actually be such a thing as a Canadian identity. Canadian individuals and groups made significant contributions to literature, art, music, dance, drama, and the media. Canadian achievements were recognized both at home and on the international scene.

Canadian governments supported the development of a distinctive Canadian culture through such organizations as the Canada Council. Regional arts councils reached people at the grassroots. The rise of national television networks like the CBC and CTV, which reported on Canadian events, fostered the growth of our identity.

Canadians travelled the country with greater ease during the 1960s, 70s and 80s. They visited all parts of Canada, from sea to sea to sea. Students biked from Toronto to Vancouver, took skiing and hiking trips to the Rocky Mountains. Some Canadians adventurers even canoed from the Rockies to Montreal for Expo '67. Families loaded children into

## THE SYMBOLS OF A NATION

**Percentage of respondents who think these factors are an important part of what makes us Canadian:**

| The Flag | Canada | Quebec | Men | Women |
|---|---|---|---|---|
| Achievements of prominent Canadians, such as artists and scientists, around the world. | 80 | 79 | 78 | 82 |
| Our climate and geography | 80 | 79 | 76 | 84 |
| Health-care system | 79 | 77 | 73 | 85 |
| Our international role | 77 | 67 | 77 | 79 |
| Our multicultural and multiracial makeup | 74 | 68 | 70 | 79 |
| Canadian ownership of businesses operating in Canada | 73 | 69 | 66 | 79 |
| The traditional family | 70 | 66 | 65 | 76 |
| English- and French-speakers sharing one country | 69 | 69 | 67 | 72 |
| Hockey | 67 | 46 | 66 | 67 |
| Our Aboriginal Peoples | 63 | 48 | 58 | 69 |
| Restrictions on gun ownership and use | 63 | 58 | 56 | 70 |
| Public broadcasting | 63 | 62 | 54 | 72 |
| The way we treat the poor and disadvantaged | 59 | 54 | 55 | 63 |
| A Christian heritage | 54 | 47 | 45 | 63 |
| Having the Queen as our monarch | 41 | 20 | 34 | 48 |

BORN: 1961, Brantford, Ontario

SIGNIFICANCE: One of Canada's best hockey players of all time.

BRIEF BIOGRAPHY: Wayne Gretzky was born in 1961, in Brantford, Ontario. His passion for hockey began early. At age two, Wayne spent hours in his family's living room shooting pucks at his grandmother. When Wayne was four years old, his father built him a rink in the family backyard, complete with overhead lights for night games. Wayne's father tutored his son night and day. The lessons paid off. Wayne became a sensation in the minor leagues. He scored 50 goals during one two-day tournament, and 78 goals during the 69 game season.

Wayne Gretzky signed with the Edmonton Oilers at age 19. He won the NHL's most valuable player award in his first season of play. He led the Edmonton Oilers to four Stanley Cups during the 1980s. Then, in a move that tore the heart from the Alberta franchise and from Canadian hockey fans across the country, Gretzky was traded to the Los Angeles Kings in 1988.

Wayne Gretzky retired in 1999 after stints with the St. Louis Blues and the New York Rangers. He holds 61 NHL records including most regular season goals (894), and most goals in a single season (92).

Wayne Gretzky is remembered for his unequalled scoring ability. He changed hockey into a more open, and exciting, game. He is an eloquent spokesperson, and a constant reminder of the best attributes of our national pastime.

## Wayne Gretzky

cars and headed off to explore the corners of the country, from Cape Spear, Newfoundland to Tofino on Vancouver Island. All of these experiences helped give Canadians a sense of Canada—an appreciation for this country that previous generations never had the opportunity to discover.

Our cultural identity is a distinct set of beliefs and values developed and accepted by Canadians across the country. These values may not be unique but, for the most part, they are values shared by us all.

As Canadians, we believe:
- every person should be given a reasonable opportunity to reach his or her full potential
- no family should be forced to bear unavoidable medical costs alone
- young children and senior citizens should not live in poverty
- people can live together successfully regardless of background
- we benefit from one another's cultural traditions
- communities are extensions of the families living within them
- conflicts are best resolved without resorting to violence
- people in other countries should have the same opportunities as we do
- democracy—the freedom to choose our

government—is a basic right and allows us to act on these values.

These values were developed in the early 1960s. We pressured our governments—no matter which political party was in power—to enact the social programs we believed were necessary. Thus Medicare, larger Baby Bonuses, Canada Pension Plan, the Charter of Rights and Freedoms, government subsidies for university and college education, Heritage Language Programs and Anti-racist Education Programs were all created.

Local governments became involved in urban renewal projects. Our sense of community, locally and nationally, was furthered by Expo '67, the Montreal Olympics in 1976 and the Calgary Winter Olympics in 1988. We began to Canadianize our national symbols: a new flag in 1965, a new anthem in 1980, recognition of the beaver as the symbol of Canadian sovereignty in 1975 and Canadian stamps with pictures other than those of Queen Elizabeth II.

Canadians were optimistic about Canada by 1968. We believed we could have anything we wanted—no matter how difficult, no matter what the cost.

We knew the world was ours. All we had to do was claim our part of it. For many Canadians, the person best suited to lead us was Pierre Elliot Trudeau.

FOCUS
1. Define "national identity?"
2. What Canadian values do you think are most important?
3. Why are shared Canadian values important to our society?
4. Why was Wayne Gretzky called "The Great One?"

# 2 Trudeaumania

*When Trudeau became leader of the Liberal Party, he ignited an outburst of excitement called Trudeaumania.*

Canadians, by 1968, wanted fresh political faces to lead them into a new Canadian era. Pierre Elliott Trudeau seemed ideal. 48 years old, much younger than most politicians of the time, Trudeau enjoyed sports, dancing and parties. He was an exciting speaker, handsome and witty. As federal justice minister, Trudeau was fluently bilingual. He was a determined, forceful leader—something Canadians discovered when he stood up to

People were thrilled by Trudeau's clear vision of a just society where the rights of all Canadians would be respected.

| 1900 | 1910 | 1920 | 1930 | 1940 | 1950 | 1960 | 1970 | 1980 | 1990 |

big business and the Quebec government during the Asbestos strike of 1949.

Trudeau had travelled around the world. He had even made a visit to communist China during a period when China was cut off from the Western world. Trudeau brought new ideas to politics. He had a strong sense of justice and a deep love for Canada.

Prime Minister Lester Pearson resigned in 1968. Trudeau was chosen as the new leader of the Liberals. He was sworn in as prime minister in 1968 and immediately called an election. Pierre Elliot Trudeau would take advantage of the mood of the country.

People were thrilled by Trudeau's clear vision of a **just society** where the rights of all Canadians would be respected—where all could enjoy the good things of life. Candidates from other parties had little chance against the Liberals. Voters were swept up in a fever of enthusiasm for the Liberal candidate; the press called it **Trudeaumania.** Canadians went to the ballot box in 1968, and gave Trudeau the majority government he needed to get things done.

*Having a prime minister with a young wife and young children was a new experience for Canadians.*

### The Just Society

The Trudeau government faced many challenges. Canada's economy was slowing down. The country faced high unemployment. The international oil crisis and inflation posed serious problems. Tensions were rising between "old" Canadians and recent immigrants. Canada's Aboriginals wanted improved status. Women demanded true equality with men. Quebec separatists were gaining public support in their challenge to Canadian unity. Many people believed Trudeau's "Just Society" election slogan in 1968 was a promise for a better world. Canadians had high expectations of the changes that Trudeau and the government would make. Many Canadians felt disappointed and angry when the prime minister could not solve all of these problems.

## Arctic Sovereignty

In the summer of 1969, the United States supertanker, *Manhattan,* travelled the Northwest Passage from east to west. The Americans were looking for a route by which they could transport Alaskan oil south.

The USS Manhattan *and the Canadian icebreaker,* Louis St. Laurent, *crunch through the snow-covered ice of Northern Baffin Bay.*

Canada regarded the mission as a threat to its sovereignty in the North. The Trudeau government passed the Arctic Waters Pollution Prevention Act. The new law established a "100-mile pollution-prevention zone in Arctic waters adjacent to the mainland and the islands of the Arctic archipelago."

## Bilingualism

Trudeau wanted to extend the rights of French-speaking Canadians in other parts of Canada. He believed French Canadians would be isolated in Quebec if the French language was not protected by law outside Quebec.

Trudeau visualized Canada as a bilingual country. He wanted English- and French-speaking Canadians to share equal language rights.

In 1969, the government passed Canada's Official Languages Act. The new law said the Canadians would be served in either French or English when dealing with the federal government. It required companies doing business in Canada to label their products in both languages. Trudeau was disappointed that he could not persuade Canada's provinces to follow the federal lead.

The new bilingualism policy met with strong opposition. Some Western Canadians felt it was a waste of money. Even some French Canadians objected. Trudeau stood firm.

In October 1970, British diplomat James Cross and Quebec cabinet minister Pierre LaPorte were kidnapped by Quebec FLQ terrorists. Trudeau invoked the War Measures Act, and sent armed soldiers to patrol the city. Many Canadians criticized this decision.

The federal government instituted several important symbolic changes during Trudeau's first term in office:

- Muriel McQueen Fergusson became the first woman Speaker of the Senate.
- Bora Laskin became the first Jewish Chief Justice of the Supreme Court of Canada.
- Pauline McGibbon became the first woman Lieutenant Governor (of Ontario).
- Ralph Steinhauer became the first Aboriginal Lieutenant Governor (of Alberta).
- Len Marchand became the first Aboriginal Cabinet Minister.
- Jeanne Sauvé became the first woman speaker of the House of Commons, and later the first woman Governor General of Canada.

*Pierre Trudeau and Bora Laskin*

*Pauline McGibbon with her husband*

*Jeanne Sauvé*

Some Aboriginal groups and feminists described these appointments as **tokenism**, but they did open the door to future opportunities for minority groups and women in Canada.

**FOCUS**

1. Why were Canadians so attracted to Trudeau in the late 1960s?
2. What did he offer that previous prime ministers did not?
3. What did Trudeau mean by a "Just Society?"
4. Name two changes Trudeau made when he was in power.

# Canada in the 1970s

Canada's postwar economic expansion began to slow down in the early 1970s. Unemployment rose. The cost of living increased. Businesses, homeowners and farmers borrowed money from the bank at interest rates

## INFLATION: THE WAGE-PRICE SPIRAL

When businesses are forced to spend more to make their products, they must raise their prices. When workers see prices going up, they demand higher wages from their employers. Workers expect to be able to keep buying the products they always have. Employers are forced to pay still higher wages, so they raise their prices once more. This is what economists call a **wage-price spiral.** The cycle seemed endless, and Canada's inflation rate rose sharply. So did the country's unemployment.

approaching 20% to pay for mortgages and new equipment.

No one knew how high prices would go. Business leaders did not want to invest in new ventures. Few new companies were looking for workers. Many older companies cut back production, and laid off people in order to survive.

The Trudeau government responded by passing a wage and price control freeze to curb inflation (1975). The new law limited increases in salaries or hourly wages; it limited the price increases stores could charge for goods. The government hoped to break the

**wage-price cycle**. Labour unions and business people were critical of the government's interference. Consumer confidence in the economy was low. Many businesses went bankrupt. Canada was in an economic recession by 1979.

## Our Mighty Neigbour

Trudeau understood the benefits and dangers of Canada's close proximity to the United States. His government was concerned about the takeover of Canadian industries by foreign (mainly U.S.) companies. Economic nationalists such as Walter Gordon warned that foreign control of Canadian resources and industries would endanger Canadian independence. The government created the Foreign Investment Review Agency (FIRA) in 1974 to screen takeover bids for any Canadian industry or resource. Canadians concerned with economic growth and jobs did not think FIRA was a good idea. The FIRA issue divided Canadians throughout the 1970s and 80s.

## Federalism

Trudeau believed in a strong federal government. He told Canadians that only a federal government with strong powers could solve the problems facing the Canadian nation. Many provincial leaders believed otherwise. Premiers Brian Peckford of Newfoundland,

Terry Fox's legacy lives on in the Terry Fox Foundation, which, in 1999, received $17.5 million, worldwide, in donations towards cancer research.

Peter Lougheed of Alberta, and William Bennett of British Columbia joined Quebec in demanding more power for the provinces. They demanded provincial control of local resource revenues, particularly those from oil and gas. Trudeau said no. He believed someone had to stand up for the powers of the central government. Many Canadians felt Trudeau was more concerned with political and constitutional matters than with economic questions.

## An Increasing Deficit

Canada's federal government has always tried to balance its budget and spend only those tax monies it collected. During the 1960s, Ottawa usually spent less money than it collected in taxes. The country had a **surplus** budget. By the 1970s, tax revenues had decreased. Unemployment was rising. More money was needed to fund unemployment insurance, job creation projects and other social programs. The government was spending more money than it raised through taxes. Soon the government was forced to borrow money in order to pay for its needs. The country was being run on **deficit** budgets. In other words, we were spending more than we earned. By the late 1970s, Canada's annual deficit was over $12 billion per year; by the 1980s it was $38 billion. Each annual deficit contributed to a high national **debt**. Canada paid large amounts of money in interest to service its national debt. Trudeau's opponents said that the country could not continue to survive if the national debt kept increasing at such an enormous rate.

## Election 1979

Canadians were ready for a change by 1979. The Liberals were defeated. The Progressive

*The Metropolitan Toronto Reference Library, built in 1977, remains one of Canada's most innovative publicly-funded projects. It earned architects, Moriyama and Teshima, the 1977 Governor General's Award for architectural design.*

Much of the world's supply of oil came from the Middle East. In 1973, Middle Eastern oil producers created the Organization of Petroleum Exporting Countries (OPEC) to control the selling price of oil around the world. Within a year, the price of oil jumped from $8 a barrel to over $12 a barrel. The price was over $30 a barrel by 1980 and it seemed to be going higher and out of control.

Oil and petroleum products are essential to the way of life of all industrial countries. This is especially true of countries like Canada, located in the colder areas of the northern hemisphere. Higher crude oil costs increased the costs of transportation, home heating and industrial production. Even the price of imported fruits and vegetables increased. Canadians were forced to pay higher prices for their needs.

The crude oil price issue gave the Trudeau government two big problems. The first concerned the West and the price of Canadian oil. The second was Canada's national inflation rate.

As an oil-producing province, Alberta felt that its oil industry should be allowed to take advantage of the higher world price. The federal government said no. It introduced the National Energy Program (NEP) This policy reduced profits for Alberta oil producers. It also reduced the **royalties** collected by the Alberta government. Westerners were furious. They accused Trudeau of protecting central Canada at the expense of the West.

*The energy crisis fuelled a bitter debate in Canada.*

Conservatives won the election and Canada's new prime minister was Joe Clark, from High River, Alberta. Clark headed a **minority government**. Eight months later, Clark was forced to call an election when his budget was defeated in the House of Commons. The Progressive Conservatives lost. Trudeau and the Liberals returned to power in 1980.

## A New Canadian Constitution

Trudeau knew that Canada's constitution needed to be more responsive to the needs of Canadians in the 1980s. He also wanted to address the concerns of Quebecers.

---

### Trudeau had three main goals:

1. **Patriation**—Canada would bring the Constitution home from England, thus giving Canadians the right to make their own changes.

2. **Amending Formula**—A formula to change or amend the Constitution, acceptable to the premiers and the federal government would be included.

3. **Charter of Rights and Freedoms**—The Constitution's Charter would protect the rights and freedoms of Canadians from abuses from existing or future laws passed by the federal government or any municipal and provincial government in the country.

---

On May 20, 1980, Quebec voters rejected the "sovereignty-association" proposal for Quebec's future put to them in a referendum by Premier Lévesque and the separatist Parti-Québècois. Trudeau promised if the referendum was rejected, Canada would have constitutional change.

His government faced an immense task. Most people supported changes to Canada's Constitution (the British North America Act of 1867), but getting universal agreement on reform from all provincial leaders was almost impossible.

The process was slow and difficult. It required much consultation and compromise. Finally an agreement was reached on November 5, 1981, which satisfied all of the premiers, except Premier Lévesque of Quebec. The new Constitution Act was signed by the Queen and came into effect in 1982.

Trudeau's dream of a new constitution had been achieved, but at a price. Premier Lévesque and other Quebec officials rejected the new constitution. They were angry that it had been imposed on Quebec in spite of their opposition.

The federal government had tried to satisfy the needs of Quebec, but it only succeeded in satisfying the wishes of the other Canadian provinces. Once again, Quebec stood alone—as dissatisfied and isolated as ever.

## International Affairs

Trudeau's ideas and efforts in foreign affairs gained him worldwide respect. Many people felt the Canadian prime minister was more popular and respected in other countries than at home. His speeches and statements on international affairs were always well received and widely reported abroad. In 1970, Canada established diplomatic relations with Communist China, one of the first

BORN: Winnipeg, Manitoba, 1958

DIED: New Westminster, British Columbia, 1981

SIGNIFICANCE: Drew nationwide and international attention to his "Marathon of Hope," a run across Canada raising money and generating publicity for cancer research.

BRIEF BIOGRAPHY: At the age of nineteen, Terry Fox lost his right leg to osteogenic sarcoma—a rare form of bone cancer. Young and idealistic, Fox took it upon himself, while recovering, to make a difference in the battle against the disease that would eventually take his life. His "Marathon of Hope" began in St. John's, Newfoundland, on April 12, 1980, with little interest from local or national news. By the time he reached Ontario, however, Fox was a media sensation. His run garnered thousands of dollars for cancer research and, when he reached Toronto, tens of thousands of people cheered him on. A few weeks later, in Thunder Bay, Ontario, on September 1, Fox's run was cut short by illness. Doctors found cancer in his lungs and, a year later, he was dead; his run unfinished. But, Fox's legacy lives on in the Terry Fox Foundation, which, in 1999, received $17.5 million, worldwide, in donations towards cancer research.

**Terry Fox**

Western countries to do so. Trudeau worked to develop new ties with Cuba and with Latin America, an area of the world long ignored by Canadians.

*Trudeau was a respected world leader.*

Trudeau embarked on a crusade for world peace during his last years in office. He sought to bring about nuclear disarmament and to reduce the threat of nuclear war. Though his efforts were praised, he was not successful in reducing hostility between the U.S. and the U.S.S.R.

## *Trudeau Retires*

On February 29, 1984, Trudeau announced his retirement from politics.

Pierre Elliot Trudeau had dominated Canadian life as had no other prime minister since Sir John A. Macdonald. He had been in office for fifteen years. Only Macdonald and Mackenzie King governed for longer. Trudeau was 65-years-old.

Many Canadians felt the retirement was long overdue. Trudeau was very unpopular in the West and among many business people across the country. His strong-willed leadership had helped to create a mood of conflict between the provinces and the federal government. Yet, Trudeau's policies had helped to change the country greatly, moving it into the electronic age.

FOCUS
1. Why did Trudeau create FIRA and the NEP? What problems did he hope to solve with these programs?
2. What changes did Trudeau make to Canada's Constitution? Why did he think these changes were necessary?
3. What does "patriation" mean?
4. In your opinion, was Trudeau a "great" prime minister? Explain.

# The Mulroney Era

In 1984, Brian Mulroney, leader of the Conservative Party, was elected prime minister. He hailed from Baie Comeau, Quebec, and had been a successful lawyer and business leader before entering politics. Mulroney was a colourful speaker. He sensed that Canada was ready for change. Mulroney's election campaign speeches and posters emphasized change. He understood the mood of the country. His 1984 election victory was one of the greatest landslides in Canadian history.

Canadians were ready for new direction. Prime Minister Mulroney promised to stimulate the economy. He promised to provide "jobs, jobs, jobs." Mulroney pledged to reduce the annual **deficit,** encourage the growth of private industry, reduce the conflict between the provinces and the federal government, strengthen the Canadian defence role, and improve relations between the United States and Canada.

Mulroney ran into problems early on. Eight of his cabinet ministers were forced to resign within the first three years because of scandals. Many Canadians withdrew their support from the new administration. The Canadian government was accused of widespread **patronage** appointments. Mulroney did not quit.

## Economic success

From 1984–1988, Canada's economy grew at a faster rate than any other Western nation. This was good news for Mulroney's government. Industries expanded. Hundred of thousands of jobs were created faster than at any time in previous years. Unemployment dropped to 7% from a national average of 11%. Canada's annual deficit

*Brian Mulroney was a tireless political campaigner.*

Prime Minister Mulroney spoke out strongly, urging all Commonwealth countries to impose economic sanctions on South Africa, thereby refusing all trade with that country.

| 1900 | 1910 | 1920 | 1930 | 1940 | 1950 | 1960 | 1970 | 1980 | 1990 | |

dropped from $38 billion per year to $28 billion a year. The Conservatives were still a long way from their goal of **deficit elimination**.

Parliament passed laws to support business growth. It reduced taxes on corporations. FIRA, which had restricted American investment, was replaced with **Investment Canada,** which actively sought more American investment. "Canada is open for business," declared Prime Minister Mulroney before an American audience. The Conservatives cancelled the NEP as Canada welcomed American investment in its oil industry.

Canada's economic nationalists strongly opposed these measures, and charged that Canada was selling-out to the United States. Our economy was booming. Most Canadians saw only the increased number of jobs, new companies and new development. They were not concerned about consequences of the increasing foreign investment in Canada.

## A CLOSER LOOK AT THE GST

The government introduced a dramatic change to the Canadian tax system on January 1, 1991. It was designed to stimulate Canada's economy. The Canadian federal sales tax on manufactured goods (FST) was replaced with a **Goods and Services Tax (GST)** of 7% on all goods and services. It would be paid directly by the Canadian consumer at time of purchase.

Most Canadians did not know about the FST because it was a tax built into the price of purchased goods. A television priced at $500 or a car at $20,000 included FST of between 9-13.5%. Consumers never saw the tax. The FST was applied to all manufactured goods including those exported to other countries.

The Mulroney government believed elimination of Canada's FST would lower the cost of Canadian exports. Canadian products would become more competitive and more exports would result. Additional Canadian jobs would be created.

The GST was not popular with Canadians. Consumer groups claimed it was unfair to poorer people because it was levied on many of the basic necessities of life. Toothpaste was taxable. So were car repairs. Small and single servings of snack foods became taxable, as did funerals, legal fees and insurance. Many people did not understand why some items were taxable, while others were not.

In the late 1990s, under the initiative of the Chrétien government, Nova Scotia, New Brunswick, Newfoundland and Labrador **harmonized** their provincial taxes with the GST. Consumers in those provinces now pay HST (harmonized sales tax) of 15%. Many people believe HST will ultimately be the universal sales tax in Canada.

BORN: 1949, Red Sucker, Manitoba

SIGNIFICANCE: As a member of the Manitoba Legislature in 1980, Harper initiated procedural delays, effectively blocking approval vote in Manitoba of the Meech Lake Accord. Harper cited the lack of adequate participation by Aboriginal people in Canada's political process as his reason for blocking the Accord.

BRIEF BIOGRAPHY: Elijah Harper, a Cree from northeastern Manitoba, was raised by his grandparents until the age of 6, when he was sent by his father to a residential school. He began attending the University of Manitoba in 1971, and afterwards was a community development worker for the Manitoba Indian Brotherhood, and program analyst for the Department of Northern Affairs. At the age of 29, he was elected chief of the Red Sucker Lake First Nation, serving from 1978-81. Harper entered politics, provincially, in 1981,

when he was elected to the Manitoba Legislature. In 1986, he was appointed Minister Responsible for Native Affairs; a year later, he became Minister of Northern Affairs for Manitoba.

Harper remains an MP, and continues to work for Aboriginal rights. He has received many humanitarian awards, including the Stanley Knowles Humanitarian Award, the Aboriginal Achievement Award, the Order of Merit from St. Paul's University, and the Order of the Sash from the Manitoba Métis Federation. In December 1995, he hosted a Sacred Assembly in Hull, Quebec, during which the idea of a national day to celebrate and recognize Aboriginal peoples was discussed. On May 23, 1996, Canada declared June 21—the first day of summer—National Aboriginal Day.

## Elijah Harper

## Meech Lake Accord

One of the more difficult problems the Conservatives inherited from Trudeau's Liberals was the very real discord between the federal government and its provincial partners in Confederation. Mulroney had campaigned on a promise to reduce this conflict. He had also promised to find a compromise which would return Quebec voluntarily to support of the Canadian constitution.

In April 1987, the prime minister invited all of the provincial premiers to attend a conference at the government's private retreat in Meech Lake, Quebec, to discuss these matters. To everyone's astonishment an agreement (subsequently called the Meech Lake Accord) was reached. The agreement proposed to de-centralize the federal government and give more power to the provinces. It also recognized the province of Quebec as a distinct society. The agreement was rejected. Although discouraged by the failure of Meech Lake, Prime Minister Mulroney vowed to make another attempt at amending the Canadian Constitution. The 1992 Charlottetown Accord was defeated by national referendum on October 26, 1992. Once more the nation was in the middle of a unity crisis, and many Canadians blamed Mulroney for moving too fast on an emotional issue.

## A CLOSER LOOK AT PRIVATIZATION

Between 1960 and the mid 1980s, Canadian governments created a number of "social safety nets." They were designed to ensure that all Canadians were protected financially and were able to maintain a respectable quality of life. Canada's safety nets included pensions, universal health care, child welfare programs, education funding and unemployment benefits.

When Brian Mulroney came to power in 1984, he was concerned with our increasing national debt and the toll it was taking on Canada's economy. He wanted to reduce government involvement in the economy and to give the provinces more power over their jurisdictions.

One way he did this was to privatize **Crown corporations**—companies that were owned by the government. Mulroney sold companies such as Petro Canada and Air Canada to private businesses. Canada's business community—its private sector—began providing services that were once the responsibility of the federal government.

## FOCUS

1. What did Mulroney promise Canadians?
2. What economic success did Canada enjoy?
3. Why was the GST introduced?
4. What was the goal of the GST?
5. Why is Elijah Harper an important Canadian?
6. Explain the term "privatization."

# Foreign Policy Changes

*Canada is a vast nation with long borders and coastlines that are difficult to defend.*

## The Armed Forces

Another promise made by the Mulroney government was to improve and increase the strength of Canada's Amed Forces. The Canadian military presence had decreased substantially under Trudeau. The situation needed correction. In 1985, Canada's Armed Forces personnel received newly designed, modern uniforms. In 1987, Defence Minister Perrin Beatty released a comprehensive government white paper outlining the future roles and goals of Canada's Armed Forces. New tanks, armored vehicles and guns were purchased. Canada ordered 138 CF-18 fighter planes. St. John Shipbuilding began construction of the first Canadian Patrol Frigate, *Halifax*, to be built at a cost of $3.9 billion.

When Nelson Mandela, South Africa's first Black president, visited Canada in 1998, he paid tribute to Canada and Canadians for opposing apartheid.

## The Arctic

In 1986, the United States sent the icebreaker *Polar Sea* through the Arctic northern passage without informing the Canadian government.

Canadian Forces on manoeuvre in the Arctic.

Arctic permafrost makes it impossible for sewage and water pipes to be buried in the ground.

The U.S. claimed that the passage was an international waterway. Russian submarines often used Arctic waters to escape detection from NATO submarines. Canadians claimed that the area was a Canadian passage, although, in reality, the government had done little to establish its control of the Arctic area. The Conservatives announced plans to review purchasing nuclear-powered submarines to patrol Canadian shores and the Arctic. The idea was well received, but the projected cost of $8 billion was not. Nevertheless, Canadians agreed that something had to be done to assert Canadian rights to the northern coastal waters. When U.S. President Ronald Reagan visited Canada in 1988, he told Prime Minister Mulroney that the U.S. would notify Canada in advance whenever an American submarine planned to use the Northwest Passage.

## The United Nations

In 1984, Prime Minister Mulroney surprised many people when he appointed Stephen Lewis, former leader of the Ontario NDP, as

*Stephen Lewis was an eloquent spokesperson for Canada at the UN.*

Canadian ambassador to the United Nations. Lewis turned out to be an inspired choice. Not since the days of Lester Pearson had there been such a strong Canadian presence in the United Nations Assembly. Lewis spoke out passionately and strongly, particularly on issues relating to the needs of developing countries. By 1989, Canada was again recognized as a leading middle power at the UN. Canada has served its fifth elected term on the United Nations Security Council.

## The Commonwealth

Canada is an important member of the Commonwealth, an association of 49 nations including Great Britain and most of its former colonies. The Commonwealth is dedicated to fostering world peace, social tolerance, racial equality and economic growth.

During the 1980s, the Commonwealth faced serious problems. There was a great need for economic aid to underdeveloped members. South Africa's racist **apartheid** policies were a source of serious concern, particularly in view of Britain's failure to condemn and oppose a system that ran counter to Commonwealth goals.

Prime Minister Mulroney spoke out strongly, urging all Commonwealth countries to impose economic **sanctions** on South Africa, thereby refusing all trade with that country.

Mulroney worked hard trying to persuade

## A CLOSER LOOK AT APARTHEID

South Africa's apartheid policies (literally the apartness of blacks and whites) not only kept Black South Africans apart, it also denied them basic rights of citizenship—the right to vote, to own property and to travel with freedom around their country. This denial of basic human rights provoked such opposition from other Common-wealth members, that South Africa was forced to withdraw from Commonwealth membership in 1961. It was not until 1991, however, that apartheid was officially repealed, and it was not until 1993 that a multiracial government was elected in South Africa. Canada was a harsh and effective critic of apartheid.

Britain's Prime Minister Thatcher to boycott all trade with South Africa as well. He was unsuccessful, although his attacks on South African policies made Mulroney one of the most respected Commonwealth leaders during the late 1980s. Canada's strong anti-apartheid stand would not be forgotten.

When Nelson Mandela, South Africa's first Black president, visited Canada in 1998, he paid tribute to Canada and Canadians for opposing apartheid. He noted that South Africa's return to democracy, and the elimination of its apartheid laws, would not have been possible without the worldwide support and encouragement of countries like Canada.

*South African President Nelson Mandela thanked Canadians for their support of a free South Africa.*

*"I have fought against white domination, and have fought against black domination. I have cherished the ideal of a democratic and free society in which all persons live together in harmony and with equal opportunities. It is an ideal which I hope to live for and to achieve. But if needs be, it is an ideal for which I am prepared to die."*

Nelson Mandela, former president of South Africa, spent 30 years in prison under the apartheid regime.

FOCUS
1. How did Mulroney change Canada's foreign policy regarding:
   a) Arctic defence?  b) the Armed Forces?  c) the Commonwealth?
2. What is apartheid? Why was it important for Canada to oppose apartheid in South Africa?

# Free Trade with the United States

**6**

> *"The dangers of free trade are to the structure of the economic base of Canada, and our sovereignty as a nation. American priorities aren't necessarily Canadian priorities."*
> Brian Mulroney, 1983

> *"I have spoken today to the President of the United States to express Canada's interest in pursuing a new trade agreement between our two countries."*
> Brian Mulroney, 1985

What had changed Prime Minister Mulroney's mind between 1983 and 1985? During the early 1980s, both the American and Canadian economies experienced a serious **recession**. Many Canadian businesspeople felt that the only route to economic recovery was Canada's ability to sell its products to the larger economic markets of the United States. They began to demand that Canada make a new trade agreement with its southern neighbour. Such an agreement, they felt, would also prevent the United States from establishing protective tariffs to prevent the entry of Canadian products and resources into the United States. By 1985, the Conservative Party had accepted free trade as the basis of its new economic policy, and after two years of negotiations, a free trade agreement between Canada and the United States was signed.

The Free Trade Agreement required ratification by the American Congress and

By 1985, the Conservative Party had accepted free trade as the basis of its new economic policy, and after two years of negotiations, a free trade agreement between Canada and the United States was signed.

the Canadian Parliament before it could go into effect. Conservatives were solidly in support of the agreement; most Liberals and New Democrats were not. Canadian voters were almost equally divided. The only solution was to let the people decide.

The debate over free trade was the leading issue in the election of 1988. Canadian voters returned Mulroney to Parliament with a clear majority.

For the first time since the days of Sir John A. Macdonald, Conservatives had won two consecutive elections. The Conservative victory in Quebec indicated French Canadians had abandoned the Liberals, after 100 years of solid support. The Free Trade Agreement between Canada and the United States came into effect in January 1989.

## THE MAIN IDEAS OF THE FREE TRADE AGREEMENT WERE:

- all remaining tariffs between the two countries would be eliminated by 1998
- any restrictions on American investment in Canada would be greatly reduced
- export of Canadian energy resources (oil, natural gas, and hydroelectricity) would be increased
- in case of an energy shortage, resources would be shared between

the two countries
- the Auto Pact was not to be affected;
- the U.S. would respect the right of Canada to protect some of its cultural industries (radio, television, magazines, newspapers) from American investment
- future trade disputes would be settled by an arbitration board consisting of Canadians and Americans

### FOCUS
1. What is free trade?
2. Why did some Canadians feel it was important to Canada's economy?
3. In your opinion, how has free trade with the United States benefited Canada? How has it hindered Canada's economy?

## Canada in Space

In 1962, Canada launched its first space satellite—the *Alouette*. It was designed to collect data about the electrically charged layer of the earth's atmosphere (the ionosphere). The ionosphere is important because radio signals sent from one location on earth can be bounced back through the atmosphere across great distances to other locations on earth.

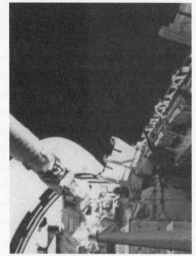

In 1972, Canada, working with the U.S. space agency NASA, was ready to launch its first communications satellite, *Anik A*. *Anik A* beamed radio, telephone and television signals across Canada. In 1976, *Anik A* was followed by *Hermes*, a joint Canadian-American project. *Hermes* was the most powerful non-military satellite of its kind. It allowed experiments in direct broadcasting to individual homes and activities. *Hermes* gave birth to tele-education and tele-medicine, via space.

Many scientists regard Dr. John Chapman (1921–1979) as the father of the Canadian space program. As Assistant Deputy Minister for Space in the Department of Communications, Chapman believed that space communications helped unite Canada: "essentially the north was plugged into the south." He believed that if Canada was going to be in space, its industry should build for space, and be competitive in the international marketplace.

*Anik D,* launched in 1982, was the first Canadian satellite *made* in Canada. It was built by Spar Aerospace, a Canadian telecommunications firm.

George John Klein (1904–1992) was another Canadian who played played a prominent role in the development of our space program. Klein, an inventor with the National Research Council (NRC), designed wind tunnels, all terrain vehicles and special wheelchairs for quadriplegics. In 1951, Klein invented the STEM—storable tubular extendible member. It would be used as a portable antenna for radio beacons used to guide bombers. NASA used the STEM regularly on Mercury, Apollo and Gemini rockets.

In 1976, Klein was consulted on the development of Canadarm—a 15-metre shuttle remote manipulator system (RMS) complete with shoulder, elbow, and simulated hand. Canadarm was commissioned by NASA under direction of the National Research Council and Spar Aerospace. It was designed to be used for work outside a space shuttle as an extension of astronauts' arms. Canadarm could carry up to 30,000 kilograms, and be moved to within 5 centimetres of any required position. The first Canadarm was completed in 1981 at a cost of $24,000,000. Canada built five Canadarms for the United States. These devices, each of which has *Canada* displayed boldly along the side, are excellent examples of the country's skill in technical development and robotics.

*In your view, what was the most important Canadian technical achievement in space science?*

BORN: 1929, Berlin, Germany

SIGNIFICANCE: John Polanyi shared the Nobel Prize for Chemistry in 1986 for the development of reaction dynamics—a new field in chemistry—in which one molecule changes energy with another. His research would form part of the basis of the development of lasers.

BRIEF BIOGRAPHY: John Charles Polanyi began his university education in 1946 at the University of Manchester, where he heard his father's last lectures on chemistry. Polanyi graduated in 1952 with his PhD in chemistry.

Polanyi worked at the National Research Council from 1952–1954, and at Princeton University from 1954–1956. In 1956, he was appointed lecturer at the University of Toronto.

After years of work on infrared chemiluminescence (infared light emission from the movement or vibration of chemical reactions) Polanyi realized that his research might be used to create a new "chemical" kind of high intensity light beam of single colour and frequency—what we now call a laser. He was appointed Professor of Chemistry at the University of Toronto in 1962.

In 1964, two scientists developed the carbon dioxide laser—one of the most powerful lasers available—based partly on Polanyi's research. In 1965, Polanyi, shared the Nobel Prize in Chemistry with Dudley Herschenbach and Yuan T. Lee for his work.

Today, the laser is a key instrument in many areas of technology. In medicine, lasers help facilitate intricate surgery; in industry, their powerful beams are used in materials forming, heat treating and marking; in communications, lasers are used as optical transmission links. In our homes and offices, lasers read the CDs we listen to. The projection of lasers has led to the science of holography or the generation of 3-D images.

John Polanyi, himself, has since been active in many aspects of science. His recent work has focused on spectroscopy—or analyzing the spectrum of light. Polanyi is a Member of the Board of the Canadian Centre for Arms Control and Disarmament, as well as founding chairman of the Canadian Pugwash Group. Polanyi believes that science is the glory and terror of mankind, and that scientists must play a role directly in public affairs, as they relate to our survival in an age of nuclear weapons and other powerful technologies.

## John C. Polanyi

# New People for a New Society

Who should be allowed to come to Canada? Clifford Sifton wanted "sturdy peasants in sheepskin coats," at the turn of the century. Canada's need for farm workers decreased once the West was settled. In 1905, Frank Oliver, the new minister of immigration, wanted only "the right class of British immigrant." Until World War II, the government made it difficult for Asians, Jews and eastern Europeans to immigrate to Canada. It did not believe they would "fit in" to Canadian society. In 1914, 376 Sikhs from India aboard the *Komagata Maru* were turned away from Vancouver. They had waited onboard ship for two months before being rejected. A few refugees from Europe were accepted into the country

*Lincoln Alexander was Ontario's Lieutenant Governor from 1986-1991. Appointed by Joe Clark, Canada's youngest prime minister, Alexander was the first Black Canadian to serve this post.*

Immigrants would be judged by a system that awarded points for education, job skills, and a knowledge of English or French. No weight would be given to race or country of origin.

1900   1910   1920   1930   1940   1950   1960   1970   1980   1990

after World War II as a humanitarian gesture, although Canada's basic immigration policy remained the same: white people from the British Commonwealth, the United States and France were preferred. Other Europeans came next, while non-white immigration into the country was severely limited.

### Changing Attitudes

By the 1970s, many Canadians felt our immigration policy was outdated and out of touch.

They believed Canada's choice of immigrants should be based on Canada's need for workers in certain fields and the ability of immigrants to fill that need. People should not be pre-judged because of the colour of their skin, their native language or the country of origin. In 1976, the Canadian government announced a new immigration policy. Immigrants would be judged by a system that awarded points for education, job skills, and a knowledge of English or French. No weight would be given to race or country of origin.

The change in Canadian immigration was immediate. Canada attracted fewer European immigrants because living conditions had improved in Europe after the war. Job opportunities in many Asian, African and Caribbean countries were poor, and it was hard to get an education. Canada, by contrast, offered social and economic opportunities, as well as civil and human rights. Many Asians, Africans and Caribbeans welcomed the new rules that would give them a chance for a new life in Canada. Over 60,000 "boat people," primarily from South Vietnam, had fled to Canada by the end of the 1980s. During the 1990s, Canada accepted displaced Romas, thousands of Kosovars, Somalians, Rwandians and Chinese refugees.

*Kim Phuc immigrated to Canada from Vietnam. The 1972 photograph of 12 year-old Kim and her family fleeing the horrors of a napalm attack during the Vietnam War is an image that continues to haunt the world.*

NEW PEOPLE FOR A NEW SOCIETY   **337**

**Individuals immigrating to Canada can apply under three categories: family class, refugee class and independent class**

**FAMILY CLASS: The "family class" process is a *sponsorship* process.**

Any Canadian citizen or landed immigrant over the age of 19 and resident in Canada may sponsor a close relative—sons or daughters, parents(s), sibling(s), fiancé(e)—living in another country. The sponsor must show financial stability. S/he must show that s/he is capable of providing financial assistance to the relative for ten years. If the sponsor's application is approved, Canadian officials will contact the Canadian visa office in the country where the prospective immigrant lives. The immigration process then begins.

**INDEPENDENT APPLICANTS: Investor, entrepreneur and self-employed**

This category was designed for people in business. Applicants must show that they have money to invest in a business in Canada. The proposed business must also benefit the Canadian economy by creating jobs for other Canadians. Generally, Canada welcomes this category of immigrant because of the economic benefits to the country.

**OTHER INDEPENDENTS:** Individuals from any part of the world can apply to became permanent residents of Canada as long as they do so from outside Canada. To determine an individual's eligibility, a point system is used. Applicants are given points on a series of categories. Some applicants may be given priority over others, depending on total points obtained. The Canada Quebec Accord gives Quebec the sole responsibility of selecting independent immigrants and refugees destined for Quebec.

The chart below shows the point system currently in use by Canadian Immigration authorities.

| CATEGORIES OF THE SELECTION SYSTEM | MAXIMUM POINTS AWARDED |
|---|---|
| education | Up to 16 |
| experience | Up to 8 |
| specific vocational preparation | Up to 18 |
| age | Up to 10 |
| knowledge of English and/or French | Up to 15 |
| personal suitability | Up to 10 |
| bonus for self-employed immigrants | Up to 30 |
| demographic factor | Up to 10 |
| arranged employment or having a designated occupation | Up to 10 |
| occupation found on the General or Designated occupations list | Up to 10 |

Changes are made to this policy from time to time. One proposal currently under discussion would use a flexible point system where transferable skills would take priority over a rigid occupation-based rating for new immigrants.

*below: Skater Elvis Stojko*

*right: Skater Emanuel Sandhu*

*Above: Senator Vivienne Poy*

*Right: Premier Ujjal Dosanijh*

*Michael Lee-Chin founded AIC Limited, one of Canada's largest mutual fund companies.*

## FOCUS

1. Which groups of people found it difficult to immigrate to Canada before the 1970s? Why?
2. How did Canada's immigration policy change during the 1970s?
3. Do you think that the three categories of applicants are efficient ways of determining who immigrates to Canada? Why or why not?

# 8 A Changing Population

As the new immigration policy took effect, the face of Canada changed. The new immigrants were a "visible minority"—easily recognized as being different. White Canadians sat next to Blacks and Asian Canadians on city buses. Children born in Canada found their new classmates were from Uganda, India or Trinidad. The line-up in the supermarket included people from all over the world. Many Canadians found this interesting and exciting. Others found it frightening. People often fear what they do not understand. Their fear can turn to prejudice and hate.

*Canadian institutions such as the RCMP have made adjustments for the traditions and values of a broad range of Canadians.*

## Assimilation or Integration?

Should immigrants forget their homeland and culture and become like other Canadians as soon as possible? Some people believe that immigrants should be assimilated (a process of quickly becoming Canadian by adopting a new language and culture). This is comparable to the American idea of the **melting pot** where all immigrants become part of one identical society.

Others suggest that immigrants should be gradually integrated into Canadian society. Immigrants should be encouraged to retain important aspects of their original culture, such as customs,

In 1988, the Mulroney government passed the Canadian Multiculturalism Act, which further emphasized the importance of Canada's rich ethnicity, and the diversity of heritage languages used throughout the country.

TIMELINE

| 1900 | 1910 | 1920 | 1930 | 1940 | 1950 | 1960 | 1970 | 1980 | 1990 |

traditions or beliefs. Today, it is generally believed that Canada is a richer society because Canadians have been free to maintain their original culture while being integrated into a Canadian identity or **cultural mosaic.**

In 1971, Prime Minister Trudeau announced that his government supported the idea of multiculturalism, or the cultural mosaic, and encouraged Canadians to take pride in their customs and traditions. It set aside money for cultural programs. New Canadians would learn "Canadian ways," while still retaining much of their cultural heritage. Multiculturalism was enshrined in the Canadian Constitution in 1982. In 1988, the Mulroney government passed the Canadian Multiculturalism Act, which further emphasized the importance of Canada's rich ethnicity, and the diversity of heritage languages used throughout the country.

## *Economic Impact of Immigration*

Some people felt that immigrants took away jobs from Canadians. They wanted the government to cut down on immigration as long as there was any unemployment in Canada. Supporters of immigration suggested that if Canada followed such a policy, the country would always have a restricted immigration policy, because Canada is likely to have some unemployment in the near future. Immigrants also create employment. Every immigrant family purchases clothing, household appliances, furniture, utensils and other necessities. Most immigrants require housing and a car, after a short period. Immigrant demand for goods and services provides employment for thousands of Canadians.

Canada's birth rate has declined dramatically since the 1960s. Economic analysts project that the Canadian population will begin to decrease by the year 2010. Some economists have suggested that Canada needs to support a much higher rate of immigration, because the Canadian economy will not maintain its current standard of living unless the population increases or, at least, remains the same.

### FOCUS
1. What does the term "visible minority" mean?
2. What is the difference between assimilation and integration?
3. Which one do you prefer? Why?
4. How does immigration benefit Canada?

# 9 Prejudice and Racism

**Prejudice**, literally, means to prejudge. Individuals sometimes pre-judge other people before they get to know them. Prejudices often result in **discrimination**. Many Canadi-an immigrants suffered from prejudice. They could not get good jobs. Some employers demanded "Canadian experience." Some immigrants found it hard to find a place to live. Landlords would refuse to rent to them, although housing discrimination is illegal in Canada. Immigrants found themselves the target of racial attacks.

Racism is a form of stereotyping. A racist believes that people of one race or culture differ significantly in intelligence or ability from people of another race or culture. Racist acts occur when people punish other people because of race or culture.

Culture is an everyday affair— what one wears, how late the kids can stay out at night, how long they stay in school, attitudes towards work, leisure activities, religion, respect and gender relationships. Different cultures have different attitudes to family life. Some cultures indulge their children. Others demand instant, unquestioned obedience. Rules for girls may not be the same as rules for boys. The relationship between older and young generations may vary. Some people ask questions when they don't understand something. Others think asking questions is pushy and rude. What seems a chance remark to one culture may be an unbearable insult to another.

*The Raven and the First Humans by Haida artist Bill Reid*

Cultures have very subtle differences, or even very obvious ones. Many people are suspicious of what they don't know. Ignorance is often a preamble to prejudice.

1900  1910  1920  1930  1940  1950  1960  1970  1980  1990

## COMMUNITY SNAPSHOT

**Africville** was founded outside Halifax, Nova Scotia, by former American slaves after the War of 1812. At its height, Africville's largest population was 400 people. All residents owned their own land. They hired themselves out, or fished and farmed to make a living. The community was tightly knit. It consisted of a few large, extended families. The community's centre was its church.

Whites living in Halifax had little use for the residents of Africville. They believed people of colour were not entitled to the same rights they enjoyed. Halifax officials allowed industries to locate in and around Africville. These industries would have been unacceptable elsewhere. Rockhead Prison was located on the outskirts of Africville. So was the Halifax raw sewage dump and a hospital for infectious diseases. Halifax opened its city dump and the incinerator was built in the same area during the 1950s. Africville nevertheless survived, and its people remained close to one another.

AFRICVILLE

Usually Halifax policemen and firemen did not consider Africville to be part of their territory. Criminals moved into the community. They brought illegal liquor, gambling, prostitution and drifters. By the early 1960s, the city of Halifax regarded Africville as an unsalvageable slum. Officials ordered the town to be destroyed, in spite of vigorous protests from its people. Africville's land was expropriated; the residents were relocated. Still, it took five years (1964-1969) for Africville to be razed to the ground.

Today, what was once a thriving community exists as a deserted park. Africville residents, although dispersed, vowed to speak out about the loss of their heritage. They came together to preserve was was left of their culture and history. Today, the Africville story is not forgotten. It has become a focus for Black Canadians everywhere: it is a symbol of "the link between social well being and community heritage."

*retold from Parks Canada backgrounder on Africville.*

BORN: 1925, Montreal, Quebec

SIGNIFICANCE: Perhaps the greatest all-time jazz musician in the world, with over 100 albums to his name.

BRIEF BIOGRAPHY: At the age of 14, Peterson won a national piano contest put on by the CBC. He soon had his own weekly radio station and was playing at local clubs in and around Montreal. He debuted in 1949 at Carnegie Hall, where this 24-year-old Canadian stole the show from more prominent performers. In his long and lustrous career as a jazz pianist, Peterson has played with Ella Fitzgerald, Dizzy Gillespie and Lester Young. He has won Grammy Awards and a Juno, and was nominated to the Juno Awards Hall of Fame in 1978. Unlike many bright Canadian musicians who move to the United States to pursue their careers, Peterson has remained in Canada. He moved to Toronto in 1958, where he briefly operated a world-famous jazz school during the 1960s. By the 1970s, Peterson was one of the most successful jazz pianists of all time. In 1986, he began teaching music part-time at York University in Toronto; in 1991, he became chancellor of the university. Peterson was made a Companion to the Order of Canada in 1985

## Oscar Peterson

Differences like these can lead to misunderstanding, fear and hate. Cultures have very small differences, or even very obvious ones. Many people are suspicious of what they don't know. Ignorance is often a cause of prejudice. Skin color, the shape of one's eyes, religious practices, eating habits, and even style of clothing can all become the focus of prejudice, and sometimes hatred.

Prejudice and racism are most severe in our large cities. People have less personal space in urban areas. Poverty is often a real concern. School boards, police forces, social workers and city governments have tried to deal with the issue. Often, their efforts have provoked charges of racism or discriminatory behavior. Many

## A CLOSER LOOK AT HATE CRIMES

Hate crimes are any acts of violence or assault directed at a person because of racial, religious, ethnic or other differences. According to a recent poll, there are about 60,000 hate crimes committed every year in Canada's major urban centres. Hate crimes, however, need not be violent to be defined as a criminal offence. Slurs, threats and vandalism all constitute a hate crime. Two Canadians have received prominent media attention for their hate crimes. James Keegstra, an Alberta teacher who was fired for giving anti-Semitic lectures, and Ernst Zundel, who was prosecuted for expressing racist ideas, have both been charged under Canada's criminal code. Some people have argued that the prosecution of Zundel and Keegstra denies them the freedom a speech—a right for Canadians under our Constitution. Canada's criminal code, however, states that anyone "who, by communicating statements, other than in private conservation, willfully promotes hatred against an identifiable group is guilty of an indictable offence and is liable to imprisonment."

Canadians do not recognize how words and actions can hurt other people.

Prejudice and racism are worldwide problems. In 1966, the United Nations designated March 21 as International Day of the Elimination of Racial Discrimination. Canada began to celebrate this event in 1989 with thousands of anti-racism activities across the country, emphasizing respect, equality and diversity for all.

Today, Canadians face a serious challenge. Our multicultural mosaic is threatened when people cannot tolerate differences. The alternative is a forced melting pot wherein everyone loses a little of his or her unique individuality.

FOCUS
1. Define: a) prejudice  b) discrimination  c) racism.
2. How did local authorities discriminate against residents of Africville?
3. What are hate crimes?

# 10 Canada's Aboriginal Peoples

Aboriginal Canadians were the first Canadians. There were many different First Nations, speaking over 50 Aboriginal languages. Before European settlers came, they lived a life in harmony with nature. This special relationship with the environment was highlighted in their religious practices. The spirit of the land was an important symbol. Conservation was the principle by which they hunted and fished. Land was like the sky, the water and the wind. It could not be sold, but it could be shared, just as the rivers, animals and fish were to be shared by all.

European traders taught the Aboriginal peoples to value fur more than the animal that bore it. Traders brought the Aboriginals whiskey, guns and disease. European settlers moved in and took over Aboriginal lands. Sometimes a treaty was made between the Aboriginal peoples and the government. Aboriginals would usually be allowed small areas of land, or reserves, a few tools and an annual pension

that was little more than welfare. Sometimes they retained hunting and fishing rights. In return, they gave up much of the vast land they regarded as their heritage. Treaties gave the government of Canada all of present day Manitoba, Saskatchewan, Alberta, the lands of the Mackenzie River Valley, plus parts of Southern Ontario. First Nations leaders of today believe their ancestors did not realize that by signing a treaty with the government, they were relinquishing all claim to their ancestral land.

By the 1970s, many native people felt the government treated them as permanent welfare cases. Their traditional way of life had vanished. Settlers had destroyed the natural forests and grazing lands where they had hunted. They had lost the customs and values they cherished. If they left the reserves to seek work, they found they did not possess the skills required in the modern cities and were often discriminated against. They were trapped in a life style that robbed them of their self-respect.

Canada's Aboriginal peoples faced a basic problem. They wanted an adequate standard of living like other Canadians. They also wanted to retain their old relationship to the land.

1900   1910   1920   1930   1940   1950   1960   1970   1980   1990

# CANADA'S INDIAN ACT

In 1876, the Canadian Parliament passed the Indian Act to establish a federal policy for governing Canada's Aboriginal population. The Act, which was developed without input from First Nations chiefs or elders, defined what an "Indian" was in the legal sense. It outlined the rights and regulations under which Canada's Aboriginal population would be required to live. Traditional ceremonies like the Sun Dance and the Potlatch were outlawed. The government hoped to assimilate Canada's First Nations into the culture established by Canadians of European descent. Residential schools for Aboriginal children were designed to speed up the assimilation process. Canada's current Indian Act was passed in 1951, and was most recently amended in 1985. It categorizes Canada's First Nations peoples as either status (registered) or non-status Indians.

Status Indians are registered under the terms of the Indian Act. Status Indians are known as Treaty Indians if they or their ancestors signed a treaty or treaties with the Canadian government. Registered Indians are status Indians whose ancestors have not signed treaties with the government, but who still fall within the regulations of the Indian Act. Most registered Indians live in British Columbia, parts of Quebec, the Northwest Territories and the Yukon. Registered Indians were not given the right to vote in federal elections until 1960. Non-status Indians are members of the First Nations who are not registered under the Indian Act.

For over one hundred years, the Indian Act contained a clause that stripped Aboriginal women of their Indian status upon marriage to non-Indian men. Loss of Indian status meant these women were no longer eligible to live on reserves and no longer entitled to government benefits received prior to marriage. Indian men who married non-Indian women did not lose Indian status. In 1981, a Maliseet woman from New Brunswick, Sandra Lovelace, asked the United Nations' Human Rights Committee to review her case. The Committee agreed that the Indian Act discriminated against women. The Indian Act was changed in 1985 to provide equal status under the law as guaranteed to all Canadians in the 1982 Canadian Constitution. A new clause was added to the Act to allow Aboriginal women who had lost Indian status prior to 1985 to regain it. Over 100,000 women have done so.

The Indian Act remains in effect today.

## Land Claims and Aboriginal Title

Canada's Aboriginal peoples faced a basic problem. They wanted an adequate standard of living like other Canadians. They also wanted to retain their old relationship with the land. Vast expanses of Canada have been claimed by Aboriginal peoples—land that the

*Ovid Mercredi is one of Canada's most eloquent Aboriginal leaders.*

government of Canada says is no longer theirs. Canada's Aboriginals have taken their case to court, in Canada and before the world.

Lawyers representing Aboriginals argued that their ancestors had never meant to give away Aboriginal lands. The government had merely acted as if they had. They also argued that the government did not live up to its side of the terms of the treaties.

Today, there are several land claim cases before the courts. The first land claim case to reach the courts was the Nisga'a First Nation's claim to 22,870 km² near the Nass River in northern British Columbia. The Nisga'a nation, which currently consists of 6,000 people, settled in Nass Valley long before the first Europeans came to Canada. They had been trying for over 100 years to have their title (ownership of) to the land recognized. British Columbia argued that the land belonged to the province, and that there was no such thing as an Aboriginal title to non-treatied lands. The Supreme Court of Canada agreed to hear the case in 1971. It was known as the Calder case. Fourteen months later, the Court rendered a split decision, with one judge stating that proper process was not followed. The Court did, however, recognize the principle of Aborigi-

| | Cree/Inuit/Naskapi | Inuit | Nisga'a |
|---|---|---|---|
| Date | 1975 | 1993 | 1998 |
| Where | Northern Quebec | Arctic | B.C. |
| Aboriginal /Inuit population | 19,200 | 25,000 | 6,000 |
| How much land was awarded | 169,902 km² | 355,842 km² | 1,992 km² |
| How | specific rights | Inuit owned | full fee simple estate |
| How much land was claimed | 981,610 km² | 1,544,158 km² | 22,870 km² |
| Cash financial payment | $225 million | $1,500 million | $230 million |
| Over how many years | 20 | 15 | 14 |
| Self government | some | make laws, tax | (evolve over 20 years) |

**LAND CLAIM SETTLEMENTS: A COMPARISON**

nal title. That decision convinced the Canadian government to negotiate land settlements or treaties for Aboriginal land claims in those areas where treaties did not exist (non-treatied lands).

The Supreme Court of Canada heard another important case about Aboriginal rights in 1997 when it reviewed the Delgamuukw decision, an Aboriginal land claim by the Gitksan and Wet'suwete'en First Nations of British Columbia. The Delgamuukw case allowed the Supreme Court to clarify the meaning of Aboriginal title and what contributes to it.

## Canadian Vision

When I was small
I used to help my father
Make ax handles.

Coming home from the wood
        with a bundle
of maskwi, snawey, aqamoq,
My father would chip away,
Carving with a crooked knife,
Until a well-made handle appeared,
Ready to be sand-papered
By my brother.

When it was finished
We started another,
Sometimes working through the night
With me holding a lighted shaving
To light their way
When our kerosene lamp ran dry.

Then in the morning
My mother would be happy
That there would be food today
When my father sold our work.

Rita Joe
reprinted with permission from
*Poems of Rita Joe*
Abanaki Press, 1978

*"Seal Hunting," felt tip drawing by Labrador artist Josephina Kalleo*

*Although most people think Aboriginal art is mainly painting and sculpture, Aboriginals have also made substantial contributions to other artistic areas—such as weaving and textiles.*

# Canadian Vision

## Aboriginal and Inuit Culture

Canada's Aboriginal and Inuit peoples have a rich heritage of oral and written literature and artistic tradition. Modern poets like Daniel David Moses and Jeanette Armstrong celebrate Aboriginal identity, culture, the natural world, conflict and change. Novelists like Thomas King argue for change by depicting Aboriginal struggle and triumph within painful reality. His novel, *Green Grass, Running Water* (1996), tells the story of five Blackfoot characters in modern-day Canada. Playwrights like

*Buffy Sainte-Marie*

Tomson Highway bring Aboriginal concerns to the stage. His play, *The Rez Sisters* (1988), is the story of seven women from a reserve on Manitoulin Island, Ontario, trying to win at bingo. Meanwhile, popular singers like Susan Aglukark and Buffy Sainte-Marie have made contributions through their music. In the world of fine arts, Aboriginal and Inuit prints, sculpture, and wall hangings continue to be exhibited and collected around the world. Self-taught painter Norval Morriseau is an originator of the style known as Woodland Indian Art—an aesthetic combining Aboriginal and Euro Canadian ideals.

*Susan Aglukark*

Daphne Odjig, a member of the Ojibwa tribe, is one of the many unique Woodland Indian artists in Canada today. Her paintings often deal with human relationships in the context of Aboriginal culture. Inuit printmaker Kenojuak Ashevak's drawing, *The Enchanted Owl*, was used on the postage stamp celebrating the 100th anniversary of the Northwest Territories. She was the first Aboriginal artist to be awarded the Order of Canada. And Pitseolak Ashoona's book, *Pitseolak: Pictures out of my Life*, published in 1971, was made into a National Film Board documentary.

Chief Joseph Gosnell of the Nisga'a tribal Council was elected for President in 1992. He was a negotiator for the Nisga'a Treaty, which was signed in principle in his village of New Aiyyansh in the Nass Valley of B.C.

He made an historic speech to the British Columbia legislature on December 2, 1998, before that body ratified the Nisga'a Treaty. Key sections of his speech follow.

*...the Nisga'a Treaty [is]—a triumph for all British Columbians —and a beacon of hope for Aboriginal people around the world....*

"To us, a Treaty is a sacred instrument. It represents an understanding between distinct cultures and shows respect for each other's way of life. We know we are here for a long time together.

A Treaty stands as a symbol of high idealism in a divided world. That is why we have fought so long, and so hard...

We have worked for justice for more than a century. Now, it is time to ratify the Nisga'a Treaty, for Aboriginal and non-Aboriginal people to come together and write a new chapter in the history of our Nation, our province, our country and, indeed, the world.

The world is our witness.
Be strong.
Be steadfast.
Be true.

**Why did Chief Gosnell feel the Treaty was such a triumph?**

## A CLOSER LOOK AT FIRST NATIONS LOBBY GROUPS

During the late 1940s, several representatives from Canada's aboriginal peoples came together to form the North American Indian Brotherhood (N.A.I.B.). They wanted to lobby for changes in federal and provincial Aboriginal policies. The N.A.I.B. was not successful. Not all First Nations supported its efforts, and government actions hindered its growth. In 1969, the National Indian Brotherhood (N.I.B) was created as a new lobby group, supported by provincial and territorial Aboriginal organizations. In 1982, the N.I.B. became the Assembly of First Nations (AFN), committed to self-determination for Status and Treaty First Nations people in Canada. The AFN has pressed successfully, and will continue to press for Aboriginal self government, for improvements in education, business opportunities and family support.

In March 1990, Mohawk warriors from the Kanesatake Reserve outside Montreal blocked off a road leading to Oka, Quebec. They were protesting construction of a golf course on lands the Mohawk had claimed since the 1700s. The police were called in when the warriors refused to leave. One officer died in the shoot out. All of Canada waited anxiously over the next eleven weeks as Mohawk protesters faced Canadian soldiers in a tense standoff. Finally, the protesters surrendered. Several were arrested. The disputed lands were ultimately turned over to the Mohawk nation by the Canadian government.

## In Their Own Words

*"I am a native who lives among whites…. Yet for most of my life my identity as an Indian wasn't clear to me. I saw no difference between myself and the people around me, and therefore took their identity as my own. If anything I felt a benefit; my face meant I had a year-round tan.*

*But by junior high school, I noticed that there was one part of my maturing that was missing. I was the only one in my group who had never been involved with a girl. I was a bit fat, so I lost weight, but that didn't help.*

*I came to realize that the problem was that I looked different from the white people around me. Once, standing before a mirror with a friend, I noticed how his wavy, blond hair hung loosely over his smooth, pinkish skin, while my hair was stiff, in thick, combed clumps above my tan skin. Around my deep black eyes was a darkness created by my high cheekbones that gave me an almost brooding look. If it were possible to symbolize our differences, my friend would have been warmth and brightness; I would have been anger and darkness. And not dark like James Dean, but more like a thug in an alley.*

*My early assumption that because I lived among whites I could shed my race had proved painfully false. …When one race dominates a population, there is going to be a boundary. That boundary in my life was around the white man's world. By some magic, whites had accepted me at a sort of mascot level, but they did not understand or respect my race. My physical difference made the females around me wary, a fact at the core of my need to be with my own kind.*

*We human beings can't help thinking about our differences. I don't know why we dwell on the thickness of our lips, the structure of cheekbones or the colour of skin….I began to die inside when I saw my situation. Everywhere I felt like an outsider. Every little stare seemed to be someone's way of telling me that they were better than me, and that I didn't belong. When I went to dances and nightclubs, the girls around me were always white. I felt they were unobtainable. This depressed me so I usually got drunk….*

*I now believe that if the society I live in does not accept me, I must take away its reasons not to. Which leads me to my desire to become a screenwriter….I went to a native screenwriting workshop and met the first native screenwriter. He was 28. He told me that there were only three other native screenwriters in all of Canada. This is when I realized why there is so much ignorance of our people. I realized I had an obligation to try and change that. This is why I have chosen screenwriting as a career."*

This memoir was written by Sean Kelly, who died in 1996 at age 22.

---

FOCUS
1. Why did this writer feel different?
2. What does he intend to do. Why?
3. What happened at Oka, Quebec?

# 11 Nunavut

On April 1, 1999, the map of Canada changed as the territory of Nunavut came into being. It had taken more than fifteen years of negotiation between the Inuit Tapirisat of Canada, the Tungavik Federation of Nunavut and the Canadian government. At issue was Inuit title to Arctic lands and Inuit Self-government. Nunavut comprises some 350,000 km$^2$ of land in the eastern Arctic between the tree line and the North Pole. Nunavut, four times as large as the state of Texas, is home to 17,000 people.

For many years, Canada's northern border was the Northwest Territories. In 1971, John Amagoalik and several other Inuit leaders founded the Inuit Tapirisat of Canada to work towards the creation of a new territory, one governed by Inuit. Because the population of the eastern Northwest Territories was 85% Inuit, the Tapirisat approached the government of the Northwest Territories to ask if

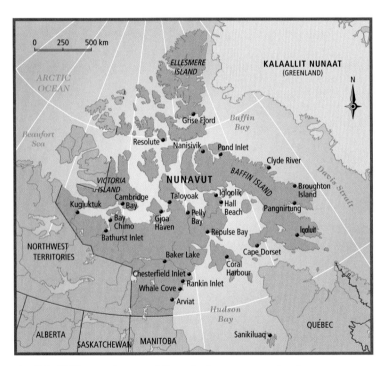

April 1, 1999, saw the map of Canada change to recognize the new territory of Nunavut.

it would divide into two. The eastern part would become Nunavut. In 1982, people in the Northwest Territories voted to divide the region. The boundaries of Nunavut were decided by another popular election in 1992.

The Inuit were given the right to hunt and fish over an area twice as big as British Columbia, and a share of royalties from mineral development in the area.

Nunvut has three official languages—

*Paul Okalik*

*This student is hard at work in a high school in Nunavut.*

Nunavut itself is the successful result of the comprehensive Nunavut Land Claims agreement enacted in 1993. In exchange for their land, the Inuit surrendered all other land claims. They also received a payment of $1.148 billion to be paid out over fourteen years. Additional funds were set aside for training in management and public service.

Inuktitut, French and English. Its capital is Iqaluit, and everyone over the age of sixteen can vote or run for public office. Paul Okalik, a 34-year-old lawyer, was elected as Nunavut's first Premier. He faces some difficult problems. The average annual per capita income is $11,000, and the unemployment rate is 22%.

**FOCUS**
1. What were the major terms of the 1993 Nunavut Land Claims Agreement?
2. What challenges face Nunavut?

# Canada in the 1990s

*Jean Chrétien has been one of Canada's most experienced and popular political figures.*

Jean Chrétien, from Shawinigan, Quebec, became prime minister in 1993. He was an experienced and popular politician. He had served under Pearson and Trudeau. His reputation for honesty and toughness made him popular with voters. Although well-to-do,

Chrétien projected a down-to-earth image in tune with the Liberal party's grassroots strength. The new prime minister was faced with two large problems: an enormous budget deficit of $46 billion, which was rising annually, and a powerful Quebec separatist move-

Canada extended economic ties to the Pacific Rim Countries (APEC).

TIMELINE

1900   1910   1920   1930   1940   1950   1960   1970   1980   1990

ment pressing for another referendum.

Chrétien set to work. He appointed Paul Martin minister of finance with instructions to reduce the deficit. Martin froze public service wages, cut defence and foreign aid, privatized Canadian National railways, and reduced the size of the government. By 1998, Martin announced a budget surplus.

Dealing with the separatists was another matter altogether. Jacques Parizeau, leader of the Parti Québécois and premier of Quebec, announced his referendum on Quebec sovereignty for October 30, 1995. The Liberals were not worried. It was almost too late before Chrétien realized his government had badly underestimated the appeal of independence to many young Québécois voters. Lucien Bouchard, former Liberal under Trudeau, then former Conservative under Mulroney, joined the "oui" side and campaigned vigorously throughout Quebec. Chrétien responded rapidly with rallies and speeches. The vote came down to the wire. The "nons" squeaked through to victory by a mere 1.2 percent

Chrétien vowed that federalist Canada would never be caught unprepared again. He appointed Stéphane Dion intergovernmental affairs minister to insure that Ottawa would have a response to the separatist movement.

Dion asked the Supreme Court of Canada to rule of the legality of separation. The court ruled that separation was legal, but that it could only be achieved with a clear majority.

In 1997, while the western Reform Party under Alberta's Preston Manning became the Liberal's official opposition, former Prime Minister Joe Clark returned to public life as leader of the Progressive Conservatives. The Chrétien government worked to expand Canada's economic ties throughout the world.

*Jean Chrétien poses with APEC leaders at a conference in British Columbia.*

The Free Trade Agreement with the United States was expanded to include Mexico (NFTA). Canada extended economic ties to the Pacific Rim Countries (APEC). Canada became a founding member of the Arctic Council. Beginning in 1994, Chrétien and the provincial premiers travelled to many parts of the world including China, South America, Cuba and Asia as part of the Team Canada effort to increase trade and investment. Chrétien also championed human rights on these tours as he urged other world leaders to adopt formal human rights policies.

## Privatization—A Continuing Trend

Chrétien and other leaders continued the trend towards privatization and less government interference. In 2000, the Ontario government drafted plans to privatize jails. In Alberta, legislation was introduced to privatize some health care services. Toll highways were built in Ontario and New Brunswick. Ontario's Highway 407 was the country's first privately-owned highway.

Unfortunately, privatization has drastically reduced Canada's safety net. Crowded emergency rooms and long waiting lists for

## THE CALGARY DECLARATION

In 1997, the federal government invited all the provincial premiers to attend a meeting in Calgary to design a framework for future constitutional change. Lucien Bouchard, premier of Quebec, refused to attend. Nevertheless, the "Calgary Declaration" was created. It said:

❏ Canada's gift of diversity includes Aboriginal peoples and cultures, the vitality of the English and French languages and a multicultural citizenry drawn from all parts of the world.

❏ In Canada's federal system, where respect for diversity and equality underlies unity, the unique character of Quebec society, including its French-

speaking majority, its culture and its tradition of civil law, is fundamental to the well-being of Canada. Consequently, the legislature and Government of Quebec have a role to protect and develop the unique character of Quebec society within Canada.

❏ If any future constitutional amendment confers powers on one province, these powers must be available to all provinces.

❏ Canada is a federal system where federal, provincial and territorial governments work in partnership while respecting each other's jurisdictions. Canadians want their governments to work cooperatively and with

flexibility to ensure the efficiency...of the federation. Canadians want their governments to work together, particularly in the delivery of their social programs. Provinces and territories renew their commitment to work in partnership with the government of Canada to best serve the needs of Canadians.

❏ All Canadians are equal and have rights protected by the law.

❏ All provinces, while diverse in their characteristics, have equality of status.

❏ Canada is graced by diversity, tolerance, compassion and an equality of opportunity that is without rival in the world.

*With which of the above are you in agreement. Why?*
*With which do you disagree? Why?*

people needing surgery became common and worrisome to Canadians in the 1990s. Funding for education was also cut substantially. Many Canadians began to fear that their social services would soon become extinct. They worried that giving more power to the individual provinces would negatively impact their social programs. Would provincial control erase the universality of their programs, for example? Would provinces with less money have inferior programs for their poor and under privileged residents? Could the provinces privatize health care? If so, would all Canadians be able to afford it?

During the latter part of the 1990s, Canada's premiers held a series of meetings to discuss how best to deliver social services such as health care, pensions and education. On February 4, 1999, they signed the Social Union Agreement in an attempt to eliminate duplication of services between the federal and provincial governments, as well as build cooperation and increase discussion between these two forms of government. All provinces, except Quebec, agreed to the principles outlined in the agreement.

Both the Social Union Agreement and the Calgary Declaration attempted to redefine Canadian values. To date, the security of our values has yet to be determined. Only time will tell how Canada will succeed in maintaining its social safety net in a society dominated by global free trade and privatization.

## A CLOSER LOOK AT THE ALLIANCE PARTY

In March 2000, the Reform Party of Canada changed its name in an attempt to shed its grassroots Alberta reputation. The new Canadian Reform Conservative Alliance Party hoped to attract disillusioned Conservatives from Ontario and Quebec, and Reformers from the West. Although the new party supports Canada's bilingualism, it does not support special status for Quebec, or the First Nations people of Canada. The new "Alliance Party" also proposes a fixed income-tax rate of 17%, a stricter criminal and parole system, and new immigration policies.

### FOCUS

1. What 2 major problems did Chrétien's Liberals face when they first came to power? How did Chrétien propose to solve them?
2. What is privatization? Name an example of this policy.
3. What are some advantages and disadvantages of privatization?
4. With which points of the Calgary Declaration do you agree? Why?

# Canadian Vision

The Legislative Assembly of the Northwest Territories opened in 1993. Designed by Yellowknife architect Gino Pinn, the 4,273 square metre building has outside walls of zinc, and was carefully constructed to ensure that the wild bird and animal population of the area would not be driven away. Its inner chamber is round to reflect the unique consensus government of the Northwest Territories .

The Confederation Bridge connecting Prince Edward Island with New Brunswick opened for business May 31, 1997. It is 12.9 km long, and took over three years to build at a cost of $1 billion Canadian dollars.

BORN: 1939, Hong Kong

SIGNIFICANCE: Canada's first Asian-Canadian Governor General.

BRIEF BIOGRAPHY: Born during the Second World War, Clarkson and her family immigrated to Canada in 1942, entering the country as refugees. She attended the University of Toronto and, after receiving a Masters degree in English, attended the Sorbonne in France to continue her post-graduate studies. From 1965 until 1982, Clarkson worked as a host, writer and producer for several CBC television programs. She left television for a few years in 1982 to serve as the Agent-General of Ontario in Paris, France, where she promoted Ontario's business and cultural interests throughout France, Spain and Italy. In 1987, she returned to Canada where she became president and publisher of McClelland and Stewart. In 1988, she returned to television as the executive producer, host and writer of Adrienne Clarkson Presents. In 1998, Clarkson served as Chairwoman of the Board of Trustees of the Canadian Museum of Civilization in Hull, Quebec. She was made an Officer to the Order of Canada in 1992 and, in 1999, Clarkson was appointed Governor General of Canada.

## Adrienne Clarkson

# 13 Women's Rights

In 1968, Prime Minister Lester Pearson established the Royal Commission on the Status of Women to report on the status of women in Canada. Chaired by Ottawa journalist Florence Bird, the Commission was asked to make recommendations on improvements the federal government could make to improve women's status. Members of the Commission travelled across the country for six months, listening to more than 450 reports. In 1970, they released their conclusions. The Commission made 167 recommendations addressing the rights of women in the workforce, in education, legal rights, and the rights of women to government and administrative positions. Many of the recommendations were implemented, particularly those which provided increased opportunity for women in the workforce. Other concerns such as maternity leave, publicly supported daycare and pay equity, "equal pay for work of equal value," became the issues of the 1980s and 1990s.

The Commission was significant because it raised public awareness about women's

*Rosemary Brown was the first Black woman to be elected to a legislature in Canada when she won a seat as MP in British Columbia in 1972. In 1975, she ran for the leadership of the NDP party, but lost. Brown's political career and influence provided young Canadian women of colour with a valuable role model. Rosemary Brown was inducted as an Officer to the Order of Canada in 1996.*

issues. In 1973, the federal government established the Advisory Council on the Status of Women, reporting to the Minister of Labour. More recently, women's issues have been represented in the federal cabinet by the Secretary of State, Status of Women & Multiculturalism portfolio.

In the 1980s, women lobbied successfully to have equal rights for women included within the Charter of Rights. Political leaders soon realized women's issues were an important factor in winning elections. The number of women in Parliament has slowly but constantly increased.

Despite occupying almost 50% of the workforce by the 1990s, women and children continued to live well below the poverty line in Canada. While the reasons for this were many, at heart was the increased divorce rate, which left many women struggling to raise families on their own; the wage gap; and the fact that women still tended to work in what was known as the "pink ghetto," clerical,

In the 1980s, women lobbied success-fully to have equal rights for women included within the Charter of Rights.

**TIMELINE**

1900   1910   1920   1930   1940   1950   1960   1970   1980   1990

retail, and "caring' profes-sions (nursing and daycare), which paid less than other jobs.

In 1996, the National Association of Women (NAC) organized a march against poverty to address these concerns. Hundreds of women marched to Ottawa in the hope of raising public awareness about the plight of poor women. They want-ed better pay equity laws, more affordable housing and economic independence for women.

Although poverty is still a grave concern for many women and children in Canada, the federal govern-ment has addressed some of the needs raised by the women at the March Against Poverty. In 1999, 230,000 federal employees including

*Kim Campbell was elected to the House of Commons as a Conservative in 1988, and served as Minister of Justice from 1990-1992. On June 25, 1993, Campbell became the first female Prime Minister in Canadian history, succeeding Brian Mulroney.*

clerks, librarians and sec-retaries, most of them women, settled their pay equity dispute with the federal government. The workers had been waiting for over fifteen years. Gov-ernment estimates regard-ing the cost of settlement ranged between $3.3 and $3.6 billion, with the aver-age worker receiving some $30,000 in back pay. To help solve the increasing day care needs of many families, the government proposed an increase to our existing maternity leave policies. By 2001, the government proposes to allow new parents a maximum fifty weeks leave by combining parental benefits, sickness benefits and maternity leave.

**FOCUS**

1. What was the purpose of the Royal Commission on the Status of Women? What was its finding?
2. What are some problems faced by women today?
3. How did the women's rights movement of the 1960s and 1970s change women's lives in the 1990s?
4. Do you think feminism in still a necessary social movement? Why or why not?

# 14 Globalization

The world seems a much smaller place than it did in our grandparents' day.

We often hear this kind of comment, but what does it mean? Surely the Earth itself hasn't shrunk.

Two major changes have occurred over the last 30 years to transform what was once a world of isolated nations into what Marshall McLuhan called a "global village."

*Marshall McLuhan, Professor of English at the University of Toronto, has been a major voice in the field of communication theory and the study of mass media. McLuhan realized in the 1960s that the Internet and computers would radically change the way we communicate. He wrote about the effects of virtual reality on relationships, and about how our lives would be affected by electronic communication.*

*Air Canada, Canada's only airline, became a member of Star Alliance, a partnership of ten of the world's leading airlines, including United and Luftansa, in 1997. In 1999, it purchased Canadian Airlines for $92 million. What does it mean for Canada to have only one national airline?*

*Nations competed at a one-day International Cricket Festival in Toronto. Modern transportation methods make events like these common today.*

Two major changes have occurred over the last 30 years to transform what was once a world of isolated nations into what Marshall McLuhan called a "global village."

T I M E L I N E

1900   1910   1920   1930   1940   1950   1960   1970   1980   1990

First, telecommunications allow people of different cultures and regions to exchange information, views, opinions, and knowledge quickly and easily. Satellite technology, the Internet, the wireless telephone, television and radio bring us to places our grandparents only dreamed about. What was once foreign and far-flung is now familiar. Canada is one of the most connected nations in the world as Canadians communicate with each other regularly by e-mail, buy goods through e-commerce, do our banking or send pictures and files over the Internet, play interactive games, or conduct medical examinations through video links. Canadian companies such as BCE dominate the telecommunications world with subsidiaries all over the world.

Many industries have moved away from localized production and consumption. People today exchange goods and services on a global scale. With the help of telecommunications and efficient forms of transportation, a company can have departments scattered throughout the world, each in the most economical location: a head office in Halifax, for example, a design department in San Diego, and a production plant in the Philippines. The daily work life that once connected individu-

> **Canada is one of the most electronically connected countries in the world**
> - In 1998, Canadians accounted for 7 percent of e-commerce in the world. Our population is only .5% of the world's total.
> - There are over one billion pages of information on the Internet. If a person spent less than 10 seconds reading each page, he or she would have to spend 24 hours a day, seven days a week for 317 years.
> - Close to 44% of all Canadian households have a computer, while 28% have Internet access.

als in the same office now connects nations. The business office of the 1920s has often become a home office with video conferencing, flex hours and Intranets.

Telecommunications help us learn more about the world around us, and the globalization of production and consumption unites our interests. Our world is indeed getting smaller.

**FOCUS**
1. What is globalization?
2. How have computers changed the way people work in Canada?

# Questions & Activities

Questions and Activities

## Test Yourself

Match the persons or group in column A with the definition in column B.

| A | B |
|---|---|
| **1.** Rosemary Brown | **a)** free trade agreement among Canada, Mexico and the United States |
| **2.** Wayne Gretzky | **b)** Manitoba MPP who stopped the ratification of the Meech Lake Accord |
| **3.** Oscar Peterson | **c)** first woman to be named Prime Minister of Canada |
| **4.** Joe Gosnell | **d)** new tax introduced by Brian Mulroney |
| **5.** Elijah Harper | **f)** role model for young women of colour |
| **6.** Kim Campbell | **f)** policy of selling Crown corporations to private businesses |
| **7.** NEP | **g)** famous hockey player |
| **8.** GST | **h)** energy program introduced by Trudeau in the 1970s |
| **9.** NAFTA | **i)** world-renowned jazz great |
| **10.** Privatization | **j)** Chief of the Nisga'a band, who signed land claim treaty |

## Ideas for Discussion

**1.** Compare the ideas and policies of Pierre Trudeau and Brian Mulroney. Use at least five of the following headings as organizers for your comparison: relations with provincial leaders; energy policy; attitudes to the national debt; attitude about powers of the federal and provincial governments; attitudes to French, English relations; attitudes towards the Meech Lake Accord; attitudes toward the United States; belief in the role of government in the economy.

**2.** Prepare one side of the argument for a class debate: Resolve that the free trade agreement will strengthen Canada's economy and cultural identity.

**3.** "There is no Canadian identity." Brainstorm arguments for and against this idea.

**4.** Name jobs that before the 1970s might have been considered "for men" or "for women" in the following areas:

**a)** offices      **d)** hospitals
**b)** factories     **e)** schools
**c)** farms       **f)** home

5. Are boys and girls treated equally in your school? Provide specific examples to support your idea. Write a letter to the school board outlining any changes you feel should be made in your school. Be sure to send a copy of the letter to your principal.

6 Some people claim that feminism is no longer a necessary social movement. Women and men, they say, are now considered equal. They both work, more women have access to jobs traditionally considered men's, and the responsibilities of raising a family are now equally distributed between men and women. Do you think feminism—the women's movement—is still necessary?

## Do Some Research

1. Analyze a recent strike in your community.
   a) What was the position of the workers?
   b) What was the position of the management?
   c) What was the final settlement? Were workers and management both satisfied?
   d) How did the strike affect your community?
   e) What are your personal reactions to this strike?

2. Do some research about one of your favorite Canadian sports or entertainment personalities. Write a Canadian Lives biocard. Pass the cards around the class and then assemble them in a class folder.

3. Do you think the "point system" of selecting immigrants is really fair? How would you change it or improve it?

4. There is prejudice in Canada not only against immigrants from other countries but also against other groups that people perceive as "different." Find out more about one such group. What can you do to help them become fully accepted as part of Canadian society?

## Be Creative

1. Write a letter to a local newspaper outlining your ideas on an aspect of one of the following:
   a) sexual equality    b) native rights
   c) Canadian culture   d) immigration policy

2. Organize a radio or television program to re-enact a famous sporting event of the 1960s or 1970s. Present your program to the rest of the class.

3. Present a visual or sound collage on one of Canada's most famous musicians, singers, artists, actors, dancers, or writers.

4. Organize a multicultural "caravan" or pageant in your class or school.

**You and the members of your class work for Alpha Corporation. Your jobs involve assembling high technology radio and radar equipment. The work force is about 75% female and 25% male. Four weeks ago, you and the other members of your union voted to go on strike. You have been walking the picket lines ever since. The union's strike fund has given you some money, but not nearly enough to cover your living expenses.**

Now your union negotiators and the company have agreed on issues affecting wages, fringe benefits and safety. Issues of special importance to women working in the plant, however, have been rejected by the company.

Union leaders have called a meeting today to decide whether to accept the company's offer or to continue to strike. As you enter the hall of a nearby community centre, you are handed a sheet summarizing the state of negotiations. You read the list of accepted and rejected demands, and make up your mind on how you will vote. When the meeting is called to order, you should be prepared to speak up for your point of view.

Would your position be any different if you were male or female? Why or why not?

## Electronic Workers' Union Local 198

Report of the Strike Committee

Fellow workers, as you know, our negotiating team has been meeting with Alpha Corporation representatives. Last night we began to feel we were getting somewhere. The company has finally agreed to some of our demands, but not all of them. Even though it is not entirely satisfactory, we felt we should put the offer to a vote.

| Union Demands | Company Position |
|---|---|
| **1.** Wage increases as requested over a two-year contract period | accepted |
| **2.** Better fringe benefits including a dental plan | accepted |
| **3.** Improved pension | accepted |
| **4.** New, tougher safety regulations | accepted |
| **5.** Six months' paid maternity leave | rejected |
| **6.** Day care facilities in the plant | rejected |
| **7.** Improvement of washroom facilities to accommodate more female employees | rejected |
| **8.** Equal pay for equal work | rejected (company says it has the right to decide pay levels of jobs) |

# Point
## Counterpoint

With which of the following statements do you most agree? Why?

With which of the following statements do you least agree? Why?

**"Canada is a collection of ten provinces with strong governments loosely connected by fear."**
Barry Broadfoot

**"Our sense of identity is our sense of identity."**
Marshall McLuhan

**"Canada is a society rather than a nation."**
Kildare Dobbs

**"Canada is the only country in the world that knows how to live without an identity."**
Marshall McLuhan

**"Canada had no cultural unity, no linguistic unity, no religious unity, no economic unity, no geographic unity. All it has is unity."**
Kenneth Boulding

**"The Canadian is often a baffled man because he feels different from his British kindred and his American neighbours, sharply refused to be lumped together with either of them, yet cannot make plain his difference."**
J.B. Priestly

**"Canadians have been accustomed to defining themselves by saying what they are not."**
William Kilbourn

**"A Canadian is someone who knows he is going somewhere, but isn't sure where."**
W.L. Morton, Canadian historian

**"Canada is less coherent than the U.S., more of a melting pot, more a "community of communities." Thus in Canada it is possible to belong to both the country as a whole and at the same time to a unique segment of it, as I belong in particular to the Maritimes."**
Alex Colville

# Introduction

## One Nation or Two?

Canada's constitution in 1867 established rules by which Aboriginals, French Canadians and English Canadians could coexist. Over the years, different problems strained the relationship among these three founding groups. Aboriginal Canadians were ignored, and struggled to regain their rights and lands. English and French Canadians experienced numerous difficulties, which prevented them from building a common heritage. The language disputes in Manitoba, Louis Riel's hanging, and the conscription crisis during the two world wars resulted in a serious division between these two groups.

During the twentieth century, differences between the French and English gave rise to the Quiet Revolution of the 60s and, in the 70s, to the first provincial separatist government—the Parti Québécois. Under the leadership of René Lévesque, the Parti Québécois held a referendum on sovereignty association in 1980. This was the first time in Canada's history that a province held a vote seeking to break up the country.

By the year 2000, the people of Quebec remained divided on the relationship Quebec should have with the rest of Canada. Québécois federalists believed their francophone heritage could survive within Canada. French Canadian separatists believed that Quebec's francophone community could prosper only by separating from the rest of Canada.

## METHODS OF HISTORICAL INQUIRY

### Computer Technology

Word processing programs, graphic art programs, spreadsheets and the Internet have greatly enhanced our ability to both research historical information, and present our findings in creative and organized ways. Students using computers can access a wide range of primary and secondary sources from all over Canada and the world. Researchers are able to download maps, obtain up-to-date statistics or census data, and find pictures related to any research topic. Many of Canada's public and academic libraries are computerized with databases that can be accessed through the Internet. In addition, CD-Rom encyclopedias are inexpensive and informative research tools.

# Chapter Seven
## Canada and Quebec: One Nation or Two?

## Expectations

### General Expectations:
**By the end of this chapter, you will be able to:**
- demonstrate an understanding of French Canadian identity
- demonstrate an understanding of French-English relations

### Specific Expectations:
**By the end of this chapter, you will be able to:**
- identify the major events that contributed to the growth of modern Quebec nationalism and separatism
- assess the changing relationship between English Canada and French Canada
- identify the events of the October Crisis
- understand the nature, implications and process of the 1980 and 1995 referendums
- define the Meech Lake and Charlottetown Accords
- summarize the terms of the Calgary Declaration and assess its implications for Quebec and Canada
- identify Acadians as a major francophone group outside Quebec and understand their struggle for recognition
- identify French-Canadian personalities

## WORD LIST

| | | | |
|---|---|---|---|
| Coexistence | Nationalism | Parti Québécois | Separatism |
| Federalism | New France | Quiet Revolution | War Measures Act |
| Language Laws | October Crisis | Referendum | |

# Chapter 7
# *Advance* **Organizer**

## 1

French Canadians can trace their roots in Quebec back over 400 years. Their culture stems from the period when New France was a French colony. Today, 7.4 million French Canadians of all races call Quebec home.

After the British assumed control of Quebec in 1763, French Canadians were granted the right to use their own language, laws and religion. French Canadians still felt threatened by the increasing number of English-speaking people moving into the country.

Confederation in 1867 created special guarantees for the French culture in Quebec. However, in the years that followed, there were clashes between the French and English over a number of issues.

## 2

By 1960, a new generation of Quebecers wanted more than just survival. They demanded equality. The "Quiet Revolution," a period of modernization, was underway. Vast natural resource projects led to economic expansion. The province took a fresh look at its education and social policies. In the new political atmosphere, some Quebecers claimed that independence was the only way to gain real equality with other Canadians.

## 3

In October 1970, headlines all over the world announced that James Cross, a British diplomat, had been kidnapped by the FLQ, a Quebec terrorist group. Pierre Laporte, a Quebec cabinet minister, was also kidnapped. He was found murdered in the trunk of a car. In response to the crisis, the federal government proclaimed the War Measures Act, which gave police special powers. Hundreds of suspected separatists were arrested without charge.

Many Canadians objected to the loss of civil rights. The crisis convinced Quebecers, however, that change should only come about through peaceful means.

## 4

In 1976, René Lévesque, the Parti Québécois leader, was elected premier. He promised to lead Quebec to independence as a separate state. On May 20, 1980, the people of Quebec voted in a referendum. They were asked whether Quebec should negotiate a new relationship with Canada—a "sovereignty association." Nearly 60% voted against the plan. The defeat of the referendum led to a temporary decline in separatist support.

## 5

Robert Bourassa returned as the Liberal Premier in 1985. He promised to work more closely with the federal government if Quebec's rights were protected and it was recognized as a "distinct society" within Canada. Prime Minister Mulroney negotiated the Meech Lake Accord to recognize Quebec's uniqueness.

When the Meech Lake Accord failed to receive unanimous provincial approval, Mulroney negotiated the Charlottetown Accord. Canadians rejected it in a national referendum. Once again English-French relations in Canada became very tense. The language rights of non-French speaking Quebecers remained a contentious issue.

## 6

The rejection of the Charlottetown Accord created a unity crisis in Canada. The separatist government of Quebec organized a second referendum on sovereignty in 1995. Quebec narrowly voted to stay within Canada. The referendum issue was of great concern to the Aboriginal communities in Quebec. Jean Chrétien, prime minister at the time, took the separation issue to the Supreme Court of Canada.

# The French
# in New France

*Arrival of Ships from France by L.R. Batchelor.*

Christopher Columbus's voyage to the Caribbean in 1492 launched European exploration of the Americas. France, England, Holland and Spain sent explorers to determine the land mass of this large continent.

Eventually, the French, Dutch and English would establish settlements in North America, while their Spanish rivals would colonize Central and South America, as well as the southern United States.

On his second voyage to the continent in 1535, French explorer Jacques Cartier became the first European to sail up the St. Lawrence River. Cartier claimed the area for France. His reports of a resource-rich land, teeming with furs, forests and fish encouraged the French government to explore this unknown continent, but early French attempts at colonization were limited.

In 1604, Sieur de Monts and Samuel de Champlain established a colony at Port Royal on the Bay of Fundy (in what is now Nova Scotia). This was the first permanent European settlement in North America. Cham-

These new settlements, collectively known as New France, were an important source of furs, fish and timber for the mother country.

plain would establish a second colony on the St. Lawrence River, at Quebec.

These new settlements, collectively known as **New France,** were an important source of furs, fish and timber for the mother country. Champlain and his associates traded for furs with the Algonquian and the Huron First Nations of the area. Champlain himself explored and charted the lands of eastern Canada, and from the Hudson River to Georgian Bay.

Samuel de Champlain and other New France leaders wanted to impose European values on Aboriginal peoples and convert them to Christianity. French missionary priests and nuns settled in the new French colony. They provided medical, educational and administrative leadership. The Roman Catholic Church became New France's most important institution. Its influence would continue for over 350 years. By 1759, the community of New France numbered only 60,000 people. New England had 1,200,000 people populating its shores.

Residents of New France thought of themselves as **Canadien,** rather than **Français.** Many had been born in North America. They had developed a unique lifestyle suitable to

*Quebec*

their environment. Some had married their Aboriginal neighbours. The new colonists established schools, a university, churches, hospitals, missions, forges, breweries, and entertainment such as horse racing. New France colonies respected their heroes and celebrities, people such as Madeleine de Verchères, Dollard des Ormeaux, Jean Nicolet, Pierre Radisson, Le Moyne d'Iberville, Louis de Frontenac, Jeanne Mance and Jean de Brébeuf. The Canadiens had developed their own identity.

*Champlain's map of Canada, 1613.*

## The Conquest of New France:

By the eighteenth century, France and England had worldwide empires, which led to intense competition between them for furs

*Samuel de Champlain charted the lands of eastern Canada and from the Hudson River to Georgian Bay.*

and trading routes. The constant conflict between New France and its Aboriginal allies, and the English and their Aboriginal allies led many to believe that war was inevitable. Sure enough, France and England declared war in 1756 (the Seven Years' War 1756-1763). Their North American colonies were pawns in this European struggle.

French forces in New France were outnumbered and outgunned. One by one, French outposts surrendered to the British. Louisbourg fell in 1758, Quebec in 1759 after the battle of the Plains of Abraham, and Montreal in 1760. Much of the French colony lay in ruins. Farms and villages had been burned to the ground. Canadiens were placed under British military rule until the British government took formal control of the colony in 1763.

Many of the wealthy seigneurs who ruled New France returned home to their families and estates in France. Most of the 60,000 Canadiens remained in the only land they had ever known and loved. They would face the challenge of surviving as an isolated French-speaking, Roman Catholic population, under the rule of English-speaking Protestants

## French-English Relations: 1763-1867

Getting along would prove to be difficult. England's first policy, the **British Proclamation Act** of 1763, attempted to assimilate French Canadians into a British culture by encouraging British immigration. It was hoped that English residents would rapidly outnumber their French counterparts, who would find it more practical to assume the English language, religion and customs.

The British policy of assimilation did not work and was replaced by the **Quebec Act** in 1774. This new law tried to win the loyalty of the French-speaking colonists by honouring and preserving their language and customs. The success of the Quebec Act was hampered by the flood of English-speaking settlers moving north to Nova Scotia, New Brunswick and Quebec. They were fleeing from the growing political unrest in the "American" colonies to

*The Fathers of Confederation at the Quebec Conference, 1864.*

the south. The new settlers, or **Loyalists** as they became known, had no interest in maintaining the Canadiens' lifestyle. It was not long before these new immigrants began to make demands on the British government. The relationship between French and English in Canada deteriorated.

To address the complaints from English-speaking settlers, Britain passed the **Constitutional Act** in 1791. It divided the colony of Quebec into Upper Canada (later Ontario, and mostly English-speaking) and Lower Canada (later Quebec, and mostly French-speaking). Under the new law, each colony had its own government. Unfortunately, Abo-

riginal claims were ignored by both French and English Canadians.

The **Canadian Rebellions** of 1837 clearly signalled that citizens in both colonies were unhappy. Many people in Upper and Lower Canada objected to representation without election. The British government dispatched John George Lambton, Earl of Durham, to investigate and report on the colonists' concerns. Durham granted amnesty to most of the rebels, and his report to the British Parliament recommended more self-government for the colonies. Durham hoped Canadiens would be assimilated by the larger English-speaking population in the country, conse-

Etienne Desmarteau (1877-1905), a Montreal policeman, was a champion at the 25.4 kg (56 lb) weight toss. He won Canada's first Olympic gold medal in 1904. French Canada has produced many "strong men."

quently relinquishing their language and customs. He proposed to increase English-speaking immigration to Canada in order that the country's French-speaking population would be outnumbered. The British government moved to adopt many of Durham's ideas. French Canadians resented Durham's conclusions.

At Lord Durham's suggestion, the British government united Upper and Lower Canada in 1841. The arrangement did not work. By the 1860s, the Canadian government was in a stalemate. French and English were evenly balanced, and neither group was able to maintain a dominant legislative position. Both moved reluctantly to the conclusion that a strong central government would be more effective in managing common services, while local affairs would benefit from local administration.

French-Canadian George Etienne Cartier, leader of Lower Canada, worked with John A. Macdonald, leader of Upper Canada, to develop a **federal** form of government. Their efforts led to a **confederation**, or federal union of four of the British North American colonies—Nova Scotia, New Brunswick, Quebec and Ontario—in 1867. Each province controlled various facets of provincial affairs within the **Canadian Confederation**, including guaranteed control over religion and education within its borders. The new national or federal government would address those concerns—national defence, transportation, money and the post office, for example—that were common to all.

## From 1867-1934

The Confederation partnership was not an easy one, particularly as Canada's boundaries expanded and the population of the new nation increased. Several new problems tested the new Canadian unity:

- Manitoba joined Confederation in 1870 as a bilingual province. Louis Riel, the fiery, compelling leader of the Métis, used armed resistance and negotiation to protect the French language in his homeland, which, at the time, was commonly referred to as the North West Territory. Riel led two armed rebellions against the Canadian government, the first in Manitoba in 1870 and the second in 1885 in Saskatchewan. He and his supporters sought self-government, and the preservation of their indigenous French heritage. Riel was captured, tried for treason and executed. English Canada believed the man was a rabble-rouser and applauded the government's action. French Canada was outraged by the execution of a hero who had been trying to protect their fellow French cultural compatriots, the Métis.

- Manitoba's English-speaking majority abolished the use of French language instruction in schools with the passage of the Manitoba Schools Act of 1890. Ontario did the same in 1912 by passing Regulation 17. French Canadians began to feel their language and culture were safe only in Quebec.

- **Conscription,** mandatory military service, was a major divisive issue between French and English Canadians during the First World War. English Canadians favoured conscription. French Canadians, however, felt that the war was a European conflict and should not involve Canada. When conscription became law, French Canadians felt betrayed by Canada's English-language majority. Conscription became a unity issue once again from 1939-1944, during World War II.

- The **Depression** (1929-1939) emphasized the fears and insecurities of French Canadians. It was easy to believe Quebec's problems had been caused by "foreign control." Many French-Canadians believed that their culture would disappear under the English domination of the province. They voted for change.

FOCUS
1. Give 2 reasons why France set up a colony in North America.
2. Why did the population of New France grow so slowly?
3. Why did the British propose assimilation for the French after conquest?
4. List the issues that divided English and French Canadians after Confederation.

Born in St. Hilaire, Quebec, in 1864, Ozias Leduc was renowned for his church murals. In total, thirty-one churches in Quebec and eastern Canada are decorated with Leduc's religious images. Being dependent on the Church for his livelihood, however, did not stop Leduc from pursuing his own artistic expression. He would retreat to his St. Hilaire studio every once in a while to paint the landscape and the community around him. This painting, "L'Enfant au Pain" (1899), is one of Leduc's most famous. Though he sold virtually nothing during his lifetime, Leduc holds a prominent position in the artistic communities of Quebec and Canada today, with paintings in the National Gallery of Canada and the Museum of Modern Art.

Born in 1865, only one year after Ozias Leduc, James Wilson Morrice enjoyed a much different career than Leduc. Traditionally Québécois, Leduc was not interested in the fashions and tastes of the art world. Morrice, on the other hand, was greatly influenced by the **aesthetic** ideas of the day, particularly those of Modernism. Spending most of his life in France, Morrice was the first Canadian painter to receive international fame. While alive, Morrice was much more popular abroad than he was in Canada.

# The Duplessis Era in Quebec: 1936–1959

*Quebec argicultural worker, 1930.*

The Union Nationale, a new political party led by Maurice Duplessis, swept into power in Quebec in 1936. Many people viewed Duplessis as a champion of French-Canadian nationalism. He promised to fight Ottawa for more power for Quebec. He assured French Canadians that decisions about Quebec's industry and resources would be made in Quebec. Duplessis pledged to preserve the French language, religion and culture.

His Union Nationale party worked closely with the Roman Catholic Church, which controlled hospitals, schools and colleges in Quebec. The Church worried that **urbanization** would make Quebec youth less religious as they left their traditional rural communities for factory jobs in towns and cities. Duplessis encouraged young people in the province to revere their past, to respect traditional values, and to maintain their Roman Catholic religion. The government discouraged modern influences. As a result, a generation of French Canadians reached adulthood with very little background in business, science and technology.

Quebec, like the rest of Canada, lived through a period of intense industrial growth following the end of the Second World War. Industrialization brought new development and investment from outside the province and, often, these develop-

Miners in Quebec's asbestos industry went on strike in 1949, demanding higher wages and better working conditions.

1900  1910  1920  1930  1940  1950  1960  1970  1980

ments were funded by English-owned businesses. Hydroelectric power and mining were strong growth sectors.

Quebec's burgeoning industrial economy and increasing urbanization contributed to the rise of trade unions, as workers united in the hopes of increasing wages and improving working conditions. This posed a challenge for Duplessis because he was anti-union. He believed that unions were communist inspired. Large corporations—largely English-speaking—supported Union Nationale policies and helped finance the Party's election campaigns. The Quebec government, the Catholic Church and many large corporations worked together to inhibit the growth of trade unions in Quebec. With weak unions, corporations did not have to improve wages or working conditions.

Miners in Quebec's asbestos industry went on strike in 1949, demanding higher wages and better working conditions. Dup-

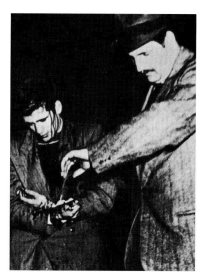

*These strikers were injured by the police during the Asbestos Strike of 1949.*

lessis, with financial support from businesses sympathetic to his cause, ordered provincial police to break up the strike and arrest its leaders. Violence resulted. The workers stood firm. When the strike ended three months later, they had gained little.

Nevertheless, the Quebec Asbestos strike

*Duplessis and Cardinal Charbonneau did not always agree on what was best for the people of Quebec.*

was an important milestone in Quebec history. Many workers objected to Duplessis' tactics and to his support of large English-owned corporations. Many workers were union members. They saw the need for laws to protect workers and unions. And some church leaders even began to question Duplessis' policies after helping workers to cope with the strike and its aftermath.

Maurice Duplessis was the premier of Quebec from 1936-1939, and again from 1944-1959. During his terms in office, he increased the Quebec government's power in education and social services. His administration created the Department of Social Welfare and Youth, which built 40 provincial technical and trade schools. The Church's involvement in Quebec's education and social services was reduced. Education in the skilled career trades was made more important. Duplessis' government introduced compulsory school attendance for children between the ages of 6 and 14 to ensure the success of educational reforms.

In spite of these improvements, there remained serious social and educational problems within the province:

*In 1946... teachers were underpaid and teaching was still considered a vocation. Despite the construction of many new schools in 1951, more than 70 percent of the 8,780 schools in the province still had only one classroom, 60 percent had no electricity and 40 percent no running water or indoor toilets. The level of schooling among francophones was still low. In the late 1950s, only 63 percent of students who started elementary school would finish the seventh grade. Under-funded and poorly organized, the education system was still undemocratic, elitist and sexist.(Quoted from the Province of Quebec website,* **www.meq.gouv.qc.ca**)

Duplessis' government increased Quebec's minimum wage, helping to create many new jobs. The government built hospitals, highways and pushed hydro development in rural areas as a means of modernizing Quebec. The most symbolic project undertaken by Duplessis was the adoption of Quebec's flag, the fleur-de-lis. It helped strengthen and symbolize the concept of Quebec unity.

## Opposition to Duplessis

Duplessis was able to keep power for a long time because political opposition to his party was weak. He was a practiced speaker, able to energize audiences, who perceived him as a champion of Quebec's survival. The Roman Catholic Church, an important influence in Quebec society, was also a strong supporter.

## Canadian Vision

*Cité libre* was a magazine of ideas created in 1950 to defend freedom of expression and put an end to the "Great Darkness" that characterized the Duplessis regime. *Cité libre* opposed the Catholic Church's stronghold on all aspects of social life in Quebec and ethnic nationalism.

*Cité libre* was a precursor of the Quiet Revolution.

quoted from *Cité libre* web site (www.citelibre.com)

Politics were corrupted under Duplessis' rule. Political ridings voting for the Union Nationale received **patronage** in the form of new roads, hospitals or other services. Ridings which voted Liberal did not. English, British, and American corporations soon discovered that the way to do business in Quebec was to support Duplessis. Sparsely populated rural regions had greater power than the densely populated cities. Labour unions were ruthlessly restricted.

Duplessis' corrupt political machine was rejected by some religious leaders in the province and by many intellectuals. Several prominent writers, artists, professors and lawyers spoke out openly against the government, and even against the powers of the Church. Pierre Trudeau, Gérard Pelletier and others realized that politics in Quebec needed to become more open and democratic. They believed that all should share in the benefits of industrialism. *Cité libre* was one medium they used to

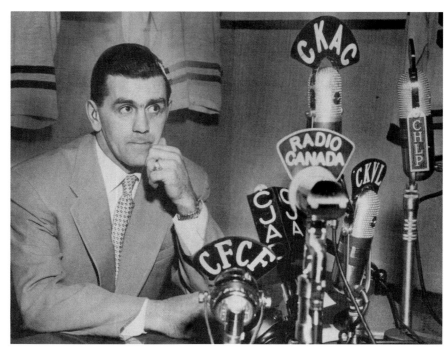

*On March 17, 1955, a riot broke out at the Montreal Forum following a decision by NHL President Clarence Campbell to suspend Canadiens' superstar Maurice (Rocket) Richard for the rest of the regular season and the playoffs. Fans spread through the streets of Montreal on a seven-hour binge of looting and destruction. Many rioters believed the English-speaking Campbell was trying to spoil Quebec's hope of another Stanley Cup. Rocket Richard became a symbol for Quebec nationalism. When he died in May 2000, the whole province mourned for their beloved idol.*

popularize their ideas.

Maurice Duplessis died on September 7, 1959. The old Quebec died with him.

FOCUS
1. How did the Union Nationale influence life in Quebec?
2. Give 2 reasons why the Duplessis government was corrupt.
3. Why did large corporations support Duplessis?
4. What groups opposed Duplessis? Why?

# Canadian Vision

Born in St. Hilaire, Quebec in 1905, Paul-Emile Borduas wanted to paint church murals like his mentor and teacher, Ozias Leduc. Economic difficulties and a growing family forced him to turn to teaching instead. In 1937, he took a teaching position at the École de Meuble in Montreal where he taught drawing. Borduas's paintings gradually shifted away from the religious tradition of Leduc toward the modern approach of the Surrealists, who were popular in the art world abroad. Greatly influenced by the writings of André Breton, a French philosopher and critic, Borduas's work began to reflect the art-for-art's-sake ideology so celebrated by such Surrealist artists as Miro and Dali. Borduas became leader of the Mouvement Automatistes in Montreal. They celebrated colour, light, line and mass as subjects of painting, and prized spontaneity in art above all else.

In 1942, Borduas published a manifesto, *Refus Global*. It would be his undoing in the Quebec art world. Though mainly about painting and aesthetics, *Refus Global* challenged traditional values of French Canadian society. Borduas wanted to minimize the influence of the Catholic Church and of Duplessis's government. Duplessis, who believed that modern art was Communist inspired, fired Borduas from his teaching post and blackballed him from Quebec

society. Unable to support himself in Quebec, Borduas fled to New York, and later Paris. Though he enjoyed some success, Borduas remained lonely and homesick for his native Quebec. He died in his Paris studio in 1960.

Born in 1923, Jean-Paul Riopelle is one of Canada's most distinguished painters. Originally a member of Borduas's *Les Automatistes,* Riopelle became famous for his gestural abstract paintings. Riopelle's works adopt many of the principles expressed by Borduas and expand them to logical extremes. He was not afraid to experiment with a variety of new techniques, including using a palette knife to apply paint to the canvas. Riopelle was one of the 15 artists to sign the *Refus global.* He received the UNESCO award for cumulative achievement in 1962, and was honoured with a retrospective at the Art Gallery of Ontario in 1963.

FOCUS
1. Why did Paul-Emile Borduas move to Paris?
2. What do you think art-for-art's sake means?
3. What was the importance of the *Refus Global*?
4. Do you think art can change society?

# Jean Lesage and the Quiet Revolution

When Duplessis died, the old Quebec died with him. The Union Nationale Party was in a state of collapse The people of Quebec were ready to reexamine their province and redefine its role in the world. In 1960, the Liberals, led by Jean Lesage, won their first Quebec election since 1939. *La Revolution Tranquille* (the Quiet Revolution) began. A period of dramatic change would revolutionize the province.

The Quiet Revolution had several goals. It was time for Québécois to be *Mâitres chez–nous* (Masters in our own house), as one of Lesage's most popular cabinet ministers, René Lévesque, put it. The phrase became a rallying point. All policy during the six years (1960-1966) of Lesage's government was designed to fulfill this goal.

Premier Lesage's most pressing problem was the erosion of social and economic conditions.

**Francophones** felt like second-class citizens in their own province. French Canadians made less money than many immigrant groups. Most of the higher paying jobs in the province went to **anglophones.** The vast majority of immigrants to Quebec learned English, not French. The province had one of the highest infant death rates in Canada. Very few francophone students majored in math, science or engineering. Most of the largest corporations in the province were owned by English Canadians or Americans. English was the language of business: people who spoke English were promoted, those who spoke French were not.

French Canadians knew they needed political and financial control over their own affairs to improve their status. Quebec needed to modernize.

The power of the Church in the province's education system was reduced with the creation of the Quebec Department of Education. Its new curriculum placed emphasis on technical skills, business, math and science. The government provided more hospitals and better health care services and reduced the Church's influence in the province's health system.

Lesage's government passed laws to protect the use of the French language, and to ensure the survival of French-Canadian culture. Other laws guaranteed the rights of labour unions and provided social benefits. The Quebec Pension Plan (QPP) was introduced in 1966 to provide pensions to Quebec workers.

The Lesage government took a more active role in developing local resources. In 1969, Quebec bought all the hydroelectric

*Jean Lesage was a powerful premier of Quebec.*

During the 1970s, the province built the world's largest hydroelectric project near James Bay.

companies in the province. It proceeded to expand availability of electricity to rural areas. During the 1970s, the province built the world's largest hydroelectric project near James Bay. Even though James Bay created major hardships for the Cree and Inuit of the area, it was only one of several hydro projects in Quebec. These projects symbolized political and economic control for the province.

Quebec developed an active society, one with increasing self-confidence. This was seen in the arts as hundreds of musicians, writers, painters and filmmakers began to use their talents to celebrate the new Quebec.

*The massive dams of the James Bay project were a source of pride and confidence for many in Quebec.*

**The Cree in Quebec** When the Quebec government proposed the James Bay hydroelectric project in 1971, the Cree were outraged. The project would flood over 176,000 square kilometres of forest and tundra in Northern Quebec— Cree land. The Cree had never given up their rights to this vast territory, because they believed their way of life would be destroyed in the process. The **Grand Council of the Cree** took their case to court. In 1975, after 4 years of intense negotiations with the Quebec government, **the James Bay and Northern Quebec Agreement** was signed. The Cree and many Inuit peoples in the area relinquished claim to large portions of Northern Quebec in return for a cash payment, uncontested land reserves, and hunting and trapping rights.

In 1986, the Quebec government proposed a new series of hydroelectric projects in the area. These would flood an additional 800 square kilometres of Cree land. These projects had been designed without the knowledge or permission of the Cree nation. The Grand Council of the Cree went to court again. It argued that the Quebec government was in breach of its James Bay Agreement, and that the new projects would result in environmental catastrophe. The court-ordered environmental assessment had still not been carried out in 1994 when Jacques Parizeau's government shelved the expensive project.

Today, the Grand Council of the Cree is a powerful international voice. The Cree have experience in Canadian and international law. Their campaign for Aboriginal rights has increased awareness of this issue in Canada and around the world.

The Cree are worried about Quebec separation. Like the Québécois, the Cree say they are a *distinct people,* with the right to protect, and promote their culture and identity. The Cree assert *Aboriginal title* to their land, which they have held *since time immemorial.* They claim the right to use their land as their ancestors did. They believe Quebec does not have the right to speak for them, and it does not have the right to take or control their land.

The Cree believe the Supreme Court decision means if Quebec cannot be forced to remain part of Canada, the Cree cannot be forced to become part of an independent Quebec. The Cree say that when

the Supreme Court recognized referenda as a democratic means of *self-determination,* it recognized their right to remain in Canada through their own referendum.

People gained a new pride in their province and began to call themselves **Québécois** (Quebecers) rather than French Canadians.

Jean Lesage and his Liberals were defeated in 1966. Some voters were dissatisfied with the rate of changes introduced during their six years in power. Others were concerned about the increasing provincial debt. The Union Nationale Party led by Daniel Johnson, Sr. returned to power.

Most French Canadians agreed with the goals of the Quiet Revolution. Some, however, had different ideas about modernization. One group—which included Jean Marchand, Pierre Trudeau, and Jean Chrétien—wanted Quebec to have more influence on the federal government in Ottawa. Another group felt Quebec would be better off with fewer ties to the rest of Canada. They believed Quebec's culture and interests were separate from those of other Canadians. They wanted Quebec to be politically independent. René Lévesque, the former Liberal, became a symbol and a leader for many people who felt this way.

A smaller group believed Quebec would only be freed through violent revolution. This group, the Front de Libération du Québec (FLQ), pledged to fight a war of liberation. The first stage in this war was terrorism.

## MUSIC

One of Quebec's most influential singers, Gilles Vigneault was born in 1928, just outside Montreal. Vigneault's Québécois ballads capture the character, isolation and the landscape of rural Quebec. In 1965 Vigneault's collection of poetry won the Governor General's Award. But, it is for his music that Vigneault is most famous. His hit, Mon Pays, a ballad about winter, is almost a national anthem in Quebec. In 1970, Vigneault became an outspoken supporter of the Parti Québécois, proudly singing about Quebec's heritage at annual Saint Jean-Baptiste Day celebrations.

FOCUS
1. What was the major goal of the Quiet Revolution?
2. List three changes made by the Lesage government.
3. How did the Cree fight against Quebec's hydroelectric industry?
4. Why do you think the people of Quebec preferred to call themselves Québécois rather than French Canadians?

*Charles de Gaulle*

The Canadian Confederation was 100 years old in 1967. Centennial celebrations were planned throughout the country. Montreal hosted the World's Fair—known as Expo '67. Charles de Gaulle, president of France, represented his country at the opening ceremonies, and gave a rousing speech from the balcony of Montreal City Hall. "Vive Montrèal, vive Québec, vive le Québec libre, vive le Canada français, vive la France." His words were greeted with a roar of applause from the crowd. De Gaulle had appealed to the deepest feelings of many Quebecers. Vive le Québec libre was a separatist slogan.

In Ottawa, however, the reaction was very different. By encouraging Quebec's independence in this way, the French president had "interfered" with Canada's internal affairs. Canadian Prime Minister Lester Pearson protested the interference, and de Gaulle promptly went back to France at the request of the Canadian government.

# Canadian Vision

In 1880, the song that would become Canada's national anthem was written by Adolphe-Basile Routhier and Calixa Lavallee to help celebrate French Canada's national day, St. Jean Baptiste Day. The song was an instant hit.

In 1908, Stanley Weir wrote English words to Lavallee's famous tune in celebration of the 300th anniversary of the founding of Quebec. His version became popular in English Canada.

In 1980, Parliament recognized *O Canada* as the national anthem. Minor changes were made to the English words, but the French version remains exactly as Routhier and Lavalle wrote it.

**FRENCH VERSION:**

O Canada!
Terre de nos aieux,
(Land of our forefathers)
Ton front est ceint de fleurons glorleux!
(Thy brow is wreathed with a glorious garland of flowers!)
Car ton bras sait porter l'épée il sait porter la croix!
(As your arm is ready to wield a sword so is it ready to carry the cross)
Ton histoire est une épopée
(Thy history is an epic)
Des plus brillants exploits
(of the most brilliant exploits)
Et ta valeur, de foi trempée,
(Thy value, steeped in faith,)
Protégera nos foyers et nos droits
(Will protect our homes and our rights)
Protégera nos foyers et nos droits.
(Will protect our homes and our rights)

**ENGLISH VERSION:**

O Canada!
Our home and native land!
True patriot love in all thy sons command.
With glowing hearts we see thee rise,
The True North strong and free!
From far and wide,
O Canada,
We stand on guard for thee.
God keep our land, glorious and free!
O Canada,
We stand on guard for thee!
O Canada,
We stand on guard for thee!

> **FOCUS**
> 1. Read both versions of O Canada! carefully and note the differences. It seems that even when French and English Canadians are singing our national anthem, they are still not in agreement!

# The October Crisis

Not all Quebecers were satisfied with the amount or pace of change during the Quiet Revolution. In the 1960s, a small group of radical separatists carried out bombings. These people were members of the Front de Libération du Québec (FLQ). They wanted to call attention to their cause by bombing federal government property. The FLQ was organized into **cells** or small groups of people. Communication between cells was by secret code. One cell did not know the individuals of another cell. If one cell was captured, it could not betray others. Despite these precautions, the police were able to arrest, try and imprison several FLQ members.

On the morning of October 5, 1970, the FLQ kidnapped James Cross, a British diplomat, from his Montreal home. They demanded a ransom of $500,000, plus TV and radio time to broadcast their views to the Quebec people. They also demanded safe passage out of Canada for themselves, and for imprisoned FLQ members. They warned that Cross would be executed if their demands were not met. The FLQ hoped the Cross kidnapping would spark a wave of violence that would result in the separation of Quebec from Canada.

French and English Canadians were numb with shock. Terrorism could be expected to happen in unstable countries, perhaps, but not in safe, quiet Canada. The police could find no clues to the Cross kidnapping.

Five days later, on October 10, the terrorists struck again. Pierre Laporte, the Quebec minister of labour, was kidnapped at gunpoint while playing football outside his suburban home. This second kidnapping drove many people in Quebec into near panic.

*Montreal's Westmount area after a bomb went off in a mailbox.*

*James Cross*

On the morning of October 5, 1970, the FLQ kidnapped James Cross, a British diplomat, from his Montreal home.

## The War Measures Act

Quebec police were frustrated by their inability to solve the two kidnappings. People feared the FLQ would strike again. Quebec Premier Robert Bourassa asked the federal government for help. Prime Minister Trudeau responded by asking Parliament to proclaim the **War Measures Act,** which suspended legal rights and freedoms. The Act was designed for emergency use when Canada was at war. It had never been used during times of peace. The act gave police special powers to search, question and arrest suspects without cause. A **curfew** was declared

*Parts of Montreal looked like an armed camp during the FLQ crisis.*

in Montreal. The army was called in to assist the police.

On October 17, police received a tip about an abandoned car. The body of Pierre Laporte was found in its trunk. He had been strangled with the chain of his own religious medal.

On November 6, one of the Laporte kidnappers was found in a closet during a search of a Montreal apartment. Police did not realize until later that the terrorists were hiding behind a partition in the same closet. These people were later found on December 28 in an abandoned farmhouse thirty kilometres southeast of Montreal.

It was grinding, routine police investigation, and not the War Measures Act, which finally found James Cross. On December 3, police and soldiers surrounded the house where Cross was being held. He had been there for nearly nine weeks. All of Canada watched as the deal for his release was nego-

*Pierre Laporte's funeral at Montreal's Church of the Notre Dame.*

tiated. Television crews in helicopters followed the kidnappers' car as it raced through downtown Montreal to "Man and his World," the site of Expo '67. There Cross was released into the custody of the Cuban Consul. The kidnappers were flown to Cuba.

The results of the October Crisis were far-reaching. Under the War Measures Act, almost 500 people were arrested and held in custody for up to three weeks. They had been imprisoned merely on suspicion: most were released without charge. People lost faith in the government's ability to protect society and their civil rights. Any sympathy most Québécois might have had for the FLQ was wiped out. The Front was in ruins. Separatists were firmly convinced that separatism for Quebec would have to be achieved through peaceful means. Other Canadians, both French and English, became truly aware of the feelings dividing the country for the first time. They resolved to work even harder at cooperation and understanding. Everyone realized that Canada, too, was vulnerable to violence and terror.

## A CLOSER LOOK AT QUEBEC'S FUTURE: CHANGE WITHIN FEDERALISM OR SEPARATISM?

Quebec **separatists** see themselves as citizens of Quebec, not as citizens of Canada. They want Quebec to leave Confederation and to establish itself as an independent country. Separatists believe that independence is the only way for Quebec to control its own affairs and protect the uniqueness of the Québécois culture. Separatists, however, do want to retain strong economic ties to the rest of Canada.

Quebec **federalists** believe that Quebec has prospered as part of the Canadian Confederation. Federalists acknowledge that the Québécois suffered injustices and discrimination in earlier times, but they believe that the French language and culture are well protected today within the Canadian union. Federalists believe that Confederation strengthens Quebec and that the province can only realize its fullest potential as a part of Canada.

Many Québécois often fall between the two groups and are neither fully separatist, nor fully federalist. These people are sometimes referred to as **soft separatists** or **nationalists.**

FOCUS

1. What was the goal of the FLQ?
2. Why did the government proclaim the War Measures Act? How did it use the powers the act gave them?
3. What were the results of the October Crisis?

# Constitutional Change: 1960s-1970s

The challenge of the Quiet Revolution forced the federal government to rethink the relationship between Canada's two main cultures. During the 1960s and 1970s, Canadian Confederation was studied and reexamined several times by various government-appointed committees or commissions. Their task was to suggest ways to modernize the politi-

*This unique photograph shows four Liberal prime ministers: Trudeau, Turner, Chrétien and Pearson.*

cal, economic and social relationship between the provinces and the federal government.

Each committee came up with recommendations for constitutional change. Few of the recommendations were adopted. Agreement among the ten provincial governments on any change to Canada's Constitution was almost impossible.

The Commission on Bilingualism and Biculturalism warned that unless "an equal partnership" between French and English Canada was formed, the country was likely to break up. It recommended that Canada be formally declared bilingual, and that French and English be given equal status in the courts, Parliament and government services.

In 1969, the new Liberal government of Pierre Elliot Trudeau passed the **Official Languages Act,** which implemented many of the Royal Commission on Bilingualism and Bicul-

In 1963, the Liberal government of Lester Pearson established the Royal Commission on Bilingualism and Biculturalism.

turalism's recommendations. This law made Canada officially bilingual. It meant the federal government and courts would carry out the business of the land in both French and English. The importance of the French language in Canada increased dramatically across the country. Canadians living in communities with a French-speaking population of more than 10% would be served in their own language at the federal level. French Canadians also had greater opportunities for jobs within the federal civil service.

The Official Languages Act was of great benefit to francophones outside Quebec. Aca-

## ROYAL COMMISSION ON BILINGUALISM AND BICULTURALISM

In 1963, the Liberal government of Lester Pearson established the Royal Commission on Bilingualism and Biculturalism to analyze the relationship between English and French Canadians, and to examine Quebec's role in Confederation. For several years, the Commission examined the needs, complaints and aspirations of each. Pearson hoped that the Commission's report would guide the government as it worked to maintain a united Canada.

dians in the Atlantic Provinces were well served by it, as were francophones in Ontario and Manitoba.

Many English Canadians felt there were not enough French-speaking people outside Quebec to justify the costs of bilingualism. They felt French Canadians already held favoured status when applying for government jobs and promotions. Anglophones in government positions objected to learning French. Not all French Canadians were universally in favour of bilingualism either. Many had mixed feelings about the policy. They wanted to promote the French Canadian culture outside Quebec, not just the French language.

FOCUS
1. What did the Commission on Bilingualism and Biculturalism say would happen if Quebec did not receive equal partnership with English Canada?
2. What is the Official Languages Act? Why were so many people unhappy with it?

**Acadia** French Canadians in the Maritimes—Acadians—have a proud heritage. They are different from their Quebec neighbours with a different history, different memories, a different culture—even a different language. At the same time, they look to the larger French-speaking population of Quebec as allies in the struggle to maintain a French identity in the often alien, English-speaking culture of North America.

Canada's francophone population in the Atlantic provinces dates back to the original settlements along the Bay of Fundy. Often ignored by France, Acadians became an agricultural community. They dyked and improved the rich farmlands around the bay. They traded with the English colonies to the south for the things they could not produce themselves.

Acadia was soon caught up in the strife between Britain and France. After 1713, much of Acadia was under British rule.

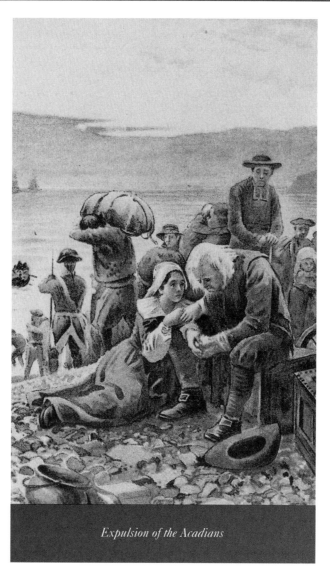

*Expulsion of the Acadians*

The Acadians tried to remain neutral, but the British did not trust them. In 1755, as tensions grew, the British decided to expel the Acadians from Canada, and send them to English colonies further south.

Very few Acadians escaped this deportation. Others slowly made their way back to their homeland. Eventually, many settled in what is now northern New Brunswick. Some Acadians remained in the American colonies and adapted to their new country. Today, Americans of Acadian ancestry are found in Louisiana, Maine, Vermont and other American states. Their modern name is Cajun, an Americanization of Acadien.

The Acadian community is as strong and vibrant as ever. Many Acadians have achieved national and international acclaim. Roméo LeBlanc, Canada's Governor General from 1995-1999, was the first Acadian to fill this post. Antoinine Maillet, a prominent Acadian writer, won France's Prix Goncourt in 1979 for her novel *Pélagie-la-charrette*—the first time in the prize's history that it was awarded to an author living outside of France.

**Franco-Ontarians** There have been French settlers in Ontario almost as long as there have been French people in Canada. The first known French voyageur to make it to what would later be Ontario was Etiene Brûlé who, in 1610, was sent on a survey mission for Champlain. By 1840, the rapidly growing population of New France began to spill into Ontario, particularly near the Ottawa River and the Sudbury regions.

Most Franco-Ontarians sought to preserve their culture, language and religion in the predominately English-speaking, Protestant world of Ontario. In 1910, they established the Association Canadien-française de l'Ontario (ACFP) and, in 1913, the first French-language paper in Ontario, the Ottawa-based daily, *Le Droit*.

One major concern for Franco-Ontarians during the early part of the twentieth century was French-language education. By 1890, French-language in schools had been mostly abolished in public

*Many Franco-Ontarians settled along the Ottawa River where they found employment in the forestry industry.*

schools when English became the compulsory subject of instruction, unless proven impractical. In 1912, the provincial government brought in Regulation 17 in an attempt to assimilate French-speaking Ontarians into the predominately English-speaking culture. This bill limited French

instruction in schools to the first 2 years of elementary school, regardless of practicality. All French-speaking children would receive English-language instruction after grade 2. Although amended in 1913 to allow for 1 hour of French study per day, Regulation 17 caused a massive outcry among Franco-Ontarians. Rallies, marches and rebellions were organized to oppose the regulation. By the time of the conscription crisis of the First World War, Ontario's language issue had become a national conflict. Although eventually abolished in 1927, Regulation 17 shaped a whole generation of Franco-Ontarians, who were never allowed to receive an education in their mother tongue. Today, Franco-Ontarians from all over the province continue to thrive, and are proud of their culture, their language and their heritage.

# René Lévesque and the Parti Québecois

The end of the FLQ crisis in 1970 did not mean the end of separatism. Many Québécois leaders still believed passionately in achieving independence by lawful means.

René Lévesque was one such person. A popular journalist and an influential minister in the Lesage government of the 1960s, Lévesque became frustrated with the Liberal's federalist policies. He resigned from the party to found the Mouvement Souveraineté Association in 1967. It joined forces with

Bourassa government was corrupt. PQ support increased dramatically.

The PQ pledged to end corruption in Quebec politics, to protect the French language, and to aid the weaker groups in society. To ease fears that independence might bring a loss of money and jobs, Lévesque stressed that an independent Quebec would have close economic ties with Canada. During the election campaign of 1976, the PQ promised good government. To attract voters who were

*René Lévesque was a forceful and dramatic speaker.*

*Trudeau and Lévesque were longtime rivals, each respecting the other's political skill.*

another separatist party in 1968 to form the **Parti Québécois** or PQ. Lévesque was elected party leader.

The popularity of the PQ coincided with the falling popularity of the Bourassa Liberals. Quebec was plagued with strikes between 1973 and 1976. Unemployment rose; so did the cost of living. People began to believe the

uneasy about voting for a separatist party, the PQ announced that the question of separation would be decided in a future **referendum,** or free and democratic popular vote.

Lévesque and the PQ won 69 out of 110 seats on election day. The Liberals won 28. Many Canadians were stunned. Even PQ members were surprised by the size of the

Lévesque became frustrated with the Liberal's federalist policies. He resigned from the party to found the Mouvement Souveraineté Association in 1967.

T I M E L I N E

1900 1910 1920 1930 1940 1950 1960 1970 1980 1990

victory. Quebec separatists were ecstatic. The world viewed the PQ victory with unease. What did it mean for Canada?

Pierre Elliot Trudeau, a strong Québécois federalist, was Canada's prime minister. Canadian federalists looked to Trudeau for leadership in fighting the Quebec separatist movement.

In 1979, the Parti Québécois announced it would hold a referendum in May, 1980. Quebecers would vote on the idea of leaving Confederation.

PQ leaders worked hard on the wording of the question they would put to voters. They knew many were afraid of separatism. They wanted to reduce voters' alarm, so they **softened** the question. Quebecers were asked to vote *oui* (yes) or *non* (no) on whether they wished to give the Quebec government the "**mandate** (or right) to negotiate **sovereignty-association** with Canada."

Both the *oui* and the *non* campaigns were hard fought. The province was bombarded with rallies, speeches, pamphlets, and radio and TV ads. Lévesque and his followers claimed a *oui* vote was needed to protect the

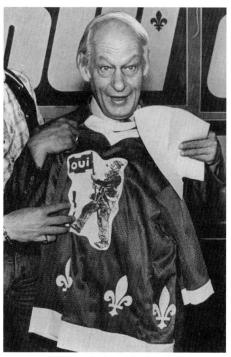

*Premier Lévesque holds a Quebec Nordiques jersey with a symbol of the rebellion of 1837 on it.*

French language and the culture of Quebec. They urged Québécois to remember their history and their pride in their homeland. They claimed a strong *oui* vote would give the province more political clout when dealing with Ottawa.

The *non* campaign was headed by the new Liberal leader, Claude Ryan, a political rookie. Ryan attacked the wording of the question. He felt the PQ was trying to disguise separatism by calling it sovereignty-association. His speeches were passionate. Ryan began to impress the voters as a sincere and dedicated man.

Members of all three federal parties supported the *non* side. Pierre Trudeau used his personal popularity in the province to persuade Quebecers to remain in Canada. One million Canadians signed a petition to tell the people of Quebec they wanted them to remain in Canada.

The turning point of the 1980 Quebec Referendum came when Lise Payette, a PQ cabinet minister, unintentionally mobilized Quebec women into the debate. Payette delivered a speech in which she called Claude Ryan's wife a "Yvette" and accused all women who voted against the PQ of being "Yvettes." Yvette was the name of the girl in a grade 2 reader used in Quebec schools. The reader showed Yvette staying at home to cook and sew while her brother had exciting adventures. Payette was implying that all women who were against sovereignty-association were submissive and could not think for themselves. Payette soon regretted her thoughtless remark.

Enraged women in Quebec started an Yvette movement. Within a week of Payette's comments, the Yvettes held a mass rally of

15,000 women. The Yvette rally was the first serious setback for the PQ. Payette's apology came too late to make a difference. From that point on, the federalist campaign gathered momentum.

On referendum day, 85% of eligible Quebec voters cast their ballots. When the polls closed, people across the nation waited in hushed suspense as the results trickled in.

Within an hour, the outcome was clear. Almost 60% of the Québécois voted to remain in Canada. They did not want to negotiate an independent Quebec. Referring to the majority of women who voted *non* to sovereignty-association, one PQ organizer commented: "the Yvettes killed us."

Lévesque and the PQ had suffered a considerable defeat, but the people of Quebec were not unhappy with Lévesque. They believed both he and the PQ party had provided good government. Both were re-elected in 1981. Claude Ryan resigned, and Robert Bourassa returned as the Liberal leader.

Canadians understood that Quebec's voice would be heard again. Political and/or constitutional change would be needed to avoid the future break up of the country.

## A CLOSER LOOK AT SOVEREIGNTY

**Sovereignty** meant that Quebec would be politically independent. No law passed in Ottawa would have any effect in Quebec. Only the Quebec government could collect taxes, and Quebec would run its own foreign affairs. **Association** meant that Quebec would still be tied to Canada economically. The two countries would use the same money. They would have the same tariffs on imports. A mandate to negotiate the question meant that a *oui* vote would not necessarily mean Quebec would leave Canada. Rather, it would mean that the Quebec government would try to work out a deal with the rest of the country. A second vote would be called after any agreement was reached.

But would the Québécois ever be satisfied within a Canadian framework? A delicate balance would be difficult to achieve.

Prime Minister Trudeau was determined to forge a binding link by **patriating** and revising the Canadian Constitution. This was a long and often bitter struggle. There was considerable debate and compromise before the Canadian Constitution Act of 1982 was finally complete. Binding on agreement from all ten provinces, the Constitution was only approved by nine. Lévesque and the PQ opposed it. The Canadian Constitution, rather than providing a binding tie, proved to be a divisive element between Quebec and the rest of the country.

When Réne Lévesque resigned from the Parti Québécois in 1985, support for the party declined. Lévesque died in 1987. Although most Québécois could not accept his ideas on separatism, they loved the man with the giant heart who had dedicated his life to them and to the survival of Québécois culture.

# Canadian Vision

First screened in 1971, Claude Jutra's film, *Mon Oncle Antoine*, is said by many to be the best film Canada has ever produced. Claude Jutra was born in Montreal in 1930 to a family of doctors. His filmmaking talent became obvious when he was only 18. Half-way through medical school, Jutra directed an award winning short film called *Perpetual Motion*, which caught the attention of the National Film Board. Jutra's first feature length film, *A Tout Prendre* which was financed privately because the NFB was unwilling to chance it, won a number of

international awards and marked the first wave of Quebec filmmaking. In 1969, Jutra began work on *Mon Oncle Antoine*. It garnered more attention in English-speaking Canada and the United States than it did in French Canada. American critics loved the film and Claude Jutra became an international film star overnight. Unfortunately, his next movies failed to attract critical or commercial attention. In 1986, Jutra disappeared from his Montreal home. Six months later, his body washed up on the banks of the St. Lawrence River.

# Quebec Language Laws

In 1977, the Lévesque government revolutionized Quebec's language practices with the passage of Bill 101 to **entrench** French as the language of business and government. French was the official language of Quebec. All communication from the Quebec government would be only in French.

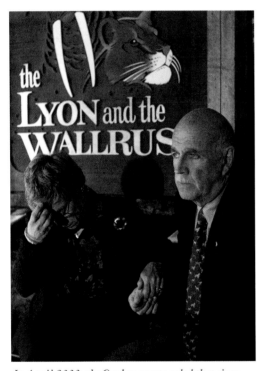

*In April 2000, the Quebec courts ruled that signs with the same size of French and English lettering were illegal under Quebec's language law.*

Consumers had the right to be served in French, and workers the right to work in French. All signs and billboards had to be written and displayed in French. French was designated the language of instruction in school. Immigrant children would learn French in the school system, not English. Only children whose parents had been educated in English would be sent to English-language schools. Bill 101 created the office of the **Commission de Surveillance,** which was given the responsibility of enforcing the law.

Many anglophones and immigrants in the province were appalled by the legislation. They claimed Bill 101 violated bilingualism. Some people banded together to form **Alliance Quebec.** They took their case to court. Others simply left the province.

In 1982, Pierre Trudeau introduced the Canadian Charter of Rights and Freedoms. It has had a significant effect on Quebec language laws and the debates they generate. Many anglophones have used the Charter to fight Quebec's language laws. Quebec politicians have used the Charter to uphold the same laws.

One hotly contested issue was the use of English language signs in Quebec stores. Anglophones were upset at the idea of French-only signs in their stores. In 1982, the Quebec Supreme Court ruled that store signs must be in French, but that they could also be bilingual.

Robert Bourassa, who had retired in the late 1970s, returned to Quebec politics in 1985 as leader of the Liberal party. His Liberals defeated the Parti Québécois in the 1985 election. Like Lévesque, Bourassa believed that Quebec should have the power to control its language law.

The store signage issue was raised again in 1988 on appeal to the Supreme Court of Canada. The Supreme Court ruled that

Anglophones were upset at the idea of French-only signs in their stores. In 1982, the Quebec Supreme Court ruled that store signs must be in French, but that they could also be bilingual.

## TIMELINE

1900  1910  1920  1930  1940  1950  1960  **1970**  1980  1990

although the government of Quebec *had* the right to require all signs to be written in French, it *did not* have the right to prevent the use of other languages on the signs.

The Quebec government promptly passed a new law. Bill 178 required *French only* signs on the outside of buildings, but permitted *bilingual* signs on the *inside* of buildings—as long as French dominated.

Bourassa was strongly supported by francophones within the province. He was denounced by the anglophones, most of whom were long-time Liberals. They began to abandon the party in droves.

Some anglophones persisted in their fight against Bourassa's legislation and took their case to the United Nations Committee on Human Rights. In 1993, it ruled against Bill 178. Bourassa's government passed Bill 86 in answer. Commercial signs in Quebec can be bilingual wherever they are, as long as the French dominates.

## A CLOSER LOOK AT THE CANADIAN CHARTER OF RIGHTS AND FREEDOM

The Charter guarantees the rights and freedoms of all Canadians. All Canadian laws (present and future) must follow the terms of the Charter and allow freedom of speech, of thought and of expression. However, the Charter places *"reasonable limits"* on the rights and freedoms Canadians enjoy.

Another section of the Charter, Section 33, the *notwithstanding clause,* gives Canadian provinces the right to pass laws which *ignore* or *override* certain Charter rights. Section 33 was added to give Canadian provinces flexibility when dealing with their respective citizens. Quebec has used this clause to justify its language laws.

The debate over Quebec's language laws continues. Even the Internet is subject to the language dispute. The Commission de Surveillance will investigate when people complain about English-only Internet communication. This has not yet been heard in the courts. In any event, it is impossible to censor the Internet.

### FOCUS

1. What is Bill 101? What did it do to Quebec's language laws?
2. What was the Alliance Quebec?
3. How has Quebec used the Charter of Rights and Freedoms to uphold its language laws?
4. What evidence is there that language continues to be a divisive issue in Quebec?

BORN: 1950, Berthierville, Quebec

DIED: 1982, Zolder, Belgium

SIGNIFICANCE: Canada's best high-speed auto racer.

BRIEF BIOGRAPHY: Villeneuve's entry into high-speed racing started in 1971, when he won the North American championship for snowmobile racing. He followed this stunning debut by winning the Quebec crown in 1972 and the Canadian title in 1973. Villeneuve's true passion, however, was car racing, and he used his earnings from racing snowmobiles to enter the Formula Ford competition in 1973, where he won the Quebec Crown. Villeneuve moved to Formula Atlantic racing in 1974, but broke his leg at his Mosport debut. He returned the following year with an outstanding performance—ranking fifth overall. During the 1976 season, Villeneuve dominated Canadian and North American Formula Atlantic racing, winning 9 out of 10 competitions. After winning the Canadian championship for CanAm class racing in 1977, Villeneuve was asked to join the Ferrari team on the world circuit. He won 6 out of the 67 races he drove for Ferrari in Formula 1. Unfortunately, he was killed during a qualifying race in Belgium, just as his international career was beginning to take off. Today, his son Jacques has become a famous racing car driver as well.

## Gilles Villeneuve

*Joseph Armand Bombardier beside an early snowmobile (1940s).*

One of Canada's most famous inventions, the snowmobile, was the brainchild of Joseph Armand Bombardier (1907–1964). Like all great inventors, Bombardier built everything from scratch himself. He created the first vehicle propelled by skis in 1936. Fully enclosed, with room for 10-12 people, Bombardier's tank-like invention soon became a common sight on snowy Quebec roads. It was used by the government during the war. Sales of Bombardier's machine declined after the war when the Quebec government announced that it would keep Quebec roads clear of snow. Not one to give up, Bombardier continued playing with his snowmobile and, in 1959, just as postwar consumerism began, introduced the ski-doo. Modeled more on a motorcycle than a bus, the ski-doo was an instant success in Canada. For the first time in history, Canada's remote Arctic communities were accessible by land.

Although Bombardier died in 1964, the ski-doo continued to sell worldwide. By the 1990s, more than 2 million had been sold. Bombardier Inc. is Canada's most important transportation company, with manufacturing plants in Montreal, Austria, Iceland and the U.S. Bombardier also makes planes and trains for the global market.

# Bourassa, Mulroney and Constitutional Change

## Meech Lake Accord

Conservative leader Brian Mulroney became prime minister in 1984. From the very beginning, Mulroney was determined to resolve the conflict between Quebec and the rest of Canada. Although the Constitution Act of 1982 was legally binding on Quebec, Mulroney found it unacceptable that Quebec had not agreed to it. He believed that recognition of Quebec's **special status** in the Canadian Constitution would bring the province into constitutional agreement with the rest of Canada.

*Brian Mulroney*

### MEECH LAKE ACCORD

**The Meech Lake Accord specified the following:**

- Quebec would be recognized as a distinct society within the Constitution.
- All provinces would have the right to recommend the appointment of Senators and Supreme Court justices.
- Changes to federal institutions (number of members in the House of Commons, Senate, and Supreme Court, for example), as well as changes from territories to provinces, would require ratification by all Canadian provinces, as well as the Canadian Parliament.
- Provinces could opt out of the newly created national social programs, and receive federal revenues for their own social programs, as long as these met national objectives.

In 1987, Mulroney invited all the provincial premiers to a government conference centre at Meech Lake, Quebec, to propose constitutional changes that would unify the country. The meetings were not easy, but an agreement—the Meech Lake Accord— was eventually reached.

The Accord was accepted by almost everyone in attendance. It had the approval of all three federal parties, and was rapidly approved by eight of the ten provinces. Only Newfoundland and Manitoba held out.

Opponents of Meech Lake felt the Accord weakened federal government powers, while awarding too much power to the provincial governments. They also felt the price paid to bring Quebec into the Constitution was too great and that the phrase 'distinct society,' which had no precise legal meaning, might give rise to future legal and constitutional disputes.

Aboriginal Canadians also opposed Meech Lake. They felt Aboriginal communities should also be recognized as distinct. They saw the survival of their communities within Canada as no less important than the survival of Quebec.

Elijah Harper, speaking on behalf of Aboriginal Canadians, prevented the Meech Lake vote from taking place in the Manitoba legislature.

1900   1910   1920   1930   1940   1950   1960   1970   1980   1990

On June 23, 1990, Manitoba MPP, Elijah Harper, speaking on behalf of Aboriginal Canadians, prevented the Meech Lake vote from taking place in the Manitoba legislature. Time had expired without unanimous approval. Prime Minister Mulroney's first attempt to bring Quebec into the Constitution had ended in failure.

*Elijah Harper*

### Charlottetown Accord

Mulroney believed a second attempt at constitutional change was justified. This time, he planned to ask Canadians for their views. Constitutional committees were established to canvas the country and to report back with specific recommendations. Bourassa's government threatened to hold a vote on separatism if the country did not address Quebec's demands. Tension mounted.

Finally, after months of discussion, an agreement was reached in Charlottetown, Prince Edward Island. This was a particularly symbolic location because the Confederation discussions of 1864 had taken place there as well.

The Charlottetown Accord was presented to Canadian voters for approval in a national referendum held in October, 1992. The Accord was defeated by 55% No to 45% Yes. Another constitutional attempt ended in failure.

Once again, Canada was caught in a unity crisis. Regionalism in western Canada blossomed, as did Quebec separatism. Many people blamed Prime Minister Mulroney for his timing of the constitutional discussions. Others blamed Quebec for not compromising its position, for demanding too much. Some Canadians blamed the provincial governments who, they felt, wanted too much power.

## CHARLOTTETOWN ACCORD

**The 1992 Charlottetown Accord consisted of several points:**

- It recognized Quebec as a distinct society with its own traditions.
- It recognized the idea of Aboriginal government on a par with federal and provincial governments.
- The Canadian Senate would be elected, not appointed.
- Canadian provinces would have extended powers, including power over social and health programs, as long as these were within "national standards."

### FOCUS

1. Why were some people against the Meech Lake Accord?
2. How did Elijah Harper prevent the Accord from taking place? Why did he do it?
3. Why did the Charlottetown Accord fail?

# Referendum 1995

*Lucien Bouchard*

Mulroney's minister of the environment, Lucien Bouchard, became disillusioned with both federalism and the Conservatives after the Meech Lake Accord. In 1990, he quit the Conservative party and sat as an independent member of the House of Commons. Soon, Bouchard was joined by several other Conservative MPs from Quebec. Together, they formed the **Bloc Québécois.**

The Bloc vowed to represent the interests of Québécois in the federal Parliament. Its popularity was confirmed during the October 25, 1993 federal election, when the Bloc won 54 seats to form the official Opposition.

In 1994, Jacques Parizeau, leader of the Parti Québécois, became premier of Quebec. Parizeau won the election because he promised voters an early referendum on separation, one that would contain clear, unambiguous wording. Parizeau moved immediately to unite the Québécois separatist

*On October 27, a huge national unity rally took place in Montreal. Observers do not agree whether this helped or hurt the federalist cause.*

On October 30, 1995, Quebec voters were asked to give the Quebec government permission to negotiate a new agreement with the rest of Canada.

**TIMELINE**

1900  1910  1920  1930  1940  1950  1960  1970  1980  1900  2000

movement. In June of 1995, he invited Lucien Bouchard and other prominent Quebec politicians to help create a document outlining how separation would be achieved

On October 30, 1995, Quebec voters were asked to give the Quebec government permission to negotiate a new agreement with the rest of Canada. Although the agreement would involve political independence, Quebec would maintain economic ties with Canada. Voters would also be giving the Parti Québécois permission to declare **unilateral independence** within one year of the referendum date, if negotiations between Quebec and Canada failed.

Daniel Johnson Jr., leader of the Quebec Liberals; Jean Charest, federal Conservative leader, and Lucienne Robillard and Michel Belanger, federal Liberal Cabinet ministers, led the campaign for the "no" vote. Momentum seemed to be with the "no" side at the beginning of the referendum campaign. The federalists underestimated the opposition, however. As voting day approached, separatists received more and more support. The

*Jacques Parizeau*

referendum looked to be a very close race. Thousands of English Canadians from all over Canada gathered in Montreal to hold a huge rally shortly before the vote. The October 27th rally was an extraordinary display of Canadian nationalism.

Voter turnout was high on Referendum Day, October 30, 1995. Canadians everywhere waited anxiously for the results. Everyone knew the decision would be a close one, but no one predicted just exactly how close it would be. 49.4% of Québécois voted in favour of the question, while 50.6% voted against it. The federalists had won, but by a very, very narrow margin indeed.

Jacques Parizeau blamed the separatist loss on big business money and "the ethnic vote." He resigned from the Parti Québécois and returned to private life.

**FOCUS**

1. Why did Lucien Bouchard quit the Conservatives?
2. What message did the people involved in the Montreal Rally hope to send to Quebecers voting in the referendum?
3. Who did Parizeau blame for the separatist loss?
4. What was the Bloc Québécois?
5. Why was the referendum result so close in 1995?

# Separatism and the Supreme Court

10

The federal government was determined never to underestimate the seriousness of the Quebec separation issue again. Prime Minister Chrétien appointed Stéphane Dion, minister of intergovernmental affairs, to

## THE REFERENDUM QUESTION

Federalists believed that the wording of the 1995 Quebec Referendum was unclear, and that most Quebecers did not know exactly what they were voting on. What do you think? Is the wording clear or ambiguous?

*Do you agree that Quebec should become sovereign after having made a formal offer to Canada for a new economic and political partnership, within the scope of the Bill respecting the future of Quebec, and the agreement signed on June 12, 1995?*

create ways of keeping Canada together. Dion was responsible for developing the federalist strategy known as **Plan B.** Dion asked the Supreme Court of Canada to decide whether the consitution legally allowed Quebec to separate.

This approach was a bold and risky one. The Supreme Court ruling would be an independent judgement, one based entirely on the law, and not on love of land or country. No one could predict what the Court's ruling might be. Many Canadians feared the decision would help the separatist cause, although Bouchard and his associates denounced the process. The Quebec government believed that the Supreme Court of Canada had no business ruling on the future destiny of Quebec. It boycotted the hearings. Quebec Liberal leader Charest thought Dion's approach heavy-handed.

Canada's Supreme Court heard the separation issue in February 1998 and released its judgement that August. The Court maintained that the voters of Quebec would determine the future of their province in a democratic manner.

Both federalists and separatists claimed victory from the Court's decision. Separatists rejoiced in the ruling that, should Quebec voters approve a separation referendum, Canada would have to negotiate separation. Federalists applauded the ruling because the Court specified a need for

**The Supreme Court of Canada ruled that:**
- Under Canadian and International law, it would not be legal for Quebec to declare unilateral separation from Canada.
- If the Quebec people voted to separate from Canada through the democratic process of a provincial referendum, the Canadian government could voluntarily negotiate separation terms with the new Quebec. This process would assure minimal disruption to Canada and to Quebec.
- A referendum vote must be a clear majority, and the vote must be made on a clear question. (The court did not define either term.)

The Supreme Court ruling would be an independent judgement, one based entirely on the law, and not on love of land or country.

a clear referendum question, and a clear majority vote in favour of separation. Both Bouchard and Charest defined a clear majority vote as 50% plus one. Prime Minister Chrétien and Stéphane Dion, however, maintained that a vote of 50% plus one was too small a majority to decide the fate of Canada.

## Clarity Act

In December 1999, Chrétien's government surprised many Canadians when it introduced the Clarity Act, Bill C-20 to the House of Commons. Based on the Supreme Court ruling on Quebec separation, the Bill outlined the conditions under which the federal government would negotiate separation of a province. The proposed law stated that negotiations would be carried out in accordance with the Supreme Court ruling. Borders, assets, liabilities, Aboriginal and minority rights would be negotiable.

The Clarity Bill marks the first time in our history that a federal government has initiated public discussions of the conditions under which it would negotiate the succession of any province.

"The French language has entered a period of slow but steady decline in Canada in face of a wave of Asian immigration and a growing number of so-called allophones in Quebec, according to two studies published this week. Allophones speak neither French nor English, Canada's official languages, at home.

The studies, undertaken by the Association for Canadian Studies in Montreal and the Conseil de la Langue Française in Quebec, predicted that Chinese would soon be spoken more than French in English-speaking Canada, while French would continue to decline slowly in Quebec, where it is predominant.

The studies said the number of French speakers had been eroded by three years of rising immigration to Ontario and British Columbia.

The study by the Conseil de la Langue Française also indicated that the French language in Quebec, a province of 7.3 million people, is threatened.

Marc Termote, who wrote the study, said the number of francophones in the province could drop by 2 percentage points, to 81 percent, in 20 years, with allophones accounting for 9.5 percent."

Quoted from *The New York Times*, October 28, 1999

## FOCUS

1. What is Plan B?
2. Why did the Quebec government denounce it?
3. What is the Clarity Bill? Why was it so significant?
4. In your view, can any province of Canada separate from the nation? Explain.

# Quebec's Changing Faces

It was 1944 before Quebec women received the right to vote in provincial elections, although they had been eligible to vote federally since 1917. Quebec suffragettes, led by Térèse Casgrain and Marie Gerin-Lajoie, were opposed by the Catholic Church. Francophone nationalists considered the suffrage movement to be Anglo-Saxon and anti-Quebec.

Quebec's women's voting preferences have had a powerful but underestimated impact on the province's politics. Women tend to see separatism as an economic risk to the province, and therefore to their personal well being. According to Statistics Canada in 1997, women over 15 years of age made up 44% of

*Gabrielle Roy*

the workforce in Quebec, but 68% were in low-paying, part-time jobs. They believe a united Canada provides them and their children greater stability, security and opportunity.

Quebec women have enjoyed great success in the arts. Céline Dion, world famous singer and celebrity, recorded her songs only in French until 1990. Authors Anne Hébert, Gabrielle Roy and Marie-Claire Blais have won Governor General's Awards for Literature. Lise Payette hosted popular radio and television shows before moving on to a successful career in politics, followed by later success as a screenwriter. Still, the gender gap is closing slowly in Quebec.

**Julie Payette** represents a new breed of Quebec women. Born October 20, 1963, she speaks 5 languages, holds a multi-engine commercial pilot licence, and has sung with the Montreal Symphonic Orchestra Chamber Choir, the Piacere Vocali in Switzerland and the Tafelmusik Baroque Orchestra in Toronto. In May 1999, Payette flew on the space shuttle *Discovery* to the International Space Station for a 10-day logistics and resupply mission. She was the first Canadian to visit the Space Station. In September 1999, Payette accompanied Prime Minister Chrétien and Quebec Premier Lucien Bouchard to Japan for trade discussions.

Authors Anne Hébert, Gabrielle Roy and Marie-Claire Blais have won Governor General's Awards for Literature.

# CANADIAN LIVES

BORN: 1896, Montreal, Quebec

DIED: 1981, Montreal, Quebec

SIGNIFICANCE: First francophone woman appointed to the Senate.

BRIEF BIOGRAPHY: Térèse Casgrain—humanist, suffragette, radio personality, reformer— played a leading role in Quebec's social and political culture during the twentieth century. She campaigned ceaselessly for women's rights and was a founding member of the Provincial Franchise Committee for woman's suffrage in 1921. During the 1930s, she hosted a radio show, Fémina, in which she discussed the role of women in Quebec society. In the 1940s, she joined the socialist group, the CCF, which mobilized opposition to Duplessis's government. In the 1960s, she founded the League of Human Rights and the Quebec branch of the Voice of Women to protest the nuclear threat.

## Térèse Casgrain

BORN: 1922, Prud'homme, Saskatchewan

DIED: 1993

SIGNIFICANCE: The first woman appointed Governor General

BRIEF BIOGRAPHY: Sauvé began her career as a journalist in print, radio and television. An ardent supporter of women's issues, she participated strongly in the political and social debates of her time. In 1972, Sauvé was elected as an MP for Montreal. She was re-elected in 1974, 1979 and 1980. Sauvé became the first female French-Canadian cabinet minister when she was made Minister of State for Science and Technology. In 1980, she became the first female Speaker of the House of Commons, a position she held until 1984. In keeping with her groundbreaking career as being the first female to achieve significant positions in federal politics, Sauvé was appointed the first female Governor General of Canada in 1984.

## Jeanne Sauvé

## New faces in Quebec

Bill 101, the Quebec language law passed in 1977, forced all immigrants to send their children to French language schools. By 2000, a whole generation of Quebec immigrant children—Blacks, Koreans, Filipinos, Chinese, Latin Americans and others—had been educated as francophones. Many of these young men and women became fully bilingual as they learned English at home or by watching TV. Some became trilingual by maintaining the cultural heritage of their parents or grandparents. This multicultural, multiracial population has developed in a Québécois culture and environment.

*Alexis Cossette-Trudel was elected president of the Parti Québécois youth wing in March, 2000. The son of former FLQ terrorists, Cossette-Trudel was born in Cuba before his parents returned to Quebec to face charges and prison terms.*

Traditionally, immigrants in Quebec have preferred federalism to separatism. Jacques Parizeau, Quebec's premier during the 1995 Referendum, cynically blamed the separatist defeat on "money and the ethnic vote." Today's youth, however, have grown up in a separatist political climate. Young Québécois of all origins, born since 1977, have lived through two sovereignty votes. They have been governed by several separatist governments that have championed Quebec independence. They heard Quebec leaders claim Canada rejected Quebec at the failure of the Meech Lake and Charlottetown Accords. Quebec's young voters grew up in an environment that saw successive Quebec governments demand more powers for Quebec. It is no surprise that the majority of Quebec youth appear to prefer the separatist option.

FOCUS
1. What are the political influences on Quebec's youth today?
2. How has Quebec's multicultural population affected the drive towards sovereignty?

**Match the people in column A with the descriptions in column B**

| A | B |
|---|---|
| **1.** Maurice Duplessis | **a)** first leader of the Parti Québécois |
| **2.** James Cross | **b)** first female Governor General of Canada |
| **3.** Jacques Parizeau | **c)** leader of the Union Nationale |
| **4.** Jeanne Sauvé | **d)** first French-Canadian women elected to the Senate |
| **5.** Térèse Casgrain | **e)** premier responsible for the 1995 Quebec referendum |
| **6.** René Lévesque | **f)** kidnap victim of the FLQ |

## Quick Recall

Identify the following in 2 sentences and explain why each is important to French-English relations:

1. FLQ
2. Quiet Revolution
3. Yvette Campaign
4. Lucien Bouchard
5. Meech Lake Accord
6. Clarity Bill
7. Franco-Ontarians
8. War Measures Act
9. Plan B
10. Acadia

## Do Some Research

1. Find out more about the expulsion of the Acadians. Why did the British government decide the Acadians had to go? How many were forcibly removed from their homes and lands? Where were they sent? How many returned to their homeland? What problems do Acadians in North America have in trying to protect their language and culture?

2. Research the circumstances that led to the War Measures Act in 1970. What powers did this give the authorities? How did this law affect the people? Was its use really necessary? In what other periods in Canadian history was the War Measures Act used? Compare these circumstances to those of 1970.

3. Separatists in Quebec claim that the Quebec government should have the right to represent the province in foreign countries. They want offices similar to Canadian embassies. Should Quebec have this right? What are the advantages for Quebec and for Canada? What are the disadvantages? Check the Quebec government website for more information supporting or rejecting this claim. Research the Parti Québécois website for more information about its goals. (www.pq.org)

4. Research the events leading up to the Quebec Referendum in 1995. What was the separatist strategy? Who did it involve, and in what capacity? What was the federalist strategy? Who organized the massive rally held in Montreal in October 1995? What was the outcome of this demonstration? Did it achieve its goals? How did separatists view this event? How did federalists view the event?

## Instant Analysis

Some statements can be labelled true or false. Others may depend on a variety of facts, opinions and special situations. Place these statements in three categories: True, False, or It Depends. Explain your answer.

1. Quebec wants to separate from Canada.
2. English and French Canadians rarely cooperate.
3. Like other provincial governments, governments of Quebec are usually prepared to defend their provincial rights and responsibilities.
4. The Quiet Revolution was a period of tremendous change for Quebec.
5. Confederation has generally been a bad deal for French Canadians.
6. Language rights will always be an issue in Quebec and Canada.

## Ideas for Discussion

1. What does the term "official bilingualism" mean? Do you support this policy? How do French-speaking Canadians benefit from this policy? How do English-speaking Canadians benefit from bilingualism? What are the disadvantages for English-speaking Canadians? Take a vote to find out the opinion of your class on official bilingualism.

2. Canada was formed with the consent of all provinces involved. Do you think its right for governments to make decisions about Canada without the consent of all the provinces.

3. What do you think would have happened if René Lévesque and the Oui force had won the Quebec referendum in 1980?

4. Organize a class discussion on the use of the War Measures Act during the October Crisis. The motion you debate might be: Resolve that the War Measures Act was an unnecessary threat to civil liberties and should not have been used.

## Be Creative

1. Make a bilingual poster advertising the benefits of living in a nation with two official languages.

2. Listen to some of the music of French Canada. Perhaps your teacher can help you translate some of the lyrics.

3. Assume you are a Canadian living in New France during the British Conquest. Write a letter to the new British governor outlining both your fears and hopes for the future.

## Web sites

**Government of Quebec:** www.gouv.gc.ca
**Cité Libre:** www.citelibre.com
**Bombardier Inc:** www.bombardier.com

*Quebec has a long history as a leader in performance art. Cirque du Soliel, founded by street performers in Quebec, now has headquarters in Los Vegas, Amsterdam and Montreal. Find out about others festivals in Quebec.*

# You Are There

**It is June 1995. In a few days, you, the people of Quebec, will be voting in a referendum on separation from Canada. A Quebec television network has brought people together from across the province for a debate. Some are prominent people in the news. Others are ordinary people. You are among them, and tonight your opinion will be heard. What would be the position of each of the following on the issue of Quebec separatism, and why would each feel that way?**

Those present include:

Jacques Parizeau — Quebec Premier and leader of the Parti Québécois

Pierre Trudeau — former Canadian Prime Minister

Jean Charest — leader of the Quebec Liberal party

Jean Chrétien — Canadian Prime Minister and leader of the Liberal party

An English-speaking Montrealer

A hotel owner from a Laurentian resort

An Acadian teacher from Moncton, New Brunswick

A dairy farmer from the Eastern Townships

A member of the Alberta cabinet

A French-Canadian miner from Sudbury, Ontario

A diplomat from Belgium, a country that also has 2 official languages (French & Flemish), chairs the debate.

Are you planning to vote oui or non? Might this debate change your mind? It's time to find out.

# Point
## Counterpoint

With which of the following statements do you most agree? Why?

With which of the following statements do you least agree? Why?

Much of Canadian history is consumed by heated debate. At the turn of the twentieth century, English and French Canadians had very different views about Canada's connection to Britain and what being Canadian was all about. At this time, few sought to consider the ideas or concerns of Aboriginal Canadians, Black Loyalists, Canada's Asian population or new immigrants arriving daily from Europe. As you read these differing selections, decide which you most/least disagree with and be prepared to defend your choice. Can you find any evidence of stereotyping in these quotes? How would you describe being Canadian today?

**"The French-Canadian population do not belong, if I may speak that way, to the same civilization as their fellow-countrymen of English origin. The French genius is not the same as the Anglo-Saxon genius. We are French, you are English. Would you permit me to add that we are Canadians to the fullest extent of the word, while on many occasions, you are more British than Canadians. If there is trouble in the future, the trouble will come out of that difference."**
Israel Tarte, French-Canadian Cabinet Minister, 1900

**"As long as I live, as long as I have the power to labour in the service of my country, I shall repel the idea of changing the nature of its different elements....I want the sturdy Scotsman to remain a Scotsman; I want the brainy Englishman to remain the Englishman; I want the warm-hearted Irishman to remain the Irishman; I want to take all these elements and build a nation that will be foremost among the great powers of the world."**
Sir Wilfrid Laurier, PM, 1900

**"In the scrolls of the future it is already written that the centre of the [British] Empire must shift—and where, if not to Canada?"**
Sara Jeanette Duncan, Canadian author, 1904

**"Canada for the British and Why Not!"**
Isaac Barr, author, 1902

# Introduction

## Sleeping with an Elephant: Canadian-American Relations

IN 1900, MANY PEOPLE STILL THOUGHT OF CANADA AS A BRITISH DEPENDENCY, not as an independent nation. Indeed, our foreign policy was controlled by Great Britain. Influence from the United States was minimal. As the twentieth century unfolded, however, there was a gradual shift from British to American influence and, some would argue, to American dependency. While on a visit to the United States, Prime Minister Pierre Trudeau once stated: "Living next to the United States is in some ways like sleeping with an elephant. No matter how friendly and even-tempered is the beast, one is affected by each twitch and grunt."

Throughout the twentieth century, Canada had something of a "love-hate relationship" with the United States. Many Canadians seemed anxious to adopt a life style that included American fashions, automobiles, entertainment, and standard of living. Yet, in doing so, there was often a fear of the loss of "Canadianisms," traits that were distinctively Canadian in nature. The Canadian tensions between being both "pro and anti" American continue as Canada enters the twenty-first century.

## METHODS OF HISTORICAL INQUIRY

### Comparisons

Comparing information is an important task for people studying history. When asked to do a comparison, you must look at both the **similarities** and the **differences** of the subject in question. For example, if you were asked to compare Canada with the United States, you would have to look at the ways in which we are similar to Americans and the ways in which we are different. You could break down the information even farther by looking at a number of different categories and asking yourself how we compare on these levels. You might compare our political system to that of the United States; our economical situation, our culture, our geography and our language. Each time, however, you must try to find similarities and differences.

# Chapter Eight: Sleeping with an Elephant

# Expectations

## General Expectations:

**By the end of this chapter, you will be able to:**

- demonstrate an understanding of the elements of Canadian identity

- explain ways in which outside forces and events have influenced Canada's policies

- demonstrate a knowledge of how and why changing economic conditions and patterns have affected Canadians

## Specific Expectations:

**By the end of this chapter, you will be able to:**

- explain how and why the federal government has tried to promote a common Canadian identity through various agencies and assess the effectiveness of these efforts

- explain how American culture and lifestyle have influenced Canadians from 1900 to the present

- summarize Canada's changing political relationship with the United States from 1900 to the present

- demonstrate knowledge of the advantages and disadvantages of American participation in the Canadian economy

- explain how the government had promoted Canada's cultural distinctiveness

## WORD LIST

| | | | |
|---|---|---|---|
| Acid rain | Canadian content | Split Run Magazine | Free Trade |
| Auto pact | Ethnic cleansing | Suez Crisis | Trade sanctions |

# Chapter 8

# *Advance* Organizer

## 1

**Although Canada and the United States share the same continent, it is surprising how little the people of each country know each other. Stereotypes have been created by movies, television and other media. Although many stereotypes are old ones, for the most part, they are still with us. A clear, unbiased image of each other would make for easier social and economic relations. With the tensions in the world today, such mutual understanding would greatly benefit both countries.**

## 2

Canadian culture is hard to define, and it faces a constant challenge, especially with so much influence from the United States—television, movies, magazines, sports, music and other forms of entertainment. Many Canadian organizations, both public and private, contribute to the recognition and preservation of Canadian culture.

## 3

The United States is our most important trading partner and shares many economic interests. However, both countries sometimes disagree over the handling of different problems. In the end, each country tries to protect its own economic interests.  Americans have invested in Canada and promoted Canadian economic growth. At the same time, Canadians are anxious to maintain control of their own companies. Still, each country is likely to become more dependent on each other in years to come. It is important that Canada and the United States keep their economic alliance an open and friendly one.

**4**

On a political level, Canadians and Americans have probably had a better relationship historically than most other countries. The world's longest undefended border has, in this century,

been almost invisible. The leaders of both countries continue to meet periodically, under friendly conditions, with a few notable exceptions. Furthermore, the two countries also established the International Joint Commission to monitor issues of mutual concern and to make recommendations.

**5**

In sports, there has been a lot of cross-border influence between Canada and the United States. At the professional level, hockey, baseball and basketball are played on a continent-wide basis, although it is often difficult for the Canadian teams to feel they are on an equal footing with the United States, which has more teams and more money.

# 1 The Geographic Link

*"Geography has made us neighbors. History has made us friends. Economics has made us partners. And necessity has made us allies."*
President John Kennedy addressing Canada's Parliament, 1961

*Waterton-Glacier International Peace Park spans the U.S.– Canada international border between Montana and Alberta.*

Canada and the United States share the same continent, and the world's longest undefended border—all 9,000 kilometres of it. We have similar immigration patterns, settlement histories and livelihoods. We often interact similarly when dealing with the rest of the world. Americans and Canadians have been working together for over 250 years. Our two nations have closer economic, social and political ties than any other two nations in the Western world. Yet Canada's population is only one-tenth that of the United States. Canada must work hard to preserve our Canadian presence. We are enriched by our close association with the United States—its highly developed culture, dynamic population, wealth and momentous history—but it is also important that Canadians not be overwhelmed by our large and prosperous neighbour to the south. Both the determination to resist the American presence, and the will to gain from it, have been conflicting passions throughout our history.

On March 18, 1998, the people of Minnesota's Northwest Angle—a small corner of land bordering Manitoba's Lake of the Woods, submitted a constitutional amendment in favour of leaving the United States and joining Canada. Visitors to the Northwest Angle must travel through Canada to get there—unless they come by boat. Northwest Angle's citizens were unhappy with the condition of their roads and with American fishing regulations. There was no Canadian response to this overture.

Canada and the United States share the same continent, and the world's longest undefended border—all 9,000 kilometres of it.

## BORDER CROSSINGS

Unlike many international boundaries, most of the border between the United States and Canada is unfenced. We rely on lakes, rivers and roadways to define the separation of our two countries. Sometimes, the border runs through the middle of a town, sometimes through the middle of a house. Most Canadians and Americans are used to crossing the border between the two countries without fuss. Some people cross it every day. During the Vietnam War, 20,000 American draft-dodgers crossed the border into Canada. Many of us have crossed the border several times. Canadian and American immigration officials check our papers and ask us how long we plan to stay, or how long we've been away.

Every once in a while, a border crossing is not routine. In 1985, Canadian author and naturalist Farley Mowat was refused entry into the United States. He was scheduled to give a series of lectures, but his outspoken views landed him on a list of "undesirables." American officials turned him back at the border. Canadians were outraged. Mowat's works have been published in over 40 countries. He is the author of such impassioned books as *Never Cry Wolf* and *A Whale for the Killing*. Mowat's rejection was later overturned, but he refused to travel to the United States again. *My Discovery of America* is a chronicle of Mowat's experiences.

### A CLOSER LOOK AT THE ALASKA BOUNDARY DISPUTE

The Alaska Boundary Dispute was one of the very few genuine arguments between the United States and Canada about our international border. When the U.S. purchased Alaska from Russia (in 1867), it claimed possession of the entire Alaskan coastline. Canada disagreed, arguing that access to the Yukon—particularly as a result of the Klondike gold rush—was under Canadian control. In 1903, both parties submitted their argument to arbitration by an international tribunal. Canada was still a British colony and did not have the power to make treaties on its own behalf. Britain represented the Canadian case to the tribunal, which found in favour of the United States. Canadians were very unhappy with the judgement, and expressed considerable anti-British feeling as a result.

### FOCUS

1. What was the Alaska Boundary Dispute?
2. Why were Canadians dissatisfied with the outcome of the dispute?
3. What are some of the dangers for Canada in living so close to the United States?

# The Political Link

Canada and the United States usually have a warm and friendly relationship. When U.S. President Franklin D. Roosevelt received an honorary degree from Queen's University in 1938, he noted that Americans and Canadians did not view each other as "foreigners." Roosevelt's "Good Neighbour" policy stated that the people of the United States would not stand idly by if the dominion of Canadian soil were threatened by any other Empire.

*A Canadian CF-18 ground crew check over a fighter jet in Quatar during the Gulf War in 1991.*

Sometimes, the relationship between Canada's prime minister and the president of the United States can turn into close personal friendships. When President Ronald Reagan met with Prime Minister Mulroney over St. Patrick's Day in 1985, the two "Irishmen" got along so well, the conference was called "The Shamrock Conference." Prime Minister Chrétien enjoyed a similar friendship with U.S. President Clinton.

## Foreign Affairs

Canada and the United States have usually agreed about how relations with other countries should be conducted. The two neighbours share many interests, have many of the same "friends," and belong to many of the same military and political alliances—APEC, NATO, OAS, Arctic Council, and NORAD—to name a few. Meetings between the two leaders are quite common, and both are regularly in telephone contact with one another. The United States maintains its embassy in Ottawa, and numerous consulates across Canada. Our Canadian embassy in Washington D.C. is aided by Canadian consulates in several American cities.

In 1956, the U.S. and Canada worked together under the leadership of Lester Pearson to end the **Suez Crisis** in 1956. Both countries wanted to prevent the Arab-Israeli hostilities from escalating to include the Soviet Union. In 1991, both countries were involved in the Gulf War—the United Nations-sponsored military action against Iraq, which had invaded oil-rich Kuwait.

In 1999, both Canada and the United States were part of NATO forces used against Yugoslavia, which had been accused of **"ethnic cleansing"** in its province of Kosovo.

Canada and the United States have usually agreed about how relations with other countries should be conducted.

Occasionally our two countries disagree about how a situation should be handled. Sometimes there are moments of tension and concern. Canada did not approve of American policy toward Cuba or of the U.S. involvement in Vietnam. The United States did not approve when Canada established diplomatic relations with communist governments in Cuba and China. In 1965, Prime Minister Pearson called for a suspension of air strikes against North Vietnam in the hope of restoring peace talks. U.S. President Johnson was furious. Other relationships between Canadian and American leaders have been so cool as to be almost uncivil. Pierre Trudeau did not get along with Richard Nixon in the 1970s. John Diefenbaker's nationalist policies were not welcomed by the United States during the 1950s and 1960s, and the Americans were not pleased when Canada began exporting wheat to Communist China.

More recently, Canada and the United States have disagreed about exports. United States' law forbids American companies from selling goods to "enemy" countries. The U.S. government believes Canadian branches of American companies must obey this law. Canadians have protested when an American parent company forces its Canadian branch to cancel a sale.

## A FRIEND IN NEED

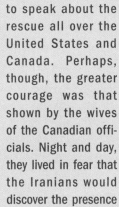

In 1979, the staff of the American embassy in Iran was taken hostage by the Iran government. Six American diplomats escaped and found refuge in the homes of Canadian embassy officials. No one knew the Americans were even alive. Over two months later in January 1980, the Americans were able to leave Iran secretly, using fake Canadian passports. The Royal Canadian Mounted Police and the American Central Intelligence Agency had worked together to prepare the documents and to smuggle them into Iran.

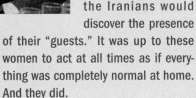

Overnight, Canadian ambassador, Ken Taylor, became a hero. He was invited to speak about the rescue all over the United States and Canada. Perhaps, though, the greater courage was that shown by the wives of the Canadian officials. Night and day, they lived in fear that the Iranians would discover the presence of their "guests." It was up to these women to act at all times as if everything was completely normal at home. And they did.

### FOCUS

1. What are some of the military and political alliances Canada shares with the United States?
2. What are some of our common interests?
3. Who was Ken Taylor?

# Technical and Environmental Links

Canada and the United States have cooperated on many projects, which have made great changes to the world in which we live. The opening of the 3,790-kilometre-long St. Lawrence Seaway in 1959 signified the end of a mammoth construction effort between the two countries. Begun in 1954, the seaway required the development of sophisticated engineering technology in order to insure a successful completion. The seaway allowed the American Midwest and the Canadian Prairies to ship goods economically across North America. Freighters could transport Canadian wheat and American corn from North America to the world.

Space exploration is another area in which Canada and the United States have worked closely together. In 1962, Canada signed an agreement with NASA for the launch of Canadian satellites into the earth's outer atmosphere. These exploratory missions would help Canadian and American scientists discover many of the mysteries of space. By 1976, Canada, working once again with NASA, was able to launch a telecommunications satellite. It broadcasted radio and TV programs directly into Canadian homes. Telecommunications is an important element of Canada's technological future because it allows us to communicate over long distances with minimal hardware support.

*In 1982, NASA contracted with Canadian scientists to develop and purchase the remote manipulation device, Canadarm. It has proved invaluable during NASA's manned space flights. New remote manipulation devices continue to be a major Canadian contribution to space exploration. NASA has invited several Canadian astronauts to participate in NASA-sponsored space flights, both as scientific experimenters and as mission control personnel. The cooperative effort between Canada and the United States is longstanding and ongoing.*

TIMELINE

1900   1910   1920   1930   1940   1950   1960   1970   1980   1990

## Environmental Link

In 1909, Canada and the United States established the International Joint Commission (IJC), consisting of three representatives from each country. The IJC is mandated to protect lake and river systems along the border between Canada and the United States. Both countries knew that the maintenance of healthy lake and river systems along their mutual border was essential to friendly cooperation. They made sure the IJC met regularly to review problems and to make decisions on issues affecting the health of the international boundary waters.

**Acid rain** is another issue faced by the International Joint Commission. The industries of central Canada and the northern United States create air pollution. This is absorbed into rain which falls on eastern North America. The resultant acid rain kills plant and animal life in lakes. In 1991, Canada and the United States signed an Air Quality Agreement. It set up an Air Quality Committee to report every two years on progress in eliminating acid rain.

*Canadian fishers blockaded an American ferry during the salmon wars.*

In 1985, Canada and the United States signed the Pacific Salmon Treaty to set up equal distribution of the Pacific salmon catch. Each country would limit its catch to quotas. By 1993, it was obvious the treaty was not working. Canadian fishermen felt that the Americans were catching too many fish. The salmon population was declining. The dispute dragged on. Finally, in 1997, Canadians blockaded an Alaskan ferry off the coast of British Columbia. It was not until June, 1999 that Canada and the United States signed a new treaty setting salmon quotas until 2009.

> ### FOCUS
> 1. Why was the St. Lawrence Seaway important for Canada-US relations?
> 2. What is the International Joint Commission?
> 3. How did Canada and the Unites States solve the salmon war?

# The Economic Link

Canada lives next door to the world's largest economic power. The American economy produces over $1.5 trillion of wealth a year. Canadians and Americans are joined together in one of the most comprehensive and extensive economic relationships in the world, a relationship that supports more than two million jobs in each country. Two-way trade more than doubled from 1989 to 1999. We are each other's largest trading partner, with more than $1.5 billion crossing the border each day. Many countries see Canada and the United States as a single economic unit.

More than 80% of Canadian exports go to the United States ($270 billion in 1998). Twenty-two percent ($234 billion in 1998) come to Canada. In fact, the United States sells twice as many goods to Canada's market of 30 million people, than it does to its next biggest trading partner, Japan—with 130 million people. Canada uses more American goods than do all 15 countries of the European Union combined.

Canada and the United States are not equal economic partners, however. Our economy is much smaller. The United States's population exceeds 280 million people. Canada's population is a little over one-tenth of that amount. Sometimes

## A CLOSER LOOK AT THE BRAIN DRAIN

Canadian "Brain Drain" to the United States may be worse than previously thought, a new federal government study has found . It shows that as many as 16,540 Canadian skilled workers have obtained temporary work visas under the North American Free Trade Agreement and are likely to stay in the United States for a long time.

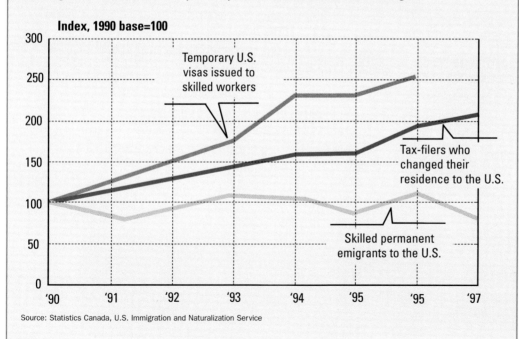

Index, 1990 base=100

Source: Statistics Canada, U.S. Immigration and Naturalization Service

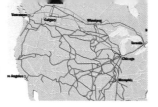

Canadians and Americans are joined together in one of the most comprehensive and extensive economic relationships in the world

1900    1910    1920    1930    1940    1950    1960    1970    1980    1990

Canadian and American interests are not the same. The close relationship between our two countries does present some problems. Many Canadians feel that Canada is too dependent on the American economy. Often, our economic well-being can rise and fall with decisions made "south of the border." This makes it very difficult for Canada to act independently of the U.S.

## The Question of Ownership

Foreigners own more than half of Canada's 500 largest corporations. Some commentators say Canadians are tenants rather than landlords in their own country. Millions of dollars in profits and resources leave Canada each year for the United States. Many multinationals, such as General Motors, IBM, Coke, Microsoft, Kentucky Fried Chicken, Random House, Allstate Insurance and McDonald's, have branch plants or stores throughout Canada, but maintain their head offices and major decision-making locations in the United States. Some of Canada's most respected companies have been sold to the Americans. Lumber giant MacMillan Bloedel, for example, went to Weyerhaeuser in 1999, while Del Rina, creators of WinFaxPro, was bought up by Symantec.

83% of Canadians responding to an annual survey conducted by *Maclean's* magazine

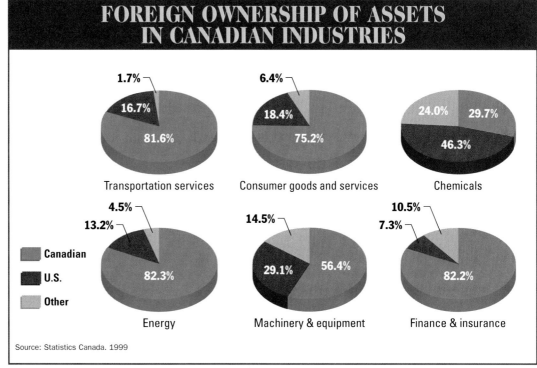

**FOREIGN OWNERSHIP OF ASSETS IN CANADIAN INDUSTRIES**

Transportation services: 81.6%, 16.7%, 1.7%

Consumer goods and services: 75.2%, 18.4%, 6.4%

Chemicals: 29.7%, 46.3%, 24.0%

Energy: 82.3%, 13.2%, 4.5%

Machinery & equipment: 56.4%, 29.1%, 14.5%

Finance & insurance: 82.2%, 7.3%, 10.5%

Legend:
- Canadian
- U.S.
- Other

Source: Statistics Canada. 1999

felt that greater Canadian control of businesses operating in Canada was important in maintaining a strong Canadian identity in the

# FOREIGN INVESTMENT REVIEW AGENCY (FIRA) AND INVESTMENT CANADA

In 1971, the Liberals introduced the Foreign Investment Review Agency (FIRA) to investigate the purchase of Canadian companies by foreign companies. The intent was to slow down the increasing U.S. control of Canadian industries and natural resources. FIRA would act as a "watchdog" to ensure any proposed Canadian takeover by a foreign firm would be in the best economic interests of Canada.

Not all Canadians supported FIRA. Canadian business owners regarded FIRA as an intrusion on their right to control their companies as they saw fit. Americans viewed FIRA as an unfriendly action towards American business. There was the possibility of American **economic sanctions** against Canada or even a trade war.

From 1971 to 1981, American ownership of Canadian corporations remained at about 25%. By 1982, FIRA appeared to be little more than a "paper tiger," as it was approving nine out of every ten applications for foreign takeovers.

Shortly after talking office in 1984, Brian Mulroney replaced FIRA with Investment Canada. The Conservatives looked to increase prosperity and create jobs through industrial expansion. They were not worried about the source of investment in Canada.

---

twenty-first century. In 1999, American purchases of Canadian companies totalled $25.6 billion Canadian—up from $5.6 billion Canadian in 1994.

Many economists point out the fact that American money has helped Canada grow strong and wealthy. Canadians have benefited from American technology and know-how. American investment has created millions of jobs in Canada. The close economic link between the two countries has helped create friendly political and military relations.

Canada must always make sure that economic ties with the U.S. are in the best interests of Canadians. The Canadian government has taken steps to exercise some control over the relationship.

## *Train Merger*

By the end of the twentieth century, increased globalization had forced many companies to reevaluate their economic position.

Many felt that merging with other companies would increase their chances of survival. CN, for example, proposed a merger with Texas-based, Burlington Northern Santa Fe Corps. The proposed alliance would create the biggest railway in North America, with a route of about 80,000 kilometres and annual revenues of about $18.5 billion. Called the North American Railway Inc., the new company would be based in Montreal. Some people, however, felt that such a merger would weaken Canada's economy as the new railway would be 80% American-owned.

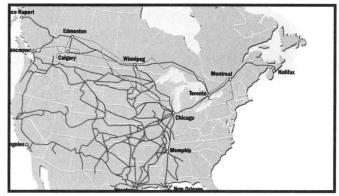

*This map shows the new route of the proposed merger between CN and Burlington Northern Santa Fe Corps.*

## A CLOSER LOOK AT THE AUTO PACT

The automotive industry—making new cars, trucks and parts—is Canada's largest manufacturing industry. In 1965, it employed 70,000 people. But there was a problem. Canada was buying more cars, trucks and car parts from the United States than it was selling back.

In 1965, Canada and the United States signed the **Auto Pact**, an agreement to establish duty-free trade in new cars and original equipment automotive parts. Canada hoped to lower Canadian consumer prices and Canadian production costs. The Auto Pact declared that the value of cars produced in Canada must equal or exceed the value of cars imported into Canada. It also said that for every American vehicle sold in Canada, 60% of the value added to its manufacture must be Canadian—this is usually in the

form of Canadian-made parts

The Auto Pact led to an expansion of automotive factories and production in Canada. American automakers could build a car in Canada and sell it to either country. The Auto Pact has worked in Canada's favour for many years. Canada has shipped a higher value of car parts to the United States than the U.S. has shipped to Canada. Canadian automotive manufacturing employs well over 130,000 people today.

In 2000, however, the World Trade Organization (WTO) ruled that the Auto Pact was unfair to foreign dealers, and that Canada must either scrap the 6.1% duty it levies on cars from Japan and Europe, or extend it to include cars from the United States.

### FOCUS
1. Why do many Canadians think they are too dependent on the United States's economy?
2. What is FIRA and why did Trudeau introduce it?
3. How has the Auto Pact helped Canada's automotive industry?

# 5 The Free Trade Agreement

Free trade with the United States has been discussed or implemented at several different times in Canadian history. From 1854 to 1866, a reciprocity treaty existed between the two countries, allowing free trade on certain goods and products. When Prime Minister Laurier proposed another reciprocity agreement with the United States in 1911, the Americans agreed but the Canadians baulked. Laurier was turned out of office, and Robert Borden's Conservatives rejected free trade.

Free trade reared its head again during the 1980s when Canadians and Americans watched as European nations forged a successful economic union—the so-called Common Market. Mulroney and his Conservatives began to champion the free trade cause, although Mulroney himself had earlier opposed it. "Free trade is terrific until the elephant twitches, and if it ever rolls over, you're a dead man," he once said.

The Canadian government worried that American duties and tariffs would restrict the flow of Canadian goods and services to the United States. **Free trade**—unrestricted passage of goods across the border—seemed the only answer.

Not all Canadians wanted free trade. Many were very vocal in their opposition. In 1988, Mulroney's government called an election and asked Canadian voters to decide the issue. Free trade won, and Canada began to negotiate with the United States.

## THE FREE TRADE DEBATE

**Supporters of free trade said that it would benefit Canada because:**

- Canadian producers gain access to a market ten times larger than our own
- Increased Canadian exports allow Canadian companies to make longer and more economical production runs
- More Canadian jobs are created
- Foreign investors are attracted to Canada
- Consumers will pay lower prices
- Economic prosperity means Canadians can spend more on research and development

**Opponents of free trade said that it would hurt Canada because:**

- We lose control of our political sovereignty
- The poorer areas of the country will get poorer
- Canadians will be Americanized
- Unemployment will increase
- Canada will send too many of its natural resources out of the country, and our supply of these is limited
- Canada's service industries will be threatened by their larger American competitors

In 1994, the FTA was expanded to include Mexico and renamed the North American Free Trade Agreement or NAFTA. This created the world's largest free-trade bloc. It linked 370 million people in three countries.

| 1900 | 1910 | 1920 | 1930 | 1940 | 1950 | 1960 | 1970 | 1980 | 1990 |

Finally, in January 1989, the Free Trade Agreement (FTA) went into effect. It signalled a decision by both Canada and the United States to pursue economic integration. President Ronald Reagan called the trade deal a new economic constitution for North America. The FTA gave Canada and the United States open access to each other's markets for most goods, either immediately or through a phase-in period of several years. From 1989 to 1999, Canadian exports to the United States increased from $101 billion to over $270 billion, although probably no more than twenty-five percent of this growth should be directly attributed to the FTA.

In 1994, the FTA was expanded to include Mexico and renamed the North American Free Trade Agreement or NAFTA. This created the world's largest free-trade bloc. It linked 370 million people in three countries, with thirty-one percent of the world's wealth, into one single trade region. By the year 2000, serious discussions were taking place among all countries in the Western Hemisphere. They were looking to unit into one gigantic free-trade partnership by 2004.

By 1999, ten years of free trade had had both positive and negative effects on Canada, but with no clear-cut overall decision. In a lead editorial *The Toronto Star* offered this assessment:

> *"In a decade in which the U.S. has been the primary engine of world economic growth, hitching our wagon to the 50 American stars appears to make a great deal of sense. If the U.S. economy falters, however, we may come to regret just how dependent we have become on a single export market. By the same token, there remains a strong possibility that the forces of integration will draw us even further into America's maw."*

The inescapable reality is that Canada is quickly becoming deeply integrated into the American economy, or a North American economic community.

This fact has enormous political, cultural and economic ramifications, including suggestions of a common currency, establishment of a customs union, and the creation of common institutions. Canada has been walking a tightrope with the United States for at least half a century. The key question seems to be—what price are Canadians willing to pay for their own Canadian distinctiveness?

### FOCUS

1. What is free trade?
2. What are its advantages for Canada?
3. What are its disadvantages?

# 6 The Cultural Link

How well do Americans and Canadians really know each other? Are they neighbours or strangers, friends or foe?

Canadians think they know a lot about Americans. They receive information about the United States from a wide variety of sources—from movies, television, magazines, music and sports, and even the Internet. Many Canadian students study American history or geography in school.

Americans receive little, if any, information about Canada and Canadians. Those who live close to the border often vacation in Canada. Others may meet our Canadian "snowbirds," those retired Canadians who spend the winters in the southern States. Some American movie fans are familiar with Canadian talent. The American music indus-

try has a sincere appreciation for the songs of Shania Twian, Randy Bachmann and Céline Dion. But, for the most part, the enormous influence the American mass media has in Canada is not reciprocated. Americans do not believe in Canadian culture. They do not need it, or as one columnist for *The Boston Globe* wrote: " Canada is like Belgium or Equador—a nice enough place, but not very important."

When Canadians go to Europe or Asia, a strange thing happens. If they are taken for Americans, they become indignant and offended. They put Canadian flags on their bags or lapels so people will not make the same mistake again. Suddenly they are proud of their country and their heritage.

---

## So What's the Difference?
**Anyone seriously comparing Canada and the United States will find very real differences:**

- the contrast between the parliamentary and congressional systems
- the Canadian duality (French and English), our tradition of multiculturalism or the Canadian **cultural mosaic,** as compared to the unity of the American vision—the American **melting pot**
- Canada's historic ties with Great Britain, which would be rejected by most Americans
- Canada's conservative tradition, one in which civil war and revolution have played no part
- Canadians's attitudes towards social welfare programs—we expect them. Americans do not
- Canadian speech and Canadian language—Americans say "What?" We say "Eh?"
- Our pronunciation of the English language is not always up to American standards— and theirs is not always up to ours
- Perhaps, however, the greatest difference between Canadians and Americans is Canada's perpetual quest for a national identity. Americans don't seem to be looking for a national identity at all. They have always seemed to have one

Canadians think they know a lot about Americans. They receive information about the United States from a wide variety of sources.

1900    1910    1920    1930    1940    1950    1960    1970    1980    1990    2000

*Canadian artist Takao Tanabe's sweeping landscapes explore space, light, and the horizon.*
*This painting is called "Columbia Plateau 5/96." It depicts the northwestern part of Washington State.*

## Canadian English is not always American English

**Canadian English might best be described as a dialect that reflects both British and American patterns of speech. Here are a few examples:**

| CANADIAN | AMERICAN |
|---|---|
| chesterfield | sofa |
| serviette | napkin |
| blinds | shades |
| schedule (pronounced shed ule) | schedule (pronounced sked ule) |
| highway | interstate |
| z (pronounced zed) | z (pronounced zee) |

**What other differences can you come up with?**

# CANADIANS TALK ABOUT AMERICANS

1  Everyone in the U.S. owns a gun, or would like to.

2  Americans all live in cities in big apartment buildings. They have to breathe their air through filters so they won't die of smog and pollution.

3  Americans just think about money and big business. They have either big homes or fast cars.

4  I can name you five thousand times when the Americans raced to the help of other people in trouble. Can you name me even one time when someone else raced to the Americans in trouble?

(Gordon Sinclair in a 1973 CFRB radio broadcast)

5  Americans get their foreign policy from those John Wayne movies: "Shoot first and ask questions later."

6  The major threat to Canadian survival today is American control of the Canadian economy.

7  Americans are so ignorant because they know almost nothing about Canada, and what they do know is usually wrong or distorted.

What is Canada? Is it just the United States moved north, or is there something about Canadian culture that is unique? When *Maclean's* magazine conducted their annual poll of Canadian attitudes in 1999, 90% of the respondents said that Canada has a unique identity as a country. 77% felt that our identity is based on a strong sense of Canadian history.

One element of life that contributes greatly to identity is culture. Canadian federal and provincial governments believe that strong support of cultural activities strengthens Canadian identity. As early as 1949, the federal government worried about the impact of American mass media on Canadian culture. It established a Royal Commission to investigate Canadian culture, education and communication. The Massey-Lévesque Commission released its report in 1951. It recommended the creation of the National Library of Canada; this was done in 1953. The Commission also recommended federal funding for the arts. In 1957, the government established the Canada Council for that purpose. Today, some 700,000 Canadians earn their living in the cultural sector. Government assistance to the arts has increased. The Heritage Canada portfolio was created "to insure access to Canadian voices and Canadian spaces, to protect Canada's heritage and to enhance pride in Canada."

# AMERICANS TALK ABOUT CANADIANS

1 Mountains. I think of mountains, and people singing.

2 Canadians are healthier than we are because they have to fight the elements to survive. Also, probably because they're mostly descended from Eskimos, Indians and Mounties.

3 The one thing I remember about Toronto is that you can read the map on the subway. In New York, I never know where I'll end up, but Toronto's such a neat, itty-bitty place you can't get lost.

4 Canadians are nice and polite, not rude and noisy like some Americans you see. 'Course, I've only met two Canadians I know of.

5 Canada will always be remembered by my generation as the nation that stood for peace, whether in the Middle East or Vietnam or Cyprus. If I were a Canadian, I'd rather have that said about me than anything else.

6 Canadians—short and fat and dark mostly, and some of them speak French.

7 Canadians are generally indistinguishable from Americans, and the surest way of telling the two apart is to make this observation to a Canadian.

8 Canadian drivers are crazy. I'm sorry, but there's no other word for it. They put their foot on the gas and their hand on the horn and look out, here I come. I wonder if it's got anything to do with their religion.

(tour guide, Williamsburg, Virginia)

9 Canadians don't have any heroes, and not much history.

(history student, U. of Rochester, New York).

**FOCUS**
1. How are we influenced by the United States?
2. In your opinion, how are Canadians and Americans different? How are they the same?
3. What was the Massey-Lévesque Commission? What did it recommend?

# Radio and Television

**7**

Radio and television have had a profound impact on Canadian culture and identity. We spend an average of 22.7 hours a week watching TV—that's 1,180 hours, or 49 days a year. Only about 40% of what we watch originates in Canada. The rest comes from the United States and Great Britain.

*SCTV was one of the most successful comedy shows ever. Here the cast, who all achieved great success south of the border, are reunited. How many do you recognize?*

## CANADIAN BROADCASTING REGULATION

**1929**    Royal Commission on Broadcasting recommended the creation of a national, state-owned broadcasting network to counter the impact of American radio.

**1936**    The Canadian Broadcasting Corporation (CBC)—La Societe Radio-Canada—is established as a crown corporation

**1951**    Massey Commission—first major investigation of Canada's culture and foreign influences

**1957**    Fowler Commission—further support for the CBC which led to the creation of the Broadcasting Act

**1968**    Canadian Radio-Television Commission (CRTC) set up to regulate broadcasting

**1970**    CRTC content rulings created

**1976**    Canadian Radio-Television and Telecommunications Commission created to recognize the expanding nature of broadcasting and telecommunications in Canada

**1996**    Canadian Television and Cable Production Fund created—with an annual budget of $200,000,000 for the creation of Canadian productions

Radio and television have had a profound impact on Canadian culture and identity.

To protect Canadian culture in the broadcasting industry, the CRTC created content regulations. Canadian-owned radio stations must play music with **Canadian content** at least 35% of their "on air" time. Canadian content means at least two of the following conditions are met: either the composer or performer is Canadian, the song has been performed in Canada or its lyrics are about Canada. Canadian-owned television stations must have 60% Canadian content, and between 6pm and midnight—(prime time for most viewers)—Canadian content must be 50% of all broadcasting.

Some critics call the CRTC's requirements a form of censorship. Others feel that without such rules, Canadian entertainment would not be widely available to Canadian audiences.

*Michael J. Fox is Canada's best-known actor. Born in British Columbia, Fox became famous as Alex Keating on the successful U.S. sitcom,* Family Ties *and went out to star in* Spin City *and the* Back to the Future *movies.*

## A CLOSER LOOK AT ROGERS COMMUNICATION

One of the largest cable-television companies in the world is Canadian-owned and operated. Rogers Communications, with sales of $3.1 billion Canadian in 1999, owns 30 radio stations, the Canadian shopping channel, 70 magazines—including *Maclean's* and *Chatelaine*, 200 video rental stores, the Cantel cellular network, a high speed Internet access provider, a search engine, and an on-line auction service. Rogers has over 4.5 million subscribers to its cable, paging and cellular services.

---

**F O C U S**

1. Why do Canadian stars often move to the United States?
2. What is the CRTC?
3. What qualifies as "Canadian content?"
4. Why do some people disagree with the CRTC over its Canadian content legislation?

# Movies and the U.S.

**8**

Many American films and TV shows are produced in Canada. Toronto, Montreal and Vancouver have become major film-producing centres. Movie producers can take advantage of the low Canadian dollar. The Toronto area plays host to so many film crews that it has been labelled "Hollywood North."

Canadian filmmakers often have a hard time competing against the American film industry. Barely one in twenty films on Canadian screens is Canadian. Some movies, Atom Egoyan's *The Sweet Hereafter,* for example, or Bruce Bereford's *Black Robe*, or Thom Fitzgerald's *The Hanging Garden,* have achieved international acclaim. But, for the most part, U.S.-based distributors control about 85% of the Canadian film market. Canadian audiences spend some $180,000,000 every year going to the movies, yet few American distributors are eager to invest in Canadian feature films. As noted Canadian filmaker Claude Jutras (*Mon Oncle Antoine*) commented, "Not making the films you want to make is awful, but making them and not having them shown is worse."

In 1967, the Canadian Film Development Corporation was established to help promote the Canadian feature film industry. This organization was later replaced by Telefilm Canada, which invested $1.4 billion, directly or indi-

Above: *Atom Egoyan, the successful Canadian director of* The Sweet Hereafter, *has stayed in Canada despite being pursued by large Hollywood studios.*
Right: *Neve Campbell has a successful career in both film and television on both sides of the border.*

In 1967, the Canadian Film Development Corporation was established to help promote the Canadian feature film industry.

TIMELINE

1900  1910  1920  1930  1940  1950  1960  1970  1980  1990

rectly in Canada's film industry between 1989 and 1999. In 1988, acclaimed Canadian film director Norman Jewison established the Canadian Film Centre for Advanced Film Studies in Toronto to further the film careers of Canadians already established in the industry. The National Screen Institute, with offices in Winnipeg and Edmonton, "provides a continuum of career-long professional development for Canadian film and television industry professionals."

Canadian films are featured at a variety of film festivals across the country. From Yorkton, Saskatchewan to Halifax, from Montreal to Vancouver to Banff, to Rimouski, Quebec, Canada has a rich tradition of regional and national film events.

*Mike Myers relocated to the United States to pursue his career in comedy.*

## A CLOSER LOOK AT THE NATIONAL FILM BOARD

In 1939, the Canadian government established the National Film Board (NFB) to produce films that reflected Canada's social and cultural life. Since that time, the NFB has produced more than 9,000 original titles. Many have been widely praised, receiving international awards. In 1989, Hollywood bestowed an honorary Oscar on the NFB, "in recognition of its 50th anniversary and its dedicated commitment to originate artistic, creative and technological activity and excellence in every area of film making."

By the end of the 1990s, more than 81,000 Canadians were employed, directly or indirectly, in the film industry. While the leading stars are often American, more than 90% of the production crew are Canadians. There is little doubt that there is a thriving film industry in Canada today, although Canadian-made films comprise less than 10% of the total Canadian film market.

**FOCUS**
1. Why is Toronto labelled Hollywood North?
2. Why was the NFB created?
3. How many Canadian stars can you name?

# 9 Publishing

Canadians are justly proud of their internationally celebrated writers: Robertson Davies, Margaret Laurence, Anne Hébert, Michael Ondaatje, Margaret Atwood, Mordecai Richler, Carol Shields, Alice Munro, W.O. Mitchell, Roch Carrier, Pierre Berton and Michel Tremblay. Our distinctive world-class literature is, in part, a testament to the success of public policy which supports the Canadian publishing sector.

There are 321 Canadian-owned book publishing houses producing 80% of new Canadian-authored books. Canadian books account for 30% of the total book market in this country. Books by American, British, and French authors, plus those of other nationalities account for 70% of our marketplace. Many Canadian publishers have close relationships with American, British and French publishers whose books they distribute to Canadian readers.

Heritage Canada provides aid to Canadian publishers, as well as money for market research and development. The Canada Council for the Arts, the Social Sciences and Humanities Research Council (SSHRC), and provincial arts councils provide assistance to publishers and writers.

Canada produces over 1,400 different magazines with total circulation of about 500 million copies. Even though Canadian publishers have close to a 30% share of the domestic market, there is an ever-present threat from foreign magazines, mainly from the United States.

Canada's federal and provincial governments believe most Canadians want to retain an identity different from our neighbours to the south. Therefore, they have looked for a number of ways to support the arts. The CBC, the National Film Board, the Canada Council, the CRTC and Telefilm Canada have all sprung from the federal government's concern. In

## SPLIT RUN MAGAZINES

In 1999, Canadians and Americans engaged in a battle over **split run** magazines—American magazines sold in Canada that use Canadian advertising as their "Canadian content" rather than any Canadian-based articles or feature stories. The Canadian government felt that split run magazines didn't satisfy the regulations surrounding Canadian content, so they proposed a bill that would have blocked the sale of U.S. magazines in Canada. Since Canadians make up a large market of these magazines, the American government was not pleased. They warned that if the bill passed they would hit back with trade sanctions. The crisis was averted when a compromise was reached by both countries.

There are 321 Canadian-owned book publishing houses producing 80% of new Canadian-authored books.

addition, many provinces fund arts councils to support regional and local cultural activities, while private corporations sponsor concerts, theatre and dance compa-

*Margaret Atwood, Canada's leading author, had her book* A Handmaid's Tale *made into a Hollywood movie.*

nies or art shows. All this helps to give Canadian artists the opportunity to be appreciated in their own country.

*Michael Ondaatje's novel* The English Patient *was turned into an international movie blockbuster.*

The real decision about the future of Canadian culture lies with average Canadians. Only Canadians can decide if they want to be different from Americans. Only Canadians can develop their own dancers, novelists and musicians. If it means something special to be Canadian, Canadians must work to discover their national cultural identity.

FOCUS

1. What are split run magazines?
2. What is Heritage Canada, and how does it help Canadian publishers?
3. Name three important Canadian authors?

# The Leisure Link

**10**

Canadians and Americans visit each other all the time. Canada sends more visitors to the United States than any other country. More Americans come to Canada than from any other country. This has been going on for

*Banff, Alberta*

some time. Did you know, for example, that most of the major peaks in the Canadian Rockies were first climbed by American tourists in the 1800s? Americans regularly purchase vacation homes and cottages in Canadian cottage country, along our sea-coasts or in the mountains. Canadian cities such as Niagara-on-the-Lake, Windsor, Ontario and Vancouver thrive on cross border shopping and traffic. American cities such as Buffalo, New York, Burlington, Vermont and Missoula, Montana are equally attractive to Canadians. During the winter, Canadian snowbirds make Florida and the southwestern United States their second home.

## Sports

The United States has had a significant impact on Canadian sports, especially in the last quarter of the twentieth century. Television has moved sports off the playing fields and into living rooms around the world.

## Hockey

While lacrosse is officially recognized as Canada's national sport, there is little doubt that hockey is our most beloved sport. When the National Hockey League (NHL) was formed in 1917, half of the six original teams were Canadian—Montreal Canadiens, Montreal Maroons and the Toronto Maple Leafs. All the players on these teams were Canadian. By 2000, the NLH had 29 teams, of which only 6 were Canadian. Canadians comprised only 60% of the player roster. The league headquarters was located in New York City (moved from Montreal), and the NHL president was an American. American TV networks dictate schedules and game times.

More Americans come to Canada than from any other country. This has been going on for some time.

T I M E L I N E

1900    1910    1920    1930    1940    1950    1960    1970    1980    1990

Canada dominated amateur hockey at the Olympic Games for many years, but recently, other countries have consistently won gold. Hockey has moved from Canada to the world. Canadian heroes—Gordie Howe, Maurice Richard, Bobby Orr, and Mario Lemieux—set standards for others to follow.

In 1999, the nine-team National Women's Hockey League began in Ontario and Quebec, with expansion into British Columbia in the fall of 2000. In Ontario alone, there are more than 20,000 women playing organized hockey. In 1998, the Canadian national team won a silver medal in the Olympics, as well as five consecutive world championships from 1995 through 1999.

*Canadian Nicole Jenkins celebrates her victory over Amy Tong, an American, in the quarter finals of the PanAm Judo Championships.*

## Football

The Canadian Football League (CFL), created in 1960, has always struggled to survive, especially since the widespread growth of the American, National Football League (NFL). The CFL enforces a quota system to ensure a large percentage of Canadian players, although many fans feel that this is unfair. Nationality should not matter, only ability. Others maintain that this quota system is necessary to preserve the league's Canadian distinctiveness.

- 87% of Canadian athletes feel that national pride is important in determining their decision to pursue sports at a high level
- 94% view their sports role in society as being representative of Canada
- 92% see sports as a source of pride for Canadians
- 98% see themselves as role models for Canadian youth

- Sports Canada survey, 1996

During the 1990s, the CFL struggled economically and some cities dropped out of the league. Seven American cities joined the CFL for three years. In 1995, Baltimore won the Grey Cup—a symbol of Canadian football supremacy. These seven American cities then dropped out of the CFL, several to join or rejoin the NFL. The Baltimore franchise moved to Montreal to recreate the earlier Alouettes team.

Many Canadians prefer the American version of football. Some would like to see the CFL merge with the NFL. Others want to preserve the CFL as it is now, arguing that they prefer this version with its unique Canadian rules and Canadian players. By 2000, the CFL was having a resurgence in popularity and fan support.

## Baseball

There has been a very long tradition of baseball in Canada with some suggestions that it was being played here before it was "invented" in the United States. Babe Ruth hit his first professional home run in Toronto and Jackie Robinson, an African-American, broke the "colour barrier" when he played for the Montreal Royals, the Brooklyn Dodgers' top farm team.

Canada now has two teams in the major baseball leagues—the Montreal Expos in the National League and the Toronto Blue Jays in the American League. Many Americans were shocked when Toronto won the coveted World Series in 1992, and again in 1993. It was almost unthinkable that America's "national pastime" could be dominated by a "foreign" country.

*Fergie Jenkins, a native of Chatham, Ontario, was the first Canadian baseball player to make it into the Hall of Fame.*

Many Canadians have played in the major leagues. Ferguson Jenkins from Chatham, Ontario, pitched for the Chicago Cubs and the Philadelphia Phillies, and was later inducted into the Baseball Hall of Fame. During the late 1990s, Larry Walker, from Maple Ridge, B.C., became one of the most dominant players in the game.

On the non-professional level, there are numerous baseball and fastball leagues throughout the country, for both males and females. It continues to rank along with soccer as being very popular summer sports.

*Toronto Raptor Vince Carter.*

## *Basketball*

Basketball was invented by a Canadian, James Naismith of Almonte, Ontario, while he was teaching in Springfield, Massachusetts in 1891. It was not until 1994, however, that Canada had teams (the Vancouver Grizzlies and the Toronto Raptors) join the National Basketball Association. As expansion teams in a well-established league, the Canadian teams have struggled to assert themselves. Only a few Canadians have so far managed to reach basketball's professional ranks.

Canada has approximately one-tenth the population of the United States, yet it has achieved considerable fame in professional sports, especially hockey. Sports scholarships, available throughout American colleges and universities, are not allowed in Canada. As a result, many of Canada's best athletes have been lured to the United States for their post-secondary education. This has seriously eroded the level of Canadian college sports, and has probably affected professional sports in Canada as well.

Strikes, escalating salaries and labour unrest in sports over the past decade have affected the public's perceptions of professional sports. This, coupled with the tremendous influence of the United States, pose a genuine challenge for the preservation of Canadian spectator sports.

**F O C U S**
1. What were the six original hockey teams?
2. How does the CFL differ from the NFL?
3. How has the United States influenced Canadian sports?

# Questions & Activities

## Questions and Activities

## Match the words in column A with the descriptions in column B

| A | B |
|---|---|
| 1. Ronald Reagan | a) supported by the United Nations |
| 2. Lyndon Johnson | b) Mulroney-Reagan meeting |
| 3. St. Lawrence | c) watchdog on broadcasting |
| 4. "Operation Desert Storm" | d) talent loss to the United States |
| 5. "Shamrock Conference" | e) confrontation with Lester Pearson |
| 6. Massey Commision | f) watchdog on foreign investment |
| 7. CRTC | g) free trade on certain goods |
| 8. sports scholarships | h) American President in the 1980's |
| 9. FIRA | i) joint Can-Am project |
| 10. Reciprocity Treaty | j) report on Canadian culture |

## Identifications

**Identify and state the importance of the following:**

1. "Trading with the Enemy" act
2. Ferguson Jenkins
3. James Naismith
4. "Quiet Diplomacy"
5. IJC
6. Bill C-55
7. Fowler Commission
8. "Cocacolonization"
9. NEP
10. Telefilm Canada
11. Investment Canada
12. NAFTA

## Ideas for Discussion

1. Hold a debate on the topic: "Canadians are Americans in everything but name."

2. Draw up two lists showing the positive and negative results of Canada's close relationship with the United States.

3. Is there any value in having a Canadian identity separate from an American counterpart?

4. What is Canadian culture? American culture? Are there any significant similarities and/or differences?

5. To what extent is Canada a partner or puppet in North American culture and economics?

6. What do you feel are the important issues facing Canada in its relationship with the United States?

7. To what extent is your lifestyle set by patterns which have been "made in the U.S.A?" How much of this influence do you resent? Welcome?

8. What efforts have been made in the cultural and economic fields by the federal government and/or other agencies to help create a distinctive Canadian culture and economy? How effective have they been? What other steps should be taken, if any?

9. How many past and current Canadian musicians, actors and television programs can you name? Which of these reflect something distinctly Canadian?

10. Listen to your favourite radio station for one hour between 4 p.m. and 10 p.m. Write down the title of the song, the performer(s), and the nationality for each song. What are the percentages for: Canadian, American, other? Which do you like most? Should nationality matter?

## Do Some Research

1. What roles were played by each of the following prime ministers in shaping Canadian foreign policy with the United States?
   **a)** Lester Pearson    **b)** Pierre Trudeau
   **c)** Brian Mulroney    **d)** Jean Chrétien

2. What is the extent of foreign ownership in various sectors of Canada's economy? How has this developed historically?

3. Listed below are some of the key historical events or issues that have shaped Can-Am relations. What has each contributed to that relationship?
   **a)** the American Revolution, 1775-1783
   **b)** the War of 1812
   **c)** the Reciprocity Treaty, 1854-1866
   **d)** Alaska Boundary Dispute, 1903
   **e)** reciprocity issue in 1911

4. What impact has the United States had on each of the following cultural areas in Canada?
   **a)** mass media—radio, television
   **b)** the arts—film, music, theatre
   **c)** publishing—books, magazines, newspapers
   **d)** sports—NHL, CFL, NBA, baseball, amateur sports
   **e)** education—textbook authors, nationality of teachers/professors

5. Draw a chart to show areas where Canadians and Americans are both similar and different. Some headings might include:
   **a)** political structure
   **b)** geography
   **c)** language characteristics (eg. accents, use of certain words)
   **d)** life style and standard of living
   **e)** basic beliefs
   **f)** national origins (American revolution versus Confederation)
   **g)** social attitudes
   **h)** others

6. The International Joint Commission was set up between Canada and the United States to resolve areas of dispute. What have been some of these areas in the past? What are the current areas of tension?

## Web sites

**NAFTA:** : www.nafta-.net.naftagre

**CRTC:** www.crtc.gc.ca

**Canadian Film and Television Producers Association:** www.cftpa.ca

**You are the members of a newly appointed cabinet in the federal parliament. Your party has won a recent election, and you are eager to begin the task of leading Canada into the next millennium.**

**One issue you wish to discuss is Canada's relationship with the United States. Your prime minister has promised that there would be a review of existing policies, and that this would lead to a statement of party policy.**

**Three experts have been brought in to give their opinions. With which do you most agree? What will the cabinet's decision be? After listening to the three positions, you must convince your colleagues to agree with your opinion.**

Dear Prime Minister:

After much research, I suggest that the following action be taken by your government:

- the free trade deal is working so well, we should have complete economic union
- we should pool our North American energy resources
- we should remove all restrictions against American television or broadcasting
- we should begin discussions to permit Canada to join the United States

I have suggested this closer relationship with the U.S. because it is our ultimate destiny. Our people and culture are basically the same. We should seek our chance to join with the U.S., the greatest and most powerful nation on earth. Only then, can our economy truly prosper. Remember, united we stand; divided we fall.

Sam Union
Continental Consultants

Dear Prime Minister:

I have made a thorough analysis of all aspects of Canadian-American relations. Quite frankly, things have never been better. I cannot see why there is a need for review.

I would suggest that we continue our present policies:

- let the Free Trade Agreement develop; it is bound to improve our economy
- maintain friendly relations with American presidents; the U.S. is our best friend and greatest ally
- continue to resolve environmental issues. The problems took years to develop; we cannot expect rapid action to solve them
- emphasize how much we have in common with Americans, rather than publicizing issues and problems

Remember, we are all North Americans, two great nations sharing the longest undefended border in the world. Let's keep it that way.

Stan Pat
Status Quo Enterprises

Dear Prime Minister:

Time is very short. The greatest crisis in Canadian history now faces us. We have become almost a colony of the United States.

Since the Free Trade Agreement went into effect, the U.S. dominates nearly every aspect of Canadian life. Americans own most of Canada's resources; our economy is linked to theirs. Canadian culture is being submerged in American television. Our foreign policy is just a reflection of U.S. policy. To save Canada's future, I recommend the following:

- revise our involvement in free trade to reduce ties to the American economy
- reclaim control over our energy resources to create a Canadian energy policy
- encourage investment and trade with the Pacific Rim countries (Japan, China, Korea, Taiwan)
- improve policies to protect Canadian culture
- place our defence emphasis on Canadian protection of the Arctic area

Act now, or Canada is lost.

Jane Canuck
Maple Leaf Enterprises

# Point
## Counterpoint

With which of the following statements do you most agree? Why?

With which of the following statements do you least agree? Why?

"We are being swallowed up by the popular culture of the United States, but then the Americans are being swallowed up by it too. It's just as much a threat to American culture as it is to ours."

Northrop Frye, University of Toronto English professor

"Americans are benevolently ignorant about Canada, while Canadians are malevolently well informed about the United States."

J. Bartlet Brebner, Canadian historian

"The Americans are our best friends— whether we like it or not."

Robert Thompson, Canadian politician.

"The Canadian is often a baffled man because he feels different from his British kindred and his American neighbours, sharply refused to be lumped together with either of them, yet cannot make plain his difference."

J. B. Priestly, British writer

"Canadians are generally indistinguishable from Americans, and the surest way of telling the two apart is to make the observation to a Canadian."

Richard Staines

# Introduction
## Hands Around the World

CANADA UNDERWENT A DRAMATIC SHIFT THROUGHOUT THE twentieth century in its relations with other countries. In 1900, Canada was a comparatively new country with strong ties primarily to Great Britain. In fact, Canada did not yet have control over its own foreign policy. As the twentieth century unfolded, Canada became far less dependent on Great Britain, and gradually emerged as an independent and respected nation. By 2000, the United Nations had named Canada as the best country in which to live.

Canada joined many organizations during the 1900s for a variety of reasons: political, defensive, economic, cultural and humanitarian. Some of these, such as the League of Nations, no longer exist, while others, such as the United Nations and NATO, have been in existence for more than half a century. Canadians continue to assess to which organizations they should belong, and which countries would assist Canada's well-being.

Canada has walked a "tightrope" in its relations with other countries. We are not a "superpower" and, indeed, most Canadians probably would not want to see us in such a role. On the other hand, we are not a developing nation, struggling to assert itself. Sometimes, we have been called a "middle power," one that has considerable influence with both the major nations of the world, but also with those which are less well developed. This has been, and continues to be, a formidable challenge for Canada in its relations with other countries.

## METHODS OF HISTORICAL INQUIRY
### Assessing Bias

History students must always be aware of the problem of bias. All writers are unintentionally influenced by their experiences and backgrounds. Although facts cannot be disputed, our interpretations of these events often reflect our **impartialities**. A Canadian of Albanian descent, for example, would interpret the NATO War of 1999 differently than a Canadian of Serbian origin. Because of bias, different historians often offer different interpretations and reach different conclusions about the same facts.

# Chapter Nine:
# Hands Around the World

# Expectations

## Overall Expectations:
**By the end of this chapter, you will be able to:**

- explain ways in which outside forces and events have influenced Canada's policies
- demonstrate a knowledge of Canada's participation in war, peace, and security
- explain why and how Canada's international status and foreign policy have changed since 1914

## Specific Expectations:
**By the end of this chapter, you will be able to:**

- describe the influence of Great Britain and Europe on Canadian policies from 1900 to the present
- describe Canada's role in Cold War activities, such as NATO, NORAD and the nuclear arms race
- demonstrate knowledge of the roles and functions carried out by the Canadian Armed Forces since 1945
- identify why certain documents such as the Treaty of Versailles and the Statute of Westminster are important in the evolution of Canada's political autonomy
- explain the significance of Canada's contributions to the United Nations

## WORD LIST

| | | | |
|---|---|---|---|
| Boycott | Indigenous | Prisoners of Conscience | Sovereign |
| Genocide | Isolationism | | Veto |
| Humanitarian | Peacemaking | Propaganda | |

# *Advance* **Organizer**

## 1

Canada's foreign policy determines how and why it associates with other countries. Throughout its history, Canada has evolved from a series of British colonies to complete independence, although the process was lengthy. Canada's foreign policy continues to change depending on current situations and our relationship with other countries.

## 2

Out of the ashes of World War II rose the United Nations. The UN was created to prevent future wars and to promote world cooperation. Most countries, including Canada, are members of the UN. Canada has solidly supported the UN with money, people and materials. Canadian soldiers have served in many UN peacekeeping operations.

## 3

Since the introduction of atomic warfare during World War II, an all-out war can now mean the destruction of our entire world. For this reason, a new form of war, "The Cold War," developed between two major rivals, the United States and the Soviet Union, and lasted until 1990. The Cold War was a war of nerves, with the major powers threatening each other with displays of military strength rather than with outright warfare.

**4**

To help keep peace and to protect Canadian interests, Canada joined two major alliances: NATO and NORAD. Canada supports NATO to protect Europe against aggression.

Canada and the U.S. formed NORAD, whose goal is to protect North America from enemy attack. Membership in these alliances could, at some time, involve Canada in a major war.

**5**

Not all of Canada's foreign ties are of a military nature. Canada is a member of two non-military organizations—the Commonwealth and la Francophonie. The Commonwealth is a free association of peoples once ruled by the British Empire. La Francophonie is a free association of French-speaking nations of the world. Both of these bodies provide Canada with friendships all over the globe.

**6**

Canada is concerned about a number of trouble spots in the world. Of increasing importance are the developing nations. These are the poor, underdeveloped nations of Africa, Asia and South America. Their people account for well over half of the world's population. Canada has given money and supplies, and has sent people as advisers to improve conditions within these countries.

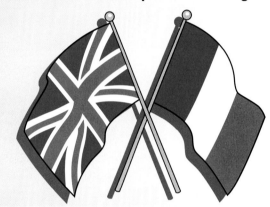

At the opposite end of the economic scale are the Arab countries of the Middle East. These countries have vast quantities of oil, and therefore hold power over other countries. Canada needs oil from the Middle East, and values the Middle East as a trading partner. To help ease tensions, Canadian soldiers have served as peacekeepers for the United Nations in the Middle East, as well as other parts of the world.

# What is Foreign Policy?

A country's foreign policy is the plan by which it conducts its relations with the rest of the world. A nation that does not have relationships with the world still has a foreign policy—we call it **isolationism**.

Foreign policies can differ greatly, but each usually includes the following:

- Objectives: the goals one nation hopes to achieve through its relations with other nations
- Methods: how that nation means to pursue those goals

Foreign policies help nations achieve prosperity—

through trade and commerce. They help nations maintain prestige or gain revenge against an enemy. Sometimes a foreign policy's goals are idealistic—Canadian aid to the poorer countries of this world. Sometimes foreign policy is shaped by a country's geographical position, military and economic power, or by its ethnic and religious ties.

As the chart indicates, the development of Canada's foreign policy has been evolutionary, rather than revolutionary. The process took place over many years as our view of the international world developed and changed.

## CANADA'S FOREIGN POLICY DEVELOPMENT

| | |
|------|------|
| 1914 | Canada entered World War I automatically as a member of the British Empire |
| 1919 | Canada signed Treaty of Versailles as a separate country, and became a charter member of the League of Nations as an independent nation |
| 1922 | Chanak Affair—Canada refused to support British action in Turkey and did not send troops as Britain requested |
| 1927 | Canada's first embassy established, in the United States |
| 1931 | Statute of Westminster gave Canada full control over its foreign affairs |
| 1939 | Canadian Parliament, without British consent, declared war on Germany in the Second World War |
| 1945 | Canada becams a charter member of the United Nations as a sovereign nation |

Foreign policies are developed because independent nations want to remain independent. They want to preserve their own integrity, and to ensure the safety of their citizens.

Canada's foreign policy falls under the direction of the Department of Foreign Affairs and International Trade, which was created in 1909. Its mandate is to:

- conduct all diplomatic and consular relations on behalf of Canada
- conduct and manage international negotiaions as they relate to Canada
- foster the expansion of Canada's international trade
- manage the Canadian Foreign Service

A visit to the departmental web page (www.dfait-maeci.gc.ca) provides an overview of its history and a statement of the key objectives of Canada's foreign policy.

*A Candian soldier serving in Bosnia looks out of a damaged window.*

*Prime Minister Chrétien has had a significant impact in the world. He applauds (left) as CIDA President Hugette Labelle and Chiness Vice-minister of foreign trade sign a Memoradum of Understanding and Cooperation in Beijing, China. Visiting Cuba's Fidel Castro (right).*

**FOCUS**
1. What is foreign policy?
2. List three reasons why countries have foreign policies.
3. List two mandates of the Department of Foreign Affairs.

# Canada and the United Nations

In 1945, Canada joined with 50 other countries around the world to found the United Nations, or UN, to maintain peace and promote friendly relations among all the countries of the world. The United Nations would become a centre of international cooperation, and its people would champion the cause of human rights around the world.

*Many member nations have contributed to the design and materials found in the UN buildings. Canada's gift was the nickel-bronze doors that lead to the General Assembly. The panels of these doors represent four themes of the United Nations—peace, justice, truth and brotherhood.*

Today, the United Nations has 188 members. It is a fascinating, gigantic, and often confusing organization divided into six main bodies.

Although its main headquarters is located in New York City, there are UN offices in countries all over the world. Discussions are held in six official languages—Arabic, Chinese, English, French, Russian and Spanish, with instantaneous translations being offered during the debates

The UN has six main organizations or branches. All are based in New York, with the exception of the International Court of Justice, which is located at the Hague, Netherlands and the United Nations Educational, Scientific and Cultural Organization (UNESCO), headquartered in Paris, France. In addition, 14 specialized agencies work in areas ranging from health to finance, agriculture, civil aviation and telecommunications.

The United Nations is an organization of independent sovereign countries. It does not pass laws like a national parliament or congress. In its meeting rooms and corridors, representatives from most countries of the world—large and small, rich and poor, with varying political views and social systems—have a voice and vote in shaping the policies of the international community.

## The United Nations' Structure

The GENERAL ASSEMBLY, sometimes referred to as a world parliament, is the UN's main body. All 188 member states are represented in it. Each has one vote. Decisions on ordinary matters are taken by simple majority. Important questions require a two-thirds majority.

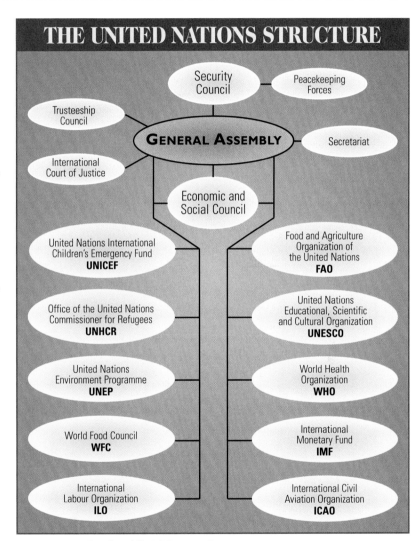

THE UNITED NATIONS STRUCTURE

- Security Council
- Peacekeeping Forces
- Trusteeship Council
- GENERAL ASSEMBLY
- Secretariat
- International Court of Justice
- Economic and Social Council
- United Nations International Children's Emergency Fund UNICEF
- Food and Agriculture Organization of the United Nations FAO
- Office of the United Nations Commissioner for Refugees UNHCR
- United Nations Educational, Scientific and Cultural Organization UNESCO
- United Nations Environment Programme UNEP
- World Health Organization WHO
- World Food Council WFC
- International Monetary Fund IMF
- International Labour Organization ILO
- International Civil Aviation Organization ICAO

Every year, the Assembly holds its regular meeting to discuss and make recommendations on all matters within the UN Charter— the organization's founding document. The General Assembly does not have the power to compel action. Its recommendations carry the weight of world opinion.

*Candian soldiers are greeted by celebrating Kosovars at the Canadian base in Urosevec, Kosovo.*

The Assembly:
- sets policies and determines programs for the UN Secretariat
- directs activities for development
- approves the UN budget, including peace-keeping operations
- admits new members
- appoints the UN Secretary-General

The SECURITY COUNCIL has the primary responsibility for maintaining peace and security. It can meet at any time, whenever peace is threatened. UN member countries are obligated to carry out Security Council decisions.

The Security Council has 15 members, five of which—China, France, the Russian Federation, the United Kingdom and the United States—are permanent. The remaining members are elected by the Assembly for two-year terms. Canada has been elected to the Security Council several times.

The five permanent Security Council members have the right of **veto**; should any of them veto a resolution, the issue is defeated.

The Security Council tries to mediate international disputes by asking opposing parties to reach agreement by peaceful means. Should that fail, the UN can use a variety of means to try to bring about a settlement:
- economic sanctions on countries that threaten peace. This usually means boycotting goods to or from that country. In recent years, a boycott has been used against Iraq which did not want to allow United Nations armament inspections
- send in peacekeeping forces to keep opposing forces apart, or put a peace agreement into effect
- use military action to deal with conflict, as in 1950 in South Korea, and as in response to Iraq's invasion of Kuwait in 1990. This is called **peacemaking**

THE SECRETARIAT works for all the branches of the UN and administers their programs. With a staff of about 8,900, the Secretariat carries out the day-to-day work of the UN. Its head is the Secretary-General.

THE ECONOMIC AND SOCIAL COUNCIL coordinates the economic and social work of the UN and its related specialized agencies. The Council has 54 members. It meets for a one-month session each year, alternating between New York and Geneva. The Council oversees UN activities and policies promoting economic growth in developing countries. It administers development projects, promoting the observance of human rights, and fostering international cooperation in areas such as housing, family planning, environmental protection and crime prevention.

THE TRUSTEESHIP COUNCIL was established to assist territories on their road to self-government or independence. This path has been followed by several countries which are now members of the UN. The Trust Territory of the Pacific Islands, now known as Palau, joined the UN as its 185th member in 1994.

THE INTERNATIONAL COURT OF JUSTICE (also known as the World Court) is the main judicial branch of the UN, settling legal disputes between member states. It consists of 15 judges, elected by the General Assembly and the Security Council. Recently the court has been actively trying soldiers accused of atrocities during conflicts in the former Yugoslavia.

## The UN's Work

The United Nations has worked hard to establish its basic principles and goals. Though not always successful, the UN has made many changes to the world.

PEACEKEEPING: Since 1948, the UN has carried out more than 40 peacekeeping operations—30 of them within the last twelve years. More than 750,000 military personnel have served with the UN forces. More than 1,500 peacekeepers have lost their lives.

In 1957, Lester Pearson became the first Canadian to receive the Nobel Peace Prize. As President of the UN General Assembly, Pearson suggested a peace plan to end the Arab-Israeli conflict over the Suez Canal. Since then, Canadian soldiers have been leading members of almost every UN peacekeeping force. They have served in places

*Canadian peacekeepers pass a horse-drawn carriage in Bosnia-Herzegovina. Most transportation in Bosnia is done without motorized vehicles because of a lack of gasoline.*

such as Cyprus, Kashmir, the Congo, Iran, Iraq, Somalia, Bosnia, and Kuwait.

Canadian armed forces were used in Rwanda from 1993 to 1996 to protect the capital city of Kigali during the Rwandan civil war. Canadian troops, under the UN flag, helped to bring food and medical supplies to starving Rwandans. Our troops worked with others to maintain UN cease-fire orders. However, serious questions were raised concerning the UN's effectiveness in this peace-keeping effort.

For more detail on past and current UN peacekeeping operations, check the United Nations Internet website at http://www. un.org.

INTERNATIONAL AID: The UN provides funds to developing countries for agricultural and industrial development, for technical, and medical and educational assistance. UN funding, however, is limited by the amount of money contributed by UN member nations. UN funding remains a constant problem as the organization's financing is far from adequate and monies received are not always spent wisely.

PEACEMAKING: In June, 1950, North Korea, encouraged by the Soviet Union, invaded South Korea, which was backed by the United States. The United Nations declared this invasion an act of aggression. It sought support from other UN members to resist the invasion. Forces from over 30 countries, including Canada, fought the war to stop the North Koreans. Over 20,000 Canadian soldiers fought in Korea. 312 were killed in action.

*A Kuwati worker kneels for midday prayers near a burning oil field outside Kuwait City.*

On January 18, 1991, United Nations' forces from 32 countries launched Operation Desert Storm against the nation of Iraq because of its invasion of Kuwait. The war lasted only 41 days as Iraqi soldiers soon abandoned the invasion, or surrendered to UN troops. This was only the second time in over forty years that the United Nations was forced to use military action to stop aggression.

The UN has often been criticized for its failure to prevent the outbreak of war, and for its inability to create world peace. Today, our world remains a hotbed of hostilities, many of which can lead to war. The UN can only work to reduce the effects of war. As the twenty-first century begins, it seems that the nations of the world may be tiring of war's constant threat, and of the need for peacekeeping forces in so many places. Today, there is renewed hope that the UN could begin to play a significant role in preserving world peace.

---

**F O C U S**
- **What type of work does the United Nations do?**
- **Why was it founded in 1945?**
- **What is the difference between peacekeeping and peacemaking?**

# A CLOSER LOOK AT LAND MINES

One of the world's most barbaric weapons is the land or anti-personnel mine—an explosive device which detonates on contact. Land mines are used widely in war, where they are planted around battlefields, roads and other areas where the enemy might be found. Land mines have become even more deadly in peace because they remain in place even after wars have ended. Today, it is estimated that there are 110 million land mines hidden in 64 countries.

*Two children hold a sign during a protest against anti-personnel mines near the American consulate in Quebec city, March 1, 2000.*

In 1996, Canada sponsored an international conference to explore ways in which land mine use could be banned. 74 nations attended. They agreed to work towards a worldwide ban. At the end of the conference, Canada announced it would host a meeting to sign a treaty banning land mines in December 1997. The International Campaign to Ban Land Mines (ICBL) worked tirelessly in support of a ban. The UN General Assembly passed a resolution urging

While land mines only cost between $5 and $15 to purchase, the cost of removing one from the landscape can be anywhere from $450-$1,500. Land mines kill 800 people a month, maiming thousands more. Most land mine victims are innocent women and children.

the ban. On December 3-4, 1997, 122 nations, including Canada, signed the Mine Ban Treaty. This number has now risen to 123. Countries which have not signed the Treaty include the United States, Russia, India, China and Pakistan.

## MOST HEAVILY MINED COUNTRIES

| Country | Number of Mines per Square Miles | Estimated Total Number of Landmines |
|---|---|---|
| Bosnia and Herzegovina | 152 | 3,000,000 |
| Cambodia | 143 | 10,000,000 |
| Croatia | 137 | 3,000,000 |
| Egypt | 60 | 23,000,000 |
| Iraq | 59 | 10,000,000 |
| Afghanistan | 40 | 10,000,000 |
| Angola | 31 | 15,000,000 |
| Iran | 25 | 16,000,000 |
| Rwanda | 25 | 250,000 |

Source: United Nations Department of Humanitarian Affairs

# 3 Human Rights

One of the primary goals of the founders of the United Nations was the protection of universal human rights. They were responding to the horrors of the Holocaust and World War II. The United Nations Charter, signed in 1945, states that the new organization's main objective is "to save succeeding generations from the scourge of war" and "to reaffirm faith in fundamental human rights. Promoting and encouraging respect for human rights and for fundamental freedoms for all without distinction as to race, sex, language or religion is one of the main goals of the United Nations."

In 1946, the UN established the Commission on Human Rights. Canadian John Humphrey, Director of Human Rights at the UN Secretariat, was one of the principal authors of the "Universal Declaration of Human Rights" adopted by the UN General Assembly in 1948.

The United Nations' work on human rights continues today.

## A CLOSER LOOK AT AMNESTY INTERNATIONAL

Amnesty International (AI) is the world's largest human rights organization with over one million members. More than 67,000 live in Canada. All AI members share a commitment to the universal protection of human rights.

Amnesty International works to abolish the death penalty worldwide, to protect religious freedoms, to protect the rights of refugees, to free political prisoners or **prisoners of conscience**, and to abolish torture and mutilation. AI does not accept government funding. It wants to be sure that its independence and impartiality are never compromised. Amnesty International's work is supported by financial donations from AI members. In 1977, Amnesty International was awarded the world's most prestigious honour—the Nobel Peace Prize. For more information about Amnesty International in Canada check out its website at www.amnesty.ca.

The "Universal Declaration of Human Rights" remains one of the UN's most important achievements today. It states that human rights are a worldwide matter, and that human rights abuses must be addressed not only locally, but also internationally.

# A CLOSER LOOK AT HUMAN RIGHTS

Human rights are such an important aspect in Canadian society that they are considered fundamental to human dignity. After the Second World War, when the international community began to regard human rights as a basic necessity for all people, Canada began to adopt comprehensive human rights codes. Ontario introduced its Ontario Human Rights Code in 1962, the first of its kind in Canada. By 1975, every province had legalized human rights. In 1976, the federal government passed the Canadian Human Rights Act, which guaranteed human rights under Canadian law.

Although human rights are a fundamental part of living in Canada, a number of groups were created to guarantee that every aspect of Canadian society received equal treatment under the law. Prison reform, for example, has long since been an important issue for Canada's human rights activists. The Elizabeth Fry Society and the John Howard Society are two international organizations involved in bettering the conditions of prisoners and ex-convicts. Both try to ensure that human rights of those in prison are respected.

*Donald Marshall spent 11 years in prison for a crime he didn't commit.*

## FOCUS

1. What was the mandate of the United Nations Charter?
2. In your opinion, what are 5 basic rights that we all should share?

# UNIVERSAL DECLARATION OF HUMAN RIGHTS

- All human beings are born free. They have equal dignity and rights.

- Everyone is entitled to all the rights and freedoms, without distinction of any kind.

- Everyone has the right to life, liberty and security of person.

- No one shall be held in slavery.

- No one shall be subjected to torture or degrading treatment.

- Everyone has the right to recognition as a person before the law.

- All people are equal before the law.

- Everyone has a right to effective legal remedy for actions which violate fundamental rights.

- No one shall be subjected to arbitrary arrest, detention or exile.

- Every person is entitled to a fair hearing by an impartial jury.

- Anyone charged with a penal offence will be presumed innocent until proven guilty according to law in a public trial.

- Every person is entitled to privacy of family, home and correspondence.

- Everyone has the right to freedom of movement, and the right to leave his or her country, and to return.

- Everyone has the right to seek and to find asylum from persecution.

- Everyone has the right to a nationality.

- Men and women, of full age, have the right to marry and have a family.

- Everyone has the right to own property.

- Everyone has the freedom of thought, conscience and religion.

- Everyone has the right of opinion and of expression.

- Everyone has the right to freedom of peaceful assembly and association.

- Every person has the right to take part in the government of one's country. The will of the people shall be the basis of the government's authority.

- Everyone has the right to social security.

- Everyone has the right to work, to free choice of employment, to just and favourable conditions of work and to protection against unemployment.

- Everyone has the right to equal pay for equal work.

- Everyone has the right to form and join trade unions for the protection of worker interests.

- Everyone has the right to rest and leisure. This includes reasonable limitation of working hours and periodic holidays with pay.

- Everyone has the right to a standard of living adequate for one's individual health and well-being, and for that of one's family.

- Everyone has the right to education, which shall be free at the earliest levels. Elementary education shall be compulsory.

- Every person has the right to participate freely in the cultural life of his or her community.

- Every person is entitled to a social and international order in which the rights and freedoms set forth in this declaration can be fully realized.

BORN: 1947, Montreal, Quebec

SIGNIFICANCE: As Chief Prosecutor for the UN International Criminal Tribunal, was responsible for prosecuting war crimes in Bosnia and Rwanda. Appointed to the Supreme Court of Canada in 1999.

BRIEF BIOGRAPHY: Born and educated in Quebec, Louise Arbour received her legal degree from the University of Montreal's Faculty of Law in 1970. She was called to the Quebec Bar in 1971. From 1971-1972, she served as law clerk for Justice Louise-Philippe Pigeon of the Supreme Court of Canada. Arbour taught law at York University's Osgoode Hall Law School from 1974-1987, when she was made Associate Dean. She was called to the Ontario Bar in 1977. In 1987, Arbour was appointed to the Ontario Supreme Court's High Court of Justice and, in 1990, to the Ontario Court of Appeal.

As a vice president of the Canadian Civil Liberties Association, she campaigned for prisoners' right to vote. Louise Arbour published many articles on human rights, criminal law, gender issues and civil liberties—in French and English.

In 1996, the United Nations Security Council

appointed Louise Arbour Prosecutor for the International Criminal Tribunals for Yugoslavia and Rwanda. Established in 1993, this was the first international body for the prosecution of war crimes since the Nuremberg and Tokyo trials after World War II. Arbour's job was to investigate and lay charges against individuals for war crimes and crimes against humanity, or **genocide**. Arbour worked tirelessly. She even observed the excavation of a mass grave site near Vukovar, Crotia. "...these bodies were thrown together indiscriminately in a hole... They were young men....I watched the bodies come out of the ground and it was like they were coming alive again. They were demanding to be identified. They were demanding that their mothers be told."

In May, 1999, Arbour announced that international warrants had been issued for the arrest of Yugoslav President Slobodan Milosevic and four other political and military leaders for crimes against humanity, including murder.

Arbour's work brought her praise internationally and in Canada. In September 1999, she was appointed to the Supreme Court of Canada by Prime Minister Jean Chrétien.

## Louise Arbour

# Children's Rights

## UNICEF and Children's Rights

The United Nations International Children's Emergency Fund (UNICEF) was founded in 1946 by the UN to provide emergency relief for millions of children in postwar Europe, China and the Middle East. Aid was given to all children without any distinction of race, creed, nationality or political conviction. In 1965, UNICEF received the Nobel Peace Prize for its work.

1979 was declared the International Year of The Child. It focused global attention on the issue of children's rights. UNICEF coordinated the year's activities. All over the world, children are regularly denied the rights that adults take for granted. Because they are dependent and vulnerable, children can easily be mistreated by adults and the society around them.

In November 1989, the UN adopted the Convention on the Rights of the Child (CRC) as an international human rights treaty. Among the specific rights for children it guarantees are the following:

- the inherent right to life
- the right to a name, an identity and a nationality
- protection from physical or mental violence, exploitation or abuse
- the right to be cared for by one's parents, if possible
- primary education
- access to information
- freedom of thought, conscience, and religion
- the right to express one's views
- the right to the highest attainable standard of health

Although these ideas are common and everyday in Canada, in poorer countries they are more difficult to institute. UNICEF continues today to be a crucial element in the battle for children's rights. Its mission statement is clear:

*"UNICEF is guided by the Convention on the Rights of the Child and strives to establish children's rights as enduring ethical principles and international standards of behaviour towards children. UNICEF insists that the survival, protection and development of children are universal development imperatives that are integral to human progress."*

The protection of children's rights around the world has been a priority concern of Canada's domestic and foreign policies for many years.

---

**FOCUS**
- **List five rights specified in the UN's Convention on the Rights of the Child.**
- **List three ways in which children's rights are violated around the world.**
- **Who is Craig Keilburger?**

**TIMELINE**

1900   1910   1920   1930   1940   1950   1960   1970   1980   1990

# CANADIAN LIVES

BORN: Thornhill, Ontario, 1982.

SIGNIFICANCE: Anti-child-labour activist and founder of the Free the Children youth movement, an international children's organization seeking to change laws affecting child labour and exploitation.

BIO: When he was 12 years old, Craig Kielburger read the story of Iqbal Masih, a young boy from Pakistan, who was sold into slavery at age four, freed, and then murdered at age 12. Craig was horrified. He became interested in worldwide injustice against children. There are 250,000,000 children labourers in the world today. Most of these children work long hours under hazardous conditions. Many are abused and starving. Craig wanted to do something. In 1995, he and his friends founded Free the Children International, a non-profit organization designed to fight the abuses of child labour. Craig began to speak out for the rights of children. He became a renowned spokesperson. When members of the Ontario Federation of Labour heard him talk, they donated $100,000 so that Free the Children could build a rehabilitation/education centre in Alwar, India for young children. Craig has travelled to over 30 countries on behalf of Free the Children. His organization has written thousands of letters as it works to raise the issue of children's rights in Canada and around the world. In 1998, Craig spoke in Calcutta as part of the "Global March to End Child Labour." Tens of thousands of people all over the world participated in the march, carrying the message, "that the time has come to guarantee every child a childhood, that no child should lose his or her chance to learn and develop by being forced to work all day long."

## Craig Kielburger

# 5 The Cold War

The world was dominated by a Cold War from 1946 to 1990, as the Soviet Union and the United States, the world's two greatest superpowers, sought to keep each other in check. The Soviet Union controlled the areas of Eastern Europe it had occupied during the Second World War. Soviet forces remained in Romania, Hungary, Bulgaria, Czechoslovakia, Poland and East Germany. Under Soviet influence, rigged elections were held in which only Soviet-sponsored candidates could run for office. The United States and its allies protested but, unless they were prepared to go to war, they could do nothing.

In the words of Winston Churchill, "From Danzig on the Baltic, to Trieste on the Adriatic, an Iron Curtain has descended on Europe."

The climate of fear in the West intensified when the Soviet Union began to build up its military strength. From 1945 to 1990, governments spent more money on the world's military than on food, housing or medicine.

The Cold War was also a struggle between conflicting values. The "Western bloc" nations led by the United States believed in a multi-party democracy with a free market economy. The "Eastern bloc" led by the Soviet Union favoured a one-party communist dictatorship with strong economic controls.

## A CLOSER LOOK AT THE ATOMIC BOMB

During World War II, a team of scientists, headed by J. Robert Oppenheimer, worked on a top secret mission. Code named "The Manhattan Project," these people were given the task of creating the world's first atomic bomb. They succeeded, and on July 16, 1945, the Americans tested the world's first atomic bomb. The atomic age had begun. Atomic bombs were used against the Japanese in August, 1945. The devastating destruction of Hiroshima and Nagasaki effectively ended World War II in the Pacific.

Russian scientists were not far behind their American counterparts, and the first Russian atomic bomb was detonated in 1949. The Soviet Union exploded its first hydrogen bomb in 1953 just 7 months after the United States. By the 1980s, each of these two superpowers had built thousands of nuclear warheads with incredibly destructive firepower. During the height of the Cold War, it was estimated that each side had an "overkill" factor of 40; that is, each side had enough nuclear firepower to kill everyone in the world 40 times over.

In spite of the expansion of nuclear weapons, there were several attempts to reduce the tensions caused by such development. In 1973, U.S. President Richard Nixon and Russian Premier Leonid Brezhnev signed two documents (Strategic Arms Limitation Treaty or "SALT") intended to limit nuclear armaments. Later agreements have dramatically reduced the world's nuclear arsenal. Today, although the risk of nuclear warfare has lessened, there are at least eight countries in the world with nuclear weapons capability.

The Cold War overshadowed the peace and prosperity of the fifties.

## The Cuban Missile Crisis

Many people believe the height of the Cold War occurred in October, 1962. The Soviet Union had built nuclear missile sites in Communist Cuba. American U-2 spy planes photographed the sites. U.S. President Kennedy, in a dramatic television address to the American people, announced that American warships would blockade Cuba until the Russian missile sites were taken down.

For two weeks, the world hung on the brink of nuclear war, waiting to see what would happen. One commentator noted: "Americans and Russians stood eyeball to eyeball, and the Russians blinked." To the relief of the world, the Soviets backed down and dismantled their missiles. A major crisis was over.

By the late 1980s, the Soviet Union was in trouble on many political and economic fronts. Soviet leader Gorbachev moved to Westernize his country. The Warsaw Pact, the Soviet's military alliance, was dissolved. Slowly, some of the former "Iron Curtain" countries returned to democratic values.

By December, 1991, the Soviet Union itself had dissolved into fifteen smaller states, leaving Russia as the largest of the former Soviet Republics. The collapse of the once-mighty Soviet Union is considered to be the final chapter in the 45-year-old Cold War.

Today, Eastern Europe is a hotbed of tension as ethnic groups struggle to assert their independence from central governments. Clashes erupted throughout the 1990s in the Balkan region of the former Yugoslavia. In 1999, NATO forces attacked Serbia in an effort to prevent the Serbian **ethnic cleansing** campaign which forced Albanians from their homes in Kosovo. The Serbian ethnic cleansing brought back memories of Nazi racism.

Czechoslovakia on the other hand, divided peacefully into the Czech Republic and Slovakia. The Cold War may be over, but its effects are still being felt throughout Europe.

**FOCUS**
1. How was the Cold War different from other kinds of war?
2. What was the Warsaw Pact?
3. Why were people so fearful of the Cold War?

# THE RACE TO SPACE:
## Competition and Cooperation

In 1957, the Soviet Union launched the world's first space satellite, Sputnik, long before the Americans were ready to do so. The Russians used this event to show that their military and educational capabilities were superior to those of the Americans. In April 1961, Soviet astronaut Yuri Gagarin became the first human to orbit the earth. American John Glenn followed a month later.

When John Kennedy became U.S. president, he was concerned the United States would lose the space race. In 1962, he stated that a major goal for his country was to put a person on the moon "before the decade is out." In July 1969, the American space mission Apollo 11 landed on the moon.

The Russians turned their attention to the development of a permanent space station that would orbit the earth. Astronauts would live in the station and conduct experiments while living in space.

In 1981, the Americans developed a series of space shuttles to carry astronauts and equipment into space. Marc Garneau became the first Canadian astronaut in space when he flew on the American space shuttle Challenger in 1984. Roberta Bondar and Stephen Maclean were the next

*Roberta Bondar was the first Canadian women in space.*

Canadians in space when they flew in two separate flights on the shuttle Discovery in 1992.

The Russians launched the Mir Space Station in 1986. It became a symbol of the Russian space program. Mir orbits the earth every 90 minutes, giving scientists an opportunity to study living in space over long periods of time. Some astronauts remained in space for as long three months. Astronauts from many countries, including Canada, have lived on Mir. Chris Hatfield was the first Canadian astronaut to visit Mir in 1995. By 1996, Canadians had participated in six space missions. In 1999, Mir was sold.

In November, 1998, the Russians launched Zarya, the first module in one of the largest, non-military exploration projects in history—the International Space Station or ISS. Sixteen countries, including Canada, have banded together to

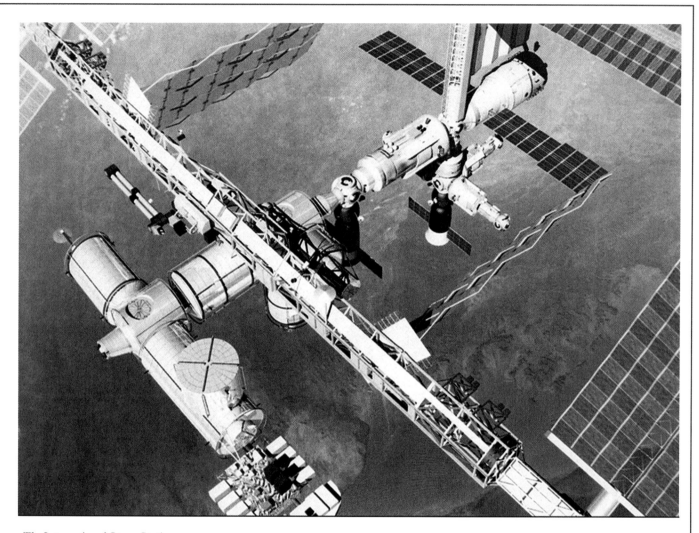

*The International Space Station.*

produce the most complex structure ever placed in orbit. In December 1998, the Americans launched the Unity module, which linked up to Zarya, forming the first part of the ISS. These two modules have already orbited the earth 8,000 times. In May 1999, astronaut Julie Payette, was the first Canadian to go aboard the ISS when the international crew of mission STS-96 spent five days re-supplying the station.

When completed (sometime in 2004), the ISS will measure 110 metres. It will have pressurized living and working space greater than the cabin and cargo hold of a 747 aircraft. There will be seven scientific laboratories. Canada's contribution to the ISS includes the MSS or Mobile Servicing System—a new generation of the innovative Canadarm.

# Canada's Alliances

Alliances with other nations are an important part of Canada's foreign policy. An alliance is formed when two or more nations agree to help one another. Canada is currently a member of several alliances. Some of these are military—for defensive purposes—others are political. Some are cultural, and others economic. Each alliance strengthens our ties to other nations with whom we share common goals. Alliances encourage cooperation and peaceful solutions to the world's problems.

### North Atlantic Treaty Organization (NATO)

Canada was a founding member of the North Atlantic Treaty Organization in 1949. Louis St. Laurent, then Canada's Prime Minister, was the first Western leader to suggest that such an organization be formed. NATO was created in response to Soviet aggression after World War II. Russian leader, Joseph Stalin, refused to remove Russian troops from the occupied countries of Eastern Europe. There was growing concern that the Soviet Union would invade the rest of Europe. Sixteen countries (Belgium, Canada, Denmark, France, Germany, Greece, Iceland, Italy, Luxembourg, Netherlands, Norway, Portugal, Spain, Turkey, United Kingdom, United States) signed the NATO charter. Its goal was to bring about peace and stability in Europe, while limiting the growth of the Soviet Union and its Warsaw Pact allies.

NATO's headquarters is in Brussels, Belgium. The Supreme Military Commander of NATO is always an American, while the political leader, or Secretary-General, is elected by the member nations. In 1999, three former Communist countries, Hungary, Poland and the Czech Republic, all previous members of the Warsaw Pact, joined NATO, bringing the current membership to 19 countries. Today, NATO works to promote peace and security for its member countries. NATO also encourages defence planning and military cooperation.

All countries in NATO pledge to support each other in the event of attack. Each member contributes to the defence of Western Europe and the North Atlantic. Thousands of Canadian troops have been stationed in Europe, the Middle East and Africa at various times over the past fifty years in support of NATO. During the Cold War, Canadian naval destroyers and frigates were used to patrol for Soviet submarines.

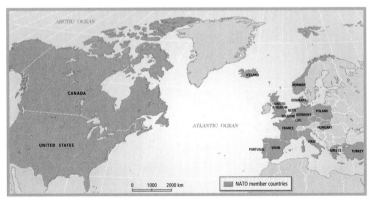

*This map shows Nato Member countries.*

Alliances encourage cooperation and peaceful solutions to the world's problems.

TIMELINE

1900   1910   1920   1930   1940   **1950**   1960   1970   1980   1990

In 1999, the objectives of NATO were put to a severe test when, acting on its own and without United Nations support, NATO forces attacked Yugoslavia in an attempt to protect ethnic Albanians in the province of Kosovo. The human cost was high, and NATO's actions remain a source of controversy today.

### North American Aerospace Defense Command (NORAD)

Canada and the United States established the North American Air Defense Alliance (NORAD) in 1958. It was designed to protect North America from attack by the Soviet Union. Three radar lines were built in Canada—the Distant Early Warning ("Dew" Line) in the far Arctic, the Mid-Canada Line, and the Pine Tree Line. These were designed to detect and intercept Russian bomber or missile attacks. The NORAD radar stations functioned through the 1960s and into the 1970s. Hundreds of NORAD missiles, aimed at targets in the Soviet Union, stood ready at an instant to respond to attack. U.S. and Canadian bombers and fighters were in the air or at the ready at all times.

Today, as technology and space exploration have developed, NORAD's focus has changed, along with its name. Now called The North American Aerospace Defense Command, NORAD monitors human-made objects in space, working to guard North America from attack by aircraft, missiles or space vehicles.

In the year 2000, the Americans invited Canada to take part in a new military venture, the creation of a sophisticated missile defence system.

### Military Alliances Today

Canada's membership in NATO and NORAD is expensive. Many Canadians feel that these alliances are dominated by the United States; they believe Canada may not be consulted before action is taken. Some feel that this country should not make alliances solely for military purposes. Others believe that with the decline of the Soviet Union and the end of the Warsaw Pact, NATO and NORAD are no longer important.

Unfortunately, the world is still not a peaceful place, and while military alliances do not necessarily provide protection from the tragedy of a nuclear war, it is hoped that they may possibly prevent such a war from happening.

**FOCUS**
1. Why are alliances with other countries important for Canada?
2. What is NATO's purpose?
3. What was NORAD?
4. Why do some people feel that membership in NATO and NORAD are no longer necessary?

# Economic and Political Alliances

*7*

## The Organization of the American States (OAS)

The Organization of American States (OAS) is the world's oldest regional organization. Originating in 1890 as the International Union of American Republics, it became the Pan American Union in 1910 and the OAS in 1948. Currently, all 35 independent countries in the Western Hemisphere are members.

Canada joined the OAS because our government believed that Canada would be able to exercise more influence within its own world hemisphere. OAS membership should lead to lower trade barriers, creating new opportunities for Canadian business. The rise of environmental concerns, and the increase in illegal drug traffic has meant that Canada needs to become more involved with other countries on the American continent.

The OAS is working to create a "Free Trade Area of the Americas," to erase poverty and discrimination while conserving our natural environment for future generations.

## The Arctic Council

Founded in 1996, the Arctic Council is an alliance of eight polar countries (Canada, the United States, Denmark/Greenland, Finland, Iceland, Norway, Russia and Sweden). It is dedicated to preserving Arctic environments and to protecting the plants and animals of the region. The Council monitors the ecological health of the Arctic. It also works to improve the economic, social and cultural well being of northern peoples. The Arctic

*Mary Simon is Canada's Ambassador for Circumpolar Affairs and chair of the newly-founded Arctic Council, an eight nation alliance designed to foster cooperation in the northernmost regions of the planet.*

Council also gives permanent participation to delegations from northern Indigenous peoples. Canada's Ambassador for Circumpolar Affairs, Mary Simon, chaired the Arctic Council from 1996-1998. Canada hosted the first Arctic Council meeting in Iqaluit in 1998.

The APEC region is home to over two billion people, and accounts for over half of the world's energy consumption, food consumption, and pollution.

1900   1910   1920   1930   1940   1950   1960   **1970**   1980   1990

## The G-7 Economic Summit

In 1976, Canada became a member of the "G-7" group of industrial nations. These include Germany, France, Italy, Japan, the U.S., European Union and the United Kingdom. Members of the G-7 meet annually to discuss international trade matters, and relations with developing countries. Their agenda often includes employment, the information highway, the environment, crime and drugs, human rights and arms control. Such conferences give the political leaders and their economic advisors the opportunity to discuss complex issues and to develop personal relationships that could help in times of world crisis. The G-7 alliance has met three times in Canada: Montebello, Quebec in 1981; Toronto, Ontario in 1988; Halifax, Nova Scotia in 1995. Beginning in 1994, the G-7 and Russia have met together as the P-8 ("Political 8") following each G-7 conference.

## Asia Pacific Economic Community (APEC)

Founded in 1994, APEC is an association of

*Leaders of the Asian Pacific Economic Cooperation (APEC), including Prime Minister Chrétien (10th from left), have their photo taken outside the Palace of Golden Horses in Kuala Lumpur, Malaysia*

21 Pacific Rim nations dedicated to achieving free trade and economic development in the Pacific region. The APEC region is home to over two billion people, and accounts for over half of the world's energy consumption, food consumption and pollution. APEC heads of state meet annually. Canada hosted the 1997 APEC summit in Vancouver. It was a controversial meeting as protestors marched against the inclusion of Indonesia's dictatorship government in the APEC talks.

## Commonwealth and Francophonie

Canada is a member of two multiracial and multicultural associations: the Commonwealth and La Francophonie. These two world-wide organizations have helped Canadians establish friendly ties with many countries.

*Mike Nolan of Windsor, Ontario is congratulated and helped up by Jamie Quarry following the decathlon at the 1998 Commonwealth Games in Kuala Lumpur. Nolan placed 6th and Quarry 10th.*

## The British Commonwealth of Nations

Britain once controlled colonies all over the world. As British colonies gained their independence, the Empire evolved into the Commonwealth in 1931 with the passing of the Statute of Westminster. Canada was one of its first members. In 1951, it was agreed that the King or Queen of Great Britain would reign as the symbolic head of the Commonwealth.

The Commonwealth is a loose economic and cultural organization.

*Every four years, athletes from Commonwealth Nations meet to compete in the Commonwealth Games. Canada was the first host for these games back in 1930 when they were held in Hamilton, Ontario.*

Members assist one another by attempting to encourage mutual trade. This has not always proved to be successful. The Colombo Plan was organized in 1950 so that richer Commonwealth nations (Great Britain, Canada, Australia and New Zealand) could give aid and technology to underdeveloped Commonwealth members. Canada made great contributions through this plan. It provided technical assistance, resources, financial assistance and scholarships to developing nations.

Commonwealth leaders usually meet on an annual basis. During the 1960s, South Africa's racist polices were a major Commonwealth concern. South Africa was asked to leave the Commonwealth, and was not allowed to return until its apartheid policy (the forced segregation of white and black peoples) ended in 1994.

By 2000, there were 54 member nations in the Commonwealth, representing one-fourth of the world's population. Gradually, Britain seemed to lose interest in its leadership role in the Commonwealth. As a result, on several occasions, Canadian prime ministers, notably Brian Mulroney in 1986 and 1988, emerged as Commonwealth leaders.

In 1999, Commonwealth members agreed to a review of the Commonwealth's role in world affairs. Most believe that the organization provides a valuable forum for the rich nations and the poor nations of this world to work together.

## La Francophonie

French is one of Canada's two official languages. After Paris, Montreal is the largest French-speaking city in the world. It is natural that Canada should be a member of La Francophonie, a voluntary association of 51 French-speaking states and governments. La Francophonie was founded in 1970. The Canadian federal government, the province of Quebec and the province of New Brunswick are all members.

La Francophonie is similar to the Commonwealth. Most of the participating nations were once part of the French Empire. While Canada has had no political links with France for over 250 years, the ties of language and culture remain deep. La Francophonie is less rigidly organized than the Commonwealth. La Francophonie

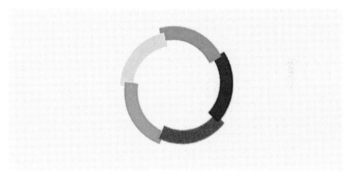

*La Francophonie is an important alliance for French-speaking nations.*

promotes cultural, scientific, technological, and legal ties with its member states or governments. The economic connection is less well developed. Canada gives aid to the poorer countries in La Francophonie, but directly rather than through the association. The cultural ties of La Francophonie are probably stronger than they are in the Commonwealth.

**F O C U S**
1. What is the British Commonwealth of Nations and what does it try to achieve?
2. What is La Francophonie? What are some of its goals?
3. Why did Canada join OAS?

# Canada's Aid to the Developing World

**8**

Over half of the world's six billion people do not have enough to eat. Home is often a crowded shack on a dirt floor in a shanty town without sewers or fresh water plumbing. Many people never have the chance to learn to read and write. Children grow up without sufficient food, or health care. Often, they fend for themselves in the local garbage dumps and become children of the streets, battered and abused, with a short life span.

Many countries have no disaster funds for emergency relief in times of war, famine flood or earthquake. Some developing nations are run by dictators who do not allow the citizens true civil or human rights. Why should Canada help the nations of the developing world?

**Humanitarian reasons**: As Canadians we believe people have the right to live in freedom, without want, and without suffering.

**Military and Political reasons:** People in great poverty can sometimes be recruited to violence. It is in Canada's interest to support a world where violence is not necessary. We do want the developing nations to be enemies of Canada.

**Economic reasons:** We can help ourselves by helping developing countries. If these countries become richer through Canadian aid programs, they may want to buy Canadian products and Canadian technology.

Canadian aid to developing nations is paid out of Canadian taxes. Canada has always been a steady contributor to needy countries either directly or through a variety

---

### Modern historians have traditionally divided our world into four communities:

1. Wealthy democratic countries with highly developed technological societies. Canada, the United States, Singapore and Japan are included in this group

2. Communist nations. This group has been shrinking since the Soviet Union fell apart in 1990. China and Cuba are included here.

3. Developing world countries. These countries are generally poor and non-white. African, Asian or South American nations are members of this group. Some have found oil and other valuable resources, which they use to improve their economic status. Most developing nations today, however, are poor and are getting poorer. Two-thirds of the world's people live in developing nations.

4. Aboriginal or indigenous peoples of the world. These communities have struggled for centuries to assert their claims to their land, which was often taken over by colonization and/or conquest. Canada's native people, who call themselves "The First Nations," are Laplanders in Scandinavia, and the Maoris of New Zealand are included in this group.

Canada has always been a steady contributor to needy countries either directly or through a variety of organizations.

1900  1910  1920  1930  1940  **1950**  1960  1970  1980  1990

of organizations. The Colombo Plan, set up in 1951 through the United Nations, was designed to help the Indian subcontinent—India, Ceylon (now Sri Lanka) and Pakistan.

In 1968, the Canadian government established CIDA—the Canadian International Development Agency—to administer our aid to developing nations. CIDA's contribution is never paid in cash. It is provided in the form of programs and projects that have been developed cooperatively with the recipient country. CIDA has given aid to regions and nations in Africa, the Middle East, Asia, the for-

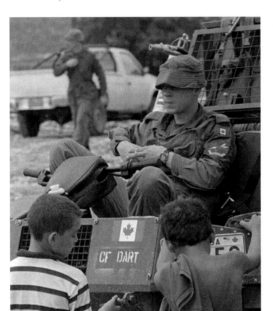

*A Canadian soldier in Honduras takes part in the Canadian Disaster Relief Team.*

mer Soviet Union and Central Europe.

Canada contributes to many UN aid programs like the World Health Organization (WHO). CUSO or Canadian Universities Overseas has sent over 10,000 Canadians all over the world. CUSO provides assistance in education, technology, agriculture, business and health. Participants work on a two-year contract at a minimal salary rate, but housing, health and dental insurance, and travel expenses are provided. Many Canadians have called their CUSO experiences unforgettable.

---

**Here is a list of more Canadian organizations that give aid to developing countries:**

- ■ Canadian Council of Churches
- ■ Canadian Red Cross Society
- ■ Canadian Save the Children Fund
- ■ Canadian Teachers' Federation
- ■ Canadian University Service Overseas

- ■ CARE Canada
- ■ Oxfam Canada
- ■ Salvation Army
- ■ World Vision
- ■ YM-YWCA

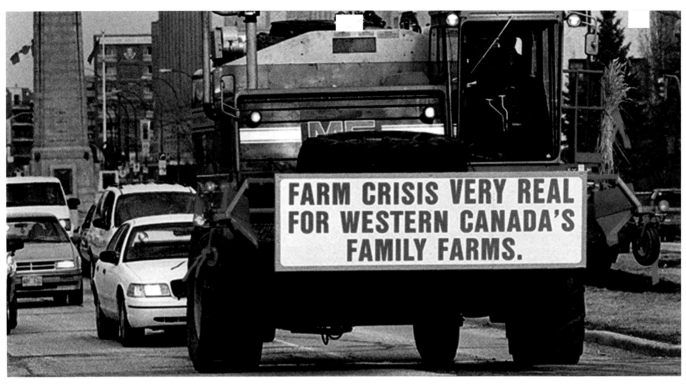

*Some people claim that Canada should spend more time and money on helping Canadians in time of need rather than developing countries. What do you think?*

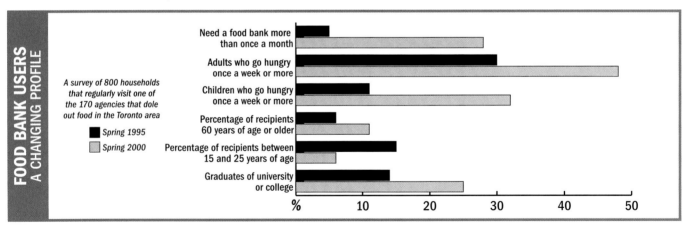

**FOOD BANK USERS**
**A CHANGING PROFILE**

*A survey of 800 households that regularly visit one of the 170 agencies that dole out food in the Toronto area*

■ Spring 1995
▨ Spring 2000

Need a food bank more than once a month

Adults who go hungry once a week or more

Children who go hungry once a week or more

Percentage of recipients 60 years of age or older

Percentage of recipients between 15 and 25 years of age

Graduates of university or college

%  10  20  30  40  50

**FOCUS**
1. List 2 reasons why Canada should help developing nations?
2. What was the Colombo Plan?
3. What is CIDA and what does it do?

BORN: 1904, Valleyfield (Salaberry-de-Valleyfield), Quebec

DIED: 1991, Montreal, Quebec

SIGNIFICANCE: One of Canada's great humanitarians, Cardinal Léger worked hard to help the humble, the sick, the weak and the poor both in Canada as Bishop of Montrea, and later Cardinal, as well as in Africa, as a missionary

BRIEF BIOGRAPHY: Cardinal Paul-Emile Léger was the oldest son of a Quebec grocer. As a young boy, he would spend hours listening to his father's friends argue about the political issues of the day. At age 12, he went to study at the Minor Seminary of Saint Thérèse. By 1923, the young student felt called to the priesthood. Léger was ordained as a priest on May 25, 1929. He left for France to serve as a teacher with the Sulpician Order. In 1933, he was sent to Japan to open a seminary for priests. When World War II broke out, he returned home to Valleyfield. In 1947, Léger was appointed Rector of the Canadian Pontifical College in Rome. The city was devastated by war, and the new Rector worked hard raising funds in Canada to help the city's poor. In 1950, Pope Pius II appointed Léger Archbishop of Montreal. The city's social problems would become his immediate concern. Léger was not afraid to speak out against the provincial government of Maurice Duplessis, although eventually the two men would work well together. In 1953, Léger became a Cardinal or Prince of the Roman Catholic Church. "A Cardinal is kind of a big chair," he once said. "You don't know where to put it in the house." He admitted, "to be a Cardinal is very convenient in a certain way, it gives you a little bit of authority."

The Second Vatican Council from 1962-1965 was an important period of change for the Roman Catholic Church. Léger argued for reform. He believed the church needed to be more relevant to the modern world. In 1963, Léger visited Africa. He set up Fame Pereo (the I am Dying of Hunger organization) to help people suffering from leprosy. Cardinal Léger resigned as Archbishop of Montreal in 1967. He travelled to Cameroon, Africa and set up the Centre for the Rehabilitation of the Handicapped. Léger spent many years in Africa, but finally, in 1979, at age 75, he returned to Montreal. He was named co-chair (with Roland Michener) of the Canadian Foundation for Refugees which was established to help Vietnamese boat people fleeing to Canada. Paul-Emile Léger died in Montreal at age 87.

## Cardinal Paul-Emile Léger

# Canadian Culture

From the folk songs of Ian and Sylvia Tyson, to the popular songs of Anne Murray, the ballads of Buffy Sainte-Marie, the corporate rock of Triumph, the irreverent songs of the Tragically Hip, the instrumentals of Hagood Hardy, to the country music of Hank Snow, Canadians have gained the respect of the music business worldwide.

Artists such as Joni Mitchell, The Band, Neil Young and The Guess Who achieved international prominence during the 1960s and 1970s. Andy Kim's "Rock Me Gently" is an oldies classic. The Guess Who, with Randy Bachman, made the phenomenally successful single "American Woman." In 1976, a new album, *August*, with a new Canadian sound from a group called RUSH caught the world's attention. The Canadian government awarded RUSH the title Ambassadors of Music.

Bryan Adams's third album, *Cuts Like A Knife*, released in 1983, rocketed him to stardom by going platinum in the U.S. His best known song remains "Everything I Do."

*Shania Twain has won many music awards. Originally from Sudbury, this country singer is the biggest selling female singer of all time.*

Canadian singers and musicians participated in both the Live Aid and the "Tears Are Not Enough" campaigns.

The 1990s were the decade for Canadian female musicians. Artists such as Sarah McLachlan, Alanis Morissette, Chantal Kreviazuk, Diana Krall, Shania Twain and Céline Dion took the music industry by storm. Each of these high-profile singers was showered with awards from their fans, as well as their peers. In 2000, one entertainment magazine called Shania Twain the biggest selling female singer of all time. Her album *"The Woman in Me"* is known by music fans everywhere. Chansonneuse Céline Dion has sold over 36 million albums worldwide.

## Literature

Canadian literature has had a world-wide impact near the end of the twentieth century. Critically-acclaimed novels like Michael Ondaatje's *The English Patient* (1992) and Margaret Atwood's *The Handmaid's Tale* (1985) were made into popular movies by for-

The 1990s were the decade for Canadian female musicians.

eign production companies. Carol Shield's *The Stone Diaries* (1993) was awarded the Pulitzer Prize, and other authors, such as Timothy Findley, *The Wars* (1977), Alice Munro, *The Love of a Good Woman* (1998), and Anne Carson, *The Autobiography of Red* (1998), continue to earn international acclaim.

At home, in the growing globalism of Canadian culture, writers from all backgrounds add to the well-roundedness of expressive voices: Trinidad-born Dionne Brand and André Alexis; Barbados-born Austin Clarke; Argentinian-born Alberto Manguel; Indian-born Bharati Mukherjee and Rohinton Mistry; Sri Lankan-born Shyam Selvadurai; and Italian-born Mary di Michele and Nino Ricci are but a few of the writers who have positioned themselves in Canada physically, but owe a debt to countries both far and near.

*Alice Munro has won major literary prizes in Canada, as well as internationally.*

## The Technical Edge

**Heartsmart** In 1941, at the age of 21, John Hopps received a degree in electrical engineering from the University of Manitoba. He began working for the National Research Council (NRC) in Ottawa. When scientists at the University of Toronto began to study hypothermia—or the process of lowering body temperature, they asked Hopps to help them by applying some of the research he had done on restoring body temperature. One scientist discovered that prodding the heart of a lab animal whose heart had stopped beating during the experiment, would cause the heart to begin beating again. Hopps found that using an electrical charge produced the same results. John Hopps took this new information and went back to the NRC. In 1950, he produced the first heart pacemaker—but the device was too large to be implanted in the human chest. After a number of attempts, Hopps finally developed a smaller version. The first pacemaker was implanted in a human in 1958. Hopps received numerous awards for his invention, including the Order of Canada in 1986. Ironically, in 1985, John Hopps had his own pacemaker implanted. It would save his life.

BORN: 1932, Toronto, Ontario

DIED: 1982, Toronto, Ontario,

SIGNIFICANCE: Internationally renowned as a concert pianist, Gould retired from the concert circuit to concentrate on the recording arts—a controversial move many, including the Beatles, would imitate in the years following his decision.

BIOGRAPHY: Glenn Gould was a child prodigy. At the age of three, he had exceptional musical genius, including perfect pitch and the ability to read staff notation. At five, he was composing for friends and family. At ten, he began studying at the Royal Conservatory of Music in Toronto. In 1945, the twelve-year-old Gould was already playing piano at a professional level. He debuted in 1946 as a soloist at the Royal Conservatory, performing Beethoven's Fourth Piano Concerto. Gould's public career was made and, over the next twenty years, he played concerts in the United States, Europe and the Soviet Union. Gould retired fom live performing because he did not think of himself solely as a pianist; he also considered himself a writer, broadcaster, composer and conductor. He also felt that live concerts were demeaning to serious artists. Although

*Gould's unique style and flair for performance, public and recorded. left an idelible mark on the world of classical music.*

he led the life of a recluse, Gould was not a hermit—he had many friends, and was renowned for his all-night phone conversations. His most famous recording, that of Bach's Goldberg Variations, still sells to a new generation of fans. In his lifetime, he won numerous Grammys and Junos. He died of a stroke only a week after his fiftieth birthday. His legacy lives on, however, in the Glenn Gould Foundation—an organization dedicated to the commemoration of celebrated Canadian musicians.

## Glenn Gould

**BORN:** 1961, E.P. Taylor's Stud Farm, North York, Ontario

**DIED:** 1990, E.P. Taylor's Farm, Maryland, U.S.

**SIGNIFICANCE:** One of the greatest racehorses in the world.

**BRIEF BIOGRAPHY:** When E.P. Taylor put his new colt, Northern Dancer, on the auction block in 1962, nobody wanted him. Not one single person put a bid up for that horse. Taylor shipped him off to trainer Tom Fleming in Fort Erie, Ontario and hoped for the best. It didn't take long for Northern Dancer to prove himself. In 1963, at the age of 2, Northern Dancer opened his career by winning the Remsen Stakes, the Flamingo and Florida Derbies, and the Summer Stakes, Coronation Futurity and Carlton Stakes. In 1964, he became the first Canadian-bred horse to win the Kentucky Derby, in a record time of 2 minutes. Only Secretariat has bettered that speed. That same year, Northern Dancer went on to win the Preakness Stakes and the Queen's Plate. Unfortunately, a tendon injury cut his stellar career short, and he was retired to the stud farm to breed future champions. As with his racing, Northern Dancer's career as a stud was unparalleled. Twenty-one percent of his progeny became Stakes winners. Indeed, Northern Dancer's statistics were so great that his stud price rose accordingly: from $21,000 in 1971 to $1,000,000 by the 1980s. At the time of his death in 1990, Northern Dancer had sired over 125 horses, including Epsom Derby winners, Njinsky and The Minstrel. His son Native Dancer won the Kentucky Derby.

## Northern Dancer

## Match the words in column A with the descriptions in column B.

| A | B |
|---|---|
| **1.** Lester Pearson | **a)** person responsible for day-to-day activities of UN |
| **2.** NATO | **b)** Canadian-American alliance |
| **3.** Security Council | **c)** winner of Nobel Peace Prize |
| **4.** NORAD | **d)** leader in aid for developing countries, especially the handicapped |
| **5.** Secretary General | **e)** alliance to defend |
| **6.** La Francophonie | **f)** body of UN responsible for maintaining peace |
| **7.** CDC | **g)** UN agency for children's welfare |
| **8.** UNICEF | **h)** association of French-speaking nations |
| **9.** Cardinal Léger | **i)** agency to promote Candian ownership |

## Word Scramble

**Unscramble the letters form words introduced in this chapter.**

**1.** INTUDE STONIAN

**2.** DHIRT RODWL

**3.** LCMTENOMAHWO

**4.** ZSEU RSCISI

**5.** LDCO RWA

**6.** ERGNIFO IDA

## Ideas for Discussion

**1.** Between 1947 and 1999, Canada participated in every UN peacekeeping mission. Do you think Canada should continue to volunteer for these activities? Why or why not?

**2.** There are still over 10,000 nuclear weapons in the world. This is enough to kill everyone on the planet many times—the so-called "overkill factor" is 10-20. In small group discussions, discuss the chances of world nuclear disarmament.

**3.** To what extent do you feel that the United Nations is an effective organization to preserve and maintain world peace?

**4.** Draw up lists outlining the good and bad points of Canada's membership in NATO and NORAD. If Canada believes itself to be a peace-loving country, should it continue to belong to these military alliances? Why or why not?.

**5.** Debate these topics:
   **a)** The Commonwealth of Nations is an outdated concept and organization. It should be dissolved.
   **b)** La Francophonie, indirectly, is a support for Quebec separatism as it supports the participation of Quebec as a "nation." Discuss the validity of this in view of Quebec's language policies, past and present.

**6.** J. S. Woodsworth, one of the founders of the CCF party in Canada, once stated that the 19th century "made the world a neighbourhood: this century (20th) must make it a brotherhood. To what extent did it succeed?

## Do Some Research

1. Find out more about the Nobel Peace Prize.
   Your report should answer the following questions:
   a) What are the origins of the prize?
   b) Besides Lester Pearson, who are some winners of the prize?
   c) Why were they awarded it?
   d) Is there anyone you think should be awarded the prize? Why do you think so?
   e) There are Nobel prizes for other achievements as well as peace. What other Canadians have won a Nobel Prize? In which field?

2. Since 1945, there have been over one hundred wars involving eighty countries, and 25 million people have been injured or killed. Examine the causes, events and results of one of these wars.

3. Find our about an agency that tries to help people in developing countries. Gather as much information as you can about the projects this agency is concerned with. Some agencies you might study are:
   a) Canadian Save the Children Fund
   b) Red Cross
   c) Oxfam
   d) Canada World Youth

4. Do further research on a developing country that has recently been in the news. Use some of the following headings as organizers for your report: Population; Type of Government; Resources; Industries; Per Capita Income; Trade; National Debt; Obstacles to Development

5. Describe at least two other examples of the Cold War not discussed in this chapter, along with an explanation of why you feel these are, in fact, Cold War examples.

6. Outline the role played by Canada in at least two developing countries since the end of World War II.

7. Canada was the last country in the Western Hemisphere to join the Organization of American States. Through further research, find out why Canada did not join until 1990.

8. Do a biographical sketch of two Canadians, other than Léger and Bethune, who have assisted in developing countries.

9. Research the historical roots of the Palestinian-Jewish tensions in modern day Israel.

## Be Creative

1. If you were creating a list of foreign policy objectives for Canada, what would they be and why?

2. Develop a list of what you consider to be the world's most important concerns. What should be Canada's responses to each of them?

3. Prime Minister Trudeau once said that he considered himself to be "a citizen of the world." What do you think he meant by this comment? To what extent do you support his assertion?

## Web sites

**The United Nations:** www.un.org
**The Organization of the American States:** www.oas.org
**NATO:** www.nato.int
**NORAD:** www.peterson.af.mil/norad
**La Francophonie:** www.francophonie.org
**The Department of Foreign Affairs:** www.dfait-maeci.gc.ca/menu-e.asp
**The Commonwealth Games Association of Canada:** www.commonwealthgames.ca
**The Arctic Council:** www.arctic-counci.usgs.gov
**UNICEF:** www.unicef.org

# You Are There

You Are There

Many people believe the height of the Cold War occurred in October, 1962. The Soviet Union had built nuclear missile sites in Communist Cuba. American U-2 spy planes photographed the sites. U. S. President John Kennedy, in a dramatic television address to the American people, announced that American warships would blockade Cuba until the Russian missile sites were taken down.

For two weeks, the world hung on the brink of nuclear war, waiting to see what would happen. One commentator noted: "American and Russians stood eyeball to eyeball, and the Russians blinked." To the relief of the whole world, the Soviets backed down, and dismantled their missiles. A major crisis was over.

In a role-playing situation, take the parts of the following people in this tense situation, and act out the position you would have likely taken during this crisis.

1. U.S. President John Kennedy
2. Soviet Chairman Nikita Krushchev
3. Cuban President Fidel Castro
4. Canadian Prime Minister John Diefenbaker
5. Private citizen of The United States
6. Private citizen of the Soviet Union
7. Private citizen of the Canada
8. Private citizen of the Cuba
9. The United Nations Secretary-General

After playing the various roles, discuss your personal views of this crisis.

# Point

## Counterpoint

With which of the following statements do you most agree? Why?

With which of the following statements do you least agree? Why?

"The test of the civilization of any people is the way they treat a foreigner; as a foreigner myself, coming as a young man to Canada, I have nothing but praise for the way I was received in Canada."
—Pierre van Paassen, 1934

"Canada is a country whose major problems are never solved."
—Canadian historian A.R.M. Lower, 1958

"The grim fact is that we prepare for war like precocious giants and for peace like retarded pygmies."
—Lester Pearson's 1957 Nobel Peace Prize acceptance speech

"The strongest pressure in the world can be friendly pressure."
—Lester Pearson, 1963

"We moved from British influence to American influence without much feeling of purely national identity in between."
—Lester Pearson upon his retirement, 1967

" The United Nations has come to expect in its debates to hear from Canada the voice of reason and enlightenment, rejecting the extreme of partisanship, seeking patiently the common ground for men of good will, yet always standing firm upon the basic principles and purposes of our world organization."
—U.N. Secretary-General Dag Hammarskjold, 1954

# Developing
## Skills in History

**T**HE STUDY OF HISTORY INVOLVES MORE THAN JUST READING, WRITING, AND TALKING about the past. Like most of the subjects you will study through school, history prepares you with certain skills which are necessary to succeed outside the classroom.

Whether you want to become a web-site designer, a union organizer, a nurse, firefighter or member of any number of professions, the skills you learn while studying history will help you meet whatever goals you set for yourself.

The skills you are learning in your course this year are life skills, not just academic skills. They will help you succeed both within and outside the classroom.

---

### The four basic skills learned by studying history are:

**1. An Ability to Process Information**
You must be able to locate and read newspapers, magazines, books, training manuals, and Internet resources, understand movies, videos, photographs, paintings and other forms of visual presentations. You must then be able to select the key ideas from the material, and record them in a meaningful and accurate manner.

**2. An Ability to Think and Organize**
You must be able to think about information, to analyze it, to make comparisons, and to assess its value and importance.

**3. An Ability to Communicate in Writing and Orally**
You will be expected to express your ideas by writing in paragraph form so that others can understand you. You will also be expected to develop more complex ideas into longer reports. You will often be expected to discuss your ideas orally, in front of others, in a group and during more formal meetings.

**4. An Ability to Work Cooperatively**
Living and working in a society—and within a democracy—requires that we all work together as community members and as citizens.

# METHODS OF HISTORICAL INQUIRY

## A New Century Dawns

**Skill:** Primary and Secondary Sources
**Practice:** Distinguishing Between Primary and Secondary Sources
- Locating Information
- Creative Writing
- Writing a Biography

## War and Recognition

**Skill:** Analysis, Evaluation and Communication
**Practice:** Recording Information in Paragraph Forms

## The Radio Age

**Skill:** The Inquiry Process and Causation
**Practice:** Constructing a Chronology
- Cause and Effect
- Writing a Newspaper Account

## The World on Trial

**Skill:** The Inquiry Process and the Research Essay
**Practice:** The Research Essay

## The Baby Boom

**Skill:** Researching and Recording Information
**Practice:** Researching Information
- Recording Information
- Group Work
- The Oral Report

## Canada Comes of Age

**Skill:** Notation Methods
**Practice:** Endnotes, Footnotes and Bibliography

## One Nation or Two

**Skill:** Computer Technology
**Practice:** Using the Internet for Research

## Sleeping With an Elephant

**Skill:** Comparisons
**Practice:** Assessing Bias and Distinguishing Fact from Opinion

## Hands Around the World

**Skill:** Assessing Bias
**Practice:** Making Comparisons
- Formulating Conclusions
- Culminating Activity

# Historical Materials

The study of history involves the gathering of information from all kinds of sources: books, essays, letters, diaries, interviews, legal documents, wills, photographs, maps, the Internet and much more. However many, all historical sources fall within two basic categories: primary and secondary sources.

## Primary Sources

A primary source is any source of information that was created during the period under study. These "first hand" accounts include parliamentary records such as Hansard, diaries, letters, an eye-witness account, legal testimony, statistics from Statistics Canada (StatsCan) and other original records.

## Secondary Sources

A secondary source is one that discusses the subject under study but was written after that period. These "second hand" accounts include essays, biographies, encyclopedia entries, textbooks and documentaries.

## Your Task

**Distinguishing Between Primary and Secondary Sources**

*Which of the following is a primary or secondary source?*

1. The poem, "In Flanders Fields."
2. The Durham Report.
3. This textbook.
4. A map drawn by a surveyor while in the field.
5. A newspaper article about Confederation, written in 1867.
6. A newspaper report about Confederation, written in 2000.
7. A copy of Canada's Constitution located on the Internet.
8. An interpretation of the Constitution, written by a professor of history.
9. A record of the debates in the House of Commons.
10. A sketch of a war scene drawn in battle by a war correspondent.

# Locating Information

Primary and secondary sources are located wherever there is printed material. In other words—everywhere. There are a number of places, though, where much of what you will need is found under one roof. These large depositories make researching much quicker and easier:

### The Library

Libraries contain a wealth of both primary and secondary material. Search for your subject in the library's digital database, or ask your librarian for help.

### Public Archives and Museums

These places specialize in preserving original, primary documents. Most archives work like libraries. You can search for material on your subject from a computer terminal. Most of the material you need is old and will be stored in a protected place, not on open shelves like your school library. You will have to ask the archivist to bring you what you want. Be careful with archival material. It is often very old and fragile. Many large public libraries have their own archival rooms. Contact you local library to see if they store any original records which might be of use.

### The Internet

The Internet is a vast network bringing together all kinds of useable information. It is proving to be a wonderful resource for all students of history. Search for the topic of choice using your favourite search engine. It is likely you will call-up all kinds of sites which are relevant to your study. Many sites post copies of primary documents, others will include secondary material. Be careful: not all Internet sources are reliable. Use information from only reputable sources like government agencies, schools and universities, and well-established companies or publishing houses. Always check the facts obtained from the Internet against textbooks, encyclopedias and other authoritative sources.

# Creative Writing

Many successful history writers use their imaginations to re-create the past and bring people, places and events back to life. All good historical work is based on extensive research. After collecting as much information as possible, historians use their imaginations to make past events as realistic and interesting as possible.

Some examples of creative writing are **diaries, letters,** and **journals.** These record facts but also provide writers with an opportunity to use their imaginations. Remember, you must research all information thoroughly and present the facts as accurately as possible before writing in a creative manner.

## Your Task

*After using your text and other sources, write one of the following:*
- A letter from the year 1900, explaining why you think the twentieth century may "belong to Canada;"
- A letter written from the perspective of an immigrant in the 1900s to a relative back in Europe describing life in Canada;
- A letter from a city dweller (rich or poor) in the 1900s, describing life in the city;
- Or another letter on your choice of topic.

# Writing a "Canadian Lives"

Biographies are basic to the study of history. They are accounts of the lives of individuals who helped shape the world around them. Throughout this textbook you will find many biographies under the heading "Canadian Lives." Each tells us when the person under discussion was born, died, something of their lives and how they contributed to the history of Canada.

## Your Task

a) Research and write a biographical sketch about one of the following individuals. You may want to use *The Canadian Encyclopedia, The Dictionary of Canadian Biography,* or search the Internet under the person's name.
   - John A. Macdonald
   - Henri Bourassa
   - Clifford Sifton
   - Emily Murphy
   - Robert Borden
   - Poundmaker
   - Wilfrid Laurier
   - Agnes Macphail
   - Reginald Fessenden
   - Another Canadian of your choice

b) While doing your research, record your information in point form.

c) After you have completed your research, record the information using some of the following organizers (you may suggest others):
   - date and location of birth
   - early childhood, family life, education
   - achievements
   - ideas
   - importance

d) Present the information in no more than three paragraphs.

# Recording Information in Paragraph Form

A history student must be able to express his or her ideas clearly in both sentence and paragraph form. Below are some suggestions to help you develop the skill of paragraph writing. After you have learned this skill, you can adapt the pattern to more creative paragraph writing.

## Writing a Paragraph

A **good paragraph** is key to any **essay** or report. It is the building block on which all written work is made.

A paragraph is a group of sentences about one topic. All paragraphs follow a pattern and include the following:

a) **Introduction** or main idea. This is called the opening or topic sentence and begins each paragraph;

b) **Body of Paragraph**—several statements which explain or support the opening sentence;

c) **Conclusion**—a statement which gives the reader an idea of why what was stated in the topic sentence is important.

*Sample Paragraph: New Inventions of the 1920s*

**Introduction**

New inventions improved the lives of most people in the 1920s.

**Body of Paragraph**

New electrical appliances cut down on some of the hard work involved in running the house. The radio permitted people to hear their favourite entertainers. Probably the most important invention was the automobile. The assembly line, perfected by Henry Ford, cut down on the costs of manufacturing a car. Many people could now afford the new "Model-T" Fords.

**Conclusion**

These new inventions made life easier and more enjoyable than in the difficult times before electricity.

When you write a paragraph, it should follow this basic pattern.

## Your Task

*Write a paragraph on one of the following topics:*

- The importance of the railroad to Canada's growth at the turn of the twentieth century;
- Residential schools;
- The Riel Rebellions;
- The use of machine guns in the First World War;
- Gas warfare in the first World War;
- Canadian soldiers at Vimy Ridge or Ypres;
- The conscription crisis;
- Women's contributions to the war.

*Remember to include:*

1) an introductory sentence
2) three or four supporting statements
3) a concluding sentence summing up the significance

# Constructing a Chronology

As you study history, you will gradually learn when things happened. You will develop a sense of time or **chronology**. The **when** in history is significant. You should know the **sequence** of events, because frequently one event **causes** a later event.

Your text provides a time line at the top of many pages to show when a particular event occurred. You should develop the skill of placing events in a sequence, and seeing how and if one event affected or caused another.

## Cause and Effect in History

Events in history do not happen in isolation. Rather, they are usually parts of a **sequence** of events. One incident or occurrence **causes** another, which in turn influences later events. This is what is referred to as cause and effect in history.

## Sequence of Events

An historical event is part of a sequence of events. Each event is one link within a chain of "happenings." You should therefore examine historical events according to the following **cause and effect** sequence:

BACKGROUND CAUSE ➡ IMMEDIATE CAUSE ➡ EVENT ➡ RESULTS ➡ LONG-TERM SIGNIFICANCE
PAST ➡ PRESENT ➡ FUTURE

## Case Study—The Depression

BACKGROUND CAUSES: During the boom of the 1920s, Canadians began to depend more on credit for their purchases. Investors bought stocks on margin, paying only a percent of the actual cost.

IMMEDIATE CAUSE: Stock Market Crash of 1929 left stock prices crumbling.

EVENT: The Depression

RESULTS: Canadians by the thousands lost their jobs. Farmers could no longer sell their produce. Many lost their farms.

LONG-TERM RESULTS: By the end of the Depression, governments realized that laissez-faire capitalism was economically risky. As a result, King's Liberals introduced unemployment insurance.

## Your Task

1. Construct a time line from 1919-1929. Locate the following events in order on the time line:
   - Soldiers returning from the First World War
   - Founding of the One Big Union
   - Winnipeg General Strike
   - Boom in Resources
   - Rise of people buying merchandise on credit
   - Rise of investors buying stocks without paying in full
   - Stock market crash

2. When you have completed your time line, write an explanation to show how each event affected a later event.

## Your Task

Analyze the Background Cause
➡Immediate Cause➡Event➡Result
➡Long-Term Results of at least one of the following:
(a) Stock Market Crash
(b) Depression
(c) Formation of the CCF
(d) Social Credit Party
(e) Changing Roles for Women

# Writing a Newspaper Account

Writing a Newspaper Account

**Newspapers are one of our main sources of information. They help us understand what is going on locally, nationally, and worldwide. What makes a newspaper important is its ability to pack a great deal of information into short, easy-to-read articles. In only a few minutes of reading we can learn a great deal about the world around us.**

A useful form of writing is to describe a historical incident as if you were a reporter at the scene of the event. By placing yourself within the context of history, you might find yourself asking questions you might otherwise have neglected: Was it warm or cold? How did things smell and taste? What were people wearing? Was it noisy? Were the streets crowded or deserted? Many of these questions and more are difficult to answer. Use your imagination based on what you have learned. The more you know about an event the better it can be described.

When you write a newspaper report, you should always:
- research and collect the necessary information
- describe the events as accurately as possible, without bias or prejudice
- answer the five "W" questions: Who, What, Where, When and Why.

## Your Task

1. Read several newspaper reports to see how reporters (journalists) write their accounts.

2. After you have read several news reports, become a reporter and write an account of one of the following (or choose a topic of your own):
   - Winnipeg General Strike
   - Persons Case
   - Stock Market Crash of 1929
   - Dustbowl in the Prairies
   - On-to-Ottawa Trek
   - Election of the Social Credit Party in Alberta
   - Winnipeg General Strike
   - Birth of the Dionne Quintuplets
   - Edmonton Grads

# Writing a Five-Paragraph Research Report or Essay

There are two common forms of reports:

## 1. Descriptive Report

Some historical reports simply describe events:

- Social Conditions of the 1920s
- Immigration into the West in the 1900s
- The Schlieffen Plan
- Trench Warfare in the First World War

These reports merely **describe** in a narrative form what happened at a given period in time.

## 2. Explanatory (or expository) Essay

Writing an explanatory (or expository) essay is more complex and difficult. It involves more varied *research, selection* of material, and *organization.*

You use this form when you are trying to **explain** an **issue,** or consider a viewpoint (or even an hypothesis) rather than just describe what happened. While your research is being completed, you must form an **opinion,** take a point of view, and try to *prove* your position.

## Organization before writing:

- Research to collect data on your topic
- Select one or two questions which allow you to focus your research
- Organize your information in a sequence
- Record your material in a rough outline (your outline should be point form and no more than 1 page long)

## Writing Your Report or Essay

Writing a five-paragraph report is an expansion of how you write a five-sentence paragraph.

## Your Task

*Write a **five-paragraph report** on one of the following topics:*

- The Holocaust
- Dieppe Raid
- Rise of Fascism
- Internment of Japanese Canadians
- The Atomic Bomb Dropped on Japan
- A topic of your choice

| WRITING A PARAGRAPH | WRITING A FIVE-PARAGRAPH REPORT |
|---|---|
| 1. **Introductory sentence** explains main idea of paragraph. | 1. **Introductory paragraph** explains main idea of report. |
| 2. **Content**—3 (or 4) sentences support the introductory sentence. | 2. **Content**—3 (or 4) supporting paragraphs—Each paragraph explains one idea supporting the introductory paragraph. |
| 3. **Concluding sentence** summarizes or gives the importance of the paragraph. | 3. **Concluding paragraph** gives conclusion or significance of the topic. |

# Research

**No textbook can provide all the information required for the study of history. To develop a complete understanding of any topic, it will be necessary to do further research in other texts, encyclopedias, the Internet and other sources. The following suggestions are offered to assist you in your research:**

1. Read your textbook coverage of the subject. This will also help you **focus** on the questions that you want to pursue in your research.
2. Consult further information sources in your library. Use the library's digital database to help you find other specific books. Consult your teacher or librarian for assistance in locating these other reference books.
3. Use the **Table of Contents** and **Index**: When you examine a book, look over the Table of Contents at the beginning. You may determine which chapters are most useful for further research. The Index at the back of the book is the most effective way of seeing whether the book has information specifically related to your topic.
4. Check out the **Internet** using a search engine of your choice. Search using the name of the person or event under study. You can also access the databases of local libraries and perhaps your school. Check with your librarian.
5. **Recording Information** When you find information that you think is worthwhile, record it in point form on your note paper or on 7.5 cm x 12.5 cm research cards.
6. **Bibliography** When you complete your written report, you will have to indicate the *sources* of your information.
7. When you have collected all of your data or information, you should *organize* your material into an acceptable, chronological order. It will help your organization if you have recorded different information on separate pages or cards.

## Your Task

Select any topic from this textbook or from the chapter you are currently studying, and do further research in the library, using at least two other sources of information.

After completing your research, write a report approximately two pages long.

# Recording Information

Recording information in an organized manner is a crucial step to researching history. Although there are as many techniques for recording information as there are historians, novice students will benefit from this tried-and-true method of note taking.

Using either note paper or 7.5 cm x 12.5 cm index cards:
- use only one side of the page only
- select the key facts or ideas
- record information in point form
- record each topic on a separate piece of paper or card
- for each point recorded write down the full bibliographical information*
  * author (First name, Last name). Title. Place of Publication: Publisher, Date of publication.

Sample notes from page 271 of *Canada, Continuity and Change*
- during the 1950s and 1960s, more children than ever attending Canadian schools
- large number of schools children resulted in radically changed ideas about education
- unlike their grandparents, who stayed in school an average of only 6 years, baby boomers began to stay in school much longer

From:
McFadden, F.C. *Canada, Continuity and Change.* Toronto: Fitzhenry and Whiteside, Ltd., 2000

## Your Task

1. On your notepaper put an appropriate **Heading** at the top.
2. Draw a **Rule** approximately 6 cm from the left side of the page. Record all of your notes in point form to the **Right** side of this rule.
3. Summarize each idea in a few words and record them to the right of the rule in **Point Form**
4. Leave at least a one-line **Space** after each note.
5. Your point form summary does not have to record *all* the information. Select the **Most Important** information.
6. The space to the Left of the rule can be used to:
   - add additional information
   - number and summarize each point in a **Key Word.**

# Group Activities

In many school activities, students "learn" from the teacher or from a textbook. At work, play, or at home, we often learn by working with other people. In fact, most of us learn more from our friends and associates than from our teachers.

## Procedure

1. Select your topic (or arrange with your teacher for another appropriate topic)
2. Divide the work among your group, so that each person is responsible for completing part of the group task.
3. Conduct research on your activity. Consult other members of your group for advice and assistance.
4. Arrange to share your reports informally with each other. You should edit each other's work before preparing a "final draft."
5. When the work has the approval of the other group members, prepare a final draft in the most effective form.
6. When your group has completed its task, prepare a cover for your folder.
7. As a group, plan the most appropriate or effective means of communicating the information to others. This might involve:
   - brief oral reports
   - overhead transparencies
   - a panel presentation
   - a rehearsed interview
   - a skit or dramatic presentation

## Your Task

Work in a group with three or four other students and prepare a folder of materials on a topic of your choice or one given to you by your teacher. For example, you might choose to work on "The changing role of women from 1914 to 1930."

*For this project you might prepare a folder of materials which includes the following:*
- a poster advertising a women's rights rally
- a report on a speech given by a supporter of the women's rights
- drawings of women's fashions and hairstyles of the 1920s, with an explanation of why women wore these new styles
- an editorial supporting (or opposing) the right of women to be involved in Parliament
- a letter to the editor disagreeing with the editorial

# Oral Reports

When we listen to a speech or lecture, the radio or television, we depend on the ability of the speaker to communicate clearly and effectively. Oral communication is important in the day-to-day lives of all Canadians. Oral communication is also very important in the study of history, for this is one of the best ways to share what we have learned.

In your history program you will be given the opportunity to:
- discuss events in small groups
- make oral reports to the rest of your class
- make reports based on your research
- participate in interviews and panel discussions

## Your Task

1) With a group of three or four other students, consider three or four interviews you have recently heard on the radio, television or Internet. After considering these interviews, write down five points which showed the people in these interviews to be good or poor communicators. Back up your remarks with examples.

2) **An Oral Report**
   a) Select an historical figure from your text or from another source. The following individuals from World War I are suggestions only:
      - General Schlieffen
      - a Canadian soldier who fought in the Battle of Ypres
      - a Canadian soldier who fought at Vimy Ridge
      - a woman who worked at a war munitions factory
      - a Canadian who opposed conscription
      - a Canadian who favoured conscription
   b) Research what your subject did and might have thought about the event or times he or she was involved in.
   c) Present your report to the class as if you were that person.

3) **An Interview**
   Work with another student to research your topic. Prepare your report with one student acting as the interviewer and the other as the subject. Present your interview to the class.

# Using the Internet

In recent years the Internet has become a valuable tool for researching history. It allows researchers to access information originating from far away places, quickly and conveniently. Students can reach a wealth of information from all provincial and territorial governments, major Canadian corporations, Canadian Labour and Congress unions, women's groups and charitable organizations.

## Your Task

A. List the following:
1) Find the Internet address for 7 search engines
2) List the websites for 10 provinces and 3 Territories
3) Find the websites for the provincial and territorial archives
4) Find the website for the public library system in your province
5) Find the websites for 5 Canadian museums
6) Find the websites for 3 large Canadian corporations (Canadian Tire, Bombardier, etc.)
7) Find the websites for all provincial and federal political parties
8) Find the website for a senior citizens' group (CARP, for example)
9) Find the websites for 4 labour groups or unions
10) Find the websites for 2 women's groups

B. Using Statistics Canada's website (*www.statcan.ca*), find the answers to the following questions:
1) What is the population of each province and territory?
2) What is the population projection for the next 2 years for each province and territory?
3) How many 15-19 year olds live in Canada? How many are male. How many are female?
4) How many people immigrated to Canada from:
   a. Asia;            b. Australia;
   c. The Netherlands;    d. Austria;
   e. Greece;          f. France;
   g. South America;      h. The West Indies?
5) How many people are employed in the primary resource industry in Canada (logging, mining, forestry, and oil)?
6) What is the average weekly salary in each industry?
7) How many people speak French in Newfoundland? New Brunswick, Quebec? Ontario? Alberta? Canada?
8) What is the average annual income of a Canadian family with children and both parents working?
9) What is the average annual income of a Canadian family with children and only one parent working?

# Notation

A history student depends a great deal on the writings of others. When we write history it is important that we acknowledge all the sources we use.

All ideas, opinions, statistics and quotations that are not our own must be referenced. Plagiarism—the act of passing off the ideas, opinions, words, or statistics of someone else as if they were our own—is a serious academic offence. To avoid plagiarism we must always reference the work of others.

Information which must be referenced within our work are:

1) **Direct Quotations**

   Evan Esar claimed that "Canada's climate is nine months winter and three months in the late fall."
   Indeed, "Canadians have been accustomed to define themselves by saying what they are not."

2) **All Opinions or Ideas Not Our Own**

   Rephrasing a quotation does not mean we do not have to reference it. For instance, the great scholar Northrop Frye once wrote: "Historically, a Canadian is an American who rejects the Revolution." We might agree with this comment and wish to express it in our own words: Canadians are very much like Americans but without the Revolutionary heritage. Although written in our own words, the above idea is not our own; it is Northrop Frye's. We must therefore make proper reference to the original source.

3) **All Statistics**

   2,510 individuals died in the war.
   49.4% of Quebecers voted for separatism in the 1995 referendum.

Information that is common knowledge, however, need not be referenced.
The war started in 1914.
Millions were killed during the Second World War.
Violence erupted during the Winnipeg General Strike.

# More about Notation

How do we reference the work of others and avoid plagiarism?
We do this in two ways, with footnotes or endnotes, and a bibliography
or works cited.

## Footnotes and Endnotes

A footnote makes clear reference to the source where original information was
obtained. Each footnote is placed at the bottom of the page below the appropriate
reference. Footnotes are numbered and run sequentially. Each contains the
following information arranged in the following manner.

Name of Author, *Title,* (Place of Publication: Publisher, Year of Publication) page
number where the information was obtained.

## Endnotes

Endnotes works just like footnotes but appear at the end of your work, just
before the bibliography or works cited.

## A Bibliography or Works Cited

A bibliography is a list of all sources used to make your essay. It may include
books, magazines, encyclopedias, newspapers, interviews, CD- ROMs and the
Internet

A bibliography appears at the end of your essay. All sources listed are
arranged alphabetically according to the last names of the authors.

A standard bibliographical reference will include the following information
arranged accordingly:

Author's Last Name, First Name. *Title.* Place of Publication: Name of Publisher, Year of Publication.

Ask your teacher for more information on how to cite primary and secondary
sources.

## Final Note

To avoid plagiarism, reference all sources that you have depended on for any
information or opinion.

# Comparison—Then and Now

Comparison—Then and Now

"The further backward you can look, the further forward you can see."
*Winston Churchill*

"Those who ignore their history, are doomed to repeat it."
*George Santayana*

Does history repeat itself?

If you know what happened previously, does that mean that you know what will happen in the future?

Most historians believe that history does not repeat itself. The complex of events and people are so varied and different that they can never be exactly duplicated.

Then, you are probably asking, "Why do we study history?"

The events of your life usually do not repeat themselves exactly. However, we would all agree that our memory of previous experiences helps us to understand present conditions and it helps us make more intelligent decisions about our current and future lives. We have all heard that one learns best from one's own mistakes. History helps us learn from the mistakes of those who came before us.

Similarly, an awareness of previous historical events may help us understand related events; it will help us to understand and to make more informed and intelligent decisions about current issues.

Conditions and events in history are often similar but are never identical. Therefore, in studying history, it is sometimes useful to compare past events with contemporary or recent events. You will usually find both similarities and differences.

Having knowledge about the Stock Market Crash of 1929 would help in understanding the Stock Market Crash of 1987. There were similarities, but also significant differences. Knowledge of the earlier crash helped some economists to predict that there would likely be another crash, but did not help in determining when, to what degree, and with which consequences.

# Facts and Bias

**History is more than the presentation of facts. It is the linking and presenting of facts to create a meaningful, accurate presentation of what happened in the past. However, the way facts are selected and organized can sometimes lead to biased writing. We need to know how history is constructed if we are to learn to recognize bias.**

## What is a Fact

A fact is something that is concrete, something which is universally agreed to be true. It is an indisputable statement of truth. Insulin is a treatment against diabetes. Kerosene was invented in Canada. World War II ended in 1945. These are facts.

## Inferences

Facts are the foundations on which history is made. Inferences are conclusions or judgements relating one fact to another. If a fact is the foundation, an inference is the bridge which links the two. Because inferences are created by individual writers, they are not all the same. This is why it is possible to read more than one history about the same subject. The facts are the same, the conclusions, or the inferences, are not.

## Bias

In an ideal world, writers would be objective in their writing. This would result in writing that is impartial. In reality, writers are really the embodiment of their own environment. The way they see things is influenced by their background, experiences, politics and beliefs. As a result, the work they produce may contain partiality. Facts cannot be disputed, but the interpretations historians make may bend or sway their conclusions to fit their own beliefs. In the world of writing we call this bias.

For example, a Canadian of Albanian origin and a Canadian of Serbian origin would probably write two different accounts of the NATO war of 1999. Likewise, a writer from a communist country would hold a different opinion of the Cold War than would someone from North America. A writer should always try to eliminate his or her bias.

# Facts and Bias

Because of bias, historians sometimes offer different interpretations and reach different conclusions from the same facts. Being able to distinguish fact from opinion helps to detect bias.

## Detecting Bias

Bias can be defined as impartiality or inclination. It is related to a writer's preference or dislike for a person, place or event. For example a hockey writer who prefers his hometown team my write the following in a newspaper article. "The Jaguars had an off night and lost the game. The goalie received no support from the defence."

A writer from another newspaper my cover the same game by stating "The Jaguars were outplayed by the opponents. The Jaguar goalie was not playing his best and should have stopped two of the opposition's goals"

Bias is shaped by an individual's background, family, environment and experiences. An adult who played organized hockey as a teenager will develop preference for hockey, and for sports in general. This might not be the same for someone who did not play sports as a child.

There have been events in Canadian history that have evoked opposing reactions from French and English Canadians. The death of Louis Riel and the conscription issues during the world wars polarized both peoples. French and English newspaper reports reflected the biases of each group.

How does one detect bias? Detecting bias is not easy. One must carefully analyze writing and look for specific clues.
- Are facts presented to support conclusions?
- Are important facts left out?
- Is the author detached from her or his writing?
- Does the writer use emotionally charged adjectives or verbs?
- Are there other sources that support the writing / opinion?
- Are both sides of the event considered or presented?

## Your Task

*Read the following.*
*Which ones are facts and which ones are opinions?*

1. Free trade is good for Canada.
2. Quebec should separate in order to survive as a French culture.
3. Hitler's ambitions helped cause WW II.
4. Canada made important contributions to the Allied war effort.
5. Chrétien was a good prime minister.
6. Quebec Separatists want to separate.
7. Newfoundland joined Canada in 1949.
8. Lester B. Pearson helped solve the Suez crisis.
9. Canada adopted a new flag.
10. Canada is still connected to Great Britain.
11. Canadian participation in world affairs is not enough.

# Comparison—Then and Now

## Your Task

*Compare two events, one historical and the other more recent. You should select your own focus questions to help you organize your comparison. Point out both the similarities and differences.*

**Select one of the following topics:**

| HISTORIC EVENT | MORE RECENT PERIOD |
|---|---|
| Problems faced by immigrants, 1890-1914 | Problems faced by immigrants today |
| Reciprocity issue of 1911 | NAFTA issue of the 1990s |
| Conscription crisis, in World War I | Conscription crisis, in World War II |
| Unemployment conditions in 1930s | Unemployment conditions today |
| Social conditions in the 1950s (or 1960s) | Social conditions today |
| Problems facing women in 1900s (or a period of your choice) | Problems facing women today |
| Values in 1900 | Values today |
| The importance of the railroad in 1900 | The importance of the railway today |
| Quebec Referendum of 1980 | Quebec Referendum of 1995 |
| Poverty and child welfare in 1900 | Poverty and child welfare today |
| The impact of technology in 1900 (or decade of your choice) | The impact of technology today |
| Canadian prime minister of the first half of the twentieth century | Canadian prime minister of the last half of the twentieth century |

### Method

1. Select focus questions to research your topic.
2. Organize a chart to show similarities and differences.
3. Research further information to clarify similarities and differences.
4. Record your information in chart form.
5. Assess your comparison to see if there are more differences than similarities or vice versa.
6. Draw your own conclusion and present supporting information.

Prepare your chart in a final copy form. You should be prepared to present your comparison to other members of the class in an oral report.

# Prepare a Two-Page Research Report

**Studying history and contemporary issues is like being a detective:**

- you are confronted with a mass of facts and events, which are often difficult to piece together like a puzzle;
- you seek to find a pattern to the mystery;
- you raise questions in your mind to focus your thoughts;
- you organize your information to tentatively answer your questions;
- if necessary, you seek more information to answer your questions;
- you draw tentative conclusions to answer your questions;
- you assess your conclusions to see if they best answer the mystery;
- you communicate your conclusions to others in oral or written form.

When you study history, you go through a process similar to a detective investigating a crime. No doubt there have been other "detectives" (historians) who have previously examined your historical question. But there is no guarantee that they have solved the case.

History, then, is in part a story. But it is also a series of "cases" still waiting to be examined. Good luck on applying your skills as a detective in studying history.

## Check List for Research Report

✔ defined my topic?
✔ completed general reading in my text or other references to the topic?
✔ raised questions to focus my thinking and research?
✔ organized my thoughts in chart or point form?
✔ completed further research to locate more information to answer my focus questions?
✔ formed a tentative conclusion (or thesis) to explain the issue or topic?
✔ assessed my ideas and information for completeness, and taken into account different viewpoints?
✔ prepared a first draft or rough outline, in point form, for the introductory paragraph, supporting paragraphs, and conclusion?
✔ edited my rough draft for corrections and clarity?
✔ prepared my final draft to communicate to the teacher or other members of the class?

## Your Task

Select a topic for a two-page research report from your history course. You may choose your own topic, or your teacher may provide a list of possible topics.

Use your skills as a detective to examine your chosen topic or question. Some possible topics for your research report:

- The Changing Role of Women, 1900 to 1920s
- The Treaty of Versailles: Cause of World War II?
- The Dieppe Raid: Triumph or Tragedy?
- The Treatment of Japanese Canadians in World War II
- The Case for (or against) Using the Atomic Bomb in 1945
- Immigration to Canada, 1945 to 1960s
- Immigration to Canada, 1970s to 1980s
- The Need for Changes in Canadian Immigration Policy Today
- The Achievements and Importance of (choose one): Mackenzie King, John Diefenbaker, Lester B. Pearson, Pierre Trudeau, Brian Mulroney
- The Need for Changes in the Role of Women in Canada Today
- Canadian Culture: Worth Preserving?
- The Changing Role of Canada in the UN
- Western Canadian Discontent Today
- What We Should Do About Our Fragile Environment

# Glossary

Glossary

**abolish** do away with.

**Aboriginal people** people living in a place from earliest times, before the arrival of colonists; in Canada, Aboriginal people are the First Nations Indians; compare with *Native Peoples.*

**abortion** an early end to pregnancy, usually caused intentionally.

**academic** of schools and colleges, and their learning.

**accord** agreement.

**ace** a war pilot who has destroyed five or more enemy aircraft.

**acid rain** rain that has become an acid because it has absorbed chemicals in polluted air.

**act** a bill that has passed through both houses of parliament and become law; compare with *bill.*

**adjacent** next to; joined to.

**aesthetic** having to do with beauty or art.

**affluence** having money, wealth.

**air raid** bombing attack by enemy planes.

**alcoholism** disease resulting from drinking too much alcohol over a long period.

**alien** people from other countries.

**alliance** agreement to cooperate, between countries, political parties or families.

**ally** friend or helper; **Allies** nations that helped one another fight Germany and its supporters during the two world wars.

**ambassador** representative of a country's government in a foreign country.

**amenable** responsive, agreeable.

**amend** change or improve.

**amplification** in radio, a device for incresing the volume of sound.

**anaesthetic** a drug or gas given to a patient before surgery to reduce the sense of pain.

**anarchy** disorder, especially political; absence of government or law.

**Anglophone** an English-speaking person.

**anti-Semitism** a hatred or dislike of Jews or other Middle East people.

**apartheid** racial segregation or discrimination, especially in South Africa.

**appeasement** giving in to some of an enemy's demands in the hopes of keeping peace.

**arbitration** settlement of a dispute by an impartial third party.

**archipelago** group of islands.

**armaments** weapons and military equipment.

**armistice** truce, the agreement to end war.

**artillery** large guns; also army units who use them.

**assassinate** murder someone (usually a public figure) in a surprise attack.

**assembly line** a way of organizing workers so that each person does the same job over and over as the product moves through the factory.

**assimilation** to become a part of something.

**asylum** protection, especially for those fleeing from the law or an enemy.

**atomic bomb** a bomb that uses energy from the splitting of atoms to cause an explosion of tremendous force.

**atrocities** terrible or cruel actions.

**Axis** an agreement between Italy, Japan and Germany to support each other against an attack by the Soviet Union.

**baby boom** temporary increase in the birthrate.

**ballot** voting paper showing the names of election candidates. The voter marks the ballot to indicate their choice of candidate.

**bankrupt** to have lost one's money in business; being unable to pay one's debts.

**barbaric** crude, savage-like, primitive.

**barter** to trade or exchange goods without using money.

**bilingual** able to speak one's own language and another equally or almost equally well.

**bill** a proposal for a law; compare with *act*.

**biography** the written story of a person's life.

**birth control** use of methods or devices to prevent pregnancy.

**blackball** to vote against, to exclude.

**black market** unofficial (often illegal) system of buying and selling goods.

**blitz** to attack suddenly with great force; **(the) Blitz** German air raids on London in 1940.

**blitzkrieg** "lightning war"; Germany's conquest of Denmark, Norway, the Netherlands, Belgium and France in 1940.

**blockade** using force to cut off supplies to an enemy.

**BNA** British North America Act, Canada's original Constitution.

**boat people** refugees who set out for other countries with very few possessions and no proper documents to allow them to enter those countries.

**bobs and shingled haircuts** short haircuts worn by women in the 1920s.

**Boer War** (1899-1902); a war between England and the Dutch settlers called Boers, fought in South Africa.

**Boers** Dutch pioneers who settled in South Africa.

**Bolsheviks** communists who took part in the Russian Revolution in 1918.

**bombardment** attack using heavy guns or bombs.

**bond** a certificate issued by a government or corporation which you buy, and can later cash at a profit.

**boom** grow rapidly; do well; **boomtown** fast-growing town.

**bootlegging** making and selling something (often liquor) illegally.

**bourgeoisie** people belonging to the middle class.

**boycott** refuse to have social or commercial relations with.

**bribery** the act of giving or taking a gift or reward to do something that is illegal or against one's wishes.

**brigade** military unit, or group organized for a special purpose.

**British Empire** colonies governed by England; compare with *commonwealth*.

**budget** an estimate of the amount of money that can be spent, and the amounts to be spent for various purposes, in a given time (e.g., a year).

**bunker** reinforced underground shelter.

**burlesque** theatrical variety show, often including comedy and striptease.

**bush pilot** pilot who flies light planes to remote areas.

**buy on time** paying for something over a period of time, usually monthly.

**cabinet** group of government members which advises the prime minister.

**cadet** young trainee in the armed services or police.

**campaign** presentation throughout the constituency, province or country to convince electors to vote for a political party or its candidate.

**Canadian Shield** vast rocky area in northeastern Canada that is rich in minerals.

**canal** man-made inland waterway.

**CANDU** a special type of atomic reactor developed in Canada and used since 1962 to produce nuclear energy.

**canvass** door-to-door or telephone approach to voters to get their support for a party or a candidate.

**capitalism** economic system in which most businesses are owned by private individuals, not the government, in order to make a profit for their owners; compare with *communism*.

**cash crop** crop grown for sale rather than for personal use by the farmer.

**casualties** soldiers who have been killed, injured or taken prisoner.

**CCF** Cooperative Commonwealth Federation, a political party founded in 1932 in Alberta as an alternative to the Liberals and Conservatives; later joined with the Canadian Labour Congress to form the New Democratic Party.

**censor** to change; to limit or deny access to.

**centennial** 100th anniversary celebration.

**chancellor** the prime minister in certain countries, such as Germany.

**cipher** secret or disguised writing or code.

**citizen** a person who by birth or acceptance by the government has full rights and responsibilities in a country.

**civilian** a person who is not in the armed forces; **civilian government** government run by civilians rather than the military.

**civil rights** freedoms and privileges of citizens guaranteed by a country's constitution or charter of rights.

**civil servant** someone who works for the government; compare with *public service*.

**civil war** war waged between citizens of the same country.

**clear-cut logging** cutting down all the trees in an area and then selecting only the best ones for timber.

**closure** a rule in parliament that lets the government cut off debate and bring about a vote on a bill.

**cold war** hostility between nations without actual fighting; **(the) Cold War** period of hostility between the United States and the Soviet Union following World War II and lasting more than four decades.

**collective bargaining** negotiation of wages and conditions by an organized body of employees; compare with *negotiation*.

**colony** territory under the political control of another country; **colonial** someone from a colony.

**commerce** buying and selling, especially between countries.

**commonwealth** a political association of a group of independent nations (including Canada) that used to be part of the British Empire.

**commune** a group of people sharing accommodation, food, and other goods.

**communism** economic and political system in which the state (political community under one government) owns all property and runs business and industry for the common good, rather than for individual profit. No opposition to the government is permitted; compare with *capitalism*.

**Communist Manifesto** published in 1848 by Karl Marx to explain his theory that unregulated capitalism or business practices exploited the working class; Marx believed that the workers should overthrow the business class and establish a classless society where everyone shared equally in the profits of labour and production.

**compensation** that which is given or received in return for services, debt, or loss; a settlement of debt.

**compromise** an agreement in which neither

side gets everything it wants, but each side gets something; splitting the difference.

**concentration camp** prison camp to hold large numbers of political enemies or unwanted people.

**confederation** the joining together of several political units into one large unit or country; especially the Canadian Confederation.

**confiscate** to take or seize private property, usually for the government treasury.

**conquest** something won or conquered.

**conscription** a system to make people join the armed forces; **conscription issue** disagreement by French-speaking Canadians with attempts by the Canadian government to make people join the armed forces during both world wars.

**conspiracy** a plot or secret plan to do something illegal or evil.

**constituency** the parliamentary representative's home district, or the group of people in that district.

**constitution** the framework or rules and traditions which sets out how something (such as a country) is run.

**consumers** people who buy things.

**controversy** prolonged argument or dispute.

**convoy** large groups of supply ships that sail together during wartime and are protected against submarines by warships.

**cooperative** a business or farm owned and run jointly by its members with profits shared.

**coordinate** to bring into proper order; make parts work or act together.

**coupon** a ticket allowing someone to buy something.

**coureur de bois** "runner of the woods"; independent fur trader.

**cremate** burn (usually a corpse) to ashes.

**cropper** (slang) fail badly; fall heavily.

**Crown corporation** Canadian company owned by the government.

**crystal radio set** a simple type of radio receiver with a crystal detector (which converts alternating current to direct current using a semiconductor in contact with a sharp conductor) instead of an electron tube detector (which depends on the motion of electrons).

**culture** *1)* way of life; *2)* the learning and arts (including painting, music, literature, drama) of a nation.

**curfew** time after which people must remain indoors.

**death camps** German prisoner-of-war camps where prisoners who were considered undesirable or enemies of the state were put to death.

**debt** something (usually money) owed to someone else.

**defect** leave one's own country for another.

**deficit** the amount of shortage of income needed to cover a budget.

**deflation** reduction in the amount of money being spent while the supply of goods is high, leading to a drop in prices; compare with *inflation*.

**delegate** representative, someone who attends a meeting on other people's behalf.

**demilitarized area** area that armed forces are not allowed to enter.

**democracy** system of government by the people or by representatives elected by the people.

**depletion** reduction in quantity (amount) or force.

**deploy** spread out troops in a line ready for action.

**depression** a period when business drops and there are few jobs.

**diabetes** disease caused when the body fails to produce enough insulin to control blood sugar levels.

**dictatorship** country under the rule of a dictator who holds all the power, and usually uses force to stay in power.

**digging-in** opposing armies fortifying their positions.

**diplomat** civil servant who looks after dealings between countries; **diplomacy** management of relations between countries.

**Dirty Thirties** period of the Great Depression, 1929 to 1939.

**discrimination** unfavourable treatment of a person or group based on racial or sexual prejudice.

**distinct** separate; different.

**diversity** variety.

**dividend** a payment that is a share of profit.

**documentary** presenting or recording factual information in an artistic fashion, such as a film or a book.

**dogfights** World War I battles involving armed aircraft.

**domestic** affairs of one's own country; also, concerning affairs of the home or family.

**Dominion** self-governing territory of the British Commonwealth, such as Canada.

**dormant** temporarily inactive or sleeping.

**Dreadnought** a heavily armoured, fast warship loaded with 30-centimetre guns able to fire 400 kilograms of shells a distance of 6,000 metres.

**drought** a long period without rain.

**dustbowl** parts of Western Canada and the United States where dust storms are frequent and violent.

**dyke** low wall, barrier or dam built to prevent flooding.

**economy** all of the business, industry, trade and financial affairs of a country.

**economy of scale** the theory that larger companies are more efficient and can produce more goods, leading to mergers and takeovers of smaller companies.

**efficiency** producing something with a minimum of effort, expense or waste.

**elect** choose someone by voting.

**elite** best, or select group or class.

**emigrate** leave one country to live in another; compare with *immigrate*.

**empire** a group of countries under one government.

**employee** someone who works for someone else in return for pay.

**employer** someone who pays other people to work for her or him.

**en masse** French for all together.

**enemy alien** an alien who is living in a country at war with his own country; compare with *alien*.

**entrench** firmly establish.

**environment** the natural world: the air, sea, countryside, lakes, rivers, etc.

**era** a certain period of time, for example, the rock and roll era.

**erosion** the act of wearing away or being worn away.

**essential services** necessary city services in times of emergency, such as fire and police departments, ambulances and hospitals.

**espionage** spying or use of spies.

**ethnic** having a common national or cultural tradition.

**expeditionary force** group of people and equipment on a journey for a particular purpose, usually exploration.

**exploit** treat someone unfairly for your own gain; to put something to profitable use, e.g., iron ore.

**export** *(v)* sell or send something to another country; *(n)* something which is sold or sent to another country; compare with *import*.

**expository** containing an explanation or description of a topic.

**exterminate** completely destroy; wipe out.

**faction** small organized group within a larger group, usually political.

**fallow** land that has been ploughed but left unplanted, usually to make the soil richer.

**famine** extreme shortage of food, leading to starvation.

**fascism** a form of dictatorship backed up by secret police and the army, based on nationalistic and racist theories.

**federal** national level of government in a country that has regional governments, such as provinces or states, as well.

**federalism** a system of government in which some powers are held by the central government, while others are held by regional governments.

**feminism** a set of beliefs that favours increased rights and activities for women.

**fiasco** complete failure; action that comes to a ridiculous end.

**fleet** a nation's warships.

**foreign affairs** government relations with other countries.

**forge** *1)* make or write an imitation, e.g., forged document; *2)* move forward steadily or rapidly; *3)* shape metal by heating and hammering.

**fortify** make stronger.

**forum** place of or meeting for public discussion.

**Francophone** a French-speaking person.

**free trade** buying and selling between countries without any tariffs or customs duties.

**frigate** naval escort vessel.

**front** battleground; the line where opposing armies meet.

**garrison** troops stationed in a place in order to defend it; fortress.

**gas warfare** to use poisonous gas as a weapon against enemy soldiers; in World War I, the Germans used chlorine and mustard gas against Canadian soldiers who were often sent to the front without gas masks.

**general strike** a strike by workers of an entire trade or industry, or of all or many of the industries in a community or country.

**generating station** place where electric power is produced

**generation gap** lack of understanding between people of different age groups.

**genesis** origin; beginning.

**genocide** deliberate extermination of a people or nation.

**Gestapo** Nazi secret police.

**ghetto** a part of a city inhabited by a racial, national, or religious minority.

**globalization** joining or connecting with similar interests (usually business) around the world; exchanging goods and services on a global scale.

**global village** term used to describe the whole world as one place.

**glossary** a list of words and definitions found in a specific book or subject.

**going over the top** soldiers in World War I would "go over the top" of the trenches and cross no-man's land when ordered to advance into enemy territory.

**governor general** representative of the Queen in Commonwealth countries such as Canada, who recognize the Queen as head of state.

**grassroots** ordinary people.

**Great Depression** period of economic depression that began with the 1929 stock market crash and ended with the beginning of World War II in 1939.

**grenade**  a small bomb thrown by hand.

**Group of Seven**  a group of Canadian painters whose aim was to paint the landscapes and beauty of Canada.

**guarantee**  be responsible for; promise to protect; promise that something will be done in the manner specified.

**gulag**  labour camp created by Josef Stalin where political prisoners were sent to serve their sentences; gulags were located in very remote areas of the USSR.

**hate crime**  act of violence or assault against a person because of race, religion or ethnic differences.

**head tax**  a tax imposed on everyone for a specific reason.

**heritage**  culture, traditions and learning handed down from the past.

**hindsight**  the ability to see, after the event, what should have been done.

**hinterland**  an area far from big cities and towns; inland region.

**hoax**  something done to deceive or fool someone; often meant as a practical joke.

**hobo**  a wandering worker or tramp; **hobo jungle**  outdoor camps where hoboes would gather to eat and sleep.

**holocaust**  total destruction, especially the Nazis' mass killing of Jews, gypsies, homosexuals, and others in World War II.

**homestead**  a piece of land given by the government to a settler to be developed as a farm; also refers to the land, house and other buildings on the property where a family lives.

**hostility**  feeling of ill will or unfriendliness; state of war or act of war.

**humanitarian**  showing kindness and concern for human beings.

**hydroelectric power**  electricity generated by water-power (e.g., waterfalls).

**hypnotize**  fascinate, capture of the mind of someone, usually through speech.

**ideal**  the way a person or group thinks things should be in a perfect world.

**identity**  distinctive character of a person or group.

**ideology**  a strongly held system of beliefs about how the world should be run.

**immemorial**  very old; extending back before memory or record.

**immigrate**  come to live in a new country; compare with *emigrate*.

**immigrant**  someone who comes to live in a new country.

**impartial**  not taking sides or showing favour to one side over the other.

**impeach**  charge with a crime against the state (treason); charge a public official with misconduct.

**imperialism**  policy of dominating other nations by establishing colonies; forming and maintaining an empire.

**import**  *(v)* to bring things into a country; *(n)* something which is brought into a country; compare with *export*.

**income tax**  a tax imposed by government on the money earned by individuals.

**Independent**  candidate in an election who does not belong to an established political party.

**indigenous**  native to, or belonging naturally to a place.

**indiscriminate**  without method or conscious choice.

**industry**  business operation that makes a special product, whether it be cars and trucks or canned lobster.

**infamous**  having a very bad reputation.

**inflation**  an increase in prices caused by an

increase in the amount of money being spent; compare with *deflation*.

**inherent**  existing in someone or something as a natural or permanent quality or characteristic.

**inhibit**  to restrict or forbid.

**initial**  first, at the beginning.

**insulin**  hormone produced naturally in most people to control blood sugar levels.  People with diabetes do not produce insulin and must receive it through injections or pills.

**intelligence**  the collecting of information, especially of military or political value.

**interest**  the money someone has to pay to use borrowed money, usually calculated as a percentage of the loan.

**interests**  a group of people with a special concern for something, for example, business interests.

**interim**  temporary.

**interior**  inland area, far from the coast.

**internal affairs**  anything that goes on within one country.

**internment**  to hold people in a confined or specific area or camp; countries often *intern* aliens in time of war.

**interpretation**  explanation of meaning.

**interrogator**  one who asks questions.

**investor**  someone who puts money into a business in the hope of making a profit.

**isolationism**  the political belief that the country should look after its own needs and not form ties with other countries.

**issue**  a point to be debated; a problem.

**job market**  the number and range of jobs available at any one time.

**journalism**  the work of writing for, editing, managing, or producing a newspaper or magazine.

**judicial**  having to do with courts, judges, or the administration of justice.

**Kristallnacht**  "the night of broken glass" when Hitler ordered his militia to destroy Jewish homes and businesses as revenge for the shooting death of a German diplomat by a Jewish student.

**laissez-faire**  economic theory that the government should not interfere with business or industry.

**landing craft**  boat designed for putting troops and equipment ashore.

**laser**  (light amplification by stimulated emission of radiation) device that generates an intense beam of light in one direction.

**League of Nations**  an association of nations formed in 1920 to promote international cooperation and peace.

**left-wing**  leaning towards a socialist political party or system of government; compare with *right-wing*.

**legal system**  organization of laws, courts, and the law enforcement in a city, province, or the whole country.

**legislature**  provincial parliament.

**legitimate**  rightful or lawful; allowed, acceptable.

**leprosy**  contagious disease that damages the skin and nerves.

**libel**  a false statement that is damaging to a person's reputation.

**lieutenant governor**  the representative of the Queen and the governor general in each province.

**literacy**  ability to read and write.

**livelihood**  the way people make their living.

**loyalty**  faithful support, especially for the government.

**Luftwaffe**  the German air force.

**mainstay** the principal means of support.

**majority** more than half of a group, especially more than half the members of parliament, as in *majority government*.

**malnutrition** condition resulting from the lack of foods necessary for health.

**mandate** authority given by voters to a government.

**manifesto** a statement of beliefs and policies by a political group.

**margin** a part payment to buy shares, with the stockbroker lending the balance to the buyer; **margin call** when the stockbroker demands payment of the balance from the buyer of the shares.

**marginalized** treated as if it were insignificant or unimportant.

**market** any area where buying and selling is done on a regular basis.

**marquis wheat** a type of wheat developed in Canada to grow well in the weather and soil conditions of the prairies.

**master race** Adolf Hitler's definition of the German people as a pure, white race.

**Medicare** health care paid for by the government.

**merchant navy** ships and sailors of a nation not in the military, engaged in commercial shipping.

**Métis** a person of mixed blood; in Canada, someone with one French parent and one Aboriginal parent.

**minimum wage** the amount set by law that is the least an employer is allowed to pay a worker.

**minister** a cabinet member who is responsible for a government department, e.g., fisheries.

**minority** less than half of a group, especially less than half the members of parliament, as in *minority government*.

**missile** a self-propelled bomb or rocket.

**missionary** someone who goes to a distant country to spread a religion.

**mobilize** set in motion; prepare for war.

**monarch** royal head of state such as king, queen, emperor, empress or czar (Russia).

**monotonous** lacking in variety; boring and repetitive.

**morale** confidence, determination, willingness to endure hardship.

**Morse code** code in which letters are represented by combinations of long and short light or sound signals.

**mortgage** a contract in which money is lent for the purchase of a house or property on the understanding that the lender may take over the property if the loan is not repaid.

**mosaic** something that is made up of many separate, distinct pieces.

**multicultural** representing many different cultures.

**multiracial** including many different races.

**municipal** of a town or city.

**munitions** guns and ammunition.

**nation** a country or the people of a particular country; a group of people with a common origin and strong cultural ties.

**nationalism** patriotic feelings or efforts; desire and plans for independence; the desire of a people to preserve its own language, religion, traditions, etc.

**nationalize** to place an industry or resource under government (as opposed to private) management, either by "buying it out" or taking it over.

**Native Peoples** the first inhabitants of a country; in Canada, the Indian and Inuit peoples; compare with *Aboriginal people*.

**naturalized citizen** an alien who has been granted the same rights and privileges of a country as someone who was born in that country.

**Nazi** member of the National Socialist German Workers' Party; supporter of an extreme type of fascism that dominated Germany from 1933 to 1945, under Adolf Hitler.

**negotiation** talks between groups or individuals to reach an agreement; compare with *collective bargaining*.

**neutrality** not taking sides in a dispute or war.

**nomadic** leading a wandering life, with no fixed home.

**no-man's land** a narrow strip of land on a battlefield between two opposing armies which is controlled by neither.

**non-aggression pact** treaty signed between Germany and the Soviet Union in 1939 agreeing not to fight each other.

**non-renewable resources** natural materials, like oil and other minerals, that do not grow back after they have been used up; compare with *renewable resources*.

**nuclear age** the period in history that began with the dropping of the atomic bomb on Hiroshima in 1945.

**nuclear power** energy created when the central "nucleus" of an atom is split, or when atoms are fused.

**nuclear reactor** device in which a nuclear fission chain reaction is used to produce energy.

**observer** someone who studies and analyses current events, usually political.

**occupied Europe** the part of Europe under the control of Germany and its allies during World War II.

**offensive** attack or movement toward a goal; invasion.

**open pit mining** the process of extracting minerals from the ground using heavy machinery to dig on the surface rather than underground.

**opposition** members of parliament who do not belong to the elected, governing party.

**oppress** to govern or treat cruelly; to overpower or subdue.

**oral history** first-hand stories told to a writer or historian by people who were involved in a historical event of period of history.

**ore** a rock or other natural substance that contains a metal.

**output** the amount of goods produced.

**over-the-top** in World War I, when troops were ordered to attack, they would climb out of trenches and go "over the top" of the piles of earth.

**Pablum** cereal for babies invented in 1931 by three doctors in Toronto; a highly nourishing mixture of wheat meal, oatmeal, cornmeal, wheat germ, bone meal, brewer's yeast and alfalfa.

**pacifist** someone who believes in solving all problems peacefully, and is especially opposed to war.

**parliament** the highest lawmaking body in certain countries.

**partisan** strong supporter of a party or cause.

**patriotism** strong love and support for one's country.

**patronage** the power to give jobs or favours, especially political jobs for favours done to help the person(s) in power.

**pauper** poor person.

**pension** money paid regularly to certain people, e.g., the elderly, the retired, and the disabled.

**penury** the condition of being extremely poor; destitute; having none of the necessities of life; compare with *poverty*.

**per capita** for each person.

**persecution** inflicting pain, punishment, or death on others, especially for reasons of race, politics or religion.

**pioneer** someone who settles in a new region; someone who investigates a new field of research.

**pluralistic** a society that contains many ethnic and cultural minority groups.

**pogrom** organized killing, originally of Jews in Russia.

**policy** a plan of action, especially in government.

**pollution** the presence of damaging chemicals and other impurities in the air, land, or water.

**poverty** the condition of being poor; having very few of life's necessities such as food, clothing and shelter; compare with *penury*.

**precursor** something or someone that goes before or precedes.

**prejudice** an opinion (usually bad) formed without knowledge, or without time to judge someone or something fairly.

**premier** person who leads the government in any one of the Canadian provinces.

**primary source** original documents such as government records, personal journals and letters which are used by historians to gather information about a time and place; compare with *secondary source.*

**prisoner of conscience** person imprisoned for his or her political or religious beliefs.

**private enterprise** businesses not under government control, but owned by individuals and run for profit.

**privatize** transfer (a business) to private ownership.

**privy council** a committee of high government officials appointed to advise the monarch or the governor general.

**profiteering** making unfair profits by taking advantage of people's needs in time of war and disaster.

**progeny** offspring, children.

**prohibition** a total ban on making and selling alcohol; **Prohibition** a period in history when making and selling alcohol was illegal.

**proletarian** a member of the class of wage-earning people; working class.

**propaganda** a systematic plan to persuade people that one political outlook is better than all the others, using radio, TV, the press, and other means.

**prospector** someone who searches for valuable mineral deposits.

**prosperity** well-being, wealth.

**public service** people who work for the Canadian government; compare with civil servant.

**pulverize** crush, defeat, demolish.

**quintuplets** five babies born to one mother at one time.

**quota** share or number of goods, people, etc. allowed.

**rabble-rouser** someone who agitates or stirs up a crowd (usually for political reasons).

**racial** connected with race, colour or nationality.

**racism** prejudice or hatred based on race, colour or nationality.

**radar** (radio detection and ranging) system for detecting the direction, range, or presence of objects, by sending out pulses of high frequency electromagnetic waves, which are reflected by the object.

**radiation** the process in which energy in the form of rays of light or heat is sent out from atoms and molecules as they undergo internal change; energy as electromagnetic waves or moving particles.

**ramification** consequence.

**rationing** restricting the distribution of food, clothing, and other goods in times of shortage.

**raw materials** the unprocessed materials used to make finished products, e.g., wood for paper or furniture.

**rebellion** an organized attempt to overthrow a government.

**recession** period of temporary business decline, shorter and less extreme than a depression.

**reciprocity** an agreement between two countries to allow imports and exports with few restrictions.

**recruit** *(v)* to enlist or hire people to join the army or navy; *(n)* a person who has just been hired in this way.

**referendum** a vote by all people to accept or reject a government proposal. Also called a *plebiscite*.

**refugees** people who have had to leave their countries to escape cruel treatment because of political disagreement with the government, other dangers, or war.

**regime** government, political or social system.

**regiment** permanent unit of an army.

**regulation** a rule, law or order; a prescribed way of doing things.

**relevant** relating to the matter being studied or discussed; pertinent.

**relief** money, food or clothes provided to people in need; now known as *welfare*.

**relief camps** camps set up in remote areas to house unemployed men; camp inmates worked 8 hours a day, 6 days a week to build roads, dig ditches and plant trees in return for food, clothing, a bed and 20¢ a day; conditions were mostly very crowded and poor.

**relinquish** give up or let go of.

**relocate** move to a new place.

**render** cause to be or become; make into something; also, to give as payment.

**renewable resources** natural products like lumber or fish, that can grow again as they are used; compare with *non-renewable resources*.

**repatriate** return to his or her native land.

**republic** state or nation in which supreme power is held by the people or their elected representatives, or by an elected or nominated president, not by a monarch.

**Residential schools** government schools in Canada where Aboriginal children, who were taken away from their families, were sent to learn to be like white people.

**resistance** organized secret groups working to throw out a foreign invader who controls their country, e.g., the French or Yugoslav resistance during World War II; compare with *underground movement*.

**resources** useful natural products such as oil, fish, iron ore, water and wood.

**resource-based economy** an economy in which industry uses and depends on natural resources to provide jobs and products.

**revenue** money collected by governments by taxation of the citizens of that country or state.

**revolution** the overthrow of a government by some of the people.

**riding the rails** travelling illegally on freight trains.

**right-wing** leaning toward a more conservative or capitalist system of government; compare with *left-wing*.

**riot** wild, often violent outburst by a large group of people; **Riot Act** a law against people gathering for the purpose of disturbing the peace or doing damage to property.

**royal commission** an invesigative group set up to study some matter or problem on behalf of the government and to make a report recommending suitable action.

**royalty** percentage of profit paid to the owner.

**rural** to do with the country, or farms; compare with *urban*.

**sabotage** deliberate damage, especially in war, to anything the enemy might use for military purposes.

**salvage** waste materials that have been saved for use.

**sanction** to give permission with authority, approval; an action against a country by other countries to force it to obey international law.

**sarcastic** using scornful and ironic language.

**satellite** a man-made object put into orbit around the earth, moon or a planet.

**scapegoat** someone who is made to take the blame for another person's mistakes or crimes.

**scourge** person or thing seen as causing suffering.

**scouts** soldiers sent to infiltrate enemy positions and report their findings to headquarters.

**secondary source** written texts such as newspaper and magazine articles, books, encyclopedias and information on the Internet which are used by historians to gather information about a time and place; compare with *primary source*.

**seditious conspiracy** a secret plan to create a rebellion against the government in power.

**segregate** separate (especially an ethnic group) from the rest of the community.

**self-deprecating** to belittle onself; to make oneself seem unimportant.

**self-determination** the right of a people to choose its own form of government.

**self-government** government of a region by the people who live there.

**Senate** the second or "upper" branch of many legislatures, such as the Canadian Parliament or the U.S. Congress.

**separatism** movement to separate Quebec from the rest of Canada and give it political independence.

**services** industries or businesses that provide a service rather than a product, such as dry cleaning, dentistry, and repairing automobiles or appliances.

**settlers** people who go to a new area and make their homes there; pioneers; colonists.

**sexism** prejudice or discrimination on the grounds of gender, especially against women.

**shanty town** area of temporary housing, usually of poor quality.

**shares** equal parts of the ownership of a business; people who buy these shares are called shareholders.

**shell** ammunition fired from large guns containing explosives.

**shrapnel** pieces of metal hurled out in all directions by a special type of shell that explodes in the air or on impact.

**sickle** a tool with a curved blade for cutting grass or grain.

**siege** surrounding and blockading a town in order to capture it.

**significance** importance, meaning.

**slaughter** killing (people) ruthlessly in large numbers; killing of animals for food or skins, or because of disease.

**Slav** member of a group of peoples from central and eastern Europe.

**slump** a period when business is poor and there are fewer jobs.

**smelter** a furnace in which metal ores are melted down to separate the metal from the rock, etc.

**snipers** soldiers in camouflage who are usually excellent shots, who fire into enemy ranks from a hidden place.

**social** of or about human beings living together as a group.

**Social Credit** a political party formed in 1932 in Alberta by William Aberhart; the party proposed to pay each Alberta citizen $25 a month to spend on things they needed.

**socialism** a political and economic system in which property and business are owned by the community rather than individuals, and all people share in both the work and the profits.

**society** 1) all the people in a community or country; 2) a group of people with similar interests, attitudes, or standards of living.

**sodbuster** settler on the prairies who broke up the ground in order to prepare the land for raising crops.

**sonar** system for detecting objects underwater using reflected sound.

**soup kitchen** a place where soup or other food is served to the poor or homeless.

**soviet** elected council of the USSR; **Soviet** citizen of the USSR.

**sovereign** self-governing; **sovereignty** supreme power or authority; the quality of being sovereign over oneself.

**special agent** an individual authorized to do a particular job for the government; often a spy.

**specialization of labour** worker or group of workers performs one function over and over on an assembly line, to produce goods (such as cars) cheaply and efficiently.

**sputnik** first Russian satellite to orbit the earth.

**stalemate** a stage in an argument, war or discussion when neither side is willing or able to make a move.

**standard of living** the level at which a person (or the average person in a group or country) lives, with respect to food, shelter, and the variety and quality of goods and services that can be expected.

**state** a nation or a political unit within a nation; the government of a nation.

**status** rank or position.

**stereotype** person or thing conforming to a fixed or conventional pattern or character.

**stock market** the buying and selling of stocks and shares; **stock exchange** where the buying and selling of stocks and shares takes place, as in The Toronto Stock Exchange.

**STOL** aircraft capable of short take-off and landing

**storm troopers** Nazi political militia.

**strike** the refusal of workers to continue working.

**stud** horses (and other valuable animals) kept for breeding.

**subdivision** land divided into small parcels for sale.

**subsidy** a grant or contribution of money, especially one made by government to support an industry or organization.

**subsoil** layer of earth underneath the topsoil that contains little or no nutrients and moisture plants need to develop.

**suburbs** the outskirts or outlying districts of a city; **suburbia** suburbs, the people who live there, and their way of life.

**suffrage** the right to vote in political elections; **suffragette** woman who fights for the right to vote in elections.

**supply-and-demand** amount of goods available to buy in relation to amount needed, as a way of determining the price.

**supreme court** the highest, most authoritative law court in Canada; the "court of final appeal."

**surplus** quantity or amount over or above what is needed.

**surreal** dreamlike; **surrealism** a modern movement in art and literature.

**swastika** ancient symbol of a cross that was altered to become the symbol of the Nazi Party in Germany in the 1930s and 1940s.

**synagogue** a building for Jewish religious worship and instruction.


**tag sale** sale of used items donated by people to raise money for a specific cause.

**tank** a huge armoured war vehicle designed to cross all sorts of rough territory.

**tank traps** obstacles (such as blocks of concrete placed close together) which tanks cannot pass.

**tariff** a special tax imposed by the government on imports and exports.

**tax** money paid to or collected by the government; **taxation** the system of arranging and collecting taxes.

**technology, technological** use of up-to-date scientific knowledge in industry and everyday life.

**temperance** *1)* refusal to drink alcohol; *2)* moderation in eating and drinking.

**tenure** the right to hold or own something; also, the length of time something is held.

**terrorism** organized use of violence and illegal acts to create an atmosphere of great fear and to put pressure on the government.

**thesis** an unproved statement or assumption to be proved in an essay or argument.

**timber** wood used for building and carpentry.

**tinderbox** box used to hold wood and kindling for starting fires.

**Tin Lizzie** nickname of Ford automobile produced on an assembly line.

**toil** work or labour.

**token** something meaningless in itself which is meant to stand for something more important; a symbol.

**topsoil** top layer of earth that contains moisture and nutrients plants need to develop.

**totalitarian** a dictatorial government that allows no competing political groups and that exercises rigid control of industry, the arts, etc.

**trade union** organized association of workers in a trade or profession.

**traitor** someone who does something to harm his or her own country, especially giving away its military or commercial secrets.

**transcontinental** spreading across a continent.

**transistor** a tiny device that controls electric current; used in many electric appliances, allowing them to be small.

**treason** betraying or acting against the interests of one's country.

**treaty** an agreement between two or more groups, intended to solve their differences.

**trench** a long, narrow ditch dug in the ground.

**trench warfare** the use of ditches 2 metres deep and topped with sandbags by soldiers in World War I to hide and protect them from the enemy.

**trestles and ties** the wood pieces that form the roadbed for a railway; ties lie crosswise under the steel track; trestles support bridges.

**turmoil** violent confusion; disturbance.


**U boat** German submarine.

**ultimatum** a final statement of conditions, rejection of which may lead to breaking off of relations or a declaration of war.

**underground movement** secret movement organized in a country to overthrow the government in power or enemy forces of occupation; compare with *resistance*.

**unemployment** being out of work; a shortage

of jobs.

**UNESCO** United Nations Educational, Scientific, and Cultural Organization; a part of the United Nations.

**unequivocal** plain; clear; unmistakable.

**unilateral** done by or affecting one side only.

**unions** organizations of workers in the same trade or industry.

**United Nations** an international organization of nations formed in 1945, pledged to promote world peace and security.

**unrepentant** without sorrow or regret for one's actions

**unscrupulous** not restrained by ideas of right and wrong; without moral principles.

**urban** in or relating to cities; compare with *rural*.

**urban planning** the process of designing cities.

**urban society** the way of life of people living in a city.

**valiant** brave.

**vaudeville** a theatrical variety show including songs, dances, comedy and acrobatics.

**ventilated** air is allowed to circulate freely in a room or enclosed space.

**veteran** a person who has served in the armed forces of a country, especially in time of war.

**veto** a legal and official refusal to allow a government bill or other proposal to take effect or become law.

**violation** the breaking of a law.

**virus** microscopic organism often causing diseases; evil or harmful influence.

**visible minority** a group within a society that looks different because of skin colour, physical features, or clothing style.

**vital** essential, indispensable.

**volatile** changeable; unstable; explosive.

**voluntarily** by one's own free choice; willingly.

**volunteer** one who offers to join the armed forces; one who works without pay for a service organization (Red Cross, political party, etc.)

**vote** choose among political candidates in an election, or between proposals in a meeting.

**voyageur** a traveller; one who transports goods and men by rivers and lakes to trading posts.

**war bride** a girl or woman who marries a soldier while he is actively engaged in war service.

**war criminal** someone who has violated the international laws of war.

**war effort** the working together of armed forces, civilians, industry, and government, all trying to win a war.

**War Measures Act** an act passed during World War I which gave the government sweeping powers to arrest and detain enemy aliens.

**Wartime Elections Act** passed in 1917, the act denied the vote to any citizen who had emigrated from any country defined as an enemy of Canada.

**welfare state** a state in which the government provides services for the people, such as health care, unemployment payment, old-age pensions.

**wheat pool** a cooperative of wheat farmers to sell and distribute their grain at a controlled price.

**wireless telegraphy** sending messages using electromagnetic waves rather than conducting wire.

**workforce** all the workers in a nation.

**zeppelin** a large airship or balloon that is long, cigar-shaped, and motor-driven, and can be steered, designed in the early 20th century.

**zero hour** the time set for an important event, such as an attack during war.

# Index

# Acknowlegements

Pg. 11 Saskatchewan Archives; pg. 12 (left) City of Toronto Archives, James Collection, (right) Glenbow Archives NA 1473-1; pg. 13 Provincial Archives of New Brunswick; pg. 14 NAC; pg. 15 NAC; pg. 16 NAC PA 29788; pg. 17 Brock Silverside; pg. 18 NAC; pg. 19 Glenbow Archives; pg. 21 Provincial Archives of Alberta OB157, Glenbow Archives; pg. 26 NAC T-2391; pg. 24 NAC C-5208; pg. 25 Glenbow Archives NA263-1; pg. 26 Vancouver Public Library; pg. 27, NAC C14118; pg. 28 Metro Toronto Reference Library; pg. 29, Glenbow Archives NA-5031-1; pg. 30, NAC PA 72527; pg. 31, Glenbow Archives NA 5031-1; pg. 32, Manitoba Archives; pg. 33, Saskatchewan Archives S-MN-B-3653, reprinted with permission from the estate of Thomas Melville Ness; pg. 34, NAC; pg. 35 (top) Glenbow Archives NA406-3, (bottom) Glenbow Archives NA 3403-13; pg. 36, Saskatchewan Archives S-MN-B-3653, reprinted with permission from the estate of Thomas Melville Ness; pg. 37, NAC PA-143204; pg. 38, Manitoba Archives; pg. 39, Glenbow Archives; pg. 40 Toronto Reference Library T-12870; pg. 41, (top) Ontario Archives, (bottom) NAC-C-30953; pg. 42 City of Toronto Archives, James Collection; pg. 43 NAC C-30936; pg. 44, Toronto Reference Library, Eaton's Collection; pg. 46, H.J. Hughes; pg. 47 NAC; pg. 48, (top) BC Archives E-05081, (bottom) NAC PA-38662; pg. pg. 52, Toronto Reference Library; pg. 53 Toronto Reference Library; pg. 54, Glenbow Archives NC53-86; pg. 56 NAC PA-37798, pg. 57, City of Toronto Archives; pg. 58, Canadian Heritage, Parks Canada; pg. 59 Ontario Ministry of Natural Resources; pg. 60, NAC C-6097; 61 NAC PA-112438; pg. 62 NAC/DND 20847; pg. 63 NAC; pg. 65 City of Toronto, James Collection; pg. 67, NAC; pg. 77, Colliers Photographic History of the War in Europe; pg. 79, (top) NAC PA-66815, (bottom) City of Toronto Archives, JC8280; pg. 80, NAC C-2468; pg. 81, (top left) City of Toronto Archives, James Collection (top right) City of Toronto Archives, James Collection (bottom) Ontario Archives; pg. 82-83 NAC C-PA648; pg. 84 RCMI; pg. 86 (bottom) NAC PA 1679, (top) NAC; pg. 87 (bottom) NAC PA 5001; pg. 88, NAC PA 042869; Pg. 89 NAC PA 3737; pg. 90 PANL; pg. 91, NAC PA 3534; pg. 92 NAC C-26340; pg. 94 NAC C26340; pg. 95 (top) NAC PA 11824, (bottom) NAC; pg. 96 NAC PA-1654; pg. 97, Glenbow Archives NA-1258-2; pg. 98-99, NAC C-19948; pg. 99 City of Toronto Archives SC-244-2456; pg. 100 NAC C-19952; pg. 101 (top) NAC PA-11264; (middle) NAC PA 1249, (bottom) NAC C-18733; pg. 102 NAC PA-25181; pg. 103 National Museum of Canada; pg. 105 NAC C-24345; pg. 108 City of Toronto, SC244-654; pg. 108, City of Toronto Archives, James Collection, 45554; pg. 110 NAC PA 4422; pg. 111, City of Toronto, James Collection; pg. 112 (top) RCMI, (bottom) NAC PA-3538; pg. 113 (top) NAC, (bottom) NAC PA-2890; pg. 114 NAC 24963; pg. 117 NAC PA-25942; pg. 128 City of Toronto Archives, James Collection SC 244-903; pg. 130 Provincial Archives of Manitoba; 131 NAC; pg. 132 NAC C-32857; pg. 133 Provincial Archives of Manitoba 2762; pg. 134, NAC C-34443; pg. 135 Cape Breton Archives; pg. 136, NAC C-54523; pg. 137, John Mardon; pg. 138, NAC PA-127295; pg. 140 Sports Hall of Fame; pg. 141, Glenbow Archives; pg. 142, NAC PA-139429; pg. 143, NAC PA-42652; pg. 144, City of Toronto Archives; pg. 146, NAC PA 33971; pg. 147, Rogers Communications Inc.; pg. 148, (bottom) NAC PA-55051; (top) Ontario Archives; pg. 149 NAC; pg. 150 City of Toronto Archives; pg. 151 Provincial Archives of Manitoba N 1888, pg. 152 Provincial Archives of Manitoba; pg. 153, Glenbow Archives NA 12955D; pg. 154 Stellerton Museum; pg. 155 (top) NAC C-820594, (bottom) Glenbow Archives NA 12955D; pg. 156 Provincial Archives of Manitoba N11765; pg. 157 Glenbow Archives NA 2308-1; pg. 159 ANC; pg. 160 NAC C-29461; pg. 161 NAC PA 35543; pg. 162 (top) NAC PA-61772, (bottom) NAC/Communist Party of Canada PA 93922; pg. 164 NAC C-7731; pg. 165 NAC C-387; pg. 168 NAC C-29298; pg. 170 NAC C-9339; pg. 172 Ontario Archives 9977; pg. 173 Glenbow Archives; pg. 174 (top) Glenbow Archives NA-1019-168, (bottom) Hockey Hall of Fame; pg. 175 Ontario Archives; pg. 177 AirCanada Archives; pg. 178 City of Toronto Archives, James Collection; pg. 180 (top) NAC C-85272, (bottom) McMichael Gallery; pg. 181 NAC C-37756; pg. 184 C-13236; pg. 191 NAC PA11471; pg. 193 NAC PA-104574; pg. 194 NAC; pg. 195 NAC C-16792; pg. 198 CBC Still Photography; pg. 200 NAC; pg. 201 NAC; pg. 202 RCAF Archives PL3053; pg. 203 NAC/DND; pg. 204 NAC PA 6478; pg. 206 DND; pg. 207 National Gallery of Canada; pg. 208 NAC; pg. 210 NAC C7490; pg. 211 (top) NAC PA 108332, (bottom) NAC; pg. 212 NAC C-31186; pg. 213 Vancouver Public Library; pg. 214 NAC C-81430; pg. 215 NAC PA 148270; pg. 216 CP; pg. 217 NAC/DND; pg. 218, Vancouver Public Library; pg. 219 NAC C-47402; pg. 220 CBC Still Photography; pg. 222 NAC/DND PA 107904; pg. 223 DND; pg. 224 National Gallery of Canada; pg. 225 private collection; pg. 226 NAC C-29452; pg. 227 (top) Toronto Transit Commission, (bottom) The Gazette; pg. 228 NAC; pg. 229 (left) NAC C-29866, (right) NAC/DND PA-114030; pg. 230 DND; pg. 232 DND 46216-N; pg. 23 DND/NAC; pg. 234

CBC Still Photography; pg. 235 AP; pg. 236 National Gallery of Canada; pg. 240-241, York University Archives; pg. 240 Toronto Star; pg. 246 NAC; pg. 252, Sports Hall of Fame; pg. 253 private collection; pg. 254, NAC C-13258; pg. 255, NAC C-692; pg. 256 de Havilland Aircraft; pg. 257 NAC C-68669; pg. 258, John Sylvester; pg. 260, NAC PA-128080; pg. 262, Provincial Archives of Alberta P-2279; pg. 263, Province of Ontario Department of Lands and Forests; pg. 264, NAC PA-167006, pg. 165, NAC C-047009; pg. 266 New Renfrew Times, pg. 267 NAC PA-116481, pg. 268 NAC/Montreal Gazette PA-136706, pg. 269 Archives of Ontario, pg. 270 NAC PA-124953, pg. 271 Toronto Telegram Archives, York University; pg. 272 (top) NAC PA-111390 (bottom) private collection, pg. 273; pg. 274 (top) private collection (bottom) NAC PA-93950; pg. 275 (top) NAC PA PA116075, (bottom) Toronto Telegram Archives, York University; pg. 276 CBC Stills Collection; pg. 277 (top) NAC PA-152117 (bottom left) NAC PA-200369 (bottom right) NAC PA-137074; pg. 278 CBC Stills Photography, pg. 279 (top) Warner Brothers Music/Chuck King (middle) Warner Brothers Music (bottom) Warner Brothers Music; pg. 280 NAC C-79009; pg. 282 NAC PA-129625; pg. 283 Diefenbunker Museum; pg. 284 NAC PA-116075; pg. 286 NAC C-75936; pg. 287 CP; pg. 288 Stratford Theatre; 289 Arrow Alliance; pg. 290 United Nations; pg. 292 Ted Grant/Canadian Museum of Contemporary Photography; pg. 294 Toronto Telegram Archives, York University; pg. 296 NAC C-36222; pg. 297 CP; pg. 298 Douglas Cardinal; pg. 299 NAC PA-167031; pg. 300 CP; pg. 310 CP; pg. 311 Macleans Magazine; pg. 312 CP; pg. 314 CP; pg. 315 CP; pg. 316 AP; pg. 317 CP; pg. 319 Metro Toronto Reference Library; pg. 320 CP; pg. 322 CP; pg. 323 CP; pg. 324 CP; pg. 326 CP; pg. 328 The Daily News; pg. 329 (left) DND (right) ;
Pg. 330 CP; pg. 331 CP; pg. 332 CP; pg. 334 CP; pg. 335 The Bulletin, University of Toronto; pg. 336 CP; pg. 337 C; pg. 339 (top left) CP (top right) CP (bottom left) CP (bottom middle) CP (bottom right) AIC Limited; pg. 340 CP; pg. 341 Bill Reid; pg. 343 Bob Brooks/Nova Scotia Archives; pg. 344 Ottawa Citizen, pg. 346 Glenbow Archives NC-7-852; pg. 347 CP; pg. 348 CP; pg. 349 Rosina Holwell; pg. 350 (left) London Free Press (right) CP; pg. 351 CP; pg. 352 CP; pg. 354 CP; pg. 355 (left) CP, (right) Inuksik High School; pg. 356 CP; pg. 357 CP; pg. 360; pg. 361 CP; pg. 362 CP; pg. 363 CP; pg. 364 CP; pg. 374 NAC; pg. 375 NAC C-2149; pg 376 NAC; pg 377 NAC; pg 378 NAC; pg 380 Estate of Ozias Leduc/SODRAC, Montreal; pg 381; pg 382 NAC PA-56391; pg 383 (left) Le Soleil (left) NAC C-53641; pg 384 Cite Libre; pg 385 The Gazette; pg 386 Art Gallery of Ontario; pg 387 Jean-Paul Riopelle/SODRAC, 2000; pg 388 CP: pg 389 Hydro Quebec; pg 390 Norman Chance/McGill Cree Project; pg 391 CP; pg 392 CP; pg 394 CP; pg 395 CP; pg 396 CP; pg 400 NAC; pg 401 NAC- PA-117531; pg 402 CP; pg 404 CP; pg 404 CP; pg 405 NFB; pg 406 CP; pg 408 CP; pg 409 Bombardier Inc.; pg 410 CP; pg 411 CP; pg 412 CP: pg 413 CP; pg 416 (top) NAC C-18347 (bottom) CP; pg 417 NAC C-68509; pg 418 Government of Canada; pg 419 CP; pg 421 CP; pg 428 ; pg 429 CP; pg 430 CP; pg 431 CP; pg 432 CP: pg 433 AP; pg 434 ; pg 435 Maclean's; pg 436 CP, Maclean's; pg 441 akao Tanabe; pg 442 Maclean's; pg 443 Maclean's; pg 444 CP;pg 445 CP; pg 446 CP; pg 447 CP; pg 449 CP; pg 450 CP; pg 451 CP; pg 452 CP; pg 453 CP; pg 462 CP; pg 463 CP; pg 464 United Nations; pg 466 CP; pg 467 CP; pg 468 CP; pg 469 CP; pg 471 CP; pg 473 CP; pg 475 Free the Children Foundation; pg 476 CP; pg 478 CP; pg 479; pg 482 CP; pg 483 CP; pg 484 CP; pg 487 CP; pg 488 CP; pg 489 NAC; pg 490 CP; pg 493 CP; pg 492 CP; pg 493 CP;